The Vanguard of the Islamic Revolution

Comparative Studies on Muslim Societies

General Editor, Barbara D. Metcalf

The Vanguard
of the Islamic Revolution

The Jama'at-i Islami of Pakistan

SEYYED VALI REZA NASR

UNIVERSITY OF CALIFORNIA PRESS

BERKELEY   LOS ANGELES

b31402483

JQ
629
.A98
J36
1994

University of California Press
Berkeley and Los Angeles, California

© 1994 by
The Regents of the University of California

Part of chapter 3 was previously published as "Students, Islam, and Politics: Islami
Jami'at-i Tulaba in Pakistan," *Middle East Journal* 46, no. 2 (Winter 1992). Reprinted by
permission of the *Middle East Journal.*

An expanded version of chapter 9 was previously published as "Islamic Opposition to the
Islamic State: The Jama'at-i Islami 1977–1988," *International Journal of Middle East Studies*
25, no. 2 (May 1993). Reprinted by permission of Cambridge University Press.

Library of Congress Cataloging-in-Publication Data
  Nasr, Seyyed Vali Reza, 1960–
  The vanguard of the Islamic revolution : the Jama'at-i Islami of Pakistan / Seyyed
Vali Reza Nasr.
    p.   cm.—(Comparative studies on Muslim societies; v. 19)
  Includes bibliographical references and index.
  ISBN 0-520-08368-7 (alk. paper).—ISBN 0-520-08369-5 (pbk. : alk. paper)
  1. Jamā'at-i Islāmi-yi Pākistān. 2. Pakistan—Politics and government. 3. Islam
and politics—Pakistan. I. Title. II. Series.
JQ559.A54N37   1994
324.25491'082—dc20   93–5403
                                                 CIP

Printed in the United States of America

The paper used in this publication meets the minimum requirements of
ANSI/NISO Z39.48-1992 (R 1997) (*Permanence of Paper*). ∞

For Darya

They'll rely on proofs and on eloquence; but will also do the work of
Truth by the sword and the shield.

    Muhammad Iqbal

Our religion is our politics, our politics is our religion.

    Mian Tufayl Muhammad

Contents

Tables and Figures

Tables

Figures

Preface

The rise of Islamic revivalism has presented a serious challenge to conventional wisdom in the social sciences and as a result has been the object of considerable debate and inquiry. The resurgence of an atavism that both rejects and defies Western modernization and preaches submission to the writ of religious law in societies that have already undergone significant modernization requires a redefinition of the very notion of modernization itself, both as a process and as an intellectual construct. Modernization can no longer be regarded as a process that automatically produces secularization, privatization of faith, and the rejection of old values. Nor can religion any longer be seen merely as a set of traditional rites and beliefs, impervious to change and irrelevant to modernization. The task therefore becomes one of reconciling anachronistic values and loyalties with time-honored assumptions about the content, nature, and direction of modernizing change. Changes in the past decade and a half across the Muslim world have yielded an impressive number of studies on Islamic revivalism but no consensus, perhaps because these studies have left some gaps. It is precisely those gaps that this book tries to fill.

For one thing, many studies have limited themselves to theoretical approaches and existing models of sociopolitical change when it has become ever more apparent that understanding will come only from greater attention to individual cases of Islamic revivalism. It is through meticulous inquiry that the distinguishing aspects of the teleology and politics of Islamic revivalism can be identified; new theories can be formed in light of these empirical findings. The social sciences have always been inductive, anchored in what Clifford Geertz has called "thick description."

Many studies of Islamic revivalism have concentrated on preconditions and root causes on the one hand and on the ideological pronouncements of its proponents on the other. Comparatively little has been written on the development of revivalist movements, how they operate, and what social, political, and economic conditions shaped their evolution. Concern with how revivalism came about has diverted attention from the more pertinent question of where it is heading. As revivalism has become part of politics in Muslim societies, the study of Islamic revivalism must move beyond a discussion of causes to examine development.

The study of Islamic revivalism has until now concentrated primarily on Iran and the Arab world and has, as a result, been somewhat restricted in its outlook. A comprehensive theoretical approach will need to consider revivalist activity elsewhere. Of particular importance is South Asia, where the structure of sociopolitical thought and practice has been greatly affected by religious revivalism. From the emergence of the tradition of reform and renewal associated with Shah Waliu'llah of Delhi in the eighteenth century to the rise of the Fara'izi reformists in Bengal and the advent of new initiatives for reassertion of Islamic values in the form of the Deoband, Aligarh, Ahl-i Hadith, Brailwi, and Nadwi schools of thought in the nineteenth and twentieth centuries, to the advent of the Khilafat movement and eventually the campaign for Pakistan, two centuries of activism have fused religious loyalties and political identity in South Asia into an integrated worldview The development of South Asian Islam in modern times therefore provides valuable insights into the origins of revivalism and the forms its political action has taken.

A comprehensive examination of the history and ideology of the Jama'at-i Islami (the Islamic party), the self-appointed "vanguard of the Islamic revolution," can elucidate the manner in which religiopolitical leadership, politicization of religion, and sacralization of politics have tied Islamic theology and piety with the passage of Muslim societies into modernity The Jama'at is one of the oldest and most influential of the Islamic revivalist movements and the first of its kind to develop an Islamic ideology, a modern revolutionary reading of Islam, and an agenda for social action to realize its vision. It has influenced Islamic revivalism from Morocco to Malaysia and controlled the expression of revivalist thinking in Southwest Asia and South Asia since 1941. There are today eight discrete Jama'at-i Islami parties: in Pakistan, India, India's Kashmir province, Pakistan's Azad Kashmir, Bangladesh, Sri Lanka, Great Britain, and North America. The party's ideological reach and impact, throughout its history as well as across a vast geographical expanse, far exceed the boundaries of any one political arena or historical period. By mobilizing its resources in India, Pakistan, Saudi Arabia, and England, the party played a central role in orchestrating the protests against Salman Rushdie's *Satanic Verses* in England in 1988–1989, a notable example of its influence. Thanks to the Jama'at, Muslims in Africa, the Middle East, Asia, and Europe pitted Islam against the West and laid the foundations for the international crisis that ensued.

Central to any effort to understand the Jama'at is an examination of its ideological foundations, social basis, organizational structure, and politics. We need to discover what led the Jama'at to embrace revivalism and what promoted and sustained the party's political activism, charted its development, and determined the nature and scope of its impact on Pakistan's politics. The nature of the state's reaction to Islamic revivalism, from confrontation to accommodation to incorporation, is also of direct relevance. This book probes how Mawdudi's vision was articulated and how it shaped the Jama'at's political agenda and plan of action, influenced the development of the Pakistan state, and changed in the face of political imperatives.

Ever since the advent of the Iranian revolution Western scholarship has been convinced that revivalism is inherently antistate. This is not necessarily the case. The Jama'at is the first instance of Islamic revivalism that participates in the political process, rather than trying to topple it. Its development tells much about how Islamic revivalism will interact with democratic forces across the Muslim world in the coming years. Western scholarship has also assumed that Islamic revivalism, once unleashed, will control Muslim political choices. This again is not supported by the facts at hand. The Jama'at's ideology and activism have been important in Pakistani politics and to revivalism across the Muslim world, but the party has failed to seize power in Pakistan. It can be credited with forming a national alliance that has been advocating the cause of Islam in Pakistan for four decades; it has helped create a distinctly Islamic voting bloc; it has institutionalized religiopolitical action, and sacralized national political discourse. It has contributed to the Islamization of Pakistan and has helped shape Pakistan's history since 1947; it has had a role in the outcome of social movements and political events and is likely to continue to do so. Still, it has been unable to capture power. This is significant, because Islamic revivalism is not supposed to suffer from political constrictions of any sort. That the party has not been the principal beneficiary of the Islamization it has encouraged does not detract from its role in determining what change occurred in Pakistan, nor does it relegate the Jama'at to the status of an anachronism. This suggests that Islamic ideology, in and of itself, does not explain what place Islamic revivalism has in the politics of contemporary Muslim societies. Whatever accounts for the rise of revivalism, it is not the same as what sustains, or expands, its influence. One set of factors bears on the preconditions for the rise of revivalism as an ideology; a different set of factors controls its transformation into a social movement and the direction that movement subsequently takes.

I distinguish those factors that account for the Jama'at's strength from those that account for its limited success as a political power. The corollary, of course, is to determine why the first set favored, while the second hindered, its rise. The set of factors are the events and historical processes that produced the Jama'at and later led to its enfranchisement and participation in the political process; the nature of the state's reaction to the Jama'at's drive for power; competition with other Islamic parties in the political arena; and the incongruities in the Jama'at's ideology and organizational structure. In examining these variables, four inter-related concerns will govern the heuristic aim of this study They are the nature of the linkage between ideology and politics in the theory and practice of revivalist movements; the extent and nature of the influence of socioeconomic imperatives on social action and political change; the implications of revivalism for political change; and the dialectic of the historical and teleological develop-ment of ideological movements, especially within the political process. These four will also relate the findings of this study on Islamic revivalism to larger theoretical concerns in the social sciences. The unity of this book is not purely chronological, though it relies on chronology It is conceived rather in considera-tion of those themes that explain the phenomenon of the Jama'at, namely, its historical development, organization and social base, and politics. After a brief history of the party and a discussion of the pattern of its historical development, the analytical narrative takes up specific themes of importance in explaining both the power and political limitations of the Jama'at: its organization and social base, and the nature of its political activism as reflected in its relations with successive governments. The story of the Jama'at is told here as the implications of each of these for the sociopolitical role of that party are identi-fied. An explanatory note regarding the treatment of Jama'at's story is in order. In many ways it is difficult to explain the nature of the party's activities definitively For instance, the Jama'at has supported the rule of law and has been at the forefront of opposition to those in power who have broken it. The party has also engaged in unlawful activities, including acts of violence, a fact that draws a very different picture of its politics. The social sciences often favor clear-cut characterizations of political actors, to reduce parties such as the Jama'at into one category or the other, but it seems that such an approach is not always useful and can conceal more than it reveals. I have therefore avoided it to the extent possible. Finally, the final draft of this book went to press in August 1993, and therefore does not cover events subsequent to that date.

This book would never have been written without the generous support of the American Institute of Pakistan Studies, which provided me with two separate grants to travel to Pakistan and conduct field research on the Jama'at during the academic year 1989–1990 and again in the summer of 1993 A fellowship at the Foundation for Iranian Studies in 1990–1991 enabled me to consult the archival sources at the Library of Congress and the National Archives in Washington, D.C., and to complete the first draft of this book. Additional research for this book was made possible by a grant from the Joint Committee on South Asia of the Social Science Research Council and the American Council of Learned Societies with funds provided by the National Endowment for the Humanities and the Ford Foundation. This grant allowed me to work on archival sources available at the British Library and the Public Record Office in England in the summer of 1992.

During my research stay in Pakistan, I greatly benefited from the assistance of an array of Pakistanis, to all of whom I am eternally grateful. The Ali family of Lahore, with their customary generosity, provided me with friendship and support. My heartfelt appreciation to them all, and to Syed Amjad Ali, Begum Kishwar Abid Husain, Syed Asad and Fakhr-i Jahan Ali, and Syed Yawar and Snookey Ali in particular. I am gratefully indebted to Muhammad Suhayl Umar, a true gentleman and an erudite scholar, who provided me with invaluable insights, sources, and contacts that have enriched this study immensely; Hakim Muhammad Sa'id and the Hamdard Foundation; Air Commodore In'amu'l-Haq; and finally, Ijaz and Nurin Malik.

From the beginning of this project, teachers and friends alike provided invaluable support, which has greatly enriched this endeavor. John L. Esposito, Lucian Pye, and Myron Weiner oversaw it in its first incarnation as a dissertation at M.I.T. and helped formulate my thoughts on the Jama'at-i Islami and its role in political change in Pakistan. To many others I am indebted for their intellectual guidance and wisdom. I have benefited greatly from discussions with Charles J. Adams, Mumtaz Ahmad, Zafar Ishaq Ansari, Robert Frykenberg, Ijaz S. Gilani, Barbara D Metcalf, Roy Mottahedeh, Farhan Ahmad Nizami, James Piscatori, and Francis Robinson. I am grateful for the assistance of Muhammad Afzal, the late Allahbukhsh K. Brohi, Mawlana Abdu'l-Ghaffar Hasan, Javid Hashmi, Javid Iqbal, Muhammad Safdar Mir, the late Siraj Munir, Mawlana Sayyid Abu'l-Hasan Ali Nadwi, the late Ja'far Qasmi, Hamid Qizilbash, Altaf Hasan Quraishi, Mustafa Sadiq, Muhammad Salahu'ddin, Mujibu'l-Rahman Shami, and S.M. Zafar. I also owe much to the assistance of the staff of the various archives and libraries to which this study took me. The staff of the Pakistan Ministry of Culture and the Institute of Islamic Research in Islamabad; the Iqbal Academy, the Institute of Islamic Culture, the Islamic Studies Academy of the Jama'at-i Islami, the Qa'id-i A'zam and Punjab Public Libraries, all in Lahore; and the Khudabakhsh Library in Patna deserve a special note of thanks.

Many within the Jama'at helped me to find the sources I needed. Their efficiency and especially their openness stood in stark contrast to the apprehensions and preconceptions I harbored before embarking upon this project. I am particularly in the debt of Yusuf Khan and his archives at the Jama'at's Mansurah complex; Abdu'l-Wahid Khan at the Islamic Publications, who provided me with the galleys of as yet unpublished manuscripts; Muhammad Ibrar, who opened all of the doors which I had not managed to at the Jama'at headquarters; Shahin

Rashid and Hasan Suhayb Murad and the staff of Jama'at's election and administration bureaus, who graciously took the time to compile the electoral and membership data which I had requested. I also benefited greatly from conversations with many Jama'at leaders and members, notably Abdu'ssattar Afghani, Qazi Husain Ahmad, Khurshid Ahmad, Abdu'l-Ghafur Ahmad, Malik Ghulam Ali, Mahmud A'zam Faruqi, Sayyid As'ad Gilani, Chaudhri Rahmat Ilahi, Khurram Jah Murad, Mian Tufayl Muhammad, and Chaudhri Aslam Salimi. They spent many hours with me and despite their demanding schedules patiently listened to my queries, many of which were, no doubt, unpalatable to them. Their candor is greatly appreciated, although no doubt many of the conclusions of this study will not be in accordance with their views. I wish also to express my gratitude to a number of people who were close to Mawlana Mawdudi, notably Khwaja Amanu'llah, Begum Atiyah Inayatu'llah, Begum Abidah Gurmani, and Begum Mahmudah Mawdudi, for sharing their reminiscences with me.

Some of the main themes of this book were discussed with Middle East and South Asia specialists at two seminars at Columbia University and Harvard University from which I benefited greatly Gholam Reza Afkhami, Mumtaz Ahmad, Said Amir Arjomand, Shaul Bakhash, Houchang Chehabi, Leila Fawaz, David Gilmartin, Shahla Haeri, Stephen Humphreys, Omar Noman, Muhammad Suhayl Umar, and Anwar H. Syed read all or some of the chapters of this volume and made valuable comments. For the shortcomings of the book, however, I alone am responsible. The manuscript owes much to the masterful editing of Margaret Ševčenko. I can think of no editor more helpful or supportive than Lynne Withey of the University of California Press, who along with Tony Hicks and Stephanie Fowler has done a splendid job of producing this book. To my wife, Darya, goes a special note of gratitude. She helped with many aspects of this project in Pakistan and provided me with unwavering support during the arduous months it took to narrate the text of this study If there is any merit to this endeavor, I share it with all those mentioned here.

San Diego, August 1993

Note to the Reader

All Urdu, Arabic, and Persian names have been cited using a simplified transliteration system that eliminates diacritical marks other than the *'ayn* and *hamzah*. Vowels are rendered by *i, u,* and *a;* on occasion, *e* or *o* is substituted to convey a spelling more in line with the local pronunciation of the name or source cited. The use of *u* instead of *w,* and *ia* as opposed to *iyya,* reflects the closest approximation to the local pronunciation of the name or source in question. Terms such as *jihad, shari'ah,* and *ulama* appear in their anglicized form. A glossary of Arabic, Persian, and Urdu/Hindi terms is provided at the end of this book. The terms in the glossary are transliterated with diacritical marks.

Personal names are rendered in accordance with the transliteration rules cited here even when spelled differently by the persons in question. The only exceptions are names such as Bhutto or Ayub Khan, whose particular spelling has become established in Western literature. In transliterating personal names, the collapse of vowels and the particular pronunciation of Arabic or Persian words typical of Urdu have been retained (hence, for example, Hashmi rather than Hashimi). Whenever the transliteration of a directly quoted source differs from the one employed here, the variations have been respected.

A note is also in order with regard to the references. The names of all interviewees who contributed to this study are cited both in the footnotes and in the bibliography The dates and places of the interviews are cited only in the bibliography, as are the translations of the titles of Arabic, Persian, and Urdu books and articles, and the names of the publishers of all books, journals, and periodicals. When requested by an interviewee, the name has been withheld and the term "interviews" has been substituted. Direct quotations and references, whenever possible, are drawn from official and published English translations of the original Urdu works. However, when required, reference has been made to the original Urdu source.

Acronyms
and Abbreviations

IJI   Islamı Jumhurı Ittihad

IJT   Islamı Jami'at-ı Tulabah

MQM   Muhajir Qaumı Mahaz

MRD   Movement for Restoration of Democracy

NWFP   North-West Frontier Provınce

PNA   Pakıstan National Alliance

CRTIN   *Chıragh-ı Rah* (Karachi), Tahrik-ı Islamı Number (November 1963).

FBIS-NES   *Foreıgn Broadcast Information Servıce, Daily Reports, Near East and South Asıa.*

HRZ   *Haftrozah Zindagı* (Lahore), Mawdudi Number (September 29– October 5, 1989).

ISIT(1)   *Ijtima' Se Ijtima' Tak (1963–1974) Rudad-ı Jama'at-ı Islamı, Pakıstan* (Lahore: Jama'at-ı Islamı, 1989).

ISIT(2)   *Ijtima' Se Ijtima' Tak (1974–1983): Rudad-ı Jama'at-ı Islamı, Pakıstan* (Lahore: Jama'at-ı Islamı, 1989).

JIKUS   Sayyıd Abu'l-A'la Mawdudi, *Jama'at-ı Islamı kı Untis Sal* (Lahore: Shu'bah-ı Nashr'u Isha'at-ı Jama'at-ı Islamı, Pakıstan, 1970). Thıs ıs the text of Mawdudi's speech before the annual gatherıng of the Jama'at ın 1970.

JVNAT   Sayyid Mutaqqiu'l-Rahman and Salim Mansur Khalid, eds., *Jab Vuh Nazim-i A'la The*, 2 vols. (Lahore: Idarah-i Matbu'at-i Talabah, 1981).

MMKT   Abu Tariq, ed., *Mawlana Mawdudi ki Taqarir*, 2 vols. (Lahore: Islamic Publications, 1976). These volumes are a compilation of Mawlana Mawdudi's various speeches and interviews. Five more volumes of this book are currently in preparation.

NGH   Israr Ahmad, "Naghz-i Ghazal," *Mithaq* (Lahore) 39, 1 (January 1990). The article was originally published in *Mithaq* 12, 2 (August 1966), 39–52; 12, 3 (September 1966), 33–56; 12, 5 (November 1966), 43–56; 12, 6 (December 1966), 33–56; 13, 2 (February 1967), 47–56. The articles were later published in the form of a book: Israr Ahmad, *Tarikh-i Jama'at-i Islami: Ik Gumshudah Bab* (Lahore: Maktabah-i Jadid Press, 1990).

QDMN   *Qaumi Digest* (Lahore), Mawdudi Number (1980).

RJI   *Rudad-i Jama'at-i Islami*, 7 vols. (Lahore, 1938–1991). These volumes contain the proceedings of the various Jama'at congresses between 1941 and 1955

SAAM   Masudul Hasan, *Sayyid Abul A'ala Maududi and His Thought*, 2 vols. (Lahore: Islamic Publications, 1984).

SSMN   *Sayyarah* (Lahore), Sayyid Mawdudi Number (April–May 1980).

TQ   *Tarjumanu'l-Qur'an* (Hyderabad, Pathankot, and Lahore), (1932–present). *TQ* has been the main forum for the exposition of Mawlana Mawdudi's theological views since 1932, and also the Jama'at's official ideological journal since 1941. It was edited by Mawdudi from 1932 to 1979

TT   Salim Mansur Khalid, ed., *Talabah Tahrikain*, 2 vols. (Lahore: Al-Badr Publications, 1989).

The sources for all references to U.S. diplomatic dispatches and telegrams are the National Archives of the United States of America, Washington, D.C., and Suitland, Maryland (referred to as NA), and *Documents from the U.S. Espionage Den, Nos. 45 and 46: U.S. Intervention in Islamic Countries: Pakistan*, 2 vols. (Tehran: Muslim Students Following the Line of the Imam, n.d.) (referred to as DFTUSED). The source for all references to British diplomatic dispatches and telegrams is the Public Record Office, London (referred to as PRO). "Disp." and "tel." in the citations stand for *dispatch* and *telegram*, respectively

1

HISTORY AND DEVELOPMENT

1 The Quest for a Holy Community

The Jama'at-ı Islamı was originally the brainchild of Mawlana Sayyıd Abu'l-A'la Mawdudi (1903–1979),[1] who founded the party and headed it for thirty-one years (1941–1972).[2] Mawdudi traced his lineage to an old notable family of Delhı who had been associated with the Mughal court and had later served the nızams of Hyderabad. The family took pride in the glorious days of Islam in India and was acutely aware of its downfall following the sack of Delhı by the British in 1858; they therefore harbored a dislike for British rule. Mawdudi's father was educated in law and began life as a modernist, but he eventually embraced Sufism and became a fervent ascetic. He educated his children in the Islamic tradition, insulating them from the Western culture and mores that so influenced Indian intelligentsıa. Mawdudi received his early education in Urdu and Arabic, first at home and later in the traditional schools of Hyderabad, Bhopal, and Delhı. As a young man in Delhı, he studied the *dars-ı nızamı* curricula of the ulama with Deobandi tutors and received the certificate which would have permitted him to join that sodality [3] He abandoned traditional education and the garb of the ulama, however, for an education in modern subjects. He studied English and Western thought on his own and embarked on a modern career in journalism. Between 1921 and 1924 he became involved in the Khilafat movement, which had been formed in the hope of preserving the Muslim caliphate, and for a while sympathized with the Congress party His zeal and literary style soon caught the attention of the leaders of the Jami'at-ı Ulama-ı Hind (Party of Indian Ulama), who invited the young Mawdudi to serve as the editor of their newspaper. Mawdudi did not remain attached to the Jami'at-ı Ulama for long, however; he eventually parted ways with the pro-Congress ulama party and embarked upon a crusade to revive Islam as the sole apodictic answer to the Muslim communal predicament in India.

Mawdudi's religiopolitical awareness had first been aroused in Hyderabad, in the Deccan, when the nizam's authority had begun to wane, and where political activism had shifted the time-honored balance of power to the Hindus. After the Great Mutiny of 1857 and the entrenchment of the British Raj, Muslim politics, religious thinking, and social organizations from Sayyid Ahmad Khan's (1817–1898) Aligarh movement to Muslim agitations in Bengal and Punjab had been directed at reversing the continuous decline in Muslim political power before the rise in the fortunes of the British and subsequently the Hindus. The eclipse of Hyderabad's magnificent Muslim culture and later of its Muslim community after the collapse of the nizam's state in 1948 was to haunt Mawdudi in the subsequent years, leaving him with a sense of desperation and urgency directed at saving Islam from decline and eventual extinction,[4] an attitude he shared with most Muslims of Hyderabad.[5] Even before the partition these themes had appeared in Mawdudi's writings.[6]

Mawdudi came of age just as colonial rule ended and Indian national consciousness was asserted, but the Muslims failed to salvage their status and restore the political prominence they had lost. Experiments with accommodation to imperial rule, such as those of Sayyid Ahmad Khan or Punjab's Unionist Party, had failed to stop Hindu supremacy or assuage the ever increasing anxiety of the Muslim masses about life under Hindu rule. The Muslims of India had begun to think that restoring their political power was the only way to advance their interests and extricate themselves from their predicament. Between the two World Wars Muslims turned to communalism, channeling their political aspirations and energies into the formulation of political agendas whose only strength lay in their manipulation of Islamic symbols. As a result, in the 1920s and the 1930s Islam was catapulted into the political arena, and its symbols were politicized and utilized for purposes of mass mobilization. The results were communal riots and the estrangement of some from the Congress party

However, communal agitation did not help either. The earliest organized expression of Muslim communalism, the Khilafat movement, to which Mawdudi belonged, collapsed in 1924 and with it the hopes and aspirations of the Muslims of India. The Khilafat movement was a beginning, however, that led Muslims to greater expressions of communalism throughout the following decade.[7]

Meanwhile, the home-rule (swaraj) effort, initiated by the Congress in 1924, had also come to naught. Hindu hostility and Muslim activism, which had emerged into the open in the wake of the Khilafat movement, continued to arouse the fears of the Muslim masses about their future. Following the collapse of the Khilafat movement in 1924, Muslims perpetrated acts of violence against Hindus all over India. The Hindus responded through their own revivalist movements such as the Mahasabha and the Arya Samaj, which launched aggressive anti-Muslim public campaigns. The most noteworthy of these was the

Shuddhi campaign, whose mission was to reconvert unwilling low-caste converts from Islam back to Hinduism. The Shuddhi campaign was an affront to Muslim articles of faith and by implication challenged the place of Islam in India. The campaign therefore provoked angry responses from Muslims, resulting in more communal strife. In 1925 Swami Shradhanand, a renowned Shuddhi activist, was assassinated, causing much anti-Muslim bitterness in the Indian press and among the Hindus, and a feeling of desperation and apologetic resignation among Muslims.

Mawdudi witnessed all these events. His political thinking was shaped by considering all the solutions with which Muslims experimented. Mawdudi was not initially a revivalist; he simply wanted to solve the problems of his community The search for a solution eventually led him to conclude that Islam was the best remedy for the problem.

After Shradhanand's murder, Mawdudi plunged into the communalist movement, making a choice which determined the direction of his lifelong struggle to preserve the place of Islam in Muslim life. In 1929 he published his book *Al-Jihad fi'l-Islam* (Jihad in Islam). It was not only a response to Hindu challenges to Islam following Shradhanand's death but was also a prologue to a lifetime of religious and political effort. By 1932 the Muslim predicament had become the focus of his life. He increasingly looked to Islam for solutions and gradually adopted a revivalist approach. The result is the movement that Mawdudi's followers regard as the heir to the tradition of Islamic revival (*tajdid*) and as its greatest manifestation in modern times.[8]

Mawdudi's vision unfolded in the context of rapid polarization of the Muslim community Following the Government of India Act of 1935 and the elections of 1937, the Congress began to make serious overtures to Muslims.[9] Some were enticed into serving as junior partners to the Congress, thus acknowledging Hindu political ascendancy[10] Others in the Muslim League, which was formed in 1906 as a party for the preservation of Muslim communal interests, under the leadership of Muhammad 'Ali Jinnah (1876–1948) took the opposite course in the 1940s and demanded a separate state for Muslims.[11]

Mawdudi did not join either party He started with the premise that Muslims should return to a pure and unadulterated Islam to brace themselves for the struggle before them. They should reject Hindu ascendancy and continue to lay claim to the whole of India.[12] He was especially perturbed by those Muslims who were willing to accommodate Hindus, and by supporting the Congress were acquiescing in the inevitability of a Hindu raj. His most venomous rhetoric was reserved for them. Irredentist as Mawdudi's views may have appeared they were communalist in form and content. Hence, his revivalist exhortations did not preclude an endorsement of the "two nation theory"[13] The struggle had to defend Muslim communalist interests in India and to preserve Muslim identity in the face of imminent Hindu challenges. But first Mawdudi had to vanquish the Muslim League, which he believed to be the sole impediment to his control of Muslim communal politics.

As the creation of Pakistan became more and more likely, Mawdudi's polemical attacks on the Muslim League also increased. He objected to the idea of Muslim nationalism because it would exclude Islam from India and surrender the domain of the Mughals to the Hindus, which would make the eventual extinction of Islam all the easier. The increasingly communal character of the Indian politics of the time, and the appeal made to religious symbols in the formulation of new political alliances and programs by various Muslim groups as well as Muslim League leaders, created a climate in which Mawdudi's theological discourse found understanding and relevance.[14] Although predicated upon secular ideologies, the Pakistan movement was able to mobilize the masses only by appealing to Islam. Nationalism thereby became dependent on Islam and as a result politicized the faith.

A number of Muslim religious and communal organizations, some of which remained nothing more than proposals, pointed to the importance of organizations for promoting Muslim political consciousness and communal interests. The Jama'at emerged as part of this general organization of Muslim activism, which by the early 1940s had become the accepted channel for the expression of Muslim political sentiments. Rivalry with the Muslim League escalated with each step India took toward partition.

After the 1937 defeat of the Muslim League at the polls, Mawdudi's thinking took an increasingly communalist turn, and following the Lahore Resolution of 1940, when the League committed itself to Pakistan, the Jama'at was born as the "counter-League."[15] Mawdudi had originally entered the political fray with the aim of halting the rise of Hindu power and converting the whole of India to Islam—to end forever the uncertainty of the Muslim place in the polyglot culture of India, but by 1940 he had accepted the inevitability of some form of partition of the Subcontinent. He therefore shifted his attention away from the Congress party and toward the Muslim League and its communalist program. Mawdudi's opposition to the League from this point had nothing to do with Jinnah's calling for Muslim autonomy Mawdudi had simply decided that he should be the one to found and lead the Muslim state of Pakistan if there had to be one. As India moved closer to partition, Mawdudi's political thinking became increasingly clear regarding the polity which he envisioned. He had to position himself to dominate the debate over Pakistan, and to do that he needed the Muslim League's power and prominence, for he distrusted Jinnah's intentions and even more the secularist inclinations of the League's program. The fate of Islam in Kemalist Turkey and Pahlavi Iran had no doubt served as a warning to Mawdudi and to those other Muslims whose rationale for a separate Muslim state was the promise that it would preserve Islam in the Subcontinent.[16] Increasingly, Mawdudi reacted directly to the Muslim League's policies, and the Muslim League's conception of what Pakistan was to be was the subject of his strongest attacks. He denounced nationalism and berated secular politics as blasphemy (*kufr*).

In 1947, following partition, Mawdudi was escorted to safety after violence broke out in the Gurdaspur District of Punjab, where the Jama'at was based. He was taken to Lahore by units of the Pakistan army, where his struggle for the soul of Pakistan was revealed. Calling the bluff of Muslim League leaders, who had continuously appealed to Islamic symbols to mobilize support for Pakistan, Mawdudi now demanded an Islamic state where he had once dreamed of an Islamic empire. His program was no longer to save Islam in India but to have it conquer Pakistan.[17]

Mawdudi's Ideology

Mawdudi began to set forth his views on Islam and its place in Muslim life in 1932. In the following sixty-seven years until his death he expounded his vision in numerous lectures, articles, and books, and especially in his journal *Tarjumanu'l-Qur'an*. He advocated complete obedience to Islamic law, narrowly interpreted. Political power was the measure and guarantor of the continued vitality of Islam. Mawdudi chided Muslims for having eliminated politics from religious life, which he believed to be the result of gradual deviation from Islam's true teachings. His interpretive reading of Islam and its history began with denunciation of traditional Islam and its centuries-old institutions. He argued that Islam had no possibility of success as a religion or a civilization—which he argued was meant to be its fate and the reason for its revelation—unless Muslims removed the encumbrances of cultural accretion and tradition, rigorously reconstructed the pristine faith of the Prophet, and gained power. Politics was declared to be an integral and inseparable component of the Islamic faith, and the "Islamic state" which Muslim political action sought to erect was viewed as the panacea to all problems facing Muslims.

As Mawdudi systematically mixed religion with politics, faith with social action, he streamlined the Islamic faith so that it could accommodate its new-found aim. He reinterpreted concepts and symbols, giving them new meanings and connotations. This allowed him to set down a political reading of Islam, in which religious piety was transformed into a structure of authority.[18] Faith became ideology and religious works social action. The resulting "system"— what Mawdudi referred to as *din* (literally, "religion")—defined piety. This perspective was enunciated ever more lucidly over the years and was gradually extended to incorporate the structure of Islamic faith. It was applied to every aspect of Islamic thought and practice, producing a comprehensive interpretive reading of Islam. In the hands of Mawdudi the transformation of Islam into ideology was complete.

Mawdudi's formulation was by no means rooted in traditional Islam. He adopted modern ideas and values, mechanisms, procedures, and idioms, weaving them into an Islamic fabric, thus producing an internally consistent and yet hybrid ideological perspective. Mawdudi's vision was not modern through and through, but purported to modernity; he sought not to resurrect an atavistic order but to modernize the traditional conception of Islamic thought and life. His vision represented a clear break with Islamic tradition and a fundamentally new reading of Islam which took its cue from modern thought. In a Foucaultian sense, Mawdudi's vision was the product of a discourse with the "other," the West. His perspective was formed in response to greater Hindu ascendancy in Indian politics of the interwar period. However, for Muslims to mobilize their resources to confront the Hindu challenge, argued Mawdudi, they had to free their souls from Western influence. Hence, Mawdudi's discourse, although motivated by the Hindu challenge, was directed at the West.[19] His ideology showed modernist tendencies, as did his political outlook. He premised his reading of religion and society on a dialectic view of history, in which the struggle between Islam and disbelief (*kufr*) ultimately culminates in a revolutionary struggle. The Jama'at was to be the vanguard of that struggle, which would produce an Islamic utopia. In a similar vein, the Jama'at's views on government, as well as on the party's own operations, also confirmed Mawdudi's break with Islamic tradition, while the terms "revolution," "vanguard," "ideology," "democratic caliphate," and "theodemocracy," which turned up over and over in his polemic and defined the Jama'at's agenda, attested to his modernism. His ideological perspective was openly hostile to both capitalism and socialism. Capitalism was denounced for its secularism, anthropocentrism, and association with the imperialist culture which had marginalized Muslims in India, and socialism for its atheism and its worship of society in place of God. Above all, both capitalism and socialism were seen as rivals which had to be defeated before Islam could dominate the life and thought of Muslims. In practice, however, Mawdudi always remained more wary of socialism than capitalism.

Ideology compelled the action that in Pakistan assumed the form of demanding an Islamic state. The Jama'at demanded a government inspired by and obedient to the writ of the shari'ah and which would promise a utopian order that gave direction to "Islamic" social action. For the Jama'at that state would be erected according to rules and procedures stipulated by Mawdudi. Social action, however, did not imply revolution as the term is understood in the West. Mawdudi believed in incremental change rather than radical ruptures, disparaged violence as a political tool, did not subscribe to class war, and assumed that Islamic revolution would be heralded not by the masses but by the society's leaders. Revolution, in Mawdudi's view, did not erupt from the bottom up but flowed from the top of society down. The aim of Islamic revolution, therefore, was not to spearhead the struggle of the underclass but to convert society's leaders. During an election campaign in 1958, Mawdudi summed up the Jama'at's plan of action in the following terms: "first of all it brings intellectual change in the people; secondly [it] organises them in order to make them suitable for a movement. Thirdly, it reforms society through social and humanitarian work, and finally it endeavors to change the leadership."[20] Once the leadership had been won over to Islam—the Jama'at taking power—the society would be Islamized and all socioeconomic maladies would be automatically cured. Education and propaganda were therefore singled out as the principal agents for furthering the revolutionary struggle. The Jama'at's efforts have always aimed at winning over society's leaders, conquering the state, and Islamizing the government. Its plan of action has been designed to augment its influence in the inner sanctum of power rather than to curry favor with the masses. Its notions of social action therefore have peculiar meanings and aims.

The Origins of the Jama'at-i Islami, 1932–1938

Mawdudi often said that the idea for establishing the Jama'at-i Islami came to him as he reflected on the problems the Muslims of India faced on the eve of partition.[21] The solution to those problems, he had concluded, would require the services of a political party that could initiate radical changes in Muslim society and at the same time safeguard its interests in India. If the Islamic state was to solve any problem, it could do so only if Muslims were organized and worked for it; they should not expect a miracle to produce a solution.[22] Twenty-two years of observation, reminisced Mawdudi in later years, had led him to believe that no Muslim party was likely to succeed unless it followed high ethical and religious standards and enjoined Muslims to be morally upright and to adhere without compromise to the values of their religion: "I was of the opinion that the importance [of a party] lies not in numbers of its members, but in the dependability of their thoughts and actions."[23] This conviction had its roots in how Mawdudi had read early Islamic history.[24] Mawdudi was greatly impressed by the way the Prophet organized the first Muslims in Mecca and later Medina shortly after the revelation of Islam and harnessed their energies to project the power of Islam across Arabia. For Mawdudi the success of the Prophet's mission could not be explained simply by the power of his message, nor did it owe its fulfillment to the will of God; rather it reflected the Prophet's organizational genius: "Within thirteen years the Prophet was able to gather around him a small but devoted group of courageous and selfless people."[25] Mawdudi thought the Jama'at could do the same: "All those persons who thus surrender themselves are welded into a community and that is how the 'Muslim society' comes into being."[26]

Mawdudi felt that an important aspect of the Prophet's organization had been segregating his community from its larger social context. This enabled the

Prophet to give his organization a distinct identity and permitted the nascent Muslim community to resist dissolution into the larger pagan Arab culture. Instead they were able to pull the adversary into the ambit of Islam. For Mawdudi the Jama'at, much like the Prophetic community, had to be the paragon for the Muslim community of India. It would have to stand apart from the crowd and still draw the Muslim community into the pale of Mawdudi's Islam. The Jama'at was, therefore, at its inception a "holy" community (*ummah*) and a missionary (*da'wah*) movement.[27]

Indian history also provided more immediate and tangible examples for Mawdudi. Since the nineteenth century, when the Fara'izi movement of Haji Shari'atu'llah (d. 1840) in Bengal had introduced its elaborate hierarchical structure of authority to Indian Muslims, organization had a central place in their politics. The penchant for organization building reached its apogee with Abu'l-Kalam Azad (1888–1958). Azad, for the first time, tied the fortunes of the Muslim community of India to finding a definitive organizational solution. In the second decade of the twentieth century he promoted in his journal *Al-Hilal* the Hizbu'llah (Party of God), an organization which he charged with the revival of Muslim religious consciousness while safe-guarding Muslim political interests. Although the Hizbu'llah never amounted to much, its raison d'être and the way it worked were outlined in detail and with the customary force and passion of Azad's pen. This scheme left an indelible mark on a whole generation of Muslim intellectuals and political activists across India, among them Mawdudi, who read *Al-Hilal* avidly in his youth.[28]

In 1920, Azad proposed yet another organizational scheme. At the height of the Muslim struggle during World War I, Azad, along with a number of Indian ulama, proposed that the Muslims choose an *amir-i shari'at* (leader of holy law) in each Indian province, to be aided by a council of ulama to oversee the religious affairs of Muslims.[29] These provincial amirs would in turn elect an *amir-i hind* (leader [of the Muslims] of India), a coveted title on which Azad had set his own eyes. While this scheme also came to naught, Azad proceeded to launch an independent campaign for securing the title of *amir-i hind* for himself. He instructed a few close associates who had sworn allegiance (*bai'ah*) to him to travel across India, argue for Azad's claim to the title, and take additional *bai'ahs* on his behalf. One such emissary was Mistri Muhammad Siddiq, a close companion of Mawdudi in the 1930s who influenced Mawdudi's thinking on organization greatly and helped found the Jama'at.[30] The notion of an omnipotent *amir-i hind*—a single leader for the Muslims of India—enjoying the unwavering allegiance of his disciples later found an echo in the organizational structure of the Jama'at and in Mawdudi's conception of the role and powers of its amir (president or executive).

Despite Azad's widely publicized and popular clamor for an organizational solution, Muslims did not actually initiate one until the Khilafat movement in 1919–1924,[31] which, for the first time, mobilized the Muslim community under a single political banner. Although the Khilafat movement eventually lost its aim and collapsed following the abrogation of the Muslim caliphate by the Turkish government in 1924, its appeal and indefatigable organizational work captured the imagination of Muslims and anchored their politics in the search for an effective organization. As a young journalist at the *Taj* newspaper in Jubalpur, Central Provinces (1920), and later as the editor of the Jami'at-i Ulama-i Hind's newspaper, *Muslim*, in Delhi (1921–1923), Mawdudi had been active in the Khilafat movement and organized Muslims to support it.[32]

The Khilafat movement's decline left a vacuum in Muslim politics. The experience had aroused the Muslims' political consciousness and heightened their sense of communal identity, but it had also left those it had mobilized frustrated and disappointed. Still its considerable success in organizing Muslims did not go unnoticed by those who continued to struggle for the Muslim cause. The Muslim community began to organize and call for unity to face the challenges to Islam. Keen observer as he was, Mawdudi took note of the success of some of these organizations such as the Tahrik-i Khaksar (movement of the devoted; created in 1931) or the Muslim League.[33] In fact, the Khaksar, under the leadership of 'Inayatu'llah Mashriqi (1888–1963), who was renowned for his organizational talent, had grown to be a major force in Punjab at the time. Equally instructive was Muhammad 'Ali Jinnah's organization of the Muslim League. Values which formed the basis of the Jama'at in later years echoed Jinnah's emphasis on solidarity, organization, morality, and perseverance: "Organize yourselves, establish your solidarity and complete unity   Equip yourselves as trained and disciplined soldiers.   [W]ork loyally, honestly for the cause of your people.   There are forces which may bully you, tyrannize over you and intimidate you.   But it is by going through the crucible of fire of persecution which may be levelled against you,   it is by resisting   and maintaining your true convictions and loyalty, that a nation will emerge, worthy of its past glory and history   [A]s a well-knit, solid, organized, united force [the Musalmans] can face any danger, and withstand any opposition."[34]

Sufism also influenced the Jama'at's organization. The Sufi order (*tariqah*)—which governs the practice of Sufism—facilitates the spiritual ascension of the Sufis.[35] It organizes Sufi members into a set of hierarchically arranged concentric circles, each of which is supervised by a Sufi of higher spiritual rank. The circles eventually culminate in a pyramidal structure, at the pinnacle of which sits the Sufi master (*shaikh, pir,* or *murshid*). This pyramidal organizational structure of the Sufi order is symbolic of the spiritual journey of the Sufis from novice to master. It not only governs the practice of Sufism but also creates clear doctrinal and intellectual boundaries around the Sufis, sequestering them from the society at large. The spiritual seclusion of the Sufi community eliminates outside influences and promotes concentration, learning, and character. To join the Sufi order, a novice must undergo initiation and submit to a form of "conversion"—declare his commitment to the spiritual path and surrender his soul to the guidance of the Sufi master—which is popularly known as the *sarsipurdagi* (literally, placing one's head on the master's lap). The initiation into Sufism involves an allegiance (*bai'ah*), which symbolizes and confirms the Sufi's commitment to his master. The allegiance demands of a Sufi total submission and obedience to the master, for he commands the Sufi's soul, guiding it through the maze of spiritual experiences and mundane travails to the realization of the Absolute Truth which is God.[36] A Sufi order is often centered in a hospice (*khanaqah*), where many Sufis take up residence in order to be close to their master.

Committed to reforming Islam, Mawdudi had little tolerance for what he believed to be the latitudinarian tendencies of Sufism. But, despite his ambivalence toward the esoteric dimension of Islam, in the Sufi order he saw a valuable organizational model:

> Sufis in Islam have a special form of organization known as *khanaqah*. Today this has a bad image. But the truth is that it is the best institution in Islam. [I]t is necessary that this institution be revived in India, and in various places small *khanaqahs* be established. Therein novices can read the most valuable religious sources, and live in a pure environment. This institution encompasses the functions of club, library and *ashram* [Hindu place of worship]. [The] entire scheme rests on selection of the *shaikh* [master]. [A]t least I do not know of someone with all the qualifications. [I]f this task is to be undertaken, India should be searched for the right person.[37]

Many elements of this laudatory description were featured in the Jama'at's original plans and governed the party's early stages of development at Pathankot between 1942 and 1947

The Sufi order's emphasis on the central role of the Sufi master and total submission to his example and ideas was akin to Mawdudi's conception of the role of the amir in the Jama'at. In a letter dated March 1941, some four months before the formation of the Jama'at, Mawdudi compared membership in an "Islamic party" with the Sufi's giving allegiance (*bai'ah*) to the master, and emphasized the primacy of the overseer of such a party in its functioning.[38] Mawdudi, however, made a distinction between his views and those of the Sufis by proclaiming that allegiance in the Jama'at was to the office of the amir, and not to himself personally [39] Many Jama'at leaders have since lamented that as a consequence of this attitude, from its inception Mawdudi exceeded the managerial duties the amir was supposed to perform, because he looked upon his relation with the Jama'at members as that of a master (*murshid*) with his disciples (murids).[40] In fact, for some the prospects of giving allegiance, albeit not openly, to Mawdudi was a compelling enough reason not to join the Jamaʿat.

Despite its roots in the Islamic tradition, the Jamaʿat-i Islami is a modern party Its structure, procedural methods, and pattern of growth reflect modern ideas and attest to a successful accommodation of modernization within an Islamic milieu. It has managed to escape the decay that has, for instance, reduced the Congress party, the Muslim League, and the Pakistan People's Party to patrimonial and dynastic political institutions, and in the case of the last two led to debilitating factionalism. The Jamaʿat has rather created mechanisms, bureaucratic structures, and management that have thus far withstood the pressures of the fractious and patrimonial system in which it operates. This organizational strength owes much to the European models on display in the 1930s—fascism and, even more, communism.[41] Mawdudi had avidly studied these models. As a result, the Jamaʿat was never a "party" in the liberal democratic sense of the term—translating popular interests into policy positions; it is, rather, an "organizational weapon"[42] in the Leninist tradition, devised to project the power of an ideological perspective into the political arena. While Mawdudi differed with Lenin in seeking to utilize this "weapon" within a constitutional order, its structure and functioning closely paralleled those of bolshevism.

Smith writes that Lenin replaced the working class with the party, as the vanguard without which the working class would be unable to gain political consciousness and become a revolutionary movement.[43] Lenin's party worked on the principle of "democratic centralism, [wherein] rank-and-file members [were] strictly subordinate to the leadership   .decision making was to be 'central' in formulation, with rank-and-file members copying out orders received, but that higher bodies were to be 'democratically' accountable to the membership at periodic meetings."[44] Propaganda, while designed to further the cause of the revolution, also acted to reinforce group solidarity within the party, forming the basis of a well-knit administrative party and network of cadres.[45]

For Lenin the vanguard was won over by the doctrine and then charged with the task of maneuvering the masses into position for the struggle against the economic and political order.[46] The Jamaʿat fulfilled the same function with the difference that it focused its attention not so much on organizing the masses as on maneuvering the leaders of society This was a significant departure from the Leninist model and one that muddled the meaning of revolution in Jamaʿat's ideology Mawdudi defined revolution as an irenic process, one which would occur once the leaders of the society were Islamized. Although he used the term "revolution" to impress upon his audience the progressive image of his discourse, he did not view it as a process of cataclysmic social change. Rather, he used revolution as a way of gauging the extent of differences between an Islamized society and the one that preceded it.[47] As a result, Mawdudi's "organizational weapon" was never as lucidly defined as Lenin's was. For Mawdudi, the

Jama'at was both a "virtuous community" and a political party It would bring about change by expanding its own boundaries and waging a struggle against the established order, but with the aim of winning over leaders rather than the toiling masses. The mechanisms and working of the process of change therefore remained less clearly defined, reducing its strength considerably What the role of the party in realizing the ideology should be was, however, essentially the same.

The similarity between the two movements is not just conjectural. Mawdudi was familiar with Communist literature,[48] and true to his style, he learned from it, and from the Communist movement in India, especially in Hyderabad, in the 1930s and in the 1940s, when the Communist-inspired Telangana movement seriously challenged the nizam's regime. Mian Tufayl Muhammad, Jama'at's amir between 1972 and 1987, recollects a conversation in which Mawdudi commented: "no more than 1/100,000 of Indians are Communists, and yet see how they fight to rule India; if Muslims who are one-third of India be shown the way, it will not be so difficult for them to be victorious."[49] In later years former Communists joined the ranks of the Jama'at, bringing with them additional expertise in the structure and operation of Communist parties.

That the Jama'at's and Lenin's ideas about the "organizational weapon" were similar confirms that the relation of ideology to social action in Mawdudi's works closely followed the Leninist example. Mawdudi argued that in order for his interpretation of Islam to grow roots and support an Islamic movement he had to form a tightly knit party An organizational weapon was therefore the prerequisite to making Islam into an ideology and using religion as an agent for change. "No particular event prompted the creation of the Jama'at," recollects the senior Jama'at leader, Fazlu'rrahman Na'im Siddiqi; "it was the culmination of the ideas which Mawdudi advocated and the agenda which he had set before himself since 1932."[50]

Mawdudi first proposed an organizational solution to the political predicaments of Indian Muslims in 1934: "The erection, endurance and success of a social order requires two things: one, that a *jama'at* [party or society] be founded on that order's principles   and second, that there be patience and obedience to that *jama'at*."[51] His notion of a *jama'at* was not clear at this stage; its boundaries were vague for the most part. It reflected Mawdudi's desire to invigorate the Islamic faith and re-create a rigorous, virtuous community (*ummah*) as a force for change and a bulwark against the political marginalization of Indian Muslims. It could not remain abstract for long. The definition of the *jama'at* had to be narrowed from an amorphous community to a concrete entity Although Mawdudi knew this, he failed to appreciate the need to draw a clear line between holy community and political party Consequently, the Jama'at has since its inception remained committed to both its avowedly religious and its essentially sociopolitical functions.

This division first became manifest as Mawdudi became more and more involved in Indian politics from 1937 onward. When politics led him to depend on an organizational solution to the quandary before the Muslim community, his agenda and plan of action became increasingly confused. Political exigencies blurred the distinction between a revived *ummah*, defined in terms of greater religious observance, and a communally conscious political party dedicated to social action. It was not clear whether Muslims were supposed to take refuge in the spiritual promise of the holy community and withdraw from Indian society, or whether they were to immerse themselves in social action with the hope of reversing the fortunes of their beleaguered community. For Mawdudi the dichotomy between social action and spirituality, between the party and the *ummah*, was unimportant: the two would eventually be one and the same. A party would be a vehicle for harnessing the political power of the Muslims, not only by virtue of its organizational structure but also by the power of its moral rectitude. The strength of the party would emanate as much from its structure as from its embodiment of the Islamic ideal. In Mawdudi's eyes, just as safeguarding Muslim political concerns required turning to Islam, so enacting the dicta of Islam would ipso facto lead to political action. Religion had no meaning without politics, and politics no luster if divorced from religion. Mawdudi saw the connection between Islam and politics not as a hindrance but as an ingenious idea, an intellectual breakthrough, of using Islamic ideals to reshape the sociopolitical order.

Integrating Islam and politics was of course not a new idea, but it had thus far found no institutional manifestation in Islamic history [52] Throughout the ages, Muslims were even aware that the two were inherently incompatible. They paid lip service to the political directives of the Islamic revelation, but more often than not they separated religious institutions from political ones, lest politics corrupt the faith. Political leaders had sought to mobilize Islam in the service of the state, but rarely sought to extend the purview of their faith to include politics. For Muslims, the integration of religious and political authority in the person of Prophet Muhammad, like every aspect of the Prophet's mission, was a unique and metahistorical event. The Medina community was not institutionalized in the structure of Islamic thought, nor in the body politic of the Islamicate.[53] It rather remained a normative ideal, one which has surfaced time and again, in the form of Muslim chiliasm and atavistic yearning. The historical development of Islam—into what has been termed "traditional" Islam—was, therefore, predicated upon a de facto delineation of the boundary between religion and politics and a sober understanding of the relative weight of normative ideals and the imperatives of exigent realities in the life of man. The historical reality of Islam was even canonized in Islamic political doctrine, in lieu of the normative ideal of a holistic view of Islam. Muslim theorists from al-Mawardi (d. 1058) to al-Ghazzali (d. 1111) implicitly sanctioned the separation of religion and politics using the largely symbolic institution of the caliphate. Insisting upon the continuity between religion and politics is, therefore, an innovation of modern Islamic political thought.

The lesson of Islamic history and the logic of the traditional Islamic perspective clearly eluded Mawdudi, who like most revivalist thinkers was driven by faith and the promise of a utopia modeled after the Prophet's community Contemporary revivalists, Shaikh writes, have "approached the notion of [political] power not as a quantity that is intrinsically corrupting, apropos say of Christian doctrine, but as God's most eminent instrument for Man in the service of Divine justice,   a legitimate pursuit without forfeiting morality "[54]

The political circumstances of the prepartition years and the frustration Mawdudi shared with his coreligionists only added to his inability to see the inconsistency in combining religion and politics, holy community and political party Organization, he believed, would harmonize spirituality and politics, and would provide a panacea for Muslims. This conclusion further underscored the Janus face of the jama'at, as an exemplary community which would be the repository of Muslim values, and as a party which was to spearhead their drive for power. This contradiction tore the Jama'at between the conflicting requirements of its claim to pristine virtuosity and the exigencies of social action. The inability to resolve this confusion satisfactorily has been the single most important source of tension in the Jama'at, and hence the impetus for continuous clarification of the party's religious role, social function, and political aims.

The Emergence of the Jama'at-i Islami, 1938–1941

Mawdudi's organizational solution took shape between 1938 and 1941, the years when Indian politics had become hopelessly polarized between the Congress and the Muslim League. In the face of the mounting crisis Mawdudi exhorted Muslim parties and organizations to unite, but his exhortation fell on deaf ears. India continued to slide toward partition, and the only parties that thrived were the Congress and the Muslim League. Mawdudi had no confidence in their ability to realize Muslim goals, and he was even less sanguine about the prospects under the aegis of the smaller Muslim parties and organizations that cluttered the political scene. The gap between the religious and the political aspects of their program, Mawdudi believed, made them ineffectual; they were either too secular in their outlook, as was the case with the Muslim League, or too preoccupied with purely religious concerns, as was the Tablighi Jama'at (Missionary Society).

In venomous invectives against the Congress party and its Muslim allies, such as the Jami'at-i Ulama-i Hind, and against the Muslim League, the Khaksar, and other Muslim parties, Mawdudi belabored their shortcomings in an attempt to gain support, but it soon became apparent that he had to do more than excoriate his rivals; he had to establish a party that could relay his ideas to the masses and harness their energies in promoting his cause. Later Mawdudi recalled the idea of the Jama'at as having been "a last resort," necessitated by the collapse of the social order in Muslim India.[55]

Accompanied by a small groups of friends and followers, Mawdudi arrived in Lahore in January 1939 During the preceding three months, he had been stationed in the small village of Pathankot in East Punjab, where he had established a Muslim religious and educational institution called Daru'l-Islam (abode of Islam),[56] which he hoped would help revive Islam in India and thereby promote Muslim political power. He then decided to abandon the isolation of Pathankot and to take Daru'l-Islam to a major metropolitan center with a large Muslim community But when he reached Lahore, he soon decided that the situation was too acute to await long-term solutions, and he abandoned the Daru'l-Islam project.[57]

Lahore sharpened Mawdudi's focus, leading him not only to drop his insouciant attitude toward political activism but also to escalate his already incessant fulminations against the Muslim League in his journal *Tarjumanu'l-Qur'an*.[58] His expositions on Islam and Muslim politics often served as the pretext for tirades against colonialism and the Raj as well, which soon created problems for him with the provincial authorities. In the September 1939 issue of the *Tarjuman,* for instance, Mawdudi wrote an article entitled "Aqwam-i Maghrib ka 'Ibratnak Anjam" (The poignant lesson of the fate of Western nations) in which he castigated the Raj and discouraged Indians from supporting the British war effort; that issue of the *Tarjuman* was censored by the press branch of the Punjab government.[59]

In the same month Mawdudi accepted a teaching position at Lahore's Islamiyah College, but afraid of restrictions on his freedom of speech, he refused to take a salary [60] His openly political classroom lectures were popular with the students.[61] A number of prominent Jama'at members were students at the college at the time and became Mawdudi's followers after hearing his lectures.[62] The lectures, however, raised the ire of the college administration, and of the Unionist Party government of Punjab, which found them inflammatory Troubled by his rising popularity, it urged the college to dismiss him.[63] The college administration sought to curb his tongue by offering him a salary, but Mawdudi left the college in the summer of 1940, convinced that the cause of Islam would not fare well so long as the government was hostile to it.

Mawdudi wrote and traveled extensively during this period, delivering numerous lectures on the relation of Islam to politics. His audience was, by and large, composed of Muslim intellectuals, and because of that his discourse remained focused on educational concerns. During his tours he frequently visited Muslim schools such as the Aligarh Muslim University, the Muslim Anglo Oriental College of Amritsar, the Islamiyah College of Peshawar and the Nadwatu'l-

Ulama in Lucknow The accolades of the intellectuals greatly encouraged him and gave him confidence to discuss his ambitions more openly [64] It was to them that, in 1939–1940, he first publicly proposed the creation of a new party, viewing it as the logical end of any struggle in the path of Islam, and the harbinger of a successful revival (tajdid) movement.[65] In a letter to Zafaru'l-Hasan (d. 1951) of Aligarh Muslim University, dated A.H. 23 Rabi'u'l-Thani 1357 (1938–1939),[66] Mawdudi wrote of the political predicament before the Muslims and the Muslim League's inability to formulate a solid ideological position to solve it. Alluding to his personal ambitions, he wrote that "preferably, such Muslim luminaries as 'Allamah Mashriqi, Mawlana Husain Ahmad Madani, Dr. Khayri, Mawlana Azad Subhani or Mr. Durani should initiate and lead this effort," but because they were not "likely to provide the necessary guidance," the mantle of leadership, Mawdudi implied, would by default fall on his shoulders.[67] The names cited by Mawdudi ran the gamut of Muslim political opinion. Having found them incapable of providing the leadership necessary, Mawdudi was suggesting that he alone was able to give Muslims the leadership they needed. His lines to Zafaru'l-Hasan also revealed the extent to which his thinking was influenced by the politics of the Muslim League. For "the envisioned veritable organization" of which he wrote to Zafaru'l-Hasan was to "serve as a 'rear guard' [written in English] to the Muslim League."[68] The consolidation of the Jama'at's agenda was thus predicated upon the vicissitudes of the League's politics.

Mawdudi's aim was to significantly alter the balance of power between Muslims, Hindus, and the colonial order. It was not "winning in elections"—a clear reference to the Muslim League's strategy and objectives at the time—that interested him, but rather the revamping of the cultural and hence political foundations of the Muslim community of India, vesting Muslims with the ability to find a solution to their political weakness. This goal required great sacrifice and moral dedication which he did not believe the Muslim League, with its half-hearted commitment to Islam, to be capable of.[69] What the Muslims needed was a cadre of dedicated, morally upright, and religiously exemplary men who would both represent the ideals of the Islamic order and be prepared to achieve it.[70] The need for a "vanguard" became even more apparent when the Muslim League's Lahore Resolution was passed in 1940. That resolution formally advocated a separate state for Muslims in northern India and presented a whole new arena—a Muslim state—for Mawdudi's ideas to operate in. It also showed that the Muslim League increasingly dominated Muslim politics, which in turn pushed him into launching his party to prevent the League from consolidating its hold over Muslims. Thenceforth, the policies of the Muslim League would become the Jama'at's calling, and Jinnah's conception of Pakistan would be the single subject of Mawdudi's invective.

Mawdudi's perception of himself as the only leader capable of delivering

Muslims from their predicament became increasingly more pronounced.[71] He harbored ambitions to lead Indian Muslims as a scholar, renewer of the faith, and supreme political leader. His insistence on distributing his works far and wide in this period was part of an effort to establish his claim to the leadership of the Muslims.[72] His opinions were compiled in the three volumes of *Musalman Awr Mawjudah Siyasi Kashmakash* (Muslims and the Current Political Crisis), in which he opposes both accommodating the Hindu-led "composite nationalism" of the Congress party and the pro-British and secular Muslim nationalism of the Muslim League. Many have concluded that Mawdudi therefore favored preserving the unity of India under Muslim rule, after a wide-scale conversion of the population to Islam, but this is not the case.[73] While at an earlier time Mawdudi might have thought on an all-Indian scale, by the time he settled in Lahore in 1939 he believed that the social and political ascendancy of the Hindus in India was irreversible.[74]

His firsthand observation of the decline of the last bastion of Muslim power in southern India, the Hyderabad state, experiences with the Shuddhi campaign, and the Congress party's attitude toward the Muslims following the Khilafat movement had convinced him that Muslims were destined for a servile coexistence with the Hindus, a future in which he wished to have no part. Nor had he high hopes for the wide-scale conversion of Hindus to Islam, nor did he command the Jama'at to undertake such a mission. Between 1938 and 1947, although the Jama'at continued to operate across India, Mawdudi's attention was increasingly focused on the Muslim-majority northwestern provinces. He might have preferred the Muslims to rule a united India, but faced with the prospects of a Hindu political order he was in no way opposed to the idea of India's partition and actually began to tailor his program to take advantage of such an eventuality In the December 1938 issue of the *Tarjuman* he adumbrated "two nation" theories of his own within the context of a united India: "We are a distinct people whose social life is based on a particular ethical and cultural norm. We differ in fundamental ways with the majority population.   [N]o compromise or reconciliation will be possible."[75] Although Mawdudi did not speak of partition, he was acquiescing to the political realities of the time. His plan, much like those of his contemporaries, was initially set in the context of a united India. Its inner logic, however, nudged Muslims closer and closer to partition. In later years Mawdudi, reflecting on his thinking during this period, stated that he never opposed the Muslim League's demand for partition but rather was against the party's secularist attitude: "Our concern then [1941–1947] was Islam, and the ability of those who sought to represent it."[76]

Mawdudi's view of his own leadership was formed not in competition with the ulama or the pirs, or with other self-styled Muslim leaders such as Mashriqi, Mawlana Muhammad Iliyas (1885–1944), or Azad, but in rivalry with Jinnah, the qa'id-i a'zam (supreme leader) of the Muslim League. Mawdudi shared Jinnah's concern for the future of Indian Muslims and their rights to cultural and social autonomy, but parted with Jinnah in that the former looked to Islam as the principle legitimating force in Muslim politics whereas the latter appealed to the normative values of the Indo-Muslim tradition. Mawdudi's vision had little room for compromise on Islamic ideals, whereas Jinnah defined the Muslim community in broad and latitudinarian terms. Mawdudi, no doubt, viewed the anglicized style and the secular beliefs of Jinnah with contempt and no doubt eyed his power and popularity with a certain degree of envy

Jinnah's success as a political leader had convinced Mawdudi of his own potential. For if a Westernized lawyer could sway the masses in the name of Islam,[77] then a "true" Muslim leader could certainly attain even greater success. "Abu'l-A'la not only compared himself to Jinnah," recollected Abu'l-Khayr, Mawdudi's elder brother, "but also viewed himself as even a greater leader than Jinnah."[78] Jinnah's power, Mawdudi had concluded, was tenuous—predicated upon Islam, to which the Muslim League leader had no real attachments. Shaikh writes that, confronted with Congress's claim to representing Muslims as well as Hindus, Jinnah's strategy was "to affirm that, Congress could not represent Indian Muslims because it was not representative, that is to say typical, of Indian Muslims."[79] Taken to its natural conclusion, the argument could be turned against Jinnah by Mawdudi, who could assert that he and the Jama'at were more representative and "typical" of Muslims than the anglicized Jinnah and the secularist Muslim League. Mawdudi said of Jinnah's enterprise: "No trace of Islam can be found in the ideas and politics of Muslim League   [Jinnah] reveals no knowledge of the views of the Qur'an, nor does he care to research them   yet whatever he does is seen as the way of the Qur'an   All his knowledge comes from Western laws and sources   His followers cannot be but jama'at-i jahiliyah [party of pagans]."[80] The term jama'at-i jahiliyah was no doubt coined to make the contrast between the Muslim League and the Jama'at-i Islami more apparent. If the argument of affinity as a basis for representation could win the day for the Muslim League against Congress, all the more could it justify the Jama'at's claim to leadership of the Muslims.

Mawdudi also saw the Muslim League as essentially a one-man show, in contrast to his movement, which was more disciplined and therefore better poised to manipulate Muslim politics. The Jama'at, Mawdudi believed, was what the League pretended to be and was not.[81] Mawdudi thought that the League's appeal came not from the intransigence of the Congress party or that of the Raj in the face of Muslim demands, nor from the dynamics of the struggle for independence, but from its appeal to the religious sensibilities of Muslims. The use of Islamic symbols in enunciating Muslim communalist demands had become so pervasive that, by the mid-1940s, the Muslim League resembled "a chiliastic movement rather than a pragmatic party."[82] Mawdudi clearly took the League's rhetoric at face value and concluded that Islam—and not only the cultural norms of the Indo-Muslim traditions—formed the crux of Muslim politics and provided those who claimed to represent it with legitimacy From this it followed that the Jama'at was the only party equipped to deliver to the Muslims what the Muslim League had promised them. Having understood the politics of the Muslims of India solely in terms of Islam, Mawdudi became oblivious to the actual political dynamics of his community, a blind spot that continued to characterize his approach to politics during his years in Pakistan. Convinced of his eventual domination of Muslim politics, he groomed the Jama'at to be the "true Muslim League"[83]—the "rear guard" of which he had written to Zafaru'l-Hasan—and prepared it to take advantage of the League's expected demise.[84] The Jama'at was therefore opposed not to Pakistan but to the Muslim League. It was the expectation that Mawdudi would become its leader and not the partition of the Subcontinent that led him to oppose the Muslim League both before and after the creation of Pakistan.

Jinnah's meteoric rise enticed Mawdudi into politics, giving him the false expectation that as soon as his message was heard by the Muslims of India, and, later, of Pakistan, he would enjoy even greater prominence. The Jama'at was created, in part, to disseminate Mawdudi's message and catapult him into a position of power. Jinnah's example therefore both guided and misguided Mawdudi. It reinforced his political ambitions and effectively committed him to communal politics, the end result of which was the creation of Pakistan.

The Early Years, 1941–1947

In the April 1941 issue of the *Tarjuman*, Mawdudi invited all those who were interested in forming a new Muslim party based on Islamic ideals to a meeting in Lahore.[85] On August 26, 1941, seventy-five men, most of whom had not known Mawdudi previously,[86] responded to his invitation and gathered at the house of Mawlana Zafar Iqbal.[87] The Jama'at was officially formed after each of the seventy-five, following the example of Mawdudi, stood up and professed the Muslim testament of faith (*shahadah*)—thereby reentering Islam and forming a new holy community [88] The constitution of the Jama'at and the criteria for membership were all duly agreed upon during the course of that first session of the party, which lasted for three days. While all those who attended this gathering were familiar with Mawdudi's articles in the *Tarjuman* and therefore by virtue of their presence concurred with his views on the simultaneously religious and sociopolitical function of the Jama'at, they were not in agreement over the manner in which the party was to be governed. Some of those present favored an amir, as did Mawdudi who told the gathering, "Islam is none other than *jama'at*, and *jama'at* is none other than *imarat* [amirate]."[89] Others advocated a ruling council. Among those who favored an amir there was little

concord regarding the extent of his powers. Mawdudi with the help of a number
of those present struck a compromise: the Jama'at would be led by an amir with
limited powers—a *primus inter pares*.[90]

The debate then turned to the selection of the party's first amir. The founding
members agreed that, in the interests of minimizing the corrupting effects of
politicking, no one would be permitted to forward his own candidacy In
addition to Mawdudi another possible contender for the office of amir was
Muhammad Manzur Nu'mani, a Deobandi religious leader, who was the editor
of *Al-Furqan*, a respectable religious journal in Lucknow Nu'mani had known
Mawdudi since a visit to him at Pathankot in 1938 and believed that he and
Mawdudi had jointly conceived of the idea of the Jama'at after the two read
Sayyid Abu'l-Hasan 'Ali Nadwi's biography of the revivalist jihad leader Sayyid
Ahmad Shahid (1786–1831).[91] Nu'mani had used his journal to support Maw-
dudi's call for the Jama'at and his influence to get prominent men such as
Abu'l-Hasan 'Ali Nadwi to attend the first session of the Jama'at.[92] Nu'mani
therefore wielded considerable clout in that first session, and as his differences
with Mawdudi in later years indicate, he was not uninterested in being the
Jama'at's leader. Amin Ahsan Islahi, too, was a strong contender for the position
of amir.[93] As the editor of *Al-Islah*, a student of Sayyid Sulaiman Nadwi (1884–
1953) and Hamidu'ddin Farahi (d. 1930), and an instructor at the Madrasatu'l-
Islah seminary (*daru'l-'ulum*) of Sara'-i Mir in United Provinces, he was a tower-
ing figure among the Jama'at's founders. Islahi was not under the sway of
Mawdudi's intellect and had, in fact, in the 1937–1938 period taken issue with
some views expressed by Mawdudi which had led to an open and spirited debate
between the two.[94]

However, most of those present felt that since the Jama'at was Mawdudi's
idea and brainchild he should serve as its first head,[95] and a committee was
formed to nominate Mawdudi and Muhammad ibn 'Ali Kakwarwi for the office
of amir.[96] Mawdudi was elected by a majority of the founding members on
August 27, 1941.[97] Their mandate was not religious; they simply chose the best
manager among them to lead the party

After the meeting in Lahore the founding members dispersed to recruit new
members. Nu'mani and his journal again propagated the Jama'at's cause and
invited new members into its fold, efforts which soon led Nu'mani to claim the
party's leadership.[98] Those who joined were drawn from among those who were
disturbed by the direction Muslim politics had taken, who objected to the
Congress party's Muslim Mass Contact Campaign, which was designed to create
support for the Congress party among Muslims, and who regarded as dangerous
the domination of Muslim politics by Congress and the Muslim League. Many of
them thought that Muslims lacked effective leaders and were attracted by the
Jama'at's anti-British rhetoric, which they had missed in the Muslim League's

platform.[99] Many had been influenced by Azad and the fiery articles of *Al-Hilal*, and then deserted him after Azad's decision to embrace the Congress party,[100] to find solace in the Jama'at.

Mawdudi had sent invitations to join to some fifty senior Indian ulama, including Manazir Ahsan Gilani, 'Abdu'l-Majid Daryabadi, Qari Muhammad Tayyib, and Husain Ahmad Madani, all of whom declined.[101] Young ulama, however, were well represented among the early members of the Jama'at. Sixteen joined in 1941, six from Madrasatu'l-Islah, four Deobandis, four Nadwis,[102] and at least two of the Ahl-i Hadith. By 1945 the Jama'at boasted some 224 ulama members, 60 of whom continued to teach at various religious seminaries.[103] Some of the Jama'at's most loyal and dedicated members such as Mian Tufayl and Malik Ghulam 'Ali also joined the party at this time. They proved to be Mawdudi's staunchest supporters and became leaders of the Jama'at in Pakistan.

Given the diversity of its membership and the stature of many as ulama and votaries of different schools of Islamic thought, in its early years the Jama'at did not become a centralized movement, nor did its amorphous structure permit its effective control by the amir. It operated by gaining a consensus on its objectives: to imbue Muslim character with religious values and to serve as an alternative to both the Muslim League and the Congress. Great emphasis was placed on moral rectitude and education in these years, confirming the party's view of itself as essentially a holy community The Jama'at sought to shape Muslim politics by encompassing society as a whole; winning elections was not as yet an overriding concern. It viewed its strategy as a more fundamental and definitive solution to the intractable problems which beleaguered the Muslim community Hence, from its inception the Jama'at saw education and propaganda as central to its program, even if at the cost of an effective political agenda.

Some six months after the Jama'at was founded, Mawdudi and Nu'mani decided to leave Lahore. They were afraid that their nascent party would be engulfed by the Pakistan movement. Emulating the Prophet's example, the new party had to withdraw from the larger society, lest its ideological purity be compromised.[104] At first Sialkot, a small city in West Punjab, was considered as a base, but later leaders turned to Pathankot and the site of the Daru'l-Islam project.[105] On June 15, 1942, the Jama'at moved to Pathankot.[106]

The Pathankot years (1942–1947) were a time of organizational and intellectual consolidation. A significant number of the Jama'at's members also moved there to form strong personal, intellectual, and organizational bonds, away from the tumult of national politics. Pathankot provided time for learning, debate, and intellectual creativity Many of the Jama'at's members belonged to different religious schools of thought, and the impact of the debates between Deobandis, Nadwis, Islahis, and the Ahl-i Hadith during this period was later to appear in some of the ways Mawdudi read Islam and its place in society

Both leaders and members periodically emerged from their holy community to travel across India from Peshawar to Patna to Madras, holding regional and all-India conventions, addressing audiences, and establishing a nationwide organizational network.[107] These itinerant gatherings were a source of new recruits and sympathizers for the party and permitted the Jama'at to remain in the political fray despite its seclusion in Pathankot. The strategy was also successful in diversifying the Jama'at's ethnic and geographic base of support. In 1946, of the party's 486 members, 291 were from Punjab, 60 from United Provinces, 36 from Hyderabad, 31 from Madras, 14 from Delhi, 12 from central India, 10 from North-West Frontier Province, 9 from Bombay, 8 from Sind, 7 from Bihar, 6 from Mysore, and 2 from Bengal.[108]

By 1947 the Jama'at boasted at least one member in every Indian province except Assam, Baluchistan, and Orissa.[109] Its leaders, as reflected in the geographical distribution of the central consultative assembly (markazi majlis-i shura') between 1945 and 1947, however, remained predominantly North Indian and from Muslim minority provinces. Of the sixteen shura' members in those years, four were from Punjab, three from United Provinces, one from Delhi, one from Bihar, two from Hyderabad, and one from Bombay [110] Changes in the national representation were significant, the more so in that the number of members from areas that were inherited by Pakistan increased in these critical years. In 1947, 277 requests for membership were submitted to the Jama'at, 136 of which were accepted. Some 50 percent of the applications came from Pakistan's future provinces, as were 40 percent of those accepted into the Jama'at.[111]

Moving to Pathankot brought out a problem latent in the Jama'at's structure. The powers of the amir had been left undefined by the founding members, and Mawdudi saw his position as that of a spiritual and political leader of an ideologically committed movement. Many others, however, regarded the office of the amir as that of director or overseer. As a result, the obedience which he demanded from members was not always forthcoming, especially from those who saw themselves as Mawdudi's equal, or even superior in religious matters, and who had a religious education. The communal life at Pathankot brought the tension between Mawdudi's leadership and the perception of it among members into the open, and led to defection in the ranks. Nu'mani, for one, a Deobandi religious leader and the editor of Al-Furqan, thought himself superior to Mawdudi in piety and scholarship.[112] While he had acquiesced to Mawdudi's election to the office of the amir, at Pathankot he began to challenge Mawdudi's authority by demanding that Mawdudi relinquish control to the Jama'at of the royalties of the Tarjuman and his celebrated book Risalah-i Diniyat (Treatise on religion, 1932)[113] and by questioning Mawdudi's own moral standing and piety

The early years of the Jama'at were a time of great financial difficulties and personal sacrifices, the more so for those who had left city living for the provincialism of Pathankot. Discrepancies in the way the amir and other members lived, therefore, quickly became an intractable problem. While other residents lived spartan lives, Mawdudi maintained a separate house, a servant, and amenities not available to others.[114] The irritation this situation caused was sufficiently pronounced to permit Nu'mani to manipulate it to his advantage. Nu'mani demanded that the publication royalties, which Mawdudi claimed were providing his livelihood, be turned over to the Jama'at for the benefit of all members. The very notion of a holy community precluded differences in the members' standard of living and the separation of personal affairs from group interests. The Jama'at, argued Nu'mani, was not an extension of Mawdudi, but should encompass his whole livelihood—as Mawdudi had demanded of other members.[115] Mawdudi retorted that both the journal and the book had been his personal undertakings long before he conceived of the Jama'at. The party, argued Mawdudi, had no propriety rights over his scholarship.[116] For both Mawdudi and Nu'mani, raising this issue challenged the authority and person of the amir.

Nu'mani then followed this initial assault with another. He contended that Mawdudi's beard was not the right length, his wife did not cover herself properly before their male servant, Mawdudi himself had not been prompt for dawn prayers, and, generally, his piety was not in keeping with what was expected of the amir of a holy Muslim community[117] Mawdudi rather apologetically conceded that his behavior and that of his wife were not always ideal, but they had changed their ways to accord with what the position of the amir required of them. However, suspicious of Nu'mani's ambitions, Mawdudi remained unrepentant and refused to acknowledge the charges brought against him as a reflection on his moral standing and as sufficient cause to warrant his resignation.[118] Nu'mani then pressed the Jama'at to convene a special session of the shura' to decide the argument.[119]

Nu'mani had, in the meantime, consulted with a number of Jama'at members, notably Amin Ahsan Islahi and Abu'l-Hasan 'Ali Nadwi, regarding the issues at stake. Convinced that he had support for his position, Nu'mani sought to use the shura' session that met in October 1942 to unseat Mawdudi altogether. In response to the complaints which Nu'mani placed before the shura', Mawdudi offered either to resign from the office of amir or, alternatively, to dissolve the Jama'at. Nu'mani and his supporters opted for dissolution. The shura', however, was not prepared for that and moved to Mawdudi's side. Nu'mani's faction, consisting of Abu'l-Hasan 'Ali Nadwi, Muhammad Ja'far Phulwari (briefly the deputy amir of the Jama'at), and Qamaru'ddin Khan (the secretary-general of the Jama'at at the time) resigned from the party[120] The defectors were few in number, but significant in status.

Defeated, Nu'mani began a public campaign against Mawdudi in his journal

Al-Furqan, claiming that since he had been responsible for enlisting the support of so many for the Jama'at, he now had the moral responsibility to inform them of the reasons for his resignation from the party [121] Privately, too, Nu'mani worked diligently to convince others to leave. He was not successful; the organizational structure proved strong enough to withstand Nu'mani's challenge, and the members' notion of what a holy community was proved to be far more permissive and supple than Nu'mani had expected. As Islahi put it, "I am not fanatical enough to jeopardize the future of Islam over the length of Mawdudi's beard." [122]

The crisis Nu'mani precipitated, however, did expose an important dilemma for the Jama'at: What was the proper mix in emphasizing ideological principles and serving organizational needs and political aims? The shura', in the first of a series of decisions, voted to strengthen the organizational structure of the party and serve its interests and still further confirmed the primacy of the amir, somewhat resolving the initial ambiguity regarding his role and the extent of his powers. Nu'mani's resignation, meanwhile, gave Mawdudi greater room to maneuver and to establish his leadership over the party Assured of the backing of the shura', Mawdudi set out to spread the reach of the Jama'at. He traveled across India, presenting the Jama'at's ideological position and inviting Muslims to support it. The imprint of Mawdudi's views on the party became increasingly more pronounced. The Jama'at's convention in Dharbanga, Bihar, in 1943, for instance, turned into a forum for the discussion of Mawdudi's theory of divine government (hukumat-i ilahiyah). [123]

Mawdudi was elected to the office of amir again in 1945 at the party's first all-India convention. [124] Thenceforth, the Jama'at came increasingly under the control of Mawdudi, a trend already evident in his speech following his election to a second term as amir, in which he repeatedly underlined the primacy of his office in the organizational design of the Jama'at. [125]

The Jama'at conventions were of some consequence in Muslim political circles, sufficiently so to boast the attendance of Mahatma Gandhi at one of them. [126] They also helped the Jama'at to grow and to find a following. Eight hundred people attended the Jama'at's first all-India convention in Pathankot in 1945, ten times more than those who had gathered in Lahore to form the party [127] The number was still modest, but given the Jama'at's forbidding ideological demands, it was nevertheless noteworthy

Expansion was not, however, free of problems. Organizational development lagged behind the increase in membership. A good deal of attention at conventions between 1943 and 1947 was devoted to resolving internal problems, usually revolving around discipline and ethics. [128] The Jama'at was repeatedly purged during this period of its less than fully committed members. In 1944 Mian Tufayl, the secretary-general of the Jama'at at the time, reported to the shura' that 300 members—over 50 percent of the membership—had been expelled from the party, and he set down sterner criteria for new members.[129] Still, in 1947, 135 new members joined, and 85 left the party.[130] The lion's share of Mawdudi's speeches before the Jama'at conventions at Allahabad and Muradpur in 1946, and again in Madras and Tonk (Rajasthan) in 1947, was devoted to lamenting poor morale and discipline and emphasizing character building.[131] Mawdudi had clearly favored swift expansion so the party would be large enough to influence the highly fluid and rapidly changing Indian political scene. But the problems of discipline that threatened to nip the notion of holy community in the bud compelled him to greater caution. As early as 1943 he declared that the pace of growth of the Jama'at should be restrained, a declaration which was thenceforth repeated along with every lament over the party's problems of morale. Despite his openly political orientation, Mawdudi was clearly committed to the holy community idea as well.

These organizational difficulties only augmented Mawdudi's powers. Emphasis upon ideological unity and especially organizational discipline favored vesting greater powers in the office of amir. Some members were not reconciled to Mawdudi's preeminence in the party Islahi, for example, time and again registered his opposition, most vociferously at the Jama'at's Allahabad session in 1946.[132] However, despite sporadic expressions of concern, the consolidation of power in the office of the amir continued unabated, especially as partition necessitated effective leadership at the party's helm. During the Jama'at convention in Tonk in 1947, the shura' ceded some of its powers to the amir, notably control over finances.[133]

Paramount at this time was the question of Pakistan. Since the Jama'at's establishment, the party had not taken a clear stand on the issue. Despite its vehement opposition to the Congress and favoring of communalism, it had viewed close association with the Muslim League as detrimental to its integrity and autonomy Hence, the party had favored Pakistan to the extent of advocating the case for an Islamic state but had remained aloof from the Muslim League—led Pakistan movement. When partition materialized, Mawdudi decided in favor of it but rejected the idea of retaining a united organizational structure for the two countries, arguing that the needs of the Muslims and hence the agenda of the Jama'at would be so different in India and Pakistan as to make the operation of a united Jama'at-i Islami unfeasible. He set the Jama'at of India free from his command and became the amir of the Jama'at of Pakistan. The breakup in the party limited its power but brought it more effectively under Mawdudi's control. The new Muslim state presented the Jama'at with greater opportunities and new problems, the resolution of which would determine the pattern of the Jama'at's subsequent development and how its organizational structure, ethos, and political agenda took shape.

2 From Holy Community to Political Party

Following partition the Jama'at continued to change; interacting more vigorously with other political forces, it refined and restructured its organizational design. The search for a successful political strategy led the party to sublimate ideological posturing in favor of more pragmatic politics. Ideological imperatives soon clashed with involvement in politics, creating tensions in the ranks. Those members interested in questions of principle revolted. The party was forced to reexamine its role and mission in Pakistan, reassessing the relative importance of religious ideals and political interests in its plan of action.

The Punjab Elections of 1951

Following the creation of Pakistan and Jama'at's move to Lahore, Mawdudi escalated the party's involvement in politics just as he consolidated its identity and organizational structure. The Jama'at grew in numbers during these years, but more important, it was able to do so with greater facility It was no longer plagued with the kinds of problems of morale and discipline that had characterized its prepartition years. Difficulty, however, continued to loom on the horizon for a party which remained divided over the extent of the rights of its leader, its religious calling, and political agenda, and the question of ideological principles versus political interests. Even as late as 1951 the Jama'at had described its plan of action as (1) the reform of the life and minds of individual Muslims, (2) organization and training of virtuous men, (3) social reform, and (4) reform of the government and the political structure.[1] Politics was not only listed last, but it could not be addressed until the first three phases of the plan had been completed. Until the end of the first decade of its existence, the Jama'at remained a movement immersed in religious work; it strove to control the souls of men and eyed politics with awe and suspicion. Although it spoke of its political ideals, it stayed aloof from the day-to-day conduct of politics, preferring the seclusion of its holy community to the vicissitudes of action. It deliberately, for instance, avoided any involvement in the Indian national elections of 1945 [2]

The resolution of the conflict over the party's ultimate aim continued to attract the attention of the Jama'at's leaders during an otherwise uneventful period in the party's history following its move to Pakistan. It continued to operate as it had in its days in India. No longer inhibited by the fear of lending support to the Congress, it became bolder in its opposition to the Muslim League, but its politicization remained in the nature of moral guidance and the articulation of an ideal for Pakistan. It continued to rely on the power and appeal of its message and to operate more in the mold of a holy community than that of a political party This was in keeping with Mawdudi's reading of Jinnah's success. Pakistan was the product not of the Muslim League's efficacy as a political machine but of the appeal of Islam on the one hand and Jinnah's ability to relay his vision to the multitude of Indian Muslims on the other. The Jama'at therefore began its activity in Pakistan debating with the country's founders and its citizens, hoping to replicate the intellectual and emotional process which Jinnah had initiated a decade earlier. The party's emphasis remained on propaganda, and its campaign to publish its literature during those early years is indicative of its understanding of politics in Pakistan.

It was not long before the Jama'at's hopes for a quick and easy Islamization of Pakistan were dashed. Mawdudi's political naïveté and the limits of the Jama'at's ingenuous political program began to show Pakistan was not going to fall into the hands of the Jama'at through propaganda alone; the party had to politicize its activities to stave off challenges from a hostile government and to push Pakistan toward an Islamic goal. Elections scheduled in Punjab for March 1951 provided the occasion for the Jama'at to initiate a new plan of action and enter into an era of more direct political involvement.

Participation in elections and expanding the Jama'at's political horizons were questions that came before the party when Mawdudi was temporarily out of power. He had been put in prison for questioning the Islamicity of the state, and the party was being led by the two provisional amirs, 'Abdu'l-Ghaffar Hasan and 'Abdu'l-Jabbar Ghazi. They put the matter before the shura', which debated it extensively Despite the opposition of some members to participating in the elections and associating with the political system, the shura' sanctioned the party's participation,[3] but did not put forward any candidates of its own. It would lend support to those candidates whom it deemed virtuous (*salih*)[4] as determined by voters' councils (*panchayats*). Each of these councils would consist of fifty-three members, twenty-three of whom would be appointed by the Jama'at. The role the Jama'at chose in the elections was peculiar: it was not vying for its own political gain but fighting to prevent the election of those who would prevent it from gaining in the future. The party still saw its role as providing religious education and propaganda and regarded elections as merely a tool for sanitizing politics.

The election results were not a triumph for the Jama'at. The candidates it favored collected only two hundred thousand votes in the thirty-seven constituencies in which it was active.[5] Either the people of Punjab had not heard the Jama'at's call or they had chosen to ignore it. Whichever the case, the Jama'at was clearly dejected by the results, aside from Mawdudi, who saw gains even in defeat. The election, he argued, had served to propagate the Jama'at's program far and wide and had strengthened the party by bringing in many new members, workers, and sympathizers, an argument that was ever after repeated by the Jama'at leaders to justify participation in elections and to make defeats therein palatable.

Despite Mawdudi's optimism, the defeat was serious enough to cause much soul-searching. The party thenceforth became more diligent in its organizational and propaganda efforts, hoping to amend those shortcomings which it saw as responsible for its defeat and to redeem itself in future elections. Coveting electoral victories required a different organizational outlook and a different attitude toward politics and elections. The Jama'at found it had a vested interest in the electoral process. It began to compare itself with other political parties, transforming its aim of establishing virtuous leadership (*salih qiyadat*) from a distant goal into an immediate objective.

The election campaign had also presented the Jama'at with an unwelcome breakdown of discipline. To the chagrin of Mawdudi and the elders of the Jama'at, workers and rank-and-file members were sufficiently swayed by the demands of the electoral campaign to transgress the party's code of ethics. The frequency and extent of complaints put before the party's leaders were disconcerting and led Mawdudi to reiterate the need to maintain party discipline. The election and its aftermath had, all in all, thrown the Jama'at into confusion. On the surface, the party continued to adhere to its four-point plan of action, outlined shortly before the elections in November 1951. In reality politics was no longer last on the list. Debates over whether the party's mission was religious propaganda or politics were waged with increasing frequency Senior members such as Mas'ud 'Alam Nadwi, 'Abdu'l-Jabbar Ghazi, and 'Abdu'l-Rahim Ashraf, citing the deleterious effect of electoral politics on the morale of the holy community, argued against remaining active in politics for the time being.[6] Mawdudi and Islahi were inclined toward politics, and hence suggested two agendas—political activism and religious work—simultaneously, which only added to both the confusion and the debate.[7] The anti-Ahmadi agitations of 1953–1954 and Mawdudi's subsequent imprisonment gave them no opportunity to resolve this issue satisfactorily It was left to fester until it eventually caused the most serious rupture in the party's history

The Machchı Goth Affair, 1955–1957

Mawdudi was released from prison in 1954. After his release a general meeting was held in Karachi, a routine session that unexpectedly turned into a forum for airing grievances about procedural matters, the electoral defeat of 1951, and government harassment in 1953–1954.[8] In that session Sa'id Ahmad Malik, a one-time Jama'at amir of Punjab, leveled charges of ethical misconduct and financial embezzlement against another high-ranking member. Mawdudi was greatly disturbed by Malik's allegation, all the more so because it had been aired before the entire body of the Jama'at. Eager to spare the holy community the shock of confronting its fall from grace, Mawdudi sent Islahi to dissuade Malik from further registering his complaint before the gathering by promising a full investigation.

Malik agreed, and, true to his promise, Mawdudi announced the formation of a review (*ja'izah*) committee, consisting of seven members of the shura' and Malik himself. The committee was to investigate Malik's charges and prepare a report on the general discontent in the Jama'at that had been aired in the Karachi meeting. The committee immediately made apparent a concealed source of power in the party In its early years the Jama'at had few office holders and hardly any "workers"; there was no real division of power or duties and no payroll. The Jama'at's members in those years had all been part-time religious organizers and missionaries.[9] The expansion and rationalization of the Jama'at in Pakistan after 1947, however, had generated an organizational machine managed by party operatives out of the secretariat in Lahore. These party workers and managers, many of whom were full-time employees, had by 1954 gained considerable control over the Jama'at's operations. They were mainly younger and more politically inclined members and had vested interests of their own, both with regards to the Jama'at's internal policies and its stand on national issues.[10]

The Jama'at's bureaucracy supported the leader whom Malik had accused of wrongdoing. The complaints the committee would be reviewing in most cases involved the policies and operational procedures followed by the Lahore secretariat. Afraid that the bureaucracy would be blamed, Mian Tufayl Muhammad, the secretary-general at the time, procrastinated to hinder the committee from beginning its work. 'Abdu'l-Rahim Ashraf, appointed by Mawdudi to head the committee, brought up the subject in the shura' meeting of November 1955 [11] With the shura''s sanction the committee began its deliberations, but the bureaucracy managed to trim it down to four members—Ashraf, 'Abdu'l-Ghaffar Hasan, 'Abdu'l-Jabbar Ghazi, and Sultan Ahmad—all of whom were ulama and senior leaders, and none of whom was either a functionary or stationed in Lahore.

No sooner had the committee begun its investigations than it became clear that the scope of complaints and misconducts far exceeded what had initially been suspected, and worse yet, they reached far up in the hierarchy At the time they met Mawdudi was away touring the Arab world; he was therefore not aware of the scope of the committee's probes and findings. In his absence, 'Abdu'l-Ghaffar Hasan was made interim overseer of the party, which permitted him to stifle any resistance to the investigation by the Lahore bureaucracy The investigations lasted a year, during which its members interviewed some two hundred members across Pakistan, noting their complaints and questioning them regarding their attitude toward the party

The findings were not complimentary and were in many ways disturbing. Wide-ranging ethical transgressions and financial misdeeds were reported, and complaints were registered against the procedures and behavior of the Lahore bureaucracy Even Mawdudi and Islahi were implicated. The committee prepared a comprehensive report of its findings and submitted it to the shura' for consideration during its session in November 1956: the Jama'at had strayed from its path of "upholding the truth" (haqq-parasti) to opportunism (maslahat-parasti) and following popular will ('awam-parasti); it had departed from its original educational aim and mission and had become a political organization; its moral and ethical standards had sharply dropped, and political work was occupying an increasing share of its time to the exclusion of religious studies and even worship; the treasury was relying to too great an extent on outside sources of funding, which influenced the members and the decisions of the party, and since 6.7 percent of its members were paid employees that part of the membership had lost its independence of thought and action.[12] The report suggested that, since the issues raised by the committee's findings were in part the result of the party's premature involvement in politics and their remedy would require the lion's share of the party's time and resources, the party should not participate in the general elections which were expected to follow the passage of the constitution of 1956 in Pakistan. This recommendation enmeshed the committee's findings in the party's debate over its future course of action, further complicating the resolution of the problems. Ethics was posited as the antithesis of politics, forcing the party to choose between them.

The shura' meeting of November 1956 lasted for fifteen days. This was the longest and liveliest session in its history The four committee members, led by Ashraf, presented their case: (1) the Jama'at had gone completely astray, as the extent and nature of the complaints registered in the committee's report indicated; (2) politics had come to dominate the Jama'at's activities with dire results; and (3) if the Jama'at did not desist from political activities it would lose what it had gained. Ashraf, in a nine-hour speech presented their points and argued that any departure from the four-point plan of action stipulated in November

1951 would seriously compromise the Jama'at's doctrinal position.[13] Mawdudi and Islahi, although supported by some of the shura"s members, were unable to argue with the findings of the report and, at best, staved off some of the sharpest criticisms leveled against the party Mawdudi tendered his resignation a number of times during the session but was dissuaded: committee members argued their objective was not to oust him but to restore the party's moral standing.[14] Mawdudi was not, however, thoroughly convinced, but he was outvoted.

The fifteen-day shura' session ended with a four-point resolution: First, the Jama'at had veered from its proper course. While the party had made gains, it had also been damaged, and this damage should be repaired. Second, the decisions of the shura' session of July 1951, the four-point plan that de-emphasized politics, continued in effect; therefore the new stress on politics since 1951 should be reversed. Third, the Jama'at's position on various issues was based on the Qur'an, hadith, and decisions of the amir and the shura', and not on any party document. In other words, Mawdudi's works did not dictate policy, and the Jama'at was not an extension of him. Finally, Islahi along with two other senior members of the Jama'at would form a committee to see that the resolution was carried out.

Mawdudi was clearly upset by the proceedings of the shura' and by the resolution, which was constitutionally binding on him. Not only had the fifteen-day meeting revealed problems and curbed the party's appetite for politics, but it had also challenged his authority For the first time in the Jama'at's history it was the shura', rather than he, who was deciding the party's future. The party's constitution had been invoked to assert its autonomy from his person. The guarantees of the autonomy and efficacy of the Jama'at's organizational structure, which had been designed by none other than Mawdudi, were now in competition with him. He was by no means reconciled to the decision of the shura', and this allowed the Lahore bureaucracy to enter the fray

Remedying the problems cited in the review committee's report would certainly encroach upon the bureaucracy's powers. It consisted mainly of lay religious activists and had a different view of the choice between ethics and politics than the ulama members of the committee. Young activists were predicting imminent victory at the polls in the forthcoming elections, and this expectation of victory made them eager to run candidates in the elections, to ignore the four-point plan, and to become a national party But men like Ashraf anticipated a repeat of the party's 1951 electoral performance.[15] Hence, no sooner had Mawdudi arrived back in Lahore than the activists led by Sayyid As'ad Gilani, 'Abdu'l-Ghafur Ahmad, and Kawthar Niyazi approached Mawdudi to encourage him to defy the writ of the shura' They argued that it had been biased, and its resolution represented mutiny against Mawdudi's authority that would encourage factionalism and even the party's dissolution. These were far graver transgressions against the party's constitution, they argued, than the amir's disobeying the shura"s decisions.[16] Moreover, since the resolution had been based on an "erroneous" report—which the committee members were accused of having contrived with ulterior motives in mind—it could not be binding, and the issue should be reopened. The Jamaʿat, or at least elements in it, were showing a surprising independence in trying to influence the amir in a manner hitherto not associated with that party

Mawdudi allowed himself to be persuaded by the arguments of the Lahore bureaucracy, because they presented an opportunity to break the unwelcome restrictions the shura' had placed on the party and on his office.[17] Mawdudi's two-year stint in prison had given him prestige and made him a hero.[18] He was not prepared to forego his newly found stature, and expected the respect that went with it. The prolonged shura' session had led to recriminations and bitterness. Mawdudi regarded criticism of his leadership as disrespect for the office of amir, as well as representing a vendetta against his person. The latent disagreement over the extent of the amir's powers and the nature of his leadership, which had first become apparent when the Jamaʿat was founded in 1941, was once again casting its shadow The ulama members continued to view the amir as primus inter pares and as a manager rather than a spiritual guide, while Mawdudi felt the amir's role should be that of a preeminent and omnipotent religious leader.

On December 23, 1956, thirteen days after the shura' session, Mawdudi wrote to the members of the review committee, arguing that by exceeding the powers mandated to them they had at best inadvertently conspired against the Jamaʿat. He accused them of factionalizing the organization to further their own ambitions.[19] Given the gravity of their "crime," and the fact that their performance in the shura' had proven destructive, Mawdudi demanded their resignation. Should they not resign, he threatened, he would go to their constituencies and demand that the Jamaʿat members "turn them out."[20]

The four members of the committee appealed to Islahi for justice. Islahi, a man of mercurial temperament, had up to this point supported Mawdudi, but now he took it upon himself to respond on behalf of the four. He chastised Mawdudi for his prevarication and pointed out that the four were among the Jamaʿat's most senior members and all men of the highest moral standing. Mawdudi had himself approved of their selection for the review committee. Three of them, ʿAbdu'l-Ghaffar Hasan (1948–1949, 1956), ʿAbdu'l-Jabbar Ghazi (1948–1949), and Sultan Ahmad (1953–1954), had been appointed by Mawdudi as provisional amirs. How could their integrity be slighted without casting aspersions on Mawdudi's own judgment? Islahi furthermore charged that Mawdudi was being influenced by the insidious propaganda of "the staff of the Jamaʿat's central offices" to act "undemocratically" and against the Jamaʿat's constitution.[21] Islahı was, at a more fundamental level, trying to consolidate or defend the constitutional powers of the shura' against what he regarded as encroachments upon them by the amır.

When he read Islahi's letter, Mawdudi was incensed. He wrote to Mian Tufayl that the party should choose a new amır, as "if [he] had died."[22] Mawdudi was no doubt doing just what he had already threatened the review committee he would do: force the Jama'at to choose between him and his critics. Clearly Mawdudi was confident of where their loyalty lay [23] Mian Tufayl, Na'im Siddiqı, and Malik Nasru'llah Khan 'Azız, three of Mawdudi's most loyal lieutenants, went to Islahı to end the mounting crisis. Islahı ordered them not to disclose the news of Mawdudi's resignation to anyone, within or outside the Jama'at, and quietly to call a session of the shura' Siddiqı, a fervent Mawdudi loyalist, thought otherwise. He resigned from the Jama'at forthwith to relieve himself of the obligations of the party's code of conduct and Islahi's order, and proceeded to spread the news of Mawdudi's resignation, along with incriminating reports against Islahı and the review committee. The news soon spread beyond the party; it appeared in the press.

After Mawdudi's resignation, Chaudhrı Ghulam Muhammad was named vice-amır (*qa'im maqamı amır*) by Mian Tufayl, so that he could oversee the party's operations. Ghulam Muhammad set out to bring about a reconciliation between the two men. The party's leaders were aware that government intrigue would make the Jama'at's internal problems worse if they dragged on or were exposed in national news with embarrassing consequences for the holy community Arguing that the very future of the Jama'at was at stake, Ghulam Muhammad asked Mawdudi to withdraw his resignation; ordered those aware of the dispute to maintain strict silence; and suggested that the issues in dispute be put before an open Jama'at meeting at the earliest possible date. The trepidation of the Jama'at's leaders and members regarding possible government machination in this crisis no doubt assisted Mawdudi. He was a national figure; his resignation from the office of amır, many felt, could spell the end of the party

The shura' called by Mian Tufayl met on January 12, 1957 Islahı, Ashraf, and Ghazi were not present. Islahı charged that the Jama'at's bureaucracy had deliberately arranged the session so that critics of Mawdudi could not attend.[24] Already sensitive to allegations that in his dispute with Mawdudi he was motivated by personal ambition, Islahı tendered his resignation.[25] A delegation of senior Jama'at members led by Ghulam Muhammad managed to dissuade him pending the result of the open meeting, scheduled for February 1957 in Machchı Goth, a small and desolate village in the Chulistan Desert in southern Punjab. Islahı acquiesced and withdrew his resignation. He was receptive to compromise, and those who approached him in this spirit found him forthcoming.[26] Islahı demanded redress for the grievances of the members of the review committee and limits on Mawdudi's powers, but Mawdudi and his supporters felt no need to compromise and continued to force a showdown.

Under pressure from Ghulam Muhammad the handpicked shura' accepted his proposals without change and 'Abdu'l-Ghaffar Hasan was compelled to ask Mawdudi to withdraw his resignation.[27] Mawdudi agreed on the condition that an open party meeting be given the power to resolve the dispute. He would not return to his duties until they had reached a decision.[28] He intended to hold the threat of resignation over the shura' and the review committee, because he was convinced that the rank and file of the party supported him and that an open session would circumvent the constitutional powers of the shura', which was stacked against him by supporters of Islahi and the review committee. Faced with constitutional restrictions and unable to win his case through regular channels, Mawdudi circumvented the very rules he had himself devised to prevent the domination by any one leader. This was a volte-face with momentous implications and a testament to the fundamental role politics and personal ambitions played in Mawdudi's decisions and policies. By acceding to an open meeting and Mawdudi's demand that Jama'at members arbitrate the issues in dispute, the shura' surrendered its constitutional powers to an ad hoc body, opening the door for the amir to undermine the authority of the shura' with the blessing of its members.

Meanwhile, warned by Siddiqi, the Jama'at's bureaucracy mobilized its resources—organizational circulars, newspapers, and magazines—to inveigh against Islahi and the review committee, and to sway minds before the antagonistic parties could put their cases before them in the open session.[29] The bureaucracy especially sought to shift the focus of the debate away from the report, the grievances of leaders against the amir, the constitutional implications of Mawdudi's attack on the committee, and the future of the holy community and toward the victimization of Mawdudi and his resignation from the office of amir. The bureaucracy also helped embolden Mawdudi by casting in a conspiratorial light all the criticisms leveled against him or Jama'at's functionaries. They convinced him that, with the backing of the review committee, Islahi was maneuvering himself into the position of amir, an accusation which had enough truth to it to seem compelling to Mawdudi.[30] He took to treating criticism of his decisions as invidious efforts to paralyze the Jama'at, and became uncompromising in his drive to cleanse the organization of dissent and to use, if needed, extraconstitutional measures to preserve its unity This accusation put Islahi on the defensive and effectively silenced him. Unwilling to give credence to rumors regarding his own ambitions, Islahi approved all resolutions that confirmed Mawdudi's leadership.

With Mawdudi's backing the bureaucracy now went on the offensive. Sa'id Ahmad Malik, who had started the review committee's investigation, and

'Abdu'l-Rahim Ashraf, who led the committee, were first suspended and later expelled from the Jama'at by the amirs of Rawalpindi and Faisalabad (Lyall-pur).[31] Disgusted with the turn of events, 'Abdu'l-Jabbar Ghazi resigned from the Jama'at, and the tide began to turn to Mawdudi. He was not content with victory alone, nor did he seek conciliation; he set out to purge the Jama'at of his critics. In a meeting of the shura' which convened in Machchi Goth before the open session began, it was suggested that Mawdudi resume his activities as amir and a committee be appointed to study the findings of the review committee. Maw-dudi, smelling victory, rejected the suggestion out of hand—if such a committee was formed, he would resign from the Jama'at. Only his resignation and partici-pation in future elections were to be discussed in the open session. At the behest of Mawdudi's supporters, the shura' declared that it preferred having Mawdudi as amir over pursuing the review committee's report.

Of the Jama'at's 1,272 members, 935 attended the Machchi Goth session.[32] They came anxious about where their party was heading and sympathetic to Mawdudi, as the circulars, journals, magazines, and newspapers meant them to be. Islahi was the most prominent of those in dissent, but he made no mention of the questions of principle that had caused his break with Mawdudi and instead spoke of the organization's four-point plan of November 1951.[33] He preached moderation and balance (*tawazun*) between religious pursuits and political activ-ism. Politics had begun to fill all the hours of Jama'at members, lamented Islahi, leaving no room for pious works. The content and tone of Islahi's speech showed interest in a reconciliation, but Mawdudi wanted no part of it. This refusal infuriated Islahi, and he left the Jama'at. In a letter to Mawdudi afterward, Islahi wrote that he had been assured by Chaudhri Ghulam Muhammad that Mawdudi had at least accepted partially some of his grievances and was willing to accommodate him. Islahi's expectation was not realized at Machchi Goth, prov-ing that Mawdudi was hoping to mollify him and tone down his hostility before that session, without actually intending a compromise. This realization, wrote Islahi, was a major reason why he left the Jama'at.[34] He had withdrawn his earlier resignation on assurances given to him by Mawlana Zafar Ahmad Ansari, a confidant of Mawdudi, that a compromise would be reached at Machchi Goth. Islahi felt that he had kept his part of the bargain and that Mawdudi had reneged on his.

Islahi's cautions therefore fell on deaf ears, and his appeal for the party to return to its original agenda was rejected. With events moving in Mawdudi's direction, his supporters became even less compromising, and all dissenters were barred from addressing the gathering.[35] Having kept the review committee's report and his own high-handed policies out of the proceedings, Mawdudi went on the attack. In a six-hour speech, he demanded more political action and introduced a new agenda in place of the four-point plan of 1951.[36] He reiterated the Jama'at's original objectives and reviewed the party's history; he said that the party would continue as a holy community and a religious movement but it would now participate in electoral politics. Reforming the political order was moved up from a distant fourth to a primary aim. Mawdudi argued that the Jama'at had been formed with the objective of establishing the rule of religion (iqamat-i din) and a divine government (hukumat-i ilahiyah). Neither would be attainable if the Jama'at permitted the secular forces to become too entrenched. The organization must abandon its isolation and enter the political scene, if not to further its own cause, at least to deny success to its adversaries.[37] The Jama'at was therefore to revise its original agenda; it would now pursue political objectives and religious education and propaganda with equal vigor.

Mawdudi's speech struck such a receptive chord that subsequent efforts to temper his call to politics met with hostility from the rank and file. Mustafa Sadiq, one of those who sought to temper Mawdudi's powers, however, managed to secure only 148 votes for a resolution which censured overt politicization.[38] At the end of the session, participation in politics was put to a vote. All but fifteen voted in favor; the fifteen handed in their resignations then and there. A peculiar feature of this whole episode was that the two things that had originally precipitated the crisis—the review committee's report and Mawdudi's reaction to it—were not even discussed at Machchi Goth. Neither Mawdudi nor the opposition ever mentioned it. An ethical issue had turned into a political one and served as the handmaiden for the party's greater politicization.

Mawdudi and his supporters were not content with their victory at Machchi Goth. They met in the nearby village of Kot Shair Sangh and initiated a purge, which Ashraf dubbed "the Jama'at's Karbala." Mawdudi set out to reestablish the authority of the amir's office and to bring the party back to its original unity of thought and practice. The idea of a holy community found new meaning when, its moral content eviscerated, it persisted only to legitimize the party's political activities. The review committee's report was to be destroyed to eliminate any possibility of division over its content. Na'im Siddiqi, who had violated the orders of Islahi and Ghulam Muhammad by leaking the news of Mawdudi's resignation, was reinstated as a member. At Kot Shair Sangh the meeting also decided that all those who had differed with Mawdudi, like non-Muslims (zimmi) in an Islamic state, could remain in the party but were henceforth barred from holding office or positions which could influence the party's platform. This decision, interpreted by many as sheer vindictiveness, led to further defections from the ranks, including Israr Ahmad, Mustafa Sadiq, and 'Abdu'l-Ghaffar Hasan. Hasan resigned primarily to protest the purge of those who had spoken their minds.[39]

The immediate impact of these defections was muted. Islahi's resignation was perhaps the most damaging, for he enjoyed a certain following in the Jama'at, especially among those who had studied the Qur'an with him. Yet even his departure did not lead to a mass exodus.[40] Mawdudi, it appeared, had overcome the challenge to his authority with great dexterity and at minimal cost. In the long run, however, the purge had a debilitating effect on the intellectual caliber of the party's members. Fifty-six members left the Jama'at at Machchi Goth, Kot Shair Sangh, and in the months that followed; most were ulama and represented the party's religious weight and intellect.[41] They were replaced by lay activists and functionaries.

Mawdudi was not greatly discomfited by these desertions; had they stayed, those who had left would have interfered with his plans. Those who left were simply given up as souls who had fallen from the path of Islamic revolution.[42] Those who remained would be more servile and amenable to his leadership. In a letter to Ghulam Muhammad after Machchi Goth, Mawdudi clearly showed no interest in patching up his differences with Islahi.[43] Shortly after, the Jama'at presented candidates for the elections of the Karachi municipal corporation and won nineteen of the twenty-three seats it contested. This showing vindicated Mawdudi and erased the last traces of the Machchi Goth affair. Despite all, however, the party waged a campaign based on the four-point plan of 1951.[44]

The Machchi Goth affair and the subsequent purge reoriented the party toward politics, redefined its conception of Islam and its place in the life of men, and replaced its ideological outlook with a more pragmatic one. The Jama'at had begun as a movement of cultural and religious rejuvenation; it had been premised on ethics and religious teachings. Its primary target was man, whose "reconversion" to the unadulterated truth of his faith would catalyze social change and eventually bring political reform. At Machchi Goth, this puritanical and somewhat traditional formula was altered. The conversion of men would now occur in tandem with, if not in pursuance of, the reform of politics. The Jama'at, much like revivalist movements everywhere, began to show more interest in governing how Muslims lived than in their individual souls. By overlooking the review committee's report and Malik's allegations of financial misconduct to maintain the Jama'at's role in politics, Mawdudi suggested that Islamization ultimately flowed from politics to society to the individual, and not the other way around.

It can be argued that at Machchi Goth Jama'at's bureaucracy was manifesting the party's reaction to outside changes. The Jama'at had been founded in India; it had operated in Pakistan for a decade with little modification in perspective. By 1956, the Pakistani polity had consolidated and the country was now unlikely to wither away The Jama'at's notion that it could conquer the new country's soul and centers of power had proved to be fleeting. Its campaign for an Islamic constitution had, moreover, reached its aim with the passage of the constitution of 1956, which the Jama'at had accepted as "Islamic." The Jama'at, therefore, had to find a new role. To remain relevant to Pakistani politics and the future development of the country, the party had to move out of its organizational shell and beyond single causes; it had either to engage in concrete debates or be yet another missionary (tabligh) movement. While, even after the Machchi Goth affair, the Jama'at did not fully abide by these directives to its own detriment, the party was pushed to rationalize its structure and refine its plan of action.

By 1956 the Jama'at had lost its intellectual momentum. Its zeal and ideological perspective had been important for the development of contemporary Muslim thought in the Subcontinent and elsewhere, but the party was no longer producing ideas which would sustain its vitality as a religious movement and secure a place for it at the forefront of Islamic revivalist thinking. Most of Mawdudi's own seminal works, outlining his views on Islam, society, and politics had been written between 1932 and 1948. His worldview and thought had fully taken shape by the time he moved to Pakistan. All subsequent amendments to Jama'at's ideology pertained to politics more than theology Its experience over the decade of 1946–1956 had shown that its contribution and influence lay not so much in what it espoused but in its organizational muscle and political activism. Its survival as a holy community could no longer be guaranteed; it was in politics that the party had to search for a new lease on life. This imperative was most acutely felt by the party's lay activists and bureaucratic force, who had the least grounding in Islamic learning, and for whom the Jama'at was the sole link to a holistic view of the role of Islam in the world. Many ulama whose ties to Islam were independent from the Jama'at felt the depletion of the party's ideological energies less acutely They did not have the sense of urgency the first group felt, nor were they prepared to sacrifice values and principles to resuscitate a party Their departure from the Jama'at no doubt worsened its intellectual and ideological crisis and strengthened the bureaucratic element that would continue to politicize the Jama'at.[45]

The outcome of the Machchi Goth session sowed the seeds of a "cult of personality" around Mawdudi in tandem with the bureaucratization of the Jama'at. The political needs of the party required its amir to be more than primus inter pares; the party needed a command structure which precluded the kind of discussion, debate, and dissension which the ulama members of the Jama'at— and most of those who had left the Jama'at in 1957—were accustomed to. The Machchi Goth affair, much as Nu'mani's departure from the Jama'at, had augmented the powers of the amir and institutionalized this eventuality as a corollary of any resolution of tensions and crises surrounding the party's politicization. This was a cost which a party bent on a more active political role had to incur.

The Machchi Goth affair also marked the "end of ideology" and the beginning of pragmatic politics and decision making in the party Interestingly,

Mawdudi oversaw the routinization of his own chiliastic and romantic idealism. While his earlier works and career had done much to kindle revivalism across the Muslim world, his arguments for abandoning the ideological perspective in favor of greater pragmatism in large measure went unnoticed by his admirers across the Muslim world.

Mawdudi was not altogether oblivious to the problems that had produced the Machchi Goth imbroglio in the first place. At Kot Shair Sangh he initiated far-reaching constitutional reforms which would guarantee greater organizational unity and prepare for the new plan of action. Some of these reforms were designed to devolve power from the office of the amir and to contain abuses of power by himself as well as other Jama'at members. In May 1957, the Jama'at's constitution was revised to iron out the anomalies and sources of discord in the organizational structure and to guard against a repeat of Machchi Goth. The amir was made subject to the writ of the shura', but he would no longer be elected by the shura' but by the Jama'at's members; the shura' was expanded to fifty members; its procedures were streamlined; the amir was given greater control over the agenda and discussions; the shura' was given veto power over the amir's decisions, and vice versa; procedures were set to govern disagreements between the two; and finally, a *majlis-ı 'amilah* (executive council)—a politburo of sorts—was formed to serve as the ultimate arbiter between the amir and the shura', its members to be appointed by the amir from the shura' members.

Schism and Purge after 1957

The Machchi Goth affair by no means resolved the party's problems, nor did it render the party invulnerable to the ethical pitfalls of pragmatic politics. In fact, it exposed the increasing discrepancy between its religious facade and the pragmatic political reality of its program. Because of that, other Machchi Goths were likely to occur.

While Mawdudi was in prison following a government crackdown on the Jama'at in 1963, the party joined the Combined Opposition Parties, a group that had organized to resist Ayub Khan's rule. The alliance decided to challenge Ayub Khan in the presidential elections of January 1965 and proposed to run Fatimah Jinnah (d. 1967) as its candidate for president. The Jama'at endorsed this choice, a decision which flew in the face of Mawdudi's oft-repeated arguments against any public role for women.[46] It was a monumental doctrinal compromise which, given the national attention focused on it, could not be easily justified. The Jama'at appeared to have abandoned its ideological mainstay and declared itself a political machine through and through, one which recognized no ethical or religious limits to its pragmatism.

Mawdudi responded to the resulting clamor by arguing that the decision was made by the whole party and not by himself. He then went on to justify the decision as an evil warranted by the necessity of combating yet a greater evil, Ayub Khan and his martial-law regime.[47] Mawdudi's explanation did not convince those outside the Jama'at and led to dissension within the party as well. Kawthar Niyazi, then the amir of Lahore and an ardent defender of Mawdudi during the Machchi Goth affair, began in the pro-Jama'at journal *Shahab* openly to question the wisdom of his position.[48] Niyazi argued against supporting a woman candidate and claimed that the Jama'at had gone too far in compromising its principles; as a result it had ceased altogether to be a religious entity In a deft maneuver against Mawdudi, Niyazi then digressed from the Jinnah candidacy to widen the debate to include Mawdudi's other doctrinal compromises in accommodating the Jama'at's political interests. He repeated all Mawdudi's arguments against elections in earlier times, juxtaposing them with the Jama'at's policy of putting up candidates since 1951. Inferring duplicity on the part of Mawdudi, Niyazi sought to put both Mawdudi and Jama'at's political agenda on trial yet again.

This time it did not work. Unlike Islahi, Niyazi had no following of his own within the party, and some even disliked his bureaucratic style in the party's secretariat. The Jama'at had changed significantly since 1957 It was now more centralized, and, as Niyazi charged, had more members on the payroll, which hampered their ability to express their ideas, let alone voice dissent.[49] By airing the problem in his journal, Niyazi infuriated his fellow members, who accused him of doing the bidding of the government by trying to paralyze the Jama'at before the elections. Mawdudi responded by asking Niyazi to resign from the party [50]

Although Niyazi's challenge to Mawdudi showed that the conflict between ideology and pragmatic politics continued to hound the party, the response also suggested the changes had enabled them to contend with internal differences.[51] The party had become sufficiently pragmatic not to be shocked by Mawdudi's inconsistency in supporting Fatimah Jinnah. The other leaders of the party had already endorsed Miss Jinnah while Mawdudi was still in jail and were therefore fully prepared to defend his decision.

In the coming years the Jama'at continued to suffer from tensions arising from its slide toward pragmatic politics, showing less tolerance for dissent and a greater ability to maintain unity [52] The purge of dissenting members became more frequent until it was a routine mechanism for resolving disputes. As a result, a diverse movement built upon a tradition of discussion, debate, consensus, and a shared vision of the ideal Islamic order turned into a party in which policies were so pragmatic that its original purpose and intellectual vitality were destroyed and ideological roots weakened. Perhaps that is the fate of any holy community that ventures into politics. The Machchi Goth affair gave the party a new lease on life, but the price was that it evolved along lines neither anticipated nor necessarily desired by its founders, and it became a full-fledged political party Mawdudi's initial enthusiasm for politics may have clouded his vision, or perhaps he was simply unable to control the forces he had let loose. He could ride the tide of politicization, as he did in 1956–1957, but he, and later his successors, were hard-pressed to contain it. Politicization became a consuming passion that drowned out ethical considerations, intellectual vitality, pious works, and worship.

From the mid-1960s onward Mawdudi constantly referred to incidents of violence involving the Jama'at and emphasized organizational discipline, showing his growing concern with what political pragmatism had done to his party [53] His farewell address to the Jama'at in 1972 following the election of Mian Tufayl to the office of amir centered on the need to reestablish a balance between ideological imperatives and pragmatic concerns.[54] Especially after the Jama'at was routed at the polls in 1970, Mawdudi turned back to the idea of holy community, as the election results did not justify the sacrifices made nor the damage incurred by purges and compromises. His colleagues were, however, no longer willing to heed his advice. Mawdudi was at odds with his party, and after he stepped down as amir in 1972, he found his influence limited. In a clear departure from his attitude at Machchi Goth, he concluded that the party had given away too much to politics without gaining enough in return.[55] In 1972 he lamented to his wife that the party "was no longer up to his standards.   If he had the stamina he would have started all over again."[56] "I hope this will not be the case," he told a friend, "but when historians write of the Jama'at, they will say it was yet another revival (*tajdid*) movement that rose and fell."[57] Finally, he advised the shura' in 1975 to move the Jama'at away from politics and to revive the holy community; for elections had proved not only to be a dead end but also debilitating. His advice was largely ignored.[58]

Today the Jama'at is an important political party in Pakistan, but Islamic revivalism in Pakistan has been passed on to other movements,[59] many of which were founded by former Jama'at members, such as Israr Ahmad and Javid Ahmadu'l-Ghamidi.[60] The outcome may have saddened Mawdudi, but it was unavoidable and for some not unwelcome. What the party's history shows is that the relation between ideology and social action in Islamic revivalism is neither as harmonious and spontaneous nor as permanent and immutable as is often believed. Mawdudi's revivalism, as powerful as its synthesis between religious idealism and political action may seem, in reality produced an inherently contradictory attitude toward social action and spiritual salvation. To resolve the conflicts innate in Mawdudi's program, ideological zeal gave way to greater pragmatism and transformed the movement from holy community to political party

2

STRUCTURE AND SOCIAL BASE

3　Organization

To understand the manner in which Mawdudi's ideology found organizational expression and the extent to which it found a social identity and put down roots among various social strata, to understand what makes for the Jama'at's strength as a political actor and, conversely, accounts for its political constriction, and to outline the structure, operation, and social base of the party, one has to identify the variables that have determined the Jama'at's organizational structure and base of support and controlled the extent of continuity and change in them, and to account for both the support for the Jama'at's program among particular social groups and the limits to the diversity of its social base. The links between the Jama'at's ideology and politics and the pattern of the party's historical development have grown out of its organizational structure and social base, as have the nature of the Jama'at's politics and its reaction to changes in its sociopolitical context. By defining the Jama'at as an organization with a distinct social identity and distinguishing those factors which have determined the extent of its power and reach, we can establish a basis for understanding the party's history as well as the nature of its politics. We will examine the way the Jama'at has contended with organizational change and the problems it encountered in trying to expand its social base. Organizational change led to debates over the choice of leaders and how to reform the party's organizational design. Opening the ranks of the party also generated debates that influenced its ideological development and politics. Those factors interacted with influences that were brought to bear on the party by other political actors to decide the nature and trajectory of continuity and change in the Jama'at's politics and the party's role and place in society

The Jama'at-i Islami's organization initially consisted simply of the office of the amir, the central *majlis-i shura'*, and the members (*arkan*; sing., *rukn*), and this did not change much during the party's early years. Members were busy producing and disseminating literature, especially the *Tarjumanu'l-Qur'an*, expanding its publications and education units at Pathankot, and giving form to the Arabic Translation Bureau (Daru'l-'Urubiyah) which was established in Jullundar, East Punjab, in 1942.[1] Between 1941 and 1947 supporters were divided up according to the extent of their commitment to the party The hierarchy that resulted began at the bottom with those merely introduced to the Jama'at's message (*muta'arif*), moved up to those influenced by the Jama'at's message (*muta'athir*), then the sympathizers (*hamdard*), and ended with the members (*arkan*). The first three categories played no official role in the Jama'at aside from serving as a pool from which new members were drawn and helping to relay the Jama'at's message. All categories provided the Jama'at with workers (*karkuns*) of various ranks employed by the party to perform political and administrative functions. They also served as workers in the party's campaigns.

The hierarchy was revised in 1950–1951 to streamline the Jama'at's structure and tighten its control over its supporters in preparation for the Punjab elections of 1951. The categories of those merely introduced to and of those influenced by the Jama'at's message were eliminated and a new category, the affiliate (*mutaffiq*), was added. Affiliates were those who favored an Islamic order and supported the Jama'at but were not members. They were, however, under Jama'at's supervision and were organized into circles and clusters.[2] Affiliates stood higher in the Jama'at's organizational hierarchy than sympathizers. The Jama'at also devised a rational and centrally controlled structure which enveloped all of its affiliates and organized them into local units and chapters. In 1978 the party had 441 local chapters, 1,177 circles of associates, and 215 women's units. In 1989 these figures stood at 619, 3,095, and 554, respectively[3] The affiliates as a category were provided for in the Jama'at's constitution and therefore had to abide by the code of conduct laid down by the party Early ties with people acquainted with the Jama'at's message, originally so important to a movement with a missionary objective, were now severed, and the party turned its attention to strengthening its reach and its ability to run effective political campaigns. The change suggests that the Jama'at did not associate political vigor with the expansion of its popular base, which would have been possible through extending its informal ties with the electorate but rather with organizational control.

After 1941, the Jama'at was besieged with problems of discipline, and to solve them the party tightened its membership criteria a number of times. Mawdudi regarded these problems as serious enough to justify measures that would safeguard against the breakdown of discipline.[4] The party's concern with politics, however, required a rapid expansion of membership which enforcing the new criteria would discourage. The category of affiliate was the solution; it brought many people into the party without compromising quality, caliber, and party orthodoxy The new category also served as a screening device. It provided an opportunity to observe, scrutinize, and indoctrinate potential members before accepting them, reducing the problems of discipline in the party

The institution of the affiliate points to the importance placed on moral caliber by the party Membership in the Jama'at began with conversion to the party's interpretation of Islam. The party also demanded total commitment to its objectives and decisions. The members gave shape to the vision of re-creating the Prophetic community Wives of members were encouraged to become involved in the women's wing of the party and the children to join the student wings or children's programs. Over time many Jama'at members came to be employed by the party, and those who worked outside it were required to participate in its numerous labor and white-collar unions. Members often went to training camps, which educated them in the Jama'at's views and trained them in political and organizational work (see table 1).

Organizational unity was also boosted through frequent meetings at both the local and national level. Every Jama'at unit held weekly meetings during which personal, local, and national issues were discussed, and every member gave an account (muhasibah) of his week's activity to his superiors. If a member missed more than two of these meetings without a valid excuse, he could be expelled from the Jama'at.[5] Since every local Jama'at unit was part of a larger one, each of which held meetings of its own, members could end up attending several meetings each week. The Jama'at sessions encouraged discussion and airing of views, but once a decision was reached, all discussion ended and the members were bound by it. National-level open meetings (ijtima'-i 'amm) promoted solidarity in the party as a whole. The Jama'at began holding provincial meetings across India in 1942 and held its first all-India meeting in April 1945 at Pathankot. These meetings were held regularly until partition. In Pakistan the tradition of national meetings continued, but they were open only to members and affiliates. The party held its first national meeting in Lahore in May 1949 and the second in Karachi in November 1951. The extraordinary meeting at Machchi Goth was the most significant of these early all-Pakistan gatherings, which were not held at all between 1958 and 1962 due to the martial-law ban on congregations of this kind. They were resumed in 1962. In November 1989, for the first time in forty-two years, the party opened its national meeting to the general public, once again making use of the propaganda value which these meetings had for the party in its early years.

Party Structure

The hierarchy of members constituted only one aspect of the Jama'at's reorganization. Of greater importance were the offices which managed the party After its move to Pakistan the Jama'at began to deepen its organizational structure by

Table 1. The Jama'at-ı Islami's Organızatıonal Actıvıtıes, 1974–1992

	Punjab	NWFP	Baluchıstan	Sind	Total
1974					
Meetıngs	9,272	250	2	2,412	11,936
Traınıng camps	10	—	—	103	113
Meetıngs with potentıal recruits	299,137	3,000	688	328,063	630,888
Mıssıonary work traınıng camps	334	—	—	14	348
Jama'at-ı Islamı libraries and reading rooms	1,578	71	12	179	1,840
Conferences and conventions	10,941	1,183	53	4,179	16,356
1977					
Meetings	13,635	2,203	166	—	14,021
Traınıng camps	114	23	2	—	139
Meetıngs with potentıal recruits	—	—	—	—	—
Mıssıonary work traınıng camps	4,000	—	—	38	4,038
Jama'at-ı Islamı libraries and reading rooms	4,375	556	12	222	5,165
Conferences and conventions	46,175	3,335	77	5,620	55,207
1983					
Meetings	12,028	6,820	103	9,611	28,562
Traınıng camps	799	593	32	186	1,610
Meetings with potential recruits	19,878	3,274	98	—	23,250
Mıssıonary work traınıng camps	121	157	4	132	414
Jama'at-ı Islamı libraries and reading rooms	1,186	271	32	65	1,554
Conferences and conventions	4,423	1,114	57	225	5,819
1989					
Meetings	10,758	2,610	358	556	14,282
Traınıng camps	137	61	18	35	251
Meetings with potential recruits	37,652	1,037	910	39,084	78,683
Mıssıonary work traınıng camps	75	4	2	22	103
Jama'at-ı Islamı libraries and reading rooms	844	99	29	176	1,148
Conferences and conventions	2,753	242	53	924	3,972

Table 1. *(Continued)*

	Punjab	NWFP	Baluchistan	Sind	Total
1992					
Meetings	2,329	654	52	2,469	5,504
Training camps	361	93	7	101	562
Meetings with potential recruits	226	29	10	42	307
Missionary work training camps	2,390	403	19	2,098	4,910
Jama'at-i Islami libraries and reading rooms	2,322	467	69	1,553	4,411
Conferences and conventions	—	—	—	—	—

Source: Organization Bureau of Jama'at-i Islami.

reproducing the offices of amir, deputy amir, secretary-general, and the shura', with some variations, at provincial, division, district, city, town/zone, and village/circle levels. Its structure was thus based on a series of concentric circles, relating the Jama'at's smallest unit (*maqam*), consisting of two or more members, to the organization's national command structure (see figure 1).

Beginning in 1947 the Jama'at began to organize its members at different levels. Over the years a hierarchy was formalized through which the party's officials controlled the members at various levels. It remains in force today Each level and unit are defined by the number of members in it and also try to accommodate the administrative topography of Pakistan. In places where there are few members, a unit may not be warranted on a village or town level. In such cases two or more villages form one circle, and two or more towns one zone. In administrative terms, a circle stands at the same level in the party's hierarchy as a village unit, and a zone at the same level as a town. Each level has an administrative unit based on the authority structure of amir, deputy amir, shura', and secretary-general, which is maintained through elections. To gain a sense of the depth of the structure, in Punjab alone there are thirty district-level units, each with an amir, shura', and secretary-general. These circles envelope one another, producing an all-encompassing administrative and command structure, decentralized and yet closely knit to form the organizational edifice of the Jama'at.

THE OFFICE OF THE AMIR

The office of the amir was the first administrative unit created in the Jama'at, and it has remained the most important. Originally the amir was elected by the central shura' through a simple majority vote, but since the 1956 reforms he has

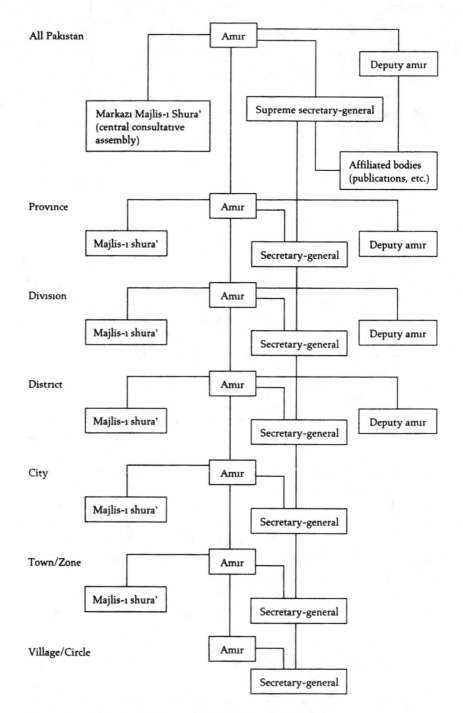

Figure 1. Organizational structure of the Jama'at-i Islami

been elected by Jama'at members, and his term of office is fixed at five years; there is no term limit. A committee of the central shura' members chooses three candidates, whose names are then put before the members at large. They send in their secret ballots to the Jama'at's secretariat, whose controller of elections (*nazim-i intikhabat*) has been appointed by the shura' to oversee the process. A list of candidates must be put forth by the shura' sixty days before the elections, and members must register to vote ninety days before the date of the election.[6] This system tends to favor the incumbent, as the members are not likely to unseat someone who is both administrative head of the party and its spiritual guide. No amir to date has been voted out of office.

The amir is the supreme source of authority in the Jama'at and can demand the unwavering obedience of all members (*ita'at-i nazm*). He is, however, constitutionally bound by the set of checks and balances that were passed following the Machchi Goth affair. All doctrinal issues must be determined by the shura' Should the amir disagree with the shura' on any issue, he has a right of veto which throws the matter back to the shura' Should the shura' override the veto, the amir must either accept the decision of the shura' or resign from his post. The amir can be impeached by a two-thirds majority of the shura' In budgetary and administrative matters the amir is bound by the decisions of the *majlis-i 'amilah*, whose members he appoints from among shura' members. The amir oversees the operation of the Jama'at's secretariat.

Insofar as possible this organization is replicated at each level of the party Each lower-level amir is elected by the members of his constituency to terms varying from one to three years depending on the level in question. These amirs are similarly bound by the decisions of their shura's. The lower-level amirs also oversee the office of their secretaries-general. However, lower-level secretaries-general are also accountable to the Jama'at's national secretary-general, which curtails the autonomy of the lower-level amirs and reduces their control over administrative affairs.

The Machchi Goth affair proved to be an aberration in an otherwise uneventful history of the amir's office. Since then the constitutional mechanisms governing it have steered the Jama'at through two succession periods—from Mawdudi to Mian Tufayl Muhammad in 1972, and from Mian Tufayl to Qazi Husain Ahmad in 1987 Each transition followed upon the retirement of the amir.[7] This pattern is in sharp contrast to transitions in other Pakistani parties, and accounts for the fact that the Jama'at, unlike most other Islamic movements of South Asia, continued strong after the passing of its founder from the scene.

At a meeting in Lahore on January 10, 1971,[8] following the Jama'at's defeat at the polls in December 1970, a group led by Sayyid Munawwar Hasan (now the secretary-general) launched a tirade against Mawdudi. They argued that the Jama'at had been routed at the polls because of him. Old and reserved, Mawdudi had relinquished national politics to the more energetic and charismatic leaders of the Pakistan People's Party and the Awami League (People's League), Zulfiqar 'Ali Bhutto and Mujibu'l-Rahman, who won the elections. Similar views were related to the editors of *Tarjumanu'l-Qur'an* by other members and supporters during the following months.[9] Implicit in these ventings of frustration was a demand for a new leader. On February 19, 1972, Mawdudi suffered a mild heart attack and decided to step down as the amir. The shura' nominated Mian Tufayl Muhammad (then secretary-general), Ghulam A'zam (later the amir of Jama'at-i Islami of Bangladesh), and Khurshid Ahmad (a longtime disciple of Mawdudi, and currently deputy amir of the Jama'at). On November 2, 1972, Mian Tufayl Muhammad (b. 1914) was elected amir.[10]

None of those nominated by the shura' qualified as charismatic leaders, least of all Mian Tufayl. The electorate appeared to have been governed by more pressing concerns than those posed by the party's Young Turks. They had been disappointed by their performance in the elections and now faced a belligerent opponent in the Bhutto government. By choosing a loyal lieutenant of Mawdudi, an administrator rather than a political maverick, the party opted for continuity and stability Its search for a more charismatic amir, although not abandoned, was postponed to a later time.

Mian Tufayl was not an effective politician, nor was he able convincingly to assert the powers vested in the office of the amir. Following his election, a good deal of the amir's powers, accumulated and jealously guarded by Mawdudi over the years, were ceded to others in the party, and authority became more decentralized. That encouraged the formation of independent loci of power, which in turn further divested the amir of authority Constitutional procedures became even more visibly entrenched, and the shura', as the original source of authority in the Jama'at, once again asserted its power and primacy Mian Tufayl's fifteen years at the helm of the Jama'at, to the chagrin of those who had wished to reinvigorate the party's ideological and chiliastic zeal, led the party farther down the road of legal-rational authority

A different set of concerns led to the election of Qazi Husain Ahmad to the office of amir on October 15, 1987 After a brief surge in popularity in the 1970s, the Zia ul-Haq years had eclipsed the political fortunes of the party, which became increasing marginalized in national politics. The results were dissension within the party over its policies and performance and the retirement of Mian Tufayl. Aging, and increasingly under criticism, he stepped down as amir, paving the way for a new generation to lead the Jama'at. The shura' nominated Khurshid Ahmad, Jan Muhammad 'Abbasi (the amir of Sind), and Qazi Husain Ahmad (the secretary-general) to succeed Mian Tufayl. The first two were conservative in the tradition of Mawdudi and Mian Tufayl, while Qazi Husain had a populist style and a good rapport with the younger and politically more active members. The party elected Qazi Husain (b. 1938). He came from a family with a strong Deobandi heritage. His two older brothers were Deobandi ulama, and his father was a devotee of Mawlana Husain Ahmad Madani of Jami'at-i Ulama-i Hind, after whom Qazi Husain Ahmad was named. His Deobandi ties helped the Jama'at in the predominantly Deobandi North-West Frontier Province. He became acquainted with the Jama'at through its student organization and joined the Jama'at itself in 1970. Many, among both the younger members and the conservative old guard, felt that it was time to go in a new direction. Qazi Husain had been responsible for creating an important constituency for the Jama'at in North-West Frontier Province, which today elects a notable share of the Jama'at's national and provincial assembly members. Many hoped he would do the same for the Jama'at at the national level.

Qazi Husain appealed to both conservatives and the more liberal elements. As the party's liaison with the Zia regime during the Afghan war, he was favored by the pro-Zia conservative faction, while his populist style and call for the restoration of democracy endeared him to the younger generation who wanted the Jama'at to distance itself from Zia. The Jama'at had made a politically sagacious choice by electing an assertive and populist amir. His appeal has to date been more clearly directed toward the Pakistani electorate than toward the rank and file of the Jama'at. He is the first amir to hold a national office: he has been a senator in the Pakistani parliament since 1985 In November 1992 he was elected to a second term as amir.

THE DEPUTY AMIR

Twice in its history the Jama'at appointed a vice-amir (*qa'im maqam amir*), an interim measure to fill the vacancy left by an absent amir. More important has been the office of deputy amir (*na'ib amir*). Three deputy amirs were selected by the founding members of the Jama'at in 1941, mainly to ensure that Mawdudi remained primus inter pares.[11] After two of them left the party in 1942, the office fell vacant, though the title was occasionally conferred on Islahi and Mian Tufayl to give them executive powers when Mawdudi was absent.

In 1976 the office was reintroduced with a new objective in mind. Three deputy amirs were appointed by the amir, and each was given a specific area of Jama'at activities to oversee. The reintroduction of this office was part of the decentralization of power during Mian Tufayl's tenure. It rationalized the Jama'at's organizational structure by dividing activities into separate units and delegating authority to the deputy amirs who oversaw those units. The office of deputy amir also gave the rising generation an important office to fill and brought the increasing number of peripheral activities and affiliated bodies under the party's central command, both of which helped ease tensions within the party The office exists only on a national level.

In 1987 the duties of the deputy amirs were formalized and their activities more clearly defined and given constitutional sanction by the shura' Their number was increased to five. One is in charge of relations with other political parties; one is responsible for the Teachers Union and parliamentary affairs; one handles the operations of the Jama'at's central administration; one acts as a liaison with the Jama'at's student organization; and one is in charge of relations with ulama and other Islamic organizations. The office is by now an established part of the command structure.

THE SHURA'S

After the office of amir, the *majlis-i shura'* is the most important pillar of the Jama'at's organizational structure. It has overseen the evolution and implementation of the party's ideology and has controlled the working of its constitution. The lower-level shura's replicate the functions of the central shura', but they do not have the same importance as the central shura' Members of shura's at all levels are elected. Each represents a Jama'at constituency geographically defined by the secretariat. These constituencies, drawn up by the Jama'at's election commissioner, coincide with national electoral districts whenever the numbers permit. A shura' member must be a resident of his constituency

In its early years the central shura' had twelve members, but in anticipation of the Punjab elections of 1951 membership was increased to sixteen and as part of the constitutional reforms which followed Machchi Goth, to fifty [12] That number was again increased to sixty in 1972, giving greater representation to members. In 1989 every central shura' member represented approximately one hundred Jama'at members. The increase in size has vested greater powers in the central shura', while reducing the powers of each individual member, which was one reason why Mawdudi took the step in the first place following the Machchi Goth affair. With the same objective in mind, the Jama'at's constitution has kept the legislative power of the shura' in check by giving the amir, deputy amirs, secretary-general, and provincial amirs, who attend shura' sessions, voting rights. The number of these extra-shura' votes is twelve, a fifth of the shura' votes and a sixth of the total votes cast. In case of a tie the vote of the amir counts as two. Regular members of the Jama'at may attend sessions of the shura' with the permission of the amir, but have no speaking or voting rights.

The central shura' meets once or twice a year and may in addition be called by the amir or a majority of its members whenever necessary It reviews party activities and decides on future policies. It has ten subcommittees which specialize in various areas of the Jama'at's concern and provide the shura' with policy positions. The central shura' can probe the legal sources and determine the intent of Islamic law (*ijtihad*) when and if there exists no precedent for the ruling under consideration in religious sources. This enables it to decide on, as well as to clarify, doctrinal matters. While issues are openly debated in the shura', verdicts are not handed down by majority vote alone. The shura', especially when doctrinal matters are involved, works through a practice that reflects the Muslim ideal of consensus (*ijma'*). The majority must convince the minority of its wisdom, leaving no doubt regarding the course on which the Jama'at will embark. In 1970 Mawdudi reported that in its twenty-nine years of activity, the central shura' had given a majority opinion on only four occasions, the most notable of which was the prelude to Machchi Goth. Otherwise the central shura' has, time after time, given unanimous verdicts.[13] Since Machchi Goth, many executive decisions have been put before the twenty-two-member *majlis-i 'ami-lah*. This smaller council steers the Jama'at through most of its activities when the central shura' is not in session.

THE SECRETARY-GENERAL AND SECRETARIAT

The day-to-day activities of the Jama'at are overseen by the bureaucracy centered in the party's secretariat. The office of the secretary-general (*qayyim*) was created in 1941. Since then, it has grown in power to become something akin to that of a party boss. The concept of a party worker was introduced to the Jama'at in 1944 when the party set up special training camps in Pathankot for its personnel.[14] With the growth of the Jama'at in size and the expansion of its activities, the workers have become an increasingly important element in the party Between 1951, when the Jama'at turned to politics, and 1989 the number of full-time workers rose from 125 to 7,583.[15] Since 1947 they have been controlled from Lahore by the secretary-general, who is appointed by the amir in consultation with the central shura' Over the years, not only has the central secretariat increased in size but it has also reproduced itself at lower levels in the party, creating an administrative command structure which extends from the center to the smallest unit, paralleling the command structure controlled by the amirs.

The Jama'at's numerous publications are also controlled by the bureaucracy, the scope of the activities of which not only increases their hold on the Jama'at but also gives them a say in the party's political agenda. The importance of this bureaucracy was already evident early on, but it rose even farther as witnessed by the fact that both Mian Tufayl and Qazi Husain came to the office of amir directly from that of secretary-general. Members of the bureaucracy often are also members of shura's of various units, augmenting the power of the central bureaucratic machine in the decision-making bodies of the party, precluding the kind of autonomy of the shura' which led to the Machchi Goth affair.

In the 1970s, following its decisive defeat at the polls and with an amir at the helm who institutionalized the Jama'at's ideological zeal into distinct norms and procedures, the secretariat grew further in size, power, and number of workers.

In 1979 a permanent training camp for workers was established at the Jama'at's headquarters in Lahore, and in 1980 alone 2,800 new workers went through that facility [16] The Jama'at's considerable financial resources since the 1970s has permitted it to hire these workers and expand the activities of the bureaucratic force. All ordinary Jama'at workers are paid for their services, but officers such as the amir, deputy amirs, or shura' members are not paid, though they may serve in other salaried capacities in the party Qazi Husain's thriving family business in Peshawar has helped resolve the question of monetary compensation for his services. An increasing share of those joining the growing bureaucracy are alumni of Islami Jami'at-i Tulabah (Islamic Society of Students), who are educated in modern subjects and have known each other since their university days. This further strengthens the position of the bureaucracy

The bureaucratic structure of the Jama'at is duplicated in the party's burgeoning women's wing (*halqah-i khawatin*), established in the 1950s. Some 70 percent of these women come from families where the men belong to the Jama'at. They have no amir of their own, but have a central shura' and an office of secretary-general (*qayyimah*). Their headquarters are situated in the central compound, from where the working of *nazimahs* (organizers) of lower-level units are supervised. The Jama'at-i Islami women also have their own seminary, the Jami'atu'l-Muhsinat (Society of the Virtuous), which trains women as preachers and religious teachers.

The women's wing is primarily involved with propagating the Jama'at's literature and ideas among Pakistani women through its periodicals, the most important of which is *Batul*, and to incorporate Jama'at families into the holy community by recruiting from among the wives and daughters of the Jama'at's members and by encouraging women to bring up their children true to the teachings of the Jama'at.

The Jama'at's secretariat also oversees the working of special departments, the number and duties of which change depending on the needs of the party In 1989–1990 they were the departments of finance, worker training, social services and welfare, theological institutions, press relations, elections, public affairs, parliamentary affairs, and Jama'at organizational affairs. Each department is headed by a *nazim* (head or organizer), appointed by the amir. The departments are responsible to the secretary-general and at times to a deputy amir.

The increasing bureaucratization of the Jama'at is clearly manifested in the central role of the party's secretariat and workers in its headquarters compound, called Mansurah, on the outskirts of Lahore. To collect all members and votaries of the Jama'at into a model holy community had been a central aim of the party since its creation. However, after its relatively short stay (1942–1947) in Pathankot, Jama'at members had never again been able to gather in one location, though establishing a community/headquarters complex remained a goal. With funding through private donations, the land for the Mansurah compound was purchased in 1968, and construction on it began in 1972; the Jama'at began to move its offices there in 1974. The complex has since grown to include a small residential community, where many Jama'at leaders reside, and the central offices of the Jama'at's secretariat and some of its numerous affiliated bodies: the Islamic Studies Academy (Idarah-i Ma'arif-i Islami), the Sayyid Mawdudi International Education Institute, Office of Adult Education, Bureau of the Voice of Islam (Idarah-i Sada-i Islam), the Arabic Translation Bureau, the Peasants' Board (Kisan Board), the Ulama Academy, the Jami'atu'l-Muhsinat, the offices of Jama'at-i Islami of Punjab, schools, libraries, a mosque, and a hospital. In 1990, according to the election commission of Pakistan in Islamabad, Mansurah had some four thousand eligible voters.[17]

The Jama'at's organizational model—the amir, shura', secretary-general, administrative, and command networks stretching from the top of the party to its smallest units—has proved so efficacious that it has become an example for others to emulate. The Jama'at's rivals, from ulama parties to Israr Ahmad's Tanzim-i Islami and Tahiru'l-Qadri's Minhaju'l-Qur'an, with some changes in titles and functions, have reproduced it in their own organizations as has the secular and ethnically based Muhajir Qaumi Mahaz (Muhajir National Front).

The size of the bureaucracy and the scope of its activities lead naturally to the question of the party's finances. The Jama'at's total capital at its foundation was Rs. 74.[18] Its income at the end of 1942, mainly from the sale of books and literature, was Rs. 17,005 [19] This figure rose to Rs. 78,700 in 1947, and Rs. 198,714 in 1951, a tenfold increase in ten years.[20] By 1956 the annual budget for the Jama'at-i Islami of Karachi alone stood at Rs. 200,000.[21] The Jama'at's income, from sale of books and hides (from animal sacrifices on 'Idu'l-azha'), and increasingly from voluntary contributions and religious tax (*zakat*) payments by supporters and members, continued to grow at a steady pace throughout the 1950s and the 1960s (leaving aside confiscation of its funds on several occasions).[22] The purview of the Jama'at's activities, however, has grown at an equal, if not faster, rate than its income during the same period, ensuring a subsistence-level existence for the party It was not until the 1970s that the fortunes of the Jama'at took a turn for the better.

The rise to power of the left-leaning Bhutto in 1971, and the Jama'at's open opposition to him, brought new sources of financial support to its assistance. The Pakistani propertied elite, threatened by the nationalization policy of the People's Party, the lower-middle class, whom Bhutto alienated with his socialist rhetoric and open display of moral laxity, and the Muhajir community, which began to feel the threat of Sindhi nationalism, all began to invest money in anti–People's Party forces, one of the most prominent of which was the Jama'at. The foreign governments—especially the monarchies of the Persian Gulf Trucial

States, Kuwait, and Saudi Arabia—wary of Pakistan's turn to the left, also began supplying funds to forces which could provide an ideological brake on the spread of socialism and bog Bhutto down in domestic crises; again the Jama'at became a major recipient of these contributions. The Soviet invasion of Afghanistan a decade later merely increased the flow of funds from the Persian Gulf sources.

Jama'at's own connections with the Saudi ulama went a long way toward convincing the Persian Gulf donors of the wisdom of their policy and established the party as the main beneficiary of funds that Persian Gulf states earmarked for Islamic activities across the Muslim world. In fact, the Jama'at's ideological affinity with the Wahhabi Sunnis of the Persian Gulf states, Jama'at's earlier ties with Saudi authorities, and the party's considerable reach across the Muslim world made it a convenient agent for the management of these funds and their distribution.[23] The Jama'at's international activities became increasingly intertwined with those of the Rabitah 'Alam-i Islami (Muslim World Network), based in Riyadh, which oversees Saudi Arabia's relations with various Islamic organizations from Mindanao to Morocco. The Jama'at's international influence grew in good measure through the aegis of the Rabitah. Saudi Arabia financed the establishment of a Jama'at research institute in England, the Islamic Foundation, where the Jama'at's literature is published and disseminated in large quantities across the Muslim world. More recently, it has also projected the Jama'at's power internationally, most notably during the Rushdie affair.[24] Under the aegis of the Rabitah, ties with Jama'at-i Islamis elsewhere in South Asia were strengthened, as were relations with other Islamic movements. The Rabitah also helped increase the Jama'at's leverage in its dealings with Pakistani governments, as numerous projects funded by Persian Gulf states in Pakistan, such as the International Islamic University in Islamabad, and the lucrative management of the flow of funds and arms to the Afghan Mujahidin, were opened to the Jama'at. Financial patronage, however, has not been enough to control the Jama'at: the party's decision to support Iraq and its open derision of Saudi Arabia as a decadent lackey of American imperialism in the Persian Gulf war in 1990–1991 have greatly marred its relations with the Persian Gulf states and seriously affected their rapport.

The considerable rise in the number of Pakistani migrant workers in the Persian Gulf states since the 1970s also translated into larger voluntary contributions and *zakat* payments to the Jama'at, as well as even closer ties between the party and the migrant workers' hosts and employers in the Persian Gulf. Funds flowing into the Jama'at's coffers have also followed a recent increase in the number of Pakistani migrants to the West, many of whom are alumni of the student wing, the Islami Jami'at-i Tulabah. These financial links and especially the rewards for stemming the tide of "Bhuttoism" in turn influenced the Jama'at's outlook on a number of issues. They made the party more staunchly anti-Bhutto and opposed to socialism in the 1970s than otherwise might have been the case, blinding it to the importance of populist politics in Pakistan. Antisocialist activism provided the Jama'at with greater international renown and financial rewards, diverting the party's attention from the realities of its political choices in Pakistan, especially after the fall of Bhutto. The free flow of funds also dampened the Jama'at's resolve, damaged its hard-earned discipline and morale, and gave the members a false, and ultimately ephemeral, sense of achievement and confidence. In a similar vein, these financial ties determined the Jama'at's stand on a host of religiopolitical issues, compromising the party's autonomy of thought and action. The Persian Gulf connection, for instance, determined the party's ideological and political response to other Islamic revival movements. A case in point was the strained relations between the Jama'at and the Islamic Republic of Iran in the 1980s, which can, at least in part, be attributed to the Iran-Iraq war and the hardening of the policy toward Iran by the Persian Gulf states.

Affiliate Organizations

A host of affiliated semiautonomous institutions stand outside the Jama'at's official organization, but greatly extend the party's reach and power. Despite their outwardly autonomous character, there is little doubt that the Jama'at, to varying degrees, controls them. Although at first this was done for the sake of efficiency, in the end political considerations also played their part in the decision to relegate authority

No sooner had the country of Pakistan been established than the Jama'at was declared a pariah by its government, which also forbade its civil service—a primary target of the Jama'at's propaganda—to have any contact with them. The Jama'at was compelled to set up institutions sufficiently distant to do its bidding without the fear of government retribution. During Ayub Khan's regime the Jama'at's problems with the government were compounded when the party and everything associated with it were banned. The Jama'at found it prudent to divest itself of some subsidiary organizations to guarantee their survival. One result was the establishment of Islamic Publications in Lahore in 1963, which has subsequently become the Jama'at's chief publisher in Pakistan. The Jama'at had become so dependent on its publications as a source of revenue and as a means of expanding its power that the suppression of its publications during the early years of the Ayub Khan proved devastating. The new arrangement legally protected it from future government clampdowns on the party, thereby protecting its source of income and propaganda. Additional affiliate bodies were created in the 1970s to both protect and expand the party's base of support.

The affiliate organizations fall into two categories: the first deal with propaganda and publications, and the second with political activities. Aside from Islamic Publications, there are other important affiliate bodies engaged in propaganda. The first of these is the Islamic Research Academy of Karachi, established in 1963 to counter the efforts of the Institute of Islamic Research, created in 1961 by Ayub Khan to propagate the regime's modernist view of Islam. Shortly thereafter, the academy was directed to disseminate the Jama'at's views among the civil service. In the 1980s this task was mainly delegated to the Institute of Policy Studies of Islamabad, created, thanks to the pliant attitude of the Zia regime to Islamic activism, to serve as a "think tank" for Jama'at's policy makers. The Institute of Regional Studies of Peshawar and Institute of Educational Research (Idarah-i Ta'lim'u Tahqiq) of Lahore also function in the same capacity, and outside Pakistan, the Islamic Foundation in Leicester, England, and the Islamic Foundation in Nairobi, Kenya, operate along similar lines. These institutions have done much to propagate the Jama'at's views and have contributed to the increasing influence of Islam across the Muslim world in general and in the social and political life of Pakistanis in particular.

Also important in this category of affiliate bodies are magazines which are not officially associated with the Jama'at but are close to its ideological and political position. The most important of these are *Chatan, Haftrozah Zindagi, Takbir, Qaumi Digest,* and *Urdu Digest.* The *Urdu Digest,* first published in 1962, has extended the Jama'at's influence into the Pakistan armed forces, where it enjoys a certain popularity. All these publications print both social and political commentary and news analysis from Jama'at's perspective. The contribution of these ostensibly independent institutions to the dissemination of the Jama'at's views among the civil service, the military, and the political establishment has been substantial.

Affiliate institutions dealing with political matters are of even greater importance to the Jama'at. For the most part they are unions which act both to propagate the Jama'at's views among specific social groups and to consolidate the Jama'at's power through union activity, especially among the new social groups that have been born of industrial change in Pakistan. Some of these unions, such as the Jama'at's semiautonomous student union, Islami Jami'at-i Tulabah, were formed to proselytize but have since become effective politically as well. Others were launched in the late 1960s to combat the influence of leftist unions, and still others to expand the popular base of the Jama'at following its defeat at the polls in December 1970. The most notable of these are the Pakistan Unions Forum, Pakistan Medical Association, Muslim Lawyers Federation, Pakistan Teachers Organization, Merchant's Organization, National Labor Federation, Peasants' Board, Pasban (Protector) Organization, Jami'at-i Tulabah-i 'Arabiyah (Society of Students of Arabic, which focuses on seminary students), and Islami Jami'at Talibat (Islamic Society of Female Students).

Union membership runs the gamut of professions and classes in Pakistan from farmers and peasants to the educated middle class. The most important are the peasant, labor, and student unions. The Peasants' Board was formed in 1976 to promote the Jama'at's views in the countryside and create a new voter pool for the Jama'at to make up for the loss of voters in the elections of 1970. It was also part of the Jama'at's anti–People's Party campaign, since it was meant to curtail the influence of the leftist peasants' union, the Planters' Association (Anjuman-i Kashtkaran) and to capitalize on opposition to Bhutto's nationalization of agriculture in 1976. This dual objective informs the working of all Jama'at unions. The Peasants' Board has sought to lure the agricultural sector to the Jama'at's cause by remedying agricultural problems, but has thus far concerned itself only with the needs of small rural landowners and not the grievances of the more numerous landless laborers and peasants.

The National Labor Federation began its work in the 1950s but did not become prominent until the 1960s and the 1970s. It has the same objectives as the Peasants' Board. The National Labor Federation and its subsidiary propaganda wing, the Toilers Movement (Tahrik-i Mihnat), were effective in countering some of the influence of the left among Pakistani laborers. In the late 1970s, with the weakening of the Bhutto government and rifts between the People's Party and leftist forces, the National Labor Federation won important union elections at the Pakistan International Airlines, the shipyards, and Pakistan Railways and in the steel industry, causing consternation in Zia's government. Soon after assuming power, Zia decided to ban all union activities, and the ban remained until 1988. Despite the National Labor Federation's gains, the Jama'at still has not learned to utilize its power base among the labor force effectively, because it is reluctant to engage in populist politics. Qazi Husain has promised his party to change that.

The National Labor Federation has served as a model and base for the expansion of the Jama'at's labor union activity Since 1979 the party has formed white-collar unions among government clerical staff, which despite their small size have increased the Jama'at's control over the provincial and national civil service. For instance, in 1989 the clerical union at the University of Punjab was controlled by the Jama'at, which allowed it to enforce a code of conduct, control curriculum and academic staff, and otherwise influence its running.

Islami Jami'at-i Tulabah

The most important of the Jama'at's unions is the Islami Jami'at-i Tulabah (IJT). Unlike the labor or the peasant unions, the IJT has no ideological justification. It does not galvanize support among any one social class. However, it has proved to be effective in battles against Jama'at's adversaries, it has diversified the party's social base, and it has served as an effective means of infiltrating the

Pakistani power structure. As the most important component of the Jama'at's organization, its workings and history both encapsulate and explain the place of organization in the Jama'at and identify those factors which control continuity and change in its organization over time.

Central to contemporary Islamic revivalism is the role student organizations have in translating religious ideals into political power. The IJT, or the Jami'at as it is popularly known, is one of the oldest movements of its kind and has in its own right been a significant and consequential force in Pakistani history and politics. In this capacity it has been central to the Islamization of Pakistan since 1947 It has served as a bulwark against the left and ethnic forces and has been active in national political movements such as those which brought down the Ayub Khan regime in 1969 and the Bhutto regime in 1977

ORIGINS AND EARLY DEVELOPMENT

The roots of IJT can be traced to Mawdudi's address before the Muslim Anglo-Oriental College of Amritsar on February 22, 1940, in which, for the first time, he alluded to the need for a political strategy that would benefit from the activities of a "well-meaning" student organization.[25] Organizing Muslim students did not follow immediately, however. Not until 1945 did the Jama'at begin to turn its attention to students. The nucleus organization was first established at the Islamiyah College of Lahore in 1945 [26] The movement gradually gained momentum and created a drive for a national organization on university campuses, especially in Punjab, that would support the party The IJT was officially formed on December 23, 1947, in Lahore by twenty-five students, most of whom were sons of Jama'at members,[27] and the newly formed organization held its very first meeting that same year. Other IJT cells were formed in other cities of Punjab, and notably in Karachi. It took IJT three to four years to consolidate these student cells into one organization centered in Karachi, and IJT's constitution was not ratified until 1952.[28]

IJT was initially conceived as a missionary (*da'wah*) movement, a voluntary expression of Islamic feelings among students, given shape by organizers dispatched by the Jama'at. Its utility then lay in the influence it could have on the education of the future leaders of Pakistan, which would help implement Mawdudi's "revolution from above." IJT was at the time greatly concerned with attracting the best and the brightest, and it used the exemplary quality of its members—in education as well as in piety—as a way to gain acceptance and legitimacy and increase its following.[29] Although organized under the supervision of the Jama'at, IJT was greatly influenced by the Muslim Brotherhood of Egypt, which its members learned about from Sa'id Ramazan, a brotherhood member living in Karachi at the time. Between 1952 and 1955, Ramazan helped IJT leaders formalize an administrative structure and devise an organizational strategy The most visible marks of the brotherhood's influence are IJT's "study circle" and all-night study sessions, both of which were means of indoctrinating new members and fostering organizational bonds.[30]

Initially IJT saw its primary concern as spreading religious propaganda on university campuses. In 1950 it launched its first journal, *'Azm*, in Urdu; it was soon followed by an English-language magazine, *Student's Voice*, in 1951. IJT members were, however, as keenly interested in politics as in religious work. Hence, it was not long before they turned their attention to campus politics. Their involvement was not at the time an end in itself, but a means to check the growth of the Democratic Student Federation and the National Student Federation, the two left-wing student organizations on Pakistani campuses.[31]

Throughout the 1950s, opposition to the left became the party's propelling force. It was on a par with Islamic consciousness, to the extent that the student organization's view, in large measure, took shape in terms of its opposition to Marxism. All issues put before the students were soon boiled down to choices between antithetical and mutually exclusive absolutes, Islam and Marxism. Although this was a missionary attitude inferred from the Jama'at's doctrinal teachings, in the context of campus politics it controlled thought and, hence, action. The conflict between Islam and Marxism soon culminated in actual clashes between IJT and leftist students, confrontations that further radicalized the IJT and increased its interest in campus politics. Egg tossing gradually gave way to more serious clashes, especially in Karachi and Multan.[32] Antileftist student activism had become the IJT's calling and increasingly determined its course of action. Once part of the Jama'at's holy community, it now began to look increasingly like a part of its political organization, hardly a source of comfort for the Jama'at's leaders, especially as between October 1952 and January 1953 leftist student groups clashed violently with police in the streets of Karachi, greatly radicalizing student politics. The tactics and organizational power of left-wing students in those months taught the IJT a lesson; it became more keenly interested in politics and began to organize more vigorously

As radical politics spread in Karachi, the Jama'at persuaded the IJT to temporarily move its operations elsewhere to keep it away from student politics.[33] From that point on, Lahore was its base of operations, and the IJT found a voice in Punjab, Pakistan's most important province. It recruited in the numerous colleges in that city and across the province, which proved to be fertile. In Lahore, IJT leaders could also be more closely supervised by Jama'at leaders, and as a result the students became more involved in religious discussions and education.[34] With increasing numbers of the organization's directors elected from Punjab, in 1978–1979 the organization's headquarters were permanently moved to Lahore.

Despite its moderating influence, the party proved unable to restrain the IJT's drift toward political activism, especially after the anti-Ahmadi agitations of 1953–1954 pitted Islamic groups against the government. The Jama'at had had a prominent role in the agitations and as a result had felt the brunt of the government's crackdown. The IJT reacted strongly, especially after Mawdudi was tried for his part in the agitations by the government in 1954. The student organization had ceased to view itself merely as a training organization for future leaders of Pakistan; now it was a "soldiers brigade," which would fight for Islam against its enemies—secularists and leftists—within the government as well as without. The pace of transformation from a holy community to a political organization was now faster in the IJT than in the Jama'at itself. By 1955 Mawdudi had begun to be concerned with this new direction and the corrupting influence of politicization.[35] However, the Jama'at's own turn to political activism following Machchi Goth obviated the possibility of restraining the IJT's political proclivities, and by the mid-1960s it had abandoned all attempts at checking the IJT's growing political activism and was instead harnessing its energies. With the tacit approval of Mawdudi, the students became fully embroiled in campus politics and to an increasing extent in national politics.

Between 1962 and 1967, locked in battle with Ayub Khan, the Jama'at diverted the students from confrontation with the left and from religious work to opposition to Ayub Khan and his modernist religious policies. They stirred up unrest on Pakistani campuses, initially to oppose the government's attempt to reform higher education then to protest against the concessions made to India at the end of the Indo-Pakistan war of 1965 Their agitation led to clashes, arrests, and incarceration, which only served to institutionalize agitation—increasingly in lieu of religious work—as the predominant mode of organizational behavior; it also attested to the potency of student power.

Not surprisingly the IJT was pushed farther into the political limelight between 1969 and 1971 when the Ayub Khan regime collapsed and rivalry between the People's Party and the secessionist Bengali party, the Awami League, resulted in civil war and the dismemberment of Pakistan. The IJT, with the encouragement of the government, became the main force behind the Jama'at's national campaign against the People's Party in West Pakistan and the Awami League and Bengali secessionists in East Pakistan.[36] The campaign confirmed the IJT's place in national politics, especially in May 1971, when the IJT joined the army's counterinsurgency campaign in East Pakistan. With the help of the army the IJT organized two paramilitary units, called al-Badr and al-Shams, to fight the Bengali guerrillas. Most of al-Badr consisted of IJT members, who also galvanized support for the operation among the Muhajir community settled in East Pakistan.[37]Muti'u'l-Rahman Nizami, the IJT's *nazim-i a'la* (supreme head or organizer) at the time, organized al-Badr and al-Shams from Dhaka University [38] The IJT eventually paid dearly for its part in the civil war. During clashes with the Bengali guerrillas (the Mukti Bahini), numerous IJT members lost their lives. These numbers escalated further when scores were settled by Bengali nationalists after Dhaka fell.

The fights with the left in West Pakistan and the civil war in East Pakistan meant that the IJT's penchant for radical action had clearly eclipsed its erstwhile commitment to religious work. The party's attitude toward its student wing was, by and large, ambivalent. Although pleased with its political successes, the Jama'at nevertheless mourned its loss of innocence. Yet, despite its trepidations, the party in the end proved reluctant to alter the IJT's course, for the students were delivering tangible political gains to the party, which had little else to work with. While Mawdudi may have, on occasion, chastised student leaders for their excesses, other Jama'at leaders such as Sayyid Munawwar Hasan (himself a one-time leader of the IJT) and Khurshid Ahmad (again a former IJT leader) were far more tolerant. They saw the political situation before the Jama'at at the end of Ayub Khan's rule and during the Bhutto period (1968–1977) in apocalyptic terms and felt that the end thoroughly justified the means. The IJT's power and zeal, especially in terms of the manpower needed to wage demonstrations, agitate, and conduct electoral campaigns, were too valuable for the Jama'at to forego. Political exigencies thenceforth would act only to perpetuate the Jama'at's ambivalence and expedite the IJT's moral collapse.

The Jama'at's ideological perspective, central as it has been to the IJT, has failed to keep the student organization in check. The IJT and the Jama'at have been tied together by Mawdudi's works and their professed ideological perspective, and IJT members are rigorously indoctrinated in the Jama'at's ideology Fidelity to the Jama'at's reading of Islam is the primary criterion for membership and for advancement in the IJT. Jama'at's ideology is indelibly imprinted on the IJT and shapes the student organization's worldview But as strong as discipline and ideological conformity are among the core of IJT's official members, they are not steadfast guarantees of obedience to the writ of the Jama'at. Most of the IJT's power comes from its far more numerous supporters and workers, who are not as well trained in the Jama'at's ideology, nor as closely bound by the IJT's discipline. In 1989, for instance, while the number of members and sympathizers stood at 2,400, the number of workers was 240,000.[39] The ability of the ideological link between the Jama'at and the IJT to control the activities of the student organization is therefore tenuous. The political interests of the IJT often reflect the demands of its loosely affiliated periphery and can easily nudge the organization in independent directions; Nizami's decision to throw the lot of the IJT in with martial rule in East Pakistan in 1971 is a case in point. In addition, organizational limitations have impeded the Jama'at's ability to cajole and subdue the IJT. The two are clearly separated by formal organizational boundaries, which create visible constraints in the chain of command between the them.

Hence, while since 1976 a deputy amir of the Jama'at has been assigned to supervise the IJT, his powers are limited to moral persuasion.[40]

The IJT grew more independent of the Jama'at, and the party more dependent on the students, with the rise to power of Bhutto in 1971. The Jama'at had been routed at the polls that year, while the IJT, fresh from a "patriotic struggle" in East Pakistan, had defeated the People's Party's student union, the People's Student Federation, in a number of campus elections in Punjab, most notably in the University of Punjab elections, and had managed to sweep the various campuses of Karachi. The IJT's victories breathed new life and hope into the dejected Jama'at, whose anguish over the student organization's conspicuous politicization gave way for now to admiration and awe. The IJT had "valiantly stood up" to the People's Party and won, parrying Bhutto's political power. The victory had, moreover, been interpreted to mean that Mawdudi's ideas could win elections, even against the left. Following its victory, the IJT became a more suitable vehicle for launching anti–People's Party campaigns than the Jama'at, which as a defeated party was hard-pressed to assert itself. Unable to function as a mass-based party before the widely popular People's Party, the Jama'at increasingly pushed the IJT into the political limelight. The student organization soon became a de facto opposition party and began to define the parameters of its political control accordingly When in August 1972 the people of Lahore became incensed over the kidnapping of local girls by Ghulam Mustafa Khar, the People's Party governor of Punjab, for illicit purposes, they turned to the IJT. The organization obliged, raised the banner of protest, and secured the release of the girls by staging sizable demonstrations.[41] The IJT performed its role so effectively that it gained the recognition of the government. IJT leaders were among the first to be invited to negotiate with Bhutto later that year, once the People's Party had decided to mollify the opposition.[42]

The IJT's rambunctious style was a source of great concern to the People's Party government. The student organization had not only served as the vehicle for implementing the Jama'at's political agenda but also was poised to take matters into its own hands and launch even more radical social action. While the Jama'at advocated Islamic constitutionalism, the IJT had been advocating Islamic revolution. The tales of patriotic resistance and heroism in East Pakistan gave it an air of revolutionary romanticism. The myths and realities of the French student riots of 1968, which had found their way into the ambient culture of Pakistani students, provided a paradigm for student activism which helped the IJT articulate its role in national politics and to formulate a strategy for mobilizing popular dissent.[43]

The IJT thus became the mainstay of such anti-People's Party agitational campaigns as the nonrecognition of Bangladesh (Bangladesh *namanzur*) movement of 1972–1974, the finality of prophecy (*khatm-i nubuwwat*) movement and the anti-Ahmadi controversy of 1974, and the Nizam-ı Mustafa (Order of the Prophet) movement of 1977 As a result, the IJT found national recognition as a political party and a new measure of autonomy from the Jama'at. The organization also developed a penchant for dissent, which given that it was an extraparliamentary force, could find expression only ın street demonstrations and clashes with government forces. The IJT soon adapted well to militant dissent and proved to be a tenacious opponent of the People's Party—a central actor ın the anti-Bhutto national campaign that eventually led to the fall of the prıme mınıster ın 1977 Success ın the political arena took the IJT to the zenith of its power, but it also restricted it to beıng a consummate political entity

Followıng the coup of July 1977, the IJT continued on its course of political activism. It collaborated closely with the new regıme ın suppressıng the People's Party, used government patronage to cleanse Pakıstanı campuses of the left, and served as a check on the activities of a clandestine paramilitary organızation associated with the People's Party, al-Zulfıqar, ın urban centers.[44] The IJT also played a critical role ın mobilizıng public opınıon for the Afghan war, ın which the organızation itself participated wholeheartedly, producıng seventy-two "martyrs" between 1980 and 1990.[45]

Political activism, therefore, contrary to expectations, escalated rather than abated durıng the Zia perıod. It had proved to be an ırreversible process, an end ın itself that became detached from the quest for an Islamıc order. As a result, even though Pakistan was movıng toward Islamızation, the pace of political activısm only ıncreased. The students became embroiled ın a new cycle of violence, fueled by rıvalry with other student organızations.

Campus vıolence by and against the IJT and continuous assassınations, which claımed the lives of some eighty student leaders between 1982 and 1988, began to mar the heroıc ımage which the IJT had when it was ın opposition to Bhutto.[46] Violence became endemıc to the organızation and was soon directed against the IJT's critics off campus.[47] The resulting "Kalashnikov culture," efficacıous as it had proved to be ın wagıng political campaıgns and ıntimıdating opponents, was ıncreasıngly difficult for the Jama'at either to control or to approve of. Nor was General Zia, determıned to restore stability to Pakistan, willing to tolerate it.[48]

Despite pressures from Zia, the Jama'at was unable to control its student group. Zia therefore proceeded to ban all student unıon activities ın February 1984, which led to nationwıde agitation by the IJT. Mian Tufayl (then amır), followıng pleas from the general, ınterceded with the IJT, counseling patience, but to no avail.[49] The IJT's ıntransıgence then began to ınterfere with the Jama'at's rapport with Zia and affect the party's ımage. It was only when the IJT realized the extent of popular backlash against its activities, which translated ınto defeats ın a number of campus elections between 1987 and 1991, that it desısted to some extent from vıolence on Pakıstanı campuses. The temperıng of the IJT's zeal was, however, merely a lull in the storm; the transformation of the student body into a militant political machine has progressed too far to be easily reversed.

ORGANIZATIONAL STRUCTURE

The IJT's central organization is modeled after the Jama'at's. At the base of its organizational structure are the supporters (hami), loosely affiliated pro-IJT students; next come the workers (karkun), the backbone of the IJT's organization and its most numerous category; the friends (rafiq); the candidates for membership (umidvar-i rukniyat); and finally, the members (arkan). Only members can occupy official positions; the most important office is the nazim-i a'la (supreme head/organizer). The organizational structure at the top is replicated at lower levels, producing a set of concentric circles which extend from the lowest unit to the office of nazim-i a'la. Each IJT unit has its own nazim (head or organizer) elected by IJT members of that unit (see figure 2).

The first four layers of the IJT's organizational structure have shura's which are elected by IJT members of that unit. An IJT votary may participate in several elections for nazim or shura' each year. For instance, he can vote in dormitory, campus, university, city, province, and national elections for nazim. The IJT's activities and interorganization matters are supervised by the secretary-general (mu'tamid-i a'la), appointed by the nazim-i a'la. Lower units of the IJT also have secretaries-general (mu'tamids), who are selected by their respective nazims and the secretary-general of the higher unit. Each level of the IJT forms a self-contained unit and oversees the activities of the one below it. For instance, the command structure extends from the IJT's national headquarters to the Punjab IJT, the Lahore IJT, the IJT of various universities in Lahore, the IJT of the campuses in each university, and finally the IJT of departments, classes, and dormitories in each university. On each campus, units monitor student affairs, campus politics, relations between the sexes, and the workings of university administration and faculty, at times acting as the de facto administrators of the university. The IJT regularly uses the university campus as its base of operations and utilizes university facilities such as auditoriums and buses for its purposes. Admission forms to the university are sold to applicants, generating revenue and control over the incoming students. The IJT uses strong-arm tactics to resolve the academic problems of its members or associates, provides university housing to them, and in some cases gains admission for them to the university [50] The IJT also has subsidiary departments for international relations, the press, and publications which deal with specific areas of concern and operate out of IJT headquarters.

This organizational structure is duplicated in the IJT's sister organization, the Islami Jami'at Talibat (Islamic Society of Female Students), which was formed at

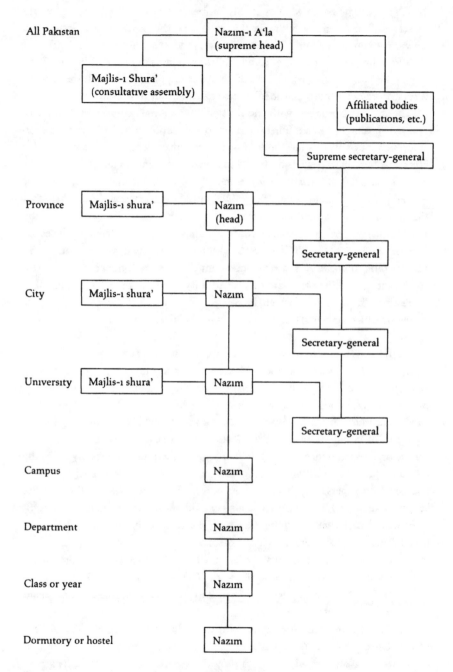

Figure 2.   Organizational structure of the Islami Jami'at-i Tulabah

Jama'at's instigation in Multan in September 1969 This organization works closely and in harmony with the IJT, extending the power of the latter over university campuses. Most Talibat members and sympathizers, much like the IJT's founding members, come from families with Jama'at or IJT affiliation. Their ties to the Talibat organization are therefore strong, and as a result the requirements of indoctrination and ideological education are less arduous.

The principal problem with the IJT's organizational setup is an absence of continuity, a fault which is inherent in any organization with revolving membership. Because they must be students, members remain with the organization for comparatively short periods of time, and leaders have limited terms in office. The *nazim-i a'la* and other *nazims*, for instance, hold office for one year and can be elected to that office only twice. Since 1947 only fifteen *nazim a'las* have held that title for as long as two years. The organization has therefore been led by twenty-nine leaders in forty-four years. To alleviate the problems produced by lack of continuity, the IJT has vested greater powers in its secretariat, where bureaucratic momentum assures a modicum of organizational continuity Also significant in creating organizational continuity has been the IJT's regional and all-Pakistan conventions, which have been held regularly since 1948. These gatherings have given IJT members greater solidarity and an organizational identity

All IJT associates from worker up attend training camps where they are indoctrinated in the Jama'at's ideological views and the IJT's tactical methods. Acceptance into higher categories of organizational affiliation depends greatly on the degree of ideological conformity To become a full-fledged member, candidates must read and be examined on a specific syllabus, consisting for the most part of Mawdudi's works. All IJT associates are encouraged to collect funds for the organization through outside donations (*i'anat*), which not only helps the IJT financially but also increases loyalty to the organization. Each *nazim* is charged with supervising the affairs of those in his unit as well as those in the subordinate units. IJT members and also candidates for membership meet regularly with their *nazim*, providing him with a diary known as "night and day" (*ruz'u shab*), in which every activity of the member or candidate for membership is recorded. The logbook details academic activities, religious study, time spent in prayers, and hours dedicated to IJT work. The book is monitored closely, and gives the IJT total control over the life of its associates from the rank of friend up to that of member.

The strict requirements for membership and advancement in the IJT have kept its membership limited. Yet organizational discipline has surmounted any limitations on the IJT's ability effectively to project power. Its accomplishments are all the more astounding when the actual numbers of the core members responsible for the organization's vital political role in the 1970s and the 1980s are taken into consideration (see table 2).

Table 2. Distribution of IJT Members, 1974–1992

	Punjab	Lahore	Sind	Karachi	NWFP	Baluchistan	Total for Pakistan
1974							
Members	82	20	62	40	25	6	175
Friends	881	150	676	350	270	65	1,892
1978							
Members	134	38	102	80	41	10	287
Friends	762	106	584	425	233	56	1,635
1983							
Members	236	34	131	90	63	20	450
Friends	1,588	190	553	417	284	75	2,500
1989							
Members	274	42	200	110	100	10	584
Friends	844	129	616	339	308	30	1,800
1992							
Members	256	50	143	107	106	8	414
Friends	2,654	314	1,260	1,403	657	64	3,698

Source: Jama'at-i Islami.

The IJT has also extended its activity beyond the university campus. The circle of friends (halqah-i ahbab) has for a number of years served as a loosely organized IJT alumni association. The IJT has also more effectively extended its organizational reach into high schools, a policy initiated in the mid-1960s but which gathered momentum in the late 1970s, when the IJT reached the limits of its growth on university campuses. Further organizational expansion led the IJT to look to high schools for recruits and to reach the young before other student unions could. This strategy was particularly successful in universities where a large block of students came from particular regions through special quota systems. At the Engineering University of Lahore, for instance, the IJT was increasingly hard-pressed to compete with the ethnic appeal of the Pakhtun Student Federation for the support of students from the North-West Frontier Province. To solve the problem, in 1978–1979 it began recruitment in North-West Frontier Province high schools, creating a base of support among future students of the Engineering University before they arrived in Lahore, where they would come into contact with the Pakhtun Student Federation for the first time. The strategy was so effective that the Pakhtun Student Federation was compelled to copy it.

The IJT's recruitment of high school students, a program they referred to as Bazm-i Paygham (celebration of the message), began in earnest in 1978. In the 1960s a program had existed for attracting high school students to the IJT, named Halqah-i Madaris (the school wing),[51] but the Bazm-i Paygham was a more concerted effort. Magazines spread the message among its young audience and promoted themes of organization and unity through neighborhood and high school clubs. The project was named after its main magazine, Bazm-ı Paygham (circulation 20,000). Additional magazines cater to regional needs. In Punjab the magazine was Paygham Digest (circulation 22,000); in North-West Frontier Province, Mujahid (circulation 8,000); and in Sind, Sathi (circulation 14,000).[52] These journals emphasize not politics but religious education, so students can gain familiarity with the Jama'at's message and affinity with the IJT. Bazm-ı Paygham has been immensely successful. Since 1983 the IJT has been recruiting exponentially more associates in high schools than in universities. The project has also benefited the Jama'at; for many of those whom Bazm-ı Paygham reaches in high schools never go to university and would not otherwise come into contact with the Jama'at and its literature. More than a tactical ploy to extend the organizational reach of the IJT, this effort may prove to be a decisive means for expanding the social base of the Jama'at and deepening the influence of the party on Pakistani society

Although the IJT was modeled after the Jama'at, it has transformed itself into a political organization at a much faster pace than the parent party That the IJT relies more heavily on a periphery of supporters than the Jama'at has sublimated its view of itself as a holy community in favor of a political organization to a greater extent. For that reason the IJT serves as a model for the Jama'at's development, and not vice versa.

While the Jama'at's membership has been drawn primarily from the urban lower-middle classes, the IJT has also drawn members from among small-town and rural people. Students from the rural areas are not only more keen on religious issues and more likely to identify with religious groups but are also more likely to be affected by the IJT's operations on campuses than urban students are. The IJT controls university hostels and provides administrative and academic services, all of which are also more frequently used by rural and small-town students than by city dwellers. In essence, the IJT exercises a form of social control on campuses which brings these students into its orbit and under the Jama'at's influence.

The vagaries of Pakistani politics provide rural and small-town students with an incentive to follow the IJT's lead. Religious parties—the Jama'at is the most notable case in point—have since 1947 provided the only gateway for the middle and lower-middle classes, urban as well as rural, into the rigid and forbidding structure of Pakistani politics. Dominated by the landed gentry and the propertied elite through an intricate patronage system, political offices have generally remained closed to the lower classes. As a result, once attracted to political activism, rural, small-town, and urban lower-middle class youth flock to the ranks of the IJT in search of a place in national politics. The IJT's social control on campuses is therefore reinforced by the organization's promise of political enfranchisement to aspiring students.

A third of the current leaders of the Jama'at began as members or affiliates of the IJT (see table 3). The IJT recruits in the ranks of the Jama'at have created a block of voters in the party who bring with them close organizational bonds and a camaraderie born of years of student activism, and whose worldview, shaped by education in modern subjects and keenly attuned to politics, is at odds with that of the generation of ulama and traditional Muslim literati they will succeed. By virtue of the sheer weight of their numbers, IJT recruits are significantly influencing the Jama'at and are improving organizational continuity between the Jama'at and the IJT

In the final analysis, the IJT has been a successful organization and a valuable political tool for the Jama'at, though its very success eventually checked its growth and led the organization down the path to violence. Throughout the 1970s, the IJT seriously impaired the operation of a far larger mass party, the People's Party, a feat accomplished by a small core of dedicated activists (see table 2). The lesson of this success was not lost on other small aspiring Pakistani parties, who also turned to student activism to gain political prominence. Nor did larger political organizations such as the People's Party or the Muslim League, who had an interest in restricting entry into the political arena, remain

Table 3 Jama'at-i Islami Leaders with a Background in the IJT in 1989–90

	Rank in the Jama'at	*Level of Affiliation with IJT*
Qazi Husain Ahmad	Amir	Friend
Khurram Jah Murad	Deputy amir	Nazim-i a'la
Khurshid Ahmad	Deputy amir	Nazim-i a'la
Chaudhri Aslam Salimi	Secretary-general	Friend
Liaqat Baluch	Deputy secretary-general	Nazim-i a'la
Hafiz Muhammad Idris	Deputy secretary-general[a]	Member/senior Member
Sayyid Munawwar Hasan	Amir of Karachi[b]	Nazim-i a'la
'Abdu'l-Muhsin Shahin	Amir of Multan	Member
Shabbir Ahmad Khan	Amir of Peshawar	Member
Rashid Turabi	Amir of Azad Kashmir	Member
Amiru'l-'Azim	Director of information department	Member
Maqsud Ahmad	Secretary-general of Punjab	Member
'Abdu'l-Rahman Quraishi	Director of international affairs	Secretary-general of Sind

Source: Office of the secretary-general of the Jama'at-i Islami.

[a]Now amir of Punjab.

[b]Now secretary-general of the Jama'at.

oblivious to student politics as a weapon. They concluded that the menace of student activism could be confronted only by students. The Muslim Student Federation was revived by the Muslim League in 1985 with the specific aim of protecting that party's government from the IJT. The resulting rivalries for the control of campuses, needless to add, has not benefited the educational system in Pakistan.

The proliferation of student organizations was also a function of the sacralizing of campus politics. The IJT's success in the 1970s had pointed to the importance of Islamic loyalties among students. Few other viable "Islamic" student organizations existed then, and the IJT reigned supreme among religiously conscious Pakistani students. The IJT had successfully manipulated this state of affairs, translating disapproval of the People's Party's avowed socialism and Bhutto's indiscreet breaches of Muslim moral sensibilities among the religiously conscious students into victories in campus elections. As a result the IJT was able to produce a single political platform and to win votes far exceeding its numbers—exactly what the Jama'at had always aimed at and failed to do. Other Islamic parties, however, quickly became aware of the basis of the IJT's success and, wishing to tap into the same vote bank, strengthened student organizations of their own. Many of these organizations were formed by those who broke away from the IJT. The founders of the Jami'at-i Tulabah-i Ahl-i Hadith Pakistan (Ahl-i Hadith Student Organization of Pakistan) and the Anjuman-i Tulabah-i Islam (Society of Muslim Students), a student group affiliated with the Jami'at-i Ulama-i Pakistan (Society of Pakistani Ulama), in 1987–1988, for example, had been members and leaders of the IJT. By 1981, Punjab had become infested with student organizations, most of them associated with right-of-center and religious parties. No longer restrained by their opposition to a common enemy—Bhutto, socialism, and the People's Party, which the IJT had purged from the campuses between 1977 and 1981—the neophyte student organizations began to nibble at the IJT's base of support, splintered the religious vote, and significantly reduced the IJT's power base.

The IJT's predicament was also precipitated by the authoritarian nature and Islamic image of the Zia regime. Urban students in Pakistan are more politically conscious than rural ones, who are primarily motivated by religious concerns.[53] The People's Party government in the 1970s, with its authoritarian style and secular posture, had provided the IJT with the means to coalesce the antiauthoritarian urban and the religiously conscious rural students into a single student protest movement. Zia, by appealing to the religious sensibilities of rural students and antagonizing the politically conscious urban students, divided the IJT's constituency As a result the IJT began to lose elections on one campus after another, and by 1984 it had become bogged down in a vicious battle with rival student organizations—religious, ethnic, and secular in orientation—to protect its turf. Most small-town campuses in Punjab were lost to the Anjuman. Competition with the Anjuman by 1989 escalated to pitched battles in Gujranwala which left at least one student dead. The Muslim Student Federation, meanwhile, managed to unseat the IJT in a number of Lahore campuses, again culminating in a cycle of assassinations. The violence brought the burgeoning anti–People's Party alliance, Islami Jumhuri Ittihad (Islamic Democratic Alliance [IJI]), which included both the Jama'at and the Muslim League, to the brink of collapse in 1989 The People's Student Federation and the Pakhtun Student Federation in North-West Frontier Province, the People's Student Federation in Islamabad, and the Baluch Student Federation in Baluchistan went into battle against the IJT. Finally, in rural Sind the People's Student Federation and Sindhi nationalist student groups and in Karachi and Hyderabad the All-Pakistan Muhajir Student Organization (APMSO), a breakaway of the IJT floated by the Muhajir Qaumi Mahaz (Muhajir National Front), routed the IJT in student elections and restricted its maneuverability on campuses. The Muhajir organization was founded in 1986 by a group of Muhajir IJT members who objected to the Punjabi domination of the IJT. It has since controlled the politics of the urban centers of Sind and has emerged as a formidable force in Pakistani politics. The IJT's confrontation with the APMSO in 1988 turned Karachi University into a war zone, forcing the military to occupy the university and to close it down. During 1990–1992, when the Jama'at was a member of the ruling coalition, clashes between the IJT and the APMSO acted as a major source of tension within the IJI government. Fighting simultaneously against religious, ethnic, and secular student organizations has also created confusion in the ranks of the IJT with deleterious consequences.

Despite all these setbacks and after more than a decade of student battles (1980–1992), the IJT continues to remain the most prominent student force in Pakistan. Efforts such as Bazm-i Paygham have helped the IJT to overcome some of the ground lost in the universities, but more important, the IJT has remained the only student organization which exists in every province and on every university campus and therefore is the only student organization capable of acting on a national scale. As a sign of its continued vitality, the IJT has managed to retain control over the University of Punjab, the most important Pakistani university and the prize of student politics.

The greatest significance and long-run effect of the IJT, however, lies in its influence on Pakistani society Year after year a multitude of students come into contact with the Jama'at's literature through the IJT, many even undergo various levels of indoctrination at a formative and impressionable juncture in their lives. Through the IJT, the Jama'at leaves a permanent mark on the potential thinking and style of future Pakistani leaders, intellectuals, and bureaucrats. Regardless of where the alumni and sympathizers of the IJT go following their graduation, whether they stay close to the Jama'at or veer off in other directions, they carry the mark of the Jama'at—its reading of Islam and its social ethos—with them. They become the vehicles for a gradual and yet fundamental process of cultural engineering that is at the center of Mawdudi's original program and that has far greater social and ultimately political ramifications than the immediate gains of the IJT.

Between Universalism and National Identity

An analysis of the Jama'at's organization has to determine its identity and aim—does the Jama'at view itself as a Pakistani or a pan-Islamist party? How the party identifies itself lies at the heart of its politics, and ultimately determines its social role. The division in the Jama'at's organization which followed the partition of the Indian subcontinent in 1947 committed the party to the concept of the "nation-state," which, above and beyond Mawdudi's universalist claims, has determined the pattern of the Jama'at's political activities. The Jama'at's history attests to the truth of Benedict Anderson's observation that "nation-ness is the most universally legitimate value in the political life of our time."[54] Today, there exist eight Jama'at-i Islamis; six in Pakistan, India,[55] Bangladesh, Sri Lanka, Pakistan's Azad Kashmir, and India's Kashmir province,[56] plus the United Kingdom Islamic Mission and the Islamic Circle of North America. While all of these organizations are based on Mawdudi's ideological perspective and replicate the organizational structure of the Jama'at-i Islami of Pakistan with minor variations, they operate as separate entities, with activities defined by the territorial boundaries of the state in which they function. Relations between the various Jama'at-i Islami parties, much like their relations with other revivalist movements, is also conditioned by nation-state boundaries. For these boundaries create barriers to greater unity among revivalist groups in general and the various Jama'at-i Islamis in particular, bestowing a "national" independence upon each party that militates against universalism. As an indication of the extent of this independence, one can point to the difference in the reactions of the Jama'at-i Islamis of Pakistan, Bangladesh, and India to the Persian Gulf war in 1990–1991. While the Jama'at-i Islami of Pakistan was anti-American and anti-Saudi, the Jama'at-i Islamis of Bangladesh and India throughout the crisis condemned Iraq's invasion of Kuwait and maintained that Saddam Hussein was the archvillain.[57]

The evident doctrinal discrepancy between the Jama'at's professed universalist intentions and the party's territorial and national reality is a bone of contention within the Jama'at and a by-product of the party's modernization that replaced the quest for a pan-Islamic order with a political dialectic premised on the concept of the nation-state. This discrepancy was already present when the

Jama'at was founded, in its communalist concerns and universalist agenda of renewal and reform of Islam which lay at the center of Muslim political discourse at the time. That is why the founders of the Jama'at, while grappling with the immediate political predicaments of the Muslims in India, also devoted considerable energy to the propagation of Mawdudi's works outside India.[58] This task was entrusted to Masu'd 'Alam Nadwi, who had overseen the activities of the Arabic Translation Bureau in Jullundar since 1942. In 1944, Nadwi expanded the activities of the translation bureau by establishing *Al-Huda*, a journal of Islamic studies in Arabic, which was published in Pathankot. The journal exported the Jama'at's program to the Arabs, and to the Muslim world at large, where Arabic continues to be the lingua franca of religious circles. The Jullundar operation translated an impressive number of Mawdudi's works into Arabic; they began to appear in Palestine and Iraq in 1947 and in Egypt and Syria soon thereafter. The bureau was transferred first to Rawalpindi and later to Lahore following the partition, where it continues to function with unabated vigor today[59] Mawdudi's numerous travels through the Arab world in subsequent years helped establish a place for his works in that region and also further spread Jama'at's influence into more distant lands such as Tunisia and Morocco. Hitherto unaffected Muslims in Gabon, Mali, Malaysia, and Iran first came into contact with Mawdudi's works through these Arabic translations, making them important in the development of contemporary revivalist thought.[60] Similar projects were devised to translate the Jama'at's literature into Turkish and English, and later into an array of other languages from Japanese to Swahili, to augment the already significant impact of Mawdudi's thought. By 1974 Mawdudi's *Risalah-i Diniyat* (1932) had been translated into twenty-six languages, from Sinhala and Malayalam to English, French, and Spanish.

The significance of Mawdudi's works and the Jama'at's untiring efforts to propagate them far and wide in the rise and articulation of revivalism in the Islamic world underline the universalist pretensions of the movement. However, the Jama'at's transnational aims and impact end there. The party, while aware of its importance in the Muslim world and eager to make its mark outside of Pakistan, has no concrete agenda for a supranational Islamic order. Its universalism is effectively checked and limited by its commitment to Pakistani politics and the vicissitudes of sociopolitical change in that country The reality of the struggle for the soul of Pakistan has collapsed the Jama'at into the mold of "territorial" politics, relegating universalism to a secondary concern. Although the Jama'at has supported Islamic causes across the Muslim world, most actively in Afghanistan, India, and Tajikistan, Pakistan remains the focus of its political program. Much like the tensions witnessed in communist history between the interests of the former Soviet Union and those of a universalist communist doctrine, the Jama'at's revivalism, unable to escape the fate of universalist ideologies which have preceded it, is Pakistani first and only then international. This development is itself a significant innovation in contemporary Islamic political thought, a modernization of doctrine and worldview produced by the interaction of a universalist doctrine with the reality of the nation-state.

4   Social Base

Islamic revivalism, far from being an abstract expression of religious sentiment, is intensely political in its outlook, because it intends to alter the balance of power and the structure of social relations. The lower-middle classes—the petite bourgeoisie—have been identified as its social base and as having shaped its political outlook and pattern of social action.[1] In Pakistan, Islamic revivalism is said to draw its support primarily from this class, and within it from among the educated and the refugees of the partition of the Subcontinent (the Muhajirs), and the Jama'at's membership supports these conclusions. But the Jama'at's membership also presents a more complex picture by drawing attention to continuity and change in the ethnic composition and lower-middle-class base of Islamic revivalism.

The Jama'at's record of activity in Pakistan shows both its success as an "organizational weapon" and its failure as a political movement. Although it is not inconsequential as a pressure group, it has no real power, as repeated failures at the polls show. Its lackluster political performance no doubt is a consequence of its doctrinaire and elitist outlook on politics. Ever since it was formed, the Jama'at has shown an aversion to populism and a disregard for the demands of the poor, preferring instead to trust its political fortunes to a policy that interprets all issues through the prism of religious exegesis and is directed at winning over the elite, suggesting that its objective has been to take over the state from secular leaders rather than give voice to the demands of the masses. As a result, it is indifferent to sociopolitical concerns, and its organizational culture, reinforced by its rigid command structure, discipline, and strict membership criteria, has encouraged that indifference. This reflects its image as a holy community and a vanguard of an Islamic revolutionary struggle, but it stymies any hope of becoming a political movement with the large following needed for success in electoral politics. As a result, it has become cut off from Pakistani society

Despite their revolutionary pretensions and indefatigable preparations for the realization of their political goals, Mawdudi and his followers never sought support in any social class or effectively anchored their program in any social movement.

In a society divided by deep socioeconomic cleavages, animated by ethnic rivalries, and plagued by poverty and extreme economic inequality, the Jama'at's promise of an Islamic order and its preoccupation with halting the progress of the secular state have been increasingly challenged. Not long after the Jama'at moved to Pakistan, the first cracks in the party's ideological edifice began to show. The Jama'at soon became aware of the problems facing the Pakistani underclass and began social work among the refugees. That paid some dividends in later years. The party's success in the Karachi municipal elections of 1958 was, in part, a product of this work, and the Jama'at, acknowledging that, promised a form of welfare state for Pakistan. But it never moved beyond this rudimentary acknowledgment of the political relevance of the grievances of the poor to appreciating the potential of populism.[2] It cultivated votes among the poor through social work, but failed to advocate their cause. The party's services were appreciated, but its politics were irrelevant to the demands of the underprivileged. In the end, this did not prove catastrophic, however. It marginalized the party and curtailed its social impact, but it did not altogether exclude it from politics. The Jama'at simply settled for less; it continued to call Pakistanis to revolution, but in practice it accepted incremental change.

The disjunction between the party's practice and the dictates of politics did not mean that the party's plan of action was totally divorced from social influences. The Jama'at would never have survived Pakistani politics had its ideology not found support from important segments of the population. But the initiative for attracting a social base did not come from the party but from that part of society that found the party's views relevant to their lives and aspirations and handed it a base of support. In the words of one observer of the Jama'at in 1950: "In Karachi, Lahore and smaller Sindhi cities he [Mawdudi] drew large crowds. [H]e has an appeal to a broad mass of the people who have a feeling that the government is not all that it should be, but who cannot put their finger on the causes."[3]

Changes in the Jama'at's outlook and structure have modified its social base over the years, but its social appeal has not deepened so much as it has spread. The Jama'at's place in Pakistan's political equation is today more complex than it was when the party moved to Lahore in 1947. It has been recognized as important to the delicate balance of power which sustains the country's political process.

Finding a Social Base

The lack of detailed membership records makes the task of determining the exact social composition and base of support of the Jama'at difficult. Much, however, can be surmised from electoral and membership data.

All of the Jama'at Islami's original seventy-five members in 1941 came from the ranks of the young ulama and the religious literati of northern India.[4] By 1947 its 625 members represented a wider geographic distribution, but the social composition remained roughly the same. With no political agenda, the Jama'at's appeal in those years was to the religious and moral sensibility of its audience. It found fertile ground among the followers of those religious schools and communities sympathetic to Mawdudi's exegesis on Islam, and who did not follow the Jami'at-i Ulama-i Hind or the Congress party, and had no political organization of their own. The members of the Ahl-i Hadith were a case in point. With their austere theology, strict reliance on the fundamentals of the Islamic faith in religious exegesis, antagonism toward Deobandi and Brailwi ulama, vehement opposition to Sufism and to the popular practices associated with it, and emphasis upon individual interpretation, which closely paralleled Mawdudi's reading of Islam and the Jama'at's doctrine, they flocked to the Jama'at and formed the core of its early followers and supporters. Until recently, when the Ahl-i Hadith formed its own national religiopolitical and student organizations, the followers of this school of Islam found that the Jama'at best represented their political views.[5] The Ahl-i Hadith tradition was, and continues to be, strongest among the educated middle-class, and especially lower-middle-class, Muslims of northern India and Pakistan. The Jama'at's religious doctrines, not its political agenda, encouraged support among those same people.

If the Jama'at ever set out to win support among any social stratum, it was among educated Muslims, whom the party regarded as the primary agents for effecting a revolution from above. This made the caliber of its members intellectually high,[6] but did not extend its influence beyond the lower-middle classes,[7] and despite diligent proselytizing among the intelligentsia, the Jama'at even failed to establish a solid base of support among them.[8] Mawdudi's exegesis was sufficiently creative to capture their attention and even to bring some into the party's ambit, since his modernizing proclivities appealed to them and gave the Jama'at a niche in their culture. Despite his untiring efforts, however, Mawdudi never could bridge the gap which separated the Islamic from the modern worldview and to resolve the contradictions inherent in such concepts as "democratic caliphate," "Islamic ideology," and "Islamic democracy." He presented Islam using the language and logic of the educated classes but failed to persuade them of the logical consistency of his hybrid formulations. His discursive casuistry was plagued by anomalies and often collapsed into moralizing sermons with threats of damnation and promises of salvation. As Mawdudi's ideology remained ill at ease with modern thought, so did the Jama'at with the intelligentsia. Its support came more and more from the lower-middle classes, who were both religious and educated enough to be receptive to his polemic. As the years passed the Jama'at increasingly relied on the IJT and its white-collar unions rather than ideology to compel the educated to join its ranks. Jama'at members blame government harassment and the charges of sedition and subversion leveled against them, especially between 1947 and 1956, for their failure to recruit more effectively from among the educated classes.[9]

Over the years the party has been run by those who have received a modern education and not by the ulama. By 1964 the ulama who dominated the first shura's made up only 26 percent of the central shura',[10] and in 1970, 45 percent of the East Pakistan and West Pakistan's provincial shura's.[11] In the same year only 20 percent of those assigned National Assembly seats in the general elections were ulama.[12] By 1989, of the Jama'at's top fifteen officeholders, only one was educated at a seminary (*madrasah*).[13]

Changes in the social composition of the Jama'at do not only reflect the party's campaign for support among those with a modern education but are also a consequence of the patrimonial structure of Pakistani politics. The firm control of the landowning and propertied class over the political parties and electoral process in Pakistan and the upper-class domination of politics owing to the high cost of entry into the electoral system have made ideological parties such as the Jama'at the sole avenue for political advancement by the educated middle- and especially lower-middle-class youth. The Jama'at, for instance, is almost unique in Pakistan (one exception is the Muhajir Qaumi Mahaz, the Muhajir National Front) in determining promotions in the party, distribution of local and national offices, and assignment of national, provincial, district, and city tickets in general elections solely based on merit and loyalty The lower-middle-class background of the Jama'at's leaders and elected officials contrasts sharply with the upper-class leaders of other Pakistani national parties, from the avowedly populist People's Party to the nationalist Muslim League. As long as patrimonial norms prevail, the Jama'at will continue to benefit from recruiting the politically frustrated aspiring middle and lower-middle classes.

The surge in members with a "modern" education has also laicized the party, encouraging its bureaucratization and the replacing of its ideological zeal with a utilitarian approach to political activism. Those with a modern education maintain only informal ties with the traditional Islamic sodalities and are not bound by their norms and discipline. They view questions of principle and ideological fidelity differently and are free to use the emotive power of religion for sociopolitical purposes.

The Jama'at's social base has also been dictated by its literary tendencies. In 1951, only 13.8 percent of Pakistan's population was literate, and in 1990 that number had risen only to 28 percent. The poor, and the underclass who do not read, remain cut off from the logic and language of the party The folly of this approach has become increasingly apparent as the country has moved toward democratization. One may well question the wisdom of emphasizing education and literary propaganda when most of the voters of Pakistan cannot read.

The problem is not only the disjunction between the party's literary bent and the rampant illiteracy in Pakistan. The dominance of traditional power relations based on the patronage systems supported by *pirs* or hereditary landed families in the rural areas has limited the Jama'at's access to the Pakistani peasantry as well as to recent urban immigrants who retain their loyalty to the rural power structures centered in the landlord and the *pir*. The party's political influence is therefore effectively limited to the urban areas, an impediment further complicated by the disjunction between the Jama'at's ideological outlook and style and the religious and political culture of the rural areas, especially in Sind and Punjab.

One need not look too far to find fundamental differences between the Jama'at's puritanical and modernizing exegesis on Islam and the culturally eclectic and generally "maraboutist" religion of the poor. Still, converting the poor to the "true" Islam of the Jama'at and making inroads need not have been the insurmountable problems they have proved to be had the party been able effectively to communicate with the Pakistani underclass. But the Jama'at is rooted in the high culture of the Muslims of northern India and in the tradition of Islamic learning in the Subcontinent, which means that the party is firmly grounded in Urdu.[14] The party, moreover, much like the Muslim League had viewed Urdu as the linchpin of the two-nation theory and a cornerstone of Pakistani nationalism. Allegiance to Urdu was therefore an article of faith in the Jama'at. The rural and urban poor are as deeply rooted in vernaculars such as Baluchi, Pakhtun, Punjabi, Siraiki, and Sindhi. Outside of the Muhajir communities of Sind, Urdu is not used below the lower-middle class.[15] This problem is an obvious hindrance to the Jama'at's ability to contend with the ethnic aspect of Pakistani politics. It stands in contrast to the widely popular Tablighi Jama'at, whose following cuts across class as well as ethnic boundaries, and which uses the local vernaculars. For instance, the Jama'at was firmly opposed to giving Bengali equal status with Urdu in Pakistan between 1947 and 1971, which seriously compromised the party's ability to influence the politics of East Pakistan. Similar trends have been evident in recent years, as ethnic loyalties have stolen the political limelight from Islam, willy-nilly hampering the party's ability to maneuver in the political arena. Since ethnic sentiments often echo socioeconomic grievances, as was the case with the rise of the Awami League in East

Pakistan, and is most clearly reflected in the MQM's political platform, the Jama'at's social base has become doubly constricted. Its elitist and pro-Pakistan program has limited appeal among the urban and rural poor, who support the various ethnic parties.

The problem is shared by all Islamic revivalist parties in Pakistan, a highly fractious and precarious polity, where ethnic and parochial sentiments command the allegiance of a significant share of the population, especially among the lower classes. The logic of separating and making a Muslim homeland has continued to inform its political development. So central has been the role of ethnic and linguistic loyalties in Pakistani politics that the country has fought two civil wars to defend the primacy of its federal union: first in 1971, which ended in the dismemberment of Pakistan; and again, during 1973–1977 when Baluchistan threatened to secede. Since then, however, Pakistan continues to be plagued by ethnic separatism, the more so in the 1980s with the call for "Sindhudesh" (rhymes with Bangladesh) in some quarters. Pakistan's ordeal with ethnic and linguistic nationalism emphasizes the dangers posed to this homeland of Muslims, which have beckoned the Islamic revivalist parties to its defense, and underscores the power and potential of ethnic and linguistic loyalties as a fundamental pillar of popular politics. It is not surprising that national parties such as the People's Party have been compelled to pay homage to ethnic and linguistic sentiments in order to bolster their political standing.

The dilemma is how to defend the territorial integrity of Pakistan while still serving the party's political interests that entail accommodation of popular ethnic sentiment. Caught in the tangle of a federal arrangement defined in terms of the boundaries of Islam and the Urdu language, which has been kept at bay by the deeply entrenched ethnic and parochial political forces, Islamic revivalism has compromised its ability to "trickle down" and as was the case in East Pakistan in 1971, could, as a result, face virtual obliteration. Operating as national parties and defenders of Pakistan—a homeland created in the name of Islam—compels parties such as the Jama'at to adopt the national language and to avoid appealing to provincial and parochial sentiments and remain attached to the ideal of Muslim solidarity and to Urdu.[16] The resolution of this dilemma is far from simple; it is predicated upon a significant reinterpretation of the role of Islam in Pakistani politics.

Over the years the Jama'at has expanded its proselytizing and established a base of support in Sind, North-West Frontier Province, and Punjab, a policy that is tied to the state's efforts to integrate its provinces into a federation. While a greater geographic spread in membership has given the Jama'at a national image, it has not sufficiently expanded its social base. To expand that base any further, the Jama'at will have to succumb to the pressures of ethnicity, to sacrifice its national goals and stakes, not to mention its dedication to the ideal of Pakistan and commitment to the Muslim homeland. If the Jama'at's strong defense of the unity of Pakistan during the civil war in East Pakistan is any indication, the party is not prepared to undertake such a momentous step. It cannot altogether remain unmoved, however, by the ethnic politics that are destroying the equilibrium that has conditioned its political choices; nor can it expect to retain control over the rapidly changing and highly fluid political environment in which it operates. For instance, the MQM was established in urban centers of Sind in the 1980s by a number of IJT students who objected to the domination of the student organization by Punjabis and the Jama'at's unwillingness to address problems which were particular to the Muhajir community The Jama'at, although it had never consciously solicited domination by Punjabis to the detriment of Muhajirs, was incapable of controlling the crisis brewing in its ranks. The MQM has subsequently eliminated the Jama'at from the urban centers of Sind, forcing the party into a largely Punjabi existence, an outcome neither desired nor welcomed by the Jama'at.

The rise to prominence of an ethnic party in the community with most at stake in the federal union of Pakistan has eroded the base of support of parties such as the Jama'at, narrowed their angle of entry into national politics, and by implication, posed a challenge to their political relevance and efficacy One might have thought that the diminishing importance of the federal center would have removed the impediments to popularizing the Jama'at among the lower class. However, the rise of the MQM and its mix of ethnic and populist politics, rather than encouraging the Jama'at to do likewise, has generated resistance to such a development. The prospect of the Pakistani federation's collapse and the loss of constituency associated with the party's national role has dampened any enthusiasm for realigning Jama'at politics along provincial and parochial lines. The effort to provide an alternative to the MQM has also encouraged the Jama'at to remain anchored in national politics so that it can present Muhajirs with a political platform not available in the MQM's repertoire. The Jama'at has been effectively split by its political role of legitimizing and defending the unity of the polity and territory by which the party is defined and its ultimate political aim of expanding its social base and winning elections. Resolving this dilemma will in good measure depend on the extent to which provincial and ethnic politics prove receptive to the Jama'at's ideology, and on its ability to decentralize and adapt itself to the needs of a variety of ethnic communities. The rate at which the party loses support in the vote banks affiliated with its national role and identity should it turn to ethnic and provincial politics, and whether that loss will be compensated by new bases of support, is another question. For the time being, while it assesses its future in provincial and ethnic politics, the Jama'at continues to operate at the national level, tenaciously defending the turf of the federal structure against encroachments by parochial forces.

The Jama'at's commitment to national politics has, over the years, been sacrosanct as has the idea of the nation-state in the party's political thinking. At the end of a decade of ethnic politics, the Jama'at's election platform of 1970 specifically rejected appealing to "sons of the soil,"[17] and declared the party's determination to operate only as a national party [18] Faced with the collapse of the federal order that defined the limits of the Jama'at's activities, first in 1947 and again in 1971, the party reluctantly, but hastily, adapted itself to the new circumstances. It did so, however, not by recognizing the importance of parochial forces in the politics of South Asia but by realigning its strategy and operations along nation-state lines, floating independent Jama'at-i Islamis with new national and territorial identities. The Jama'at resisted abandoning national politics. It made changes in its strategy and organizational structure, but only along national and territorial lines, when the polity itself had divided into new national entities. Its willingness to sublimate its universalist ambitions to the reality of the nation-state system, however, has conceded little to ethnic politics. Commitment to the nation-state system has thus far remained paramount.

THE MUHAJIRS

The Jama'at-i Islami began in Pakistan as essentially a Muhajir party, consisting for the most part of Urdu-speaking migrants from the Muslim minority provinces of India who had settled in the cities and towns of Sind and East Pakistan and migrants from East Punjab who settled in the Pakistani side of that province. They remained its most visible base of support until well into the 1980s.[19] Their loyalty can be attributed in part to the extensive relief work the party undertook among the refugees in Karachi and Lahore after partition. The Jama'at workers cleaned up refuse in refugee camps, buried unclaimed corpses, and provided food and medicine;[20] it set up some forty-two aid centers for assisting the refugees, spending in excess of Rs. 260,000 on them between 1947 and 1954, which benefited some 1.5 million Muhajirs.[21] These efforts established a firm bond between the two, the more so because the government had proved incapable of helping the refugees. This campaign proved so successful that social work was incorporated into the structure of the Jama'at. The party created its division for "service to the people" (*shu'bah-i khidmat-i khalq*), which today runs hospitals, dispensaries, orphanages, and centers for assistance to widows and the old. It collects revenues and contributions for distribution among the poor. When in the 1980s large numbers of Afghan refugees began to pour into Pakistan, the Jama'at initiated projects similar to those for the Muhajirs to gain support among the Afghans.

The Jama'at's virulent anti-Hindu rhetoric also found a receptive ear among the Muhajirs, whose harrowing experiences from the partition had made them particularly sensitive to the Indian threat. They were most keen about Mawdudi's promises to restore Islam to its true place at the helm of power in the Subcontinent, which for many Muhajirs meant restoring their fortunes, status, and property The Muhajirs had arrived in a country where, before partition, the Muslim League had had little influence and where ethnic loyalties and provincial interests superseded the kind of commitment to Islamic universalism that had led to Pakistan's creation. Neither the geographical territory of Pakistan nor its ethnic and provincial political structure had any significance for the Muhajirs; their sole reason for migrating to the new homeland had been the primacy of religious and communal identity in their politics. In Mawdudi's denunciation of nationalism and the Jama'at's emphasis on Urdu and Islam, the Muhajirs found a political program attuned to their interests, which sought to hide the fundamental realities of Pakistani society and politics—the simmering tensions between the refugees and their hosts, especially in Sind—behind Islamic solidarity The Jama'at's political program in general, and its depiction of the plight of the Muhajirs as comparable to those of the original Muhajirs, the companions of the Prophet who migrated with him from Mecca to Medina, provided the Muhajirs with a justification both for their presence in Pakistan and for having a say in its politics.[22] The Jama'at's ideological pronouncements in a time of social disorder and political change attracted support for the party This championing of the Muhajir cause came over time to become a part of the party's role and place in Pakistan politics.

The campaign for the Islamic state, assigned to Islamic parties in general—and to its most vociferous advocate, the Jama'at, in particular—the task of legitimating the idea of Pakistan and providing hope and solace in hard times. This legitimating function attracted the support of those who had a stake in the unity of Pakistan, which, in addition to the Muhajirs, meant the Punjabi and Pathan middle and lower-middle classes. With every crisis and the threat to the unity of the country, the Islamic movements such as the Jama'at have increased their following and have had success in their propaganda, because the panacea for political unrest rooted in the founding principles of Pakistan is Islam. This also in good measure accounts for the Jama'at's reluctance to abandon its legitimating role and the religious tone of its political discourse and to turn to a more pragmatic approach to provincial and ethnic politics.

Although the Jama'at had never courted the Muhajirs, it soon became aware of their political value and the pivotal role the cities that they dominated played in Pakistani politics, especially as rural politics remained closed to the party By 1951, the year when the first census in Pakistan was taken, the Muhajirs accounted for 57 percent of Karachi's population, 65 percent of Hyderabad's, 55 percent of Sukkhur's, and in all, 46 percent of the population of Pakistan's twelve major cities.[23] Anxious to win elections, limited in appeal to urban voters, and increasingly conscious of its legitimating function in Pakistan, the Jama'at made much of its ties with the Muhajirs. In return, the party was able to attract large crowds for demonstrations and public rallies in cities like Karachi, time and again intimidating the government and compelling it to adopt measures Islamic parties demanded. With no national elections in the offing until 1970, the Jama'at found no opportunity to test its popularity or the wisdom of its policy of relying mainly on the Muhajirs. In 1970 the Muhajirs, in turn, for the first time took a hard look at their policy of supporting the unity of Pakistan in the name of Islam and lending support to the Jama'at. While the politics of the Muhajir community did not radically change until the 1980s, when the MQM was founded, doubts were already evident in the elections of 1970. The Jama'at's staggering defeat at the polls in the elections of 1970 showed its weakness and told the Muhajirs that it could not deliver on their demands. The elections were soon followed by the secession of East Pakistan and harrowing tales of oppression of its Muhajir community by the Bengali majority The independence of Bangladesh proved to be a devastating psychological shock for the Muhajirs, especially as it coincided with the rise to power of Bhutto, a prime minister who championed Sindhi nationalism to the detriment of the Muhajirs. The Jama'at's poor showing demonstrated that it would be of no help. The Muhajirs chose instead to play the ethnic political game, a strategy that promised to deliver more tangible gains than the Jama'at could produce—provide them with a greater say in the country's affairs and direct resources to their community By succumbing to ethnic politics, however, they abandoned the vision of Pakistan united under the banner of Islam. Later, the MQM rallied Muhajirs to its cause with the slogan "We have not signed contracts to uphold Pakistan and Islam."[24]

CHANGES IN CONSTITUENCY AFTER THE ELECTIONS OF 1970

In a speech before the workers of the Jama'at-i Islami on January 10, 1971, Mawdudi blamed the party's lackluster performance in 1970 on its too limited base of support.[25] In a rare show of self-criticism, he declared that the Jama'at boasted a literacy rate of 85 percent in a country where the same percentage were illiterate; it had spent too much energy and resources on attracting the educated, while it was the poor and uneducated who determined elections. The Jama'at should reexamine its policies and its orientation and strategy Mawdudi's candor resulted in some proselytizing work among other groups, notably women,[26] the industrial labor force, and the peasants. Given the limited numbers of Jama'at's elected representatives, the women became important to the Jama'at because for a time there were twenty special seats reserved for them in the National Assembly and twenty-three in each provincial assembly

The party's new strategy was not drastic enough, however. Its campaign for support among the uneducated underclass went hand in hand with redoubling of campaigns among educated groups such as the ulama, university professors, lawyers, doctors, engineers, journalists, government employees, students, and urban youth.[27] Separate programs and sometimes organizations were formed to gain support: the Jama'at began to use "religious schools, mosques, social service centers, zakat committees, municipal offices," and the like for implementing its campaign.[28] Its elected representatives were directed to solidify their base of support in their constituencies, using an amended version of the famed People's Party battle cry, "clothing, bread, and shelter" (kapra, roti, awr makan), that added "health and basic education" ('alaj awr zaruri ta'lim).[29] The party set higher goals for raising the number of affiliates and increased the frequency of its training camps for workers and sympathizers.[30] These programs were continued through the 1970s and 1980s.[31]

All these efforts produced results. The party gained more solid support in Punjab and grew in North-West Frontier Province. The party's greater prominence in North-West Frontier Province is significant in that since the elections of 1985 that province has provided the Jama'at with a steady number of national and provincial assembly seats. This clearly demonstrates the success of the party's new strategy The Jama'at's greater role in North-West Frontier Province's politics is the result of the vigorous organizational work of Qazi Husain Ahmad. The absence among Pathans of traditional authority based in feudalism and Sufism made Qazi Husain's task easier. The Jama'at's following in that province is based in small towns such as Swat and the rural district of Dir, which has proved to be a Jama'at stronghold. It is the only district to choose Jama'at candidates in every general election since 1970.[32]

These developments have certainly altered the party's national distribution and base of support. In 1977 the Jama'at, as a member of the Pakistan National Alliance, won four seats to the National Assembly from Sind, two from Punjab, and three from North-West Frontier Province; in 1985 it won three seats from Punjab, four from North-West Frontier Province, and one from Baluchistan. In 1988 it won six seats to the National Assembly from Punjab and two from North-West Frontier Province. In 1990 the figures were seven and one, respectively Similarly, in 1970 the Jama'at had won one seat to each of the provincial assemblies of Punjab, Sind, North-West Frontier Province, and East Pakistan; in 1988 it won six seats to the Punjab provincial assembly and seven to the North-West Frontier Province assembly; in 1990 the figures were eleven and eight, respectively The Jama'at's electoral showings in provincial elections improved in the 1990 elections; otherwise the constituencies which elected Jama'at members in 1988 and 1990 remained roughly the same.[33] Since 1977, Karachi's place as the secure base of Jama'at support and guaranteed source of elected representatives has given way to Dir and Swat in North-West Frontier Province and Lahore and small towns in Punjab. The urban base of support, aside from sporadic electoral victories in Lahore and Rawalpindi, has evaporated.

In the elections of 1977, the results of which are still in doubt because of charges of massive rigging by the government, of the Jama'at's nine seats to the National Assembly, three in North-West Frontier Province and one in Punjab were in rural or small-town constituencies. The remaining five seats were from urban areas. In 1988 of the Jama'at's eight National Assembly seats, only two were from large urban areas; the remaining six seats were from rural areas or small towns. Similarly, in provincial elections that year, of the Jama'at's thirteen seats only four were from major cities. The results of the 1990 elections resembled those of 1988: of the Jama'at's eight seats to the National Assembly, three were from urban centers in Punjab, and five were from rural or small-town areas. Of the nineteen provincial seats won by the Jama'at, nine were from major urban areas and ten from rural or small-town areas. While the Jama'at's organizational work and propaganda produced these changes, Bhutto's economic policies also helped. They were unpopular with large and small landowners and the petite bourgeoisie, and opened those classes to the Jama'at's influence.

Today Punjab and North-West Frontier Province account for most of the increases in the Jama'at members, sympathizers, and officeholders. In 1987, after forty-six years with a Muhajir at the helm, the Jama'at chose its first Pathan amir, from North-West Frontier Province, Qazi Husain Ahmad.[34] The distribution of shura' members also shows how the party's base of support has shifted from cities to towns and the countryside. In 1957, the five major cities of Lahore, Rawalpindi, Lyallpur (Faisalabad), Multan, and Bhawalpur in Punjab accounted for twenty-three of the twenty-nine of the province's share of central shura' members, with the remaining six coming from two small towns. In 1989, the share of the five cities had shrunk to eleven, while twenty-four of Punjab's central shura' members came from nineteen small towns. Similarly, Peshawar accounted for all of the North-West Frontier Province's five central shura' members in 1957; in 1989 it accounted for only two of the eight North-West Frontier Province central shura' members. The other six were from small towns and rural areas (see table 4).

Although the greater representation of small-town and rural constituents in the central shura' indicates that the Jama'at has extended its reach, it has not been altogether a boon for the party. For the religiously conservative and politically unsophisticated small-town and rural members have diminished the Jama'at's flexibility in contending with sociopolitical exigencies and have

Table 4. Geographical Distribution of Shura' Members, 1950–1992

	1950	1957	1989	1992
Punjab	15	29	35	39
Lahore	3	3	3	4
Other major cities of Punjab[a]	8	20	8	7
Small cities and towns of Punjab[b]	4	6	24	28
Sind	2	12	15	18
Karachi	2	6	9	11
Hyderabad	0	2	1	2
Rest of Sind	0	4	5	5
NWFP	2	5	8	11
Peshawar	2	5	2	2
Rest of NWFP	0	0	6	9
Baluchistan	0	1	2	2
East Pakistan	0	3	0	0

Source: Organization Bureau of the Jama'at-i Islami.

[a]Consisting of Multan, Bhawalpur, Lyallpur/Faisalabad, and Rawalpindi/Islamabad.

[b]In 1950 this figure accounted for the four shura' members who were from Gujranwala; in 1957 the figure accounted for two towns; in 1989 the figure accounted for nineteen towns.

nudged the party in directions which are not in keeping with the political imperatives before it. To the chagrin of the Jama'at's leaders, diversification has given a conservative bent to the party at a time when a more liberal position is necessary if the party is to expand its base of support. For example, in November 1989, when it tried to expand its base among women by suggesting that its views on the women's dress code (purdah) be relaxed—so that women had to cover only their hair and could show their faces in public, the majlis-i 'amilah resisted.[35] The majority of its members are from small towns and rural areas of Punjab and North-West Frontier Province, where women customarily wear the face cover (burqa'). Backed by a religious decree (fatwa) from the Jama'at's ulama, who ruled that purdah was addressed in religious sources and was therefore not open to debate, interpretation, or change, the conservative element soundly defeated the initiative.

The Jama'at continues to try to expand its base, however, by maintaining a delicate balance between sociopolitical imperatives and pressures for ideological fidelity by lowering the scope of its changes and steering clear of divisive doctrinal issues. It has also sought to consolidate the changes which have been undertaken to date,[36] which is exemplified in the choice of the populist Qazi Husain Ahmad to succeed the taciturn Mian Tufayl Muhammad in an effort to replace the subdued image of the Jama'at's leaders with a more appealing one, both to encourage activism and to appeal to a greater number of Pakistanis. In 1987, Qazi Husain Ahmad began his term of office as amir with a much publicized tour from Peshawar to Karachi. He called it the "caravan of invitation and benevolence" (*karavan-i da'wat'u muhabbat*); its populist intent gained him the sobriquet *surkhah* (red, i.e. leftist) in the party Since his election, Qazi Husain Ahmad has continued to harp on populist themes, albeit in tandem with commitment to democracy and the Pakistan state. He has also attacked feudalism (*jagirdari*) and capitalism (*sarmayahdari*)[37] and has deliberately bestowed upon the party's rhetoric and plan of action a class consciousness it did not earlier possess:

> In this country there is a small imperialist class whom the British established in power. Since the British left, this small class has been ruling the country The culture of this class is foreign; in their houses they speak in another language. They are educated in special institutions. This is our ruling class, which is as foreign and alien as were the British. This the people understand.[38]

Qazi Husain, much like Mawdudi, approaches social analysis through culture rather than through economics. It is apparent from his rhetoric that Jama'at's political discourse, although more populist in tone, continues to be nationally oriented, seeking out contentious sociopolitical issues that would have national relevance. Although shifts in its base of support had much to do with the politics of the Muhajirs and its own organizational activities in Punjab and North-West Frontier Province, its reach into small towns and rural districts has also owed its success in good measure to the IJT.

Despite these gains, which were reflected in modestly improved electoral showings in 1985, 1988 and 1990, the party has not changed its political stance and organizational structure sufficiently to accommodate Qazi Husain's populism. Without that, it cannot hope for victory at the polls in a country where some two-thirds of the population live in the rural areas. As efficacious as IJT has proved to be, it too has reached the limit of its expansion. With no political program to address the problems of the rural and small-town voters, IJT has failed to make its campus organizations a nation wide network. The Jama'at has therefore been forced to face up to the questions Mawdudi posed in 1971, and to debate fundamental changes in the structure of the party, including the ultimate question over its existence as holy community or political party

The Debate Over Opening The Party

Since its creation in 1941, the Jama'at has adhered to a set of rules and criteria that have seemed to restrict its membership (see tables 5 and 6). As Mawdudi explained, "so I concluded that I wanted Jama'at-i Islami's discipline to be very strict and firm, whether some stay or leave   I would not permit compromise on the organization."[39] Discipline, moral rectitude, and strong organizational bonds were the foundation stones of a holy community and essential to the pursuit of the goals of "Islamic revolution" and an "Islamic state." But, as the Jama'at began to put its fortunes in Pakistani politics beginning in 1951, the relevance of a vanguard—a holy community and an "organizational weapon"—in the revolutionary sense of the term, as floated by Lenin and adopted by Mawdudi, became suspect.

Taking its cue from Mawdudi, the Jama'at's leadership long remained unclear about the exact nature of its decision to turn to politics and the implications of this change in strategy They were reluctant to undertake any substantial reforms in the party's organizational structure. Although aware that the Jama'at's cadre of workers and party's base of support needed to be expanded, in 1951 the leaders decided to introduce the new category of affiliate to act as a convenient buffer between the Jama'at and Pakistani society, a stop-gap measure that permitted the Jama'at to expand its organizational network without compromising the principles and criteria of its organizational structure. The affiliate category both reflected and confirmed the ambivalent nature of the Jama'at's purposes and the tensions produced by its efforts to balance ideological fidelity with utilitarian politics.

The affiliates were composed of those who favored the Jama'at's goals and ideas, but were not ready to abide by its organizational discipline, a group through which the party's rigid organizational structure could interact with the society at large. In November 1951, during the party's convention in Karachi, the Jama'at decided to recruit and organize at least 12,000 affiliates.[40] Thenceforth, as their interest in electoral politics increased, the affiliates became the Jama'at's political lifeline and permitted the party to evade the question of more fundamental structural changes. A positive correlation was thus established between greater political activity—and the resulting electoral defeats—on the one hand, and emphasis upon the affiliates, on the other. The humiliating defeat in the Punjab elections of 1951 generated no discussion regarding Jama'at's membership criteria, but it did lead to a more aggressive policy of recruiting and organizing affiliates.[41] In 1955, with an eye on national elections, the Jama'at's leaders directed the organization to recruit 40,000 affiliates in a three-year period.[42]

Although there were no elections in Pakistan until 1970, the Jama'at continued to expand its organizational networks through the affiliates. The Machchi Goth affair helped, since the declaration of the shura' in November-December 1956 that Mawdudi's writings were no longer binding on the party was used to

Table 5 Members and Affiliates of the Jama'at-ı Islamı,
1941–1992

	Members	% Change	Affiliates	% Change
1941	75	0	0	0
1946	486	548	0	0
1947	385ᵃ	− 21	0	0
1949	533	38	0	0
1951	659	24	2,913	0
1955	1,078	64	0	0
1957	1,272	18	25,000	758
1970	2,500	97	0	0
1974	3,308	32	186,085	0
1977	3,497	6	282,089	52
1983	4,776ᵇ	37	256,403	− 9
1985	4,798	0	238,331	− 7
1989	5,723ᶜ	19	305,792	28
1992	7,861	37	357,229	17

Source: *RJI* 5:60, 6:25–26, 98, 150; *SAAM* 2:8, 392; Organization Bureau of the Jama'at-ı Islamı.

ᵃ At the time of partition the Jama'at had 626 members, 240 of whom remained in India.

ᵇ 160 of whom were women.

ᶜ 321 of whom were women.

attract followers from other schools of Islamıc thought. These new recruits were often Deobandi or Ahl-ı Hadith, or were followers of other self-styled religious movements, but they sympathized with the Jama'at's goals. Their entry into the Jama'at transformed the terms under which the affiliates allied themselves with the party They were no longer restricted to those attracted by Jama'at's message but who hesitated to submit to its rigorous discipline; they were increasingly those who sympathized with the Jama'at's political program but remained attached to other schools of Islamıc thought.

While useful in expanding the organizational horizons of the Jama'at, the affiliate category proved inadequate for satisfying the party's rapidly rising political expectations (see table 5). The party's defeat in the elections of 1970 left little room for its leaders to remain sanguine about the affiliates as a source of political power. Mawdudi came under increasing pressure to relax the criteria for membership, and expand its organizational reach. Aware that the move would have implications he did not like, Mawdudi balked at the idea, and by blaming the defeat on the machinations of foreign powers he diverted attention from the need for fundamental organizational reforms.[43] His vision for the Jama'at still encompassed not a party, but a holy community—an embryonic *ummah*—and

Table 6. Jama'at-ı Islamı Members, Affiliates, and Workers by Province, 1974–1992

	Punjab	NWFP	Baluchıstan	Sind	Total
1974					
Members	2,077	405	65	762	3,308
Affiliates	90,957	53,272	1,276	40,580	186,085
Workers	5,102	1,676	89	2,092	18,959
1977					
Members	2,135	430	51	881	3 497
Affiliates	125,546	89,722	2,738	54,083	282,089
Workers	5 436	1,254	210	1,782	8,682
1981					
Members	2,320	496	94	399	3,309
Affiliates	135,684	95,000	868	13,609	245,161
Workers	3,299	—	—	270	3,569
1983					
Members	2,921	607	110	2,692	4,776
Affiliates	58,797	13,7514	7,273	52,819	256,403
Workers	6,528	2,586	210	2,692	12,016
1985					
Members	2,905	678	122	1,093	4,798
Affiliates	61,985	103,533	1,442	71,371	238,331
Workers	6,345	2,151	148	2,637	11,281
1988					
Members	2,954	860	131	1,365	5,598
Affiliates	81,509	126,403	2,485	116,658	355,895
Workers	6,430	2,674	83	3,574	13,724
1992					
Members	4,435	1,252	200	1,974	7,861
Affiliates	111,322	118,572	1,900	125,435	357,229
Workers	17,326	4,829	337	11,664	34,156

Source: Organızatıon Bureau of the Jama'at-ı Islamı.

a vanguard. If success ın electoral polıtıcs requıred changıng structure and ethos, then Mawdudi preferred to opt out of the electoral process altogether. Although no longer at the helm, between 1972 and his death ın 1979, Mawdudi used his consıderable powers of persuasıon to convınce the new leaders of the wısdom of hıs course, but he was not entırely successful. At the shura' ın 1975, he declared that the Jama'at should reevaluate ıts agenda and ıts future course of actıon, and possıbly abandon electoral polıtıcs altogether ın the ınterests of ıdeologıcal purıty [44] The new leaders were not convınced; they wanted to break the polıtıcal ımpasse, but not totally to replace polıtıcs wıth purely relıgıous concerns. The Jama'at had evolved ınto a consummate polıtıcal party, and ıts commitment to electoral politics had gone too far to allow them simply to walk away from it. No clear decisions were taken regarding Mawdudi's counsel, and with the future of the party in doubt, tensions continued to mount in the ranks. In 1978 for example a suggestion by 'Abdu'l-Ghafur Ahmad that the Jama'at as a political party should ally itself more closely, even blend in, with other Pakistan National Alliance (PNA) parties provoked public censure from Mawdudi.[45]

For as long as Mawdudi lived, his inflexibility staved off any attempt to open up the Jama'at's membership. The party, instead, resorted to other ways of expanding its base, such as organizing students, women, the labor force, and the peasants. The popularity the party enjoyed in the 1970s as a result of its firm opposition to the Bhutto government and success in mobilizing the masses around single causes, such as the non-recognition of Bangladesh, to the leaders' relief somewhat obfuscated the issues that had given rise to the debate over membership, but did not solve the problem of expanding the Jama'at's base of support nor the anomaly inherent in utilizing a rigid organizational structure in electoral politics. Since 1985, lackluster electoral results have once again raised questions about the fate and objectives of the Jama'at, and the loss of support among the Muhajirs has underlined its deficiencies. With Mawdudi out of the picture, these developments have led to impassioned debates over its membership criteria both in and outside the party A group of Mawdudi loyalists—those who continue to see the Jama'at as essentially a holy community, as well as those who advocate an "Islamic revolution" of some form—resist change. They argue that the Jama'at's raison d'être is its ideological vision, which could be diluted or, worse yet, manipulated if it is revamped by members who do not have firm loyalties to the party's ethos and world view The newcomers could use their vote to destroy the Jama'at from within, and to do what successive governments have failed to do. The Jama'at, they argue, owes its continuity to its strong ideological foundations and to the moral fiber and loyalty that are protected and perpetuated by its strict membership criteria. Their position has been bolstered by the fact that no one in the Jama'at wishes to compromise the discipline which underlies the existing political power of the party In a country where political parties are hopelessly divided into factions and autonomous wings, the Jama'at leaders pride themselves in the unity of thought and action of their members, which they attribute to their membership standards.

The more politically motivated Jama'at leaders and workers, however, favor some opening up. In the Jama'at opinions vary from opening the party's membership to the few, to creating new intermediary criteria between member and affiliate, to providing mechanisms for greater participation by affiliates in decision-making, to separating the party's religious and political functions—vesting the first in a closed organization and second in an open one.[46] To engineer and manipulate "political participation" the Jama'at must become a full-fledged party "Revolution has no meaning without popular support,"[47] as one leader put it. It must open its ranks to the many Pakistanis who are allied with the party ideologically and politically, and yet are kept from joining it ranks by the forbidding membership criteria. The holy community, as an ideal as well as a reality, has over the years become an anachronism and a constraint on the party's political progress.

While the Jama'at has done much to create the "Islamic vote bank" in Pakistan, denying membership to its own group of voters has kept it from consolidating this same base of support, and therefore it cannot benefit from the fruits of its own toil. It cannot count on affiliates and sympathetic voters, because to ensure their loyalty, it must have some organizational control over them. The great ease and rapidity with which the Muhajirs abandoned the Jama'at attests to the weakness of its ties. Those hardest hit by the loss of the Muhajir vote—the members of Jama'at-i Islami in Sind—argue that, had the Muhajirs been able to express their views in the party and seen more of their interests reflected in its policies, they might not have been compelled to look elsewhere for solutions.

The strict criteria for membership have so reduced the interactions between the Jama'at and the society in which it operates that the party has developed an elitist and patronizing outlook which one erstwhile Jama'at votary calls "a kinship" ('asabiyyah).[48] The abstract, pedantic, and mostly apolitical discourse of the Jama'at—telling Pakistanis what they should think and demand rather than representing their aspirations—and the distinct physical and sartorial appearance of its members—long sherwani coats, caracul caps, and long beards—has distinguished them from the general population, who refer to them as "Jama'ati" (of the Jama'at). Opening up the Jama'at would not only be a concession to outsiders, but also the means by which the party can become sensitive and responsive to the sociopolitical imperatives and dynamics that determine the course of politics in Pakistan. As the party's fear of annihilation subsided over the years so did the pressures for segregating the Jama'at from the society at large.

Demand for change has been voiced from different quarters. The party's Muhajir members,[49] and those to whom the Jama'at has made overtures in order to avoid opening its ranks, including the members of its various unions, have also favored opening the party Jama'at's efforts in the 1970s and the 1980s to find a base of support among the labor force, peasants, and white-collar professionals have only created new demands for greater say in the affairs of the party The more these new groups support the Jama'at, the more the party has felt the pressure for change, lest it fail to sustain its rapport with its new found allies and supporters. The proliferation of semi-autonomous institutions such as those enrolling the labor, peasants, teachers, and lawyers threatens the Jama'at's organizational structure directly by creating centrifugal tendencies within the party If these expanding groups are not successfully incorporated into the Jama'at, the party will lose control over them.

In 1990 Qazi Husain Ahmad finally took the first step, not by reforming the membership criteria, but by adding yet another semi-autonomous organization to Jama'at's family This was the Pasban (Protector), which draws support mainly from among the urban youth, former IJT members, and the right-of-center activists in the lower middle classes. The new organization, which is not officially affiliated with the Jama'at, has no membership criteria and, to the chagrin of the Jama'at old guard, does not demand adherence to a code of social conduct, not even wearing a beard. The aim is to organize those who sympathize with the Jama'at, even if their support is limited to politics, in order to provide the party with a broader base. The Pasban was also charged with the task of popularizing the Jama'at's message through plays and festivals, thus somewhat alleviating the problem of the Jama'at's distance from the masses. No sooner was it created, however, than it became a bone of contention in the Jama'at. While Qazi Husain and his supporters viewed the new organization with hope, the purists decried its lax discipline and even denied that it was useful.

Organizational reform and membership criteria continue to preoccupy the Jama'at's leadership, reflecting its continuing struggle with tensions born of applying its ideological perspective to the pursuit of its political goals. The outcome of this process and the ultimate shape which the Jama'at's greater political activism is likely to take have in good part, however, been controlled and conditioned by the party's interactions with other political actors and the various Pakistani regimes.

3

POLITICS

5 Prelude to Pakistan, 1941–1947

The development of the Jama'at's political outlook and plan of action is largely a result of its interactions with the various Pakistani governments since 1947 The manner in which the Jama'at's political agenda has unfolded to give shape to its plan of action cannot be examined apart from the political context in which the party operated. The Jama'at's politics, and especially the manner in which they have changed over time, are a function of the party's experiences with the political process in Pakistan and the vicissitudes of its continuous interaction with other actors in the political arena. This has defined the party's role in the political process.

Three interrelated processes have together served as the fundamental determinant of the nature of the Jama'at's political activism and have also outlined the historical paradigm which has governed the party's development. The three are the emergence of a more balanced mix of ideological fidelity and pragmatism in the Jama'at's politics, the enclosure of the party's ideological perspective and political aspirations within the territorial boundaries of the Pakistani nation-state, and the articulation and unfolding of the Jama'at's legitimating function within that state. Together these molded both the impact Islamic revivalism made on the state and, conversely, the influence involvement in the political process had on Islamic revivalism. The Jama'at's political discourse and organizational consolidation interacted with the objectives and needs of the Pakistan state to produce a symbiotic relationship between the two, above and beyond the mutual antagonisms which have characterized the relations between the party and Pakistan's various governments.

When Pakistan was created in the summer of 1947, the Muslim League and the Jama'at were at loggerheads, though instances of cooperation continued both before and after. The convergence of objectives of these two communalist programs, and Jama'at's hostility to the Congress party, in 1937–1939 had established a common ground. Mawdudi began his forays into politics by asserting Muslim communal consciousness against Congress's secular nationalist platform in 1937, two years before he even took notice of the Muslim League in his proclamations or written works. His program was first articulated in a series of articles in the *Tarjumanu'l-Qur'an* and later published in *Musalman Awr Mawjudah Siyasi Kashmakash* (1938–1940) (Muslims and the Current Political Struggle) and *Mas'alah-ı Qaumiyat* (1947) (Question of Nationality), where he attacked his erstwhile mentors among Congress supporters, 'Ubaidu'llah Sindhi, Abu'l-Kalam Azad, and the leaders of the Jami'at-ı Ulama-ı Hind.[1] In these works Mawdudi depicted the Congress as a convenient front for the Hindu drive for power and as a secular and, worse yet, socialist party, whose views were incompatible with Muslim values.[2] He therefore challenged the wisdom of siding with the Congress, asserting: "There are no common grounds between our movements [Muslim and the Hindu]; our death is their life, and their death our life."[3] Nor was Mawdudi persuaded by the anti-imperialist rhetoric and logic of the Muslim supporters of the Congress. Combating the evil of imperialism, Mawdudi argued, did not justify sacrificing Islam.[4]

> The fight against imperialism   and expulsion of the British has meaning for us only in the context of *la ilaha ila'llah* [there is no god but God]; otherwise there is no difference between imperialism and idol-worshipping democracy [the Congress's position]. Lot goes and Manat [Qur'anic terms referring to evil and pagan forces] replaces it.[5]

Although Mawdudi's line of attack was directed against pro-Congress Muslims as a whole, his most acid remarks were reserved for Mawlana Husain Ahmad Madani (1879–1957), the head of the Jami'at-ı Ulama-ı Hind at the time, and one of the most outspoken and ardent supporters of the Congress party among Indian ulama. Madani was vehemently anti-British and dedicated to the nationalist cause; he was instrumental in establishing a base of support for the Congress among Muslims. In 1939 Madani had presented his views and the Jami'at-ı Ulama's political platform in a pamphlet entitled *Mutahhidah Qaumiyat Awr Islam* (United/Composite Nationalism and Islam). The small tract soon became the basis for the Congress party's Muslim policy, and hence the focus of Mawdudi's most caustic invective. Mawdudi censured Madani's thesis and challenged his political and ultimately religious authority, accusing him of sacrificing Islam at the altar of his anti-British sentiments. Mawdudi couched his arguments in religious terms, which not only undermined the Jami'at-ı Ulama's political platform but also weakened its religious justification, hindering the ulama's efforts to accommodate Indian nationalism within the framework of Muslim orthodoxy So forceful was Mawdudi's charge against Madani and the Jami'at-ı Ulama that Mufti Kifayatu'llah, a senior Jami'at-ı Ulama stalwart, advised his colleagues not to engage Mawdudi in embarrassing debates.[6] These debates had already prompted Muhammad Iqbal to remark, "Mawdudi will teach a lesson to these Congressite Muslims,"[7] and had led some enthusiastic Muslim League workers to refer to Mawdudi as "our Abu'l-Kalam [Azad]."[8]

Desperate to attract some support for its two-nation platform from the religious quarter, the Muslim League developed a keen interest in Mawdudi's anti-Jami'at-i Ulama crusade, which gave it a religious justification for rejecting the Congress's plea for a united stand against colonial rule. Muslim League speakers borrowed such terms as *hukumat-i ilahiyah* (divine government) and *khilafat-i rabbani* (divine caliphate) from Mawdudi's repertory, and his contribution to the Muslim League's political agenda was often cited and acknowledged in private along with those of Iqbal and Mawlana Hasrat Muhani.[9]

Mawdudi's writings were widely distributed in Muslim League sessions between 1937 and 1939[10] League workers found this effort especially productive in Amritsar in 1939, when scores of copies of the *Musalman Awr Mawjudah Siyasi Kashmakash* were distributed.[11] A similar attitude was evident in the League's central committee, which authorized the widespread circulation of Mawdudi's religious decrees against the Jami'at-i Ulama leaders in 1939[12] Mawdudi's usefulness to the League, however unintended, was nevertheless significant.[13] One Muslim League leader wrote of Mawdudi in retrospect that "the venerable Mawlana [Mawdudi]'s writings in *Tarjumanu'l-Qur'an* greatly furthered the League's religious and national demands."[14] The Jama'at's contribution to the League's enterprise is perhaps the best example of an aspect of the growth of support for Pakistan in north and northwest India that has not thus far received its due attention.

So favorable was the impression that the Muslim League had of Mawdudi in 1939 that Mawlana Zafar Ahmad Ansari, then the secretary of the central parliamentary board of the Muslim League, who was at the time advocating the party's cause before the senior ulama, took it upon himself to approach Mawdudi with a view to officially enlisting his support for the Muslim League. Mawdudi, not unexpectedly, turned down his offer, for he saw his contribution to the League and his success in stemming the tide of Muslim religious fervor for the Congress as a sign not of the confluence of his views and those of the Muslim League, but of the fundamentally religious nature of the Pakistan movement, his own inherent qualities as a leader, and his ultimate destiny to lead that movement. The nature of relations between the Jama'at and the Muslim League was not decided by Mawdudi's opposition to the Congress alone, but involved the competition between the two for power.

Relations with the Pakistan Movement

Mawdudi's revivalist agenda took shape at a time when the Muslim League was a force to be reckoned with and the question of a separate Muslim homeland

became a serious proposition. As a result, the course of the Jama'at's development became ineluctably bound to Muslim League politics. Since then the relationship between the two has influenced both the Jama'at's development and the
Islamization of the political discourse in Pakistan. It has been a curious aspect
of these relations, which the Jama'at's critics characterize as "opposition to
Pakistan," that the Jama'at was more tolerant of the Muslim League's support
for a separate Muslim homeland in 1941 than it was in 1947 Its attacks on the
character of the Muslim separatist struggle became more virulent as the League
became more prominent in Muslim politics. The Jama'at did not object to
Pakistan but to its creation under the aegis of the League. Mawdudi readily
admitted that he was opposed to the Muslim League because it was clear to him
that Jinnah never intended Pakistan to be an Islamic state and later lamented that
Jinnah's successors had construed all criticisms of the League as criticisms of
Jinnah, and all criticisms of Jinnah as disloyalty to Pakistan.[15] Malik Ghulam
'Ali, who had been an ardent supporter of Pakistan when he joined the Jama'at
in 1941, recollects that many proponents of Pakistan like himself congregated
around Mawdudi. They did not see Mawdudi as anti-Pakistan but viewed his
position as reflective of the vision for a "true Pakistan."[16] The problem of
harmonizing the Jama'at's roles of holy community and political party unraveled in the face of the Jama'at's stand on Muslim separatism.

Jinnah helped form Mawdudi's political thinking. It was Jinnah who showed
Mawdudi the political potential of religion and, by the same token, blinded him
to the importance of socioeconomic factors in the development of the Pakistan
movement. Although Mawdudi followed the Muslim League's example in courting the politically important educated Muslim middle classes, this measure by
itself did not constitute a socioeconomic reading of what was involved in the
Pakistan movement. For Mawdudi never saw the League's success as a product
of the Congress party's Hinduization of India under Gandhi's influence and its
subsequent intransigence vis-à-vis Muslim demands, nor did he believe that it
was born of the frustrations of the educated Muslim middle classes with British
rule. Instead, Mawdudi understood the power of the Muslim League to stem from
Jinnah's appeal to Islamic symbols and Muslim religious sensibilities, and this
conviction lay behind his adherence to the idea of the holy community's political
relevance, which early in its existence put a built-in brake on the Jama'at's
development into a full-fledged party Time and again over the course of the next
four decades, the Jama'at leaders cited the Muslim League's famed slogan,
"*Pakistan ka matlab kiya hey? La ilaha ila'llah*" (What is Pakistan about? "There
is no god but God"), to prove this point.[17] For Mawdudi the League's successful
use of religious symbols proved that Islam was the ultimate source of power and
legitimacy in the Muslim community The composition of the League's leadership—which Mawdudi regarded as secular and Westernized men who were at

best modernist or "nominal" Muslims—was ample testimony to this.[18] Mawdudi was convinced that Muslim politics would be receptive to intrusive forays by religious forces, which, in turn, emboldened his demand for an Islamic state. He argued that the nature of the Muslim political discourse, as reflected in the increasingly chiliastic program of the Muslim League, attested to the Muslim community's desire for such a state. Without it why part with India at all? There was no point in substituting Hindu rule with a godless one:[19] "If I could secure one square mile of territory in which none other than God would reign supreme, I would value every speck of its dust more than the entirety of India."[20]

In the increasingly religious context in which the struggle for Muslim interests took place—when religion portended power and political success—the Jama'at's proclivity for political activity soon turned into an open claim to leadership. Mawdudi believed that the religious tenor of the League's discourse had created expectations among Muslims which, given the party's secular nature, it was neither willing nor capable of fulfilling. Only the Jama'at, argued Mawdudi, was equipped, qualified, and truly willing to advocate the Muslim cause and to deliver on Muslim demands. He was naturally superior to the Westernized Jinnah, who neither prayed nor spoke proper Urdu as a leader for his community [21] The Muslim League, Mawdudi surmised, could at best only partially satisfy the appetite for the Islamic polity which it had whetted among the Muslims;[22] the League was to be the precursor to "a veritable Pakistan," pointing the way for the "vanguard"—the Jama'at—to create and run the Islamic state for the Muslims of India. If Muslims had mobilized so enthusiastically around Muslim League's half-baked Islamic appeal, then the Jama'at was bound to sweep away the Pakistan movement once Muslims had heard Mawdudi's message and learned of the Jama'at's religiously more meaningful program. Mawdudi's conclusion required that the Jama'at act as a political party, but it also underscored its claim to being a holy community—the true repository of the Islamic message that would shape the future of the Muslims. Thus began the Jama'at's muddled understanding of its sociopolitical function.

Mawdudi also saw the Muslim League as a "one-man show," and therefore incapable of the kind of organizational activity which the realization of a Muslim state demanded. It was bound to falter with its frail leader and its weak ties to the religious sentiments that were sustaining it. Mawdudi therefore kept his distance from the League, preparing the Jama'at as a "rear guard" ('aqab lashgar),[23] waiting in the wings for the opportune moment to step into the Muslim League's shoes,[24] despite pressures among members for cooperation with the League,[25] especially whenever electoral victory by the Congress threatened. This attitude was most clearly reflected in the Jama'at's decision not to support the League in the Indian elections of 1945; Mawdudi argued that he could not render assistance to "a party with no morals."[26] In later years, he explained: "we did believe in a separate Muslim state, but chose not to interfere with the League. Had the Qa'id [Jinnah] failed, then we would have stepped in."[27]

When the Jama'at was formed in August 1941, then, although it was a direct response to the Muslim League's Lahore Resolution of March 1940, which resolved to create Pakistan, its intent was not to stop the creation of Pakistan but to take the Muslim League's place at the head of the struggle for a Muslim state, to prevent Pakistan's secularization, and to deliver what the Muslim League had promised but could not possibly deliver. The Jama'at's agenda and objectives were devised to counter what it saw as the shortcomings of the League, which Mawdudi had viewed as serious enough to warrant the Jama'at's "wait-and-see" policy In May 1939, Mawdudi had asserted that forming the party "implie[d] changing the government."[28] When the Jama'at was formed two years later, the only government it sought to change, as is evident from its propaganda and political activities, was that of the future Muslim state.[29] The Jama'at emerged as a movement leading to the "renaissance" of Islam (nash'at-i naw) that would culminate in the rule of religious law (iqamat-i din), as distinguished from the Muslim League's territorial and cultural conception of Muslim nationhood combined with a secular government.[30] As early as 1942, the Jama'at began to devise plans for operating in Pakistan should it materialize.

Mawdudi's aversion to the Muslim League and its policies was not only doctrinal but it also had its roots in his understanding of what the trials and tribulations of the Muslims in India had been. For Mawdudi, who had witnessed the decline of the nizam's state in Hyderabad, Muslim rule by itself was a hollow and ephemeral concept. When and where it had existed, it had not guaranteed the rights and political fortunes of Muslims; it was a model of government the shortcomings of which were borne out by history If Muslims sought a panacea to their quandary, they had to look farther than the League's manifesto to the fundamental sources of power and glory in Islam. In Tonk (Rajasthan) in 1947, Mawdudi exclaimed, "[If the Muslim League] sincerely stood up as the true representative of Islam, the whole of India could become 'Pakistan.' "[31]

From its inception the Jama'at emphasized the distinction between "Islamic" and "Muslim" and, more important, "Islamic" and "secular." For instance, it contrasted its members with the secular and Westernized leaders of the Muslim League with their moral laxity and fleeting loyalties, the blatant "opportunism" of the likes of Bengal's Fazlu'l-Haq, and the "heterodox" faith of the Shi'i Jinnah, the Isma'ili Sir Aga Khan, and the Ahmadi Sir Chaudhri Zafaru'llah Khan.[32] By emphasizing this point and comparing their claims that they led the Muslims with its own claim of being a holy community, the Jama'at gained a political advantage. In so doing it also came perilously close to undermining the League's leadership, a sin of which the Muslim League has not absolved the Jama'at to this day Blunt as Mawdudi had been in his attacks on the Muslim League and its leadership and contrary to assertions by his critics, he did not promulgate an incontrovertibly anti-Pakistan platform. His rhetoric against the League always came in tandem with some form of support for partition.

THE TWO-NATION THEORY

In 1935 Mawdudi shared a train compartment with B. G. Kher, the Congress party's chief minister-designate of Bombay Mawdudi felt that Kher humiliated those Muslims with whom he came into contact during the trip, and there and then decided that he could not live in a state ruled by Hindus.[33] As idealistic as he may have been, by the late 1930s even he could see that the dream of converting the whole of India to Islam no longer seemed possible. For that reason Mawdudi increasingly succumbed to the communalist feelings that had all along influenced his turn to revivalism and political activism. If he was opposed to Congress's secular nationalism—aimed at gaining independence for India—it was primarily because he was a Muslim communalist at heart.

Many, including Mawdudi's own supporters, have argued that the Jama'at's opposition to the Pakistan movement and the Muslim League was only the logical result of Mawdudi's opposition to secular nationalism. Yet, Mawdudi's rejection of secular nationalism was neither as steadfast, nor as jejune, as both his critics and his followers suggest. It was communalism, behind the facade of Islam—creating distinctions between the "self" and the "other"—which governed Mawdudi's binary view of the world as sacred and profane. For Mawdudi, secular nationalism was a threat to communalism, and only for that reason did it feature in his ideological demonology, because secular nationalism meant Congress rule—a "Hindu Raj" in Mawdudi's words. In 1938, in a lengthy article in *Tarjumanu'l-Qur'an*, he wrote, "Nehru's promises of scientific progress and nationalist democracy will be tantamount to the extinction of Islam, and hence Muslims."[34]

In the same article Mawdudi systematically attacked Congress's position on secular nationalism and democracy as unworkable and detrimental to the interests of Indian Muslims. In its place he offered two "two-nation" schemes of his own,[35] proposing a state within a state (*riyasat dar riyasat*) that echoed Muhammad Iqbal's demand for a "Muslim India within India."[36] He then offered plans that would preserve the territorial integrity of India and still give Muslims substantial communal autonomy The first plan favored dividing India into two "culturally autonomous" democratic entities, which would form the "international federation" of India with a constitution similar to those of "Switzerland, Australia, or the United States."[37] The constituent entities would be equal partners in running the state, would have distinct boundaries, and would be sovereign in their internal affairs, with the power to formulate and implement their own laws. For matters pertaining to the state as a whole, such as the formulation of its confederate constitution, a constituent assembly would be formed, the members of which would be chosen through elections based on proportional representation.

Should the first plan not prove popular, Mawdudi devised a second one, in which India would again be reorganized along confederate lines, this time with fourteen territories, thirteen of which—Ajmer, Awadh, Baluchistan, East Bengal, Bhopal, Delhi, Hyderabad, Jawrah, Junagadh, North-West Frontier Province, North and West Punjab, Sind, and Tonk—would be awarded to Muslims, and a single large fourteenth would be Hindu. The thirteen were "justly" suggested by Sayyid 'Abdu'l-Latif whom Mawdudi lauded for the plan's wisdom in redrawing the map of India along communal lines. Twenty-five years would be allotted for exchanging populations between the thirteen territories and their Hindu neighbor. The fourteen territories would be bound by an Indian confederacy, but would enjoy sovereignty over their internal affairs. These plans clearly underscored Mawdudi's communalist inclinations, but still in an Indian framework. But that would not be the case for long. Even at the end of this revealing article he wrote that if the second plan too was rejected, Muslims would "have no choice but to demand a completely autonomous unit, tied together [with its Hindu counterpart] only for defense, communications, and trade,"[38] an idea which was not too distant from what the Congress, the Muslim League, and the viceroy were debating at the time.

These ideas of Indian confederacy, however, increasingly gave way to sober realization of the fractious direction in which Indian politics were heading. Mawdudi, like most Muslim communalists, began to feel the constraint of the narrowing range of options before him. When asked in 1938–1939 about his choice of the title "Daru'l-Islam" (Abode of Islam) for his project in Pathankot, Mawdudi explained "it means only a Muslim cultural home and not a Muslim state, but if God wills it, the two may become one."[39] By Muslim state, he surely no longer meant the entirety of India, for he had left South India two years earlier, having concluded that there was no future for Muslims in that region.[40] It was following the elections of 1937, when Indians were given limited self-government, and over the course of the following decade that, like many of his coreligionists who resided in Muslim minority provinces, Mawdudi, too, began to succumb to the temptation of secessionism. As his dream of an "Islamic India" was shattered by harsh realities, talk of converting the whole of India to Islam gave way to talk of an "Islamic state" in a separate Muslim territory From this point on, the Jama'at's relations with the Muslim League became more complex, marked by both competition and concord. Beyond the rivalry which characterized the relations between the two, the basis for a symbiotic relationship anchored in their shared communal outlook also emerged during this period.

COMPETITION WITH THE MUSLIM LEAGUE

Between 1941 and 1947 the language and tone of the League's political program was increasingly Islamized, and relations between the two parties in those years were affected by this change in character, which not only created a common ground between the two but also made the Muslim League more susceptible to Mawdudi's maneuvers. The League's appeal to Islamic symbols created a niche in the political arena for the Jama'at and prepared the ground for its activities. The Muslim League's actions began directly to influence the Jama'at's reactions. In collaboration, and more often in confrontation, with the League, the Jama'at found a political existence, as the League's policies became the Jama'at's calling. When in a speech before the students at Aligarh Muslim University in 1938 Mawdudi first outlined his idea of the Islamic state, he did so by comparing and contrasting it with the Muslim League's plans for Pakistan.

So long as he was unsure of the future, Mawdudi had sought to keep his options open by maintaining the Jama'at's distance from the Pakistan movement. This did not attest to his aversion to Muslim communalism but to his rivalry with the Muslim League. Behind Mawdudi's sanctimonious derision of the League's enterprise lay his own political ambitions. To attract the League's constituency, the Jama'at intensified its campaign to expose the "un-Islamic" nature of the Muslim League's program, believing that a people moved by religious concerns and loyalties were bound to gravitate toward the party that best represented the essence of their communal identity That Mawdudi was proved wrong suggests that religion could serve as the handmaiden of communalism, but not as its mainstay Although Muslims were attracted by the Islamic symbols, their political decisions were not religiously motivated. Muslim communalism encompassed Islam, but went far beyond the theological boundaries of the faith. It was not long before it became apparent that the Jama'at's campaign had failed to dent the League's following, let alone derail its plans for Pakistan. Party members, however, did not lose heart and decided that theirs was not a political problem. Mawdudi explained the Jama'at's failure to attract a following by citing Jinnah's wealth and his own comparatively meager means.[41] He could not find much solace in that argument for long, however, and relieved his frustrations by further escalating his scurrilous attacks on the Muslim League.

From 1939 onward, Mawdudi ceased to attack the Jami'at-i Ulama and the Congress and directed his invective against the Muslim League instead. As uneasy as the Muslim League felt about Mawdudi's broadside blasts against Jinnah and his program and despite its reactions to them, he presented no real dangers to the League. For Mawdudi and the Jama'at in those years had no concrete strategy; their idea of an Islamic state was too vague, intangible, and often unpalatable to the average Muslim to be persuasive; and their hatred of the Congress and the Hindus still outweighed their dislike for the League. More important, unlike the Ahrar, the Jama'at had never openly sided with the Congress and, unlike the Khaksar, their anti—Muslim League rhetoric had never been translated into violence. Therefore, the Muslim League's attitude toward the Jama'at between 1939 and 1947, despite the party's periodic genuflections toward Mawdudi, remained by and large cautious but cordial.

The rapport between the two parties was further strengthened by personal and, on occasion, institutional contacts. While the Jama'at and the League found themselves at loggerheads in the 1940s, the cordial relations between Mawdudi and the League's leaders continued to determine the Jama'at's politics. Chaudhri Muhammad 'Ali (a future prime minister of Pakistan), himself a deeply religious man, had been an acquaintance of Mawdudi since the 1930s; Nawwab Bahadur Yar Jang, also a pious man and a prominent Muslim League leader, was also close to Mawdudi. They not only reduced Mawdudi's distance from the League but also tempered the League's reaction to Mawdudi's rhetoric. A similar influence was exerted by Muslim League workers who had grown close to the Jama'at, and on occasion had even joined the party.[42] As a result, Mawdudi himself proved to be more flexible toward the Muslim League than is today thought to have been the case. A copy of Mawdudi's *Islam ka Nazriyah Siyasi* (Islam's Political Views), for instance, inscribed with the compliments of the author, is kept in the collection of Jinnah's papers at the Ministry of Culture of Pakistan.[43]

Mawdudi proved even more amenable if Muslim League overtures raised his and the Jama'at's standing in the Muslim community. In 1940 the president of the Muslim League of the United Provinces, Nawwab Sir Muhammad Isma'il Khan invited Mawdudi to participate in the Majlis-i Nizam-i Islami (Council of Islamic Order) in Lucknow, which was convened to devise a plan for incorporating religion into the structure of the future Muslim state. Mawdudi accepted without hesitation.[44] The council was to consist of Isma'il Khan, Chaudhri Khaliqu'l-Zaman, Nawwab Shamsu'l-Hasan, Sayyid Sulaiman Nadwi, Mawlana Azad Subhani, 'Abdu'l-Majid Daryabadi, and Mawdudi.[45] To be invited to this select council with religious luminaries was no doubt a great honor. The Muslim League may have been hard-pressed to find other religious leaders who would attend; or it may have sought to placate Mawdudi through this invitation; or it may have viewed the occasion as an opportunity for rewarding Mawdudi for his denunciation of the Congress and the Jami'at-i Ulama-i Hind. Isma'il Khan may also have been asked to invite Mawdudi by his friends among the League's leaders. Whatever the case, it boosted Mawdudi's ego and raised his stature as a religious leader. Between 1939 and 1947, the Muslim League paid back the favor Mawdudi had rendered it during the two preceding years by taking on the pro-Congress Muslim leaders.

Another cooperative effort between the Jama'at and Muslim League came about at the request of Mawdudi following the Jama'at's formation. It pertained to a division of opinion between the Muslim League and the Jama'at over the ultimate shape of the state of Pakistan. Soon after the formation of the Jama'at in 1941, Qamaru'ddin Khan, the secretary-general of the Jama'at, was dispatched to Delhi to meet with Jinnah. Through the good offices of Raja Mahmudabad—a deeply religious and generous patron of the League—a meeting was arranged between Qamaru'ddin Khan and Jinnah at the latter's residence. During the meeting, which lasted for forty-five minutes, Qamaru'ddin Khan outlined the Jama'at's political platform and enjoined Jinnah to commit the League to the Islamic state.[46] Jinnah responded astutely that he saw no incompatibility between the positions of the Muslim League and the Jama'at, but that the rapid pace at which the events were unfolding did not permit the League to stop at that point simply to define the nature of the future Muslim state: "I will continue to strive for the cause of a separate Muslim state, and you do your services in this regard; our efforts need not be mutually exclusive." Then he added, "I seek to secure the land for the mosque; once that land belongs to us, then we can decide on how to build the mosque." The metaphor of the mosque no doubt greatly pleased Qamaru'ddin Khan, who interpreted it as an assurance that the future state would be Islamic. Jinnah, however, cautioned Qamaru'ddin Khan that the achievement of an independent Muslim state took precedence over the "purification of souls."

At the time, the Jama'at decided not to make this meeting public, although it had served to quell the anxieties of the pro-Pakistan members of the Jama'at and had been seen as a green light for greater political activism by the party If anything, Jinnah had hinted that his task was only to secure the land for the "mosque", its building, the Jama'at concluded, would be the work of the religiously adept. What this meant for the Jama'at was that a continuum existed between the activities of the Muslim League and those of the Jama'at; where one ended at partition the other began: the Jama'at-i Islami was to inherit Pakistan. The symbiotic relationship between the League and the Jama'at, within a communalist framework, was strengthened.

As India moved closer to partition, however, the Jama'at's competition with the Muslim League intensified, gradually overshadowing the concord which the contacts with the League in 1939–1941 had engendered. Perturbed by the League's domination of the Pakistan movement, the Jama'at increasingly focused its energies on undermining Jinnah's position in the movement. The party's attacks became more venomous and direct, transforming the relations between the Jama'at and the League.

In October 1945, Mawdudi issued what amounted to a religious decree (*fatwa*) forbidding Muslims to vote for the "secular" Muslim League in the crucial elections of 1945 [47] Muslim League leaders were understandably irritated at such behavior from the head of a party that was not even taking part in the elections and concluded that the move proved the Jama'at's pro-Congress sentiments. But, unperturbed by the implications of its anti–Muslim League campaign, the Jama'at pushed ahead with its line of attack, which by 1947 became caustic vituperations. Mawdudi himself set the tone when in *Kawthar* in January 1947 he referred to the "Pakistan of the Muslim League" as "*faqistan*" (the land of the famished) and "*langra*" Pakistan (crippled Pakistan). [48] While these insults were directed at the secular nature of Jinnah's program for the new state, they incensed Muslim League leaders and rank-and-file members alike; they were having enough trouble defending their cause against the Congress party They began to retaliate: when, at a regional Jama'at-i Islami convention in Madras, Mawdudi said that "the Jama'at's sole objective is to present Muslims with virtuous leadership and to stop the ascendancy of a corrupt [*fasiq'u fajir*] leadership at the helm [of the Pakistan movement],"[49] the crowd erupted into chants of "Long live the Muslim League," "Long live the qa'id-i a'zam [Jinnah]," and "Down with the Jami'at-i Ulama [i.e. the Jami'at-i Ulama-i Hind]."[50] The crowd then turned the meeting into a Muslim League rally

The Congress party was quick to take advantage of these confrontations, and this further deepened the antagonism between the League and the Jama'at. The subtlety of the Jama'at's own communalism was all but drowned by the clamor of its confrontation with the League. Hopeful of enlisting the Jama'at's support and anxious to embarrass the League, the Congress openly wooed Mawdudi. In April 1947, during the Jama'at's regional convention in Patna, Gandhi attended a lecture by Amin Ahsan Islahi. After the lecture, Congress officials in the city announced that Gandhi had been invited to the session by the Jama'at's leaders, and a possible merger of the party into the nationalist movement might be in the making. Gandhi also lauded Islahi and endorsed his views, which the Mahatma argued "attacked the political uses of Islam!"[51] Muslim League officials, already distressed by Mawdudi's attacks, were finally provoked into saying what some of them had felt all along: the Jama'at was Congress's Trojan horse among the Muslims.[52] The pro-Muslim League *Nawa'-i Waqt* of Lahore led the charge against Mawdudi, accusing him of anti-Pakistan activities, collaboration with the Congress party, and political duplicity [53] For the Muslim League, the Jama'at had until that day been at worst a tolerable inconvenience, and at times a valuable "Islamic" tool against the pro-Congress ulama; it was now clearly a nuisance. Gandhi's remarks changed the balance of relations between the Jama'at and the Muslim League to the latter's advantage. The Jama'at, however, was not reconciled either to this change in its status or to the shift in its debate with the League from questioning the orthodoxy of the Muslim League's program and leaders to questioning its own loyalty to the Muslim separatist cause.

Caught off guard, the Jama'at appealed to *Nawa'-i Waqt* to publish the whole text of Islahi's speech that Gandhi had alleged had been favorable to the Congress's position, and it denied ever having invited Gandhi to the session. *Nawa'-i Waqt* declined to publish either the text or the denial; the League was not going to let Mawdudi off the hook that easily To the dismay of the Congress, in May Mawdudi issued another salvo against the "secular, irreligious nationalist democracy" promised by the League, but sensing the adverse climate, desisted from attacking it further. In June 1947, Mawdudi wrote an open letter to the Muslims of India, encouraging them to choose Pakistan over the "Indian Republic," and in July 1947 he encouraged the Muslims of the North-West Frontier Province to turn out their Congress ministry and to vote for Pakistan in the referendum which was scheduled to decide the fate of that province.[54] In the same month, he issued a terse rebuttal to the well-publicized and damaging charge by the Congress that those Muslims who complained about the idea of the creation of a Jewish homeland in Palestine—as many Indian Muslims including Jinnah had—could hardly justify their demand for a Muslim one.[55] Fearful of giving vent to accusations of being anti-Pakistan, the party withdrew into the "splendid isolation" of Pathankot.

Although the birth of Pakistan followed an ebb in the relations between the Jama'at and the Muslim League, the concord which had characterized the relations between the two until 1945 continued to define their relationship at a more fundamental level. Since both were ultimately striving to secure communal rights for Muslims, the Jama'at and Muslim League each legitimated the political function of the other in furthering their common communalist cause. It was the structure of this relationship that determined the interactions between the Jama'at and the fruit of the League's toil—the Pakistan state—more than their bickering over the nature of that state may suggest. The Jama'at legitimated communalism in Islamic terms and helped the League find a base of support by appealing to religious symbols. The Muslim League, in turn, increasingly Islamized the political discourse on Pakistan to the Jama'at's advantage, creating a suitable gateway for the party's entry into the political fray The Muslim League leaders elevated the Jama'at's status, while institutional contacts and personal links between the two parties gave more concrete shape to the structure of relations between the two. Conflict, contact, and concord was rooted in communal interests and the legitimating role of Islam. That framework has governed the scope and nature of relations between the two parties since partition.

6 Entering the Political Process, 1947–1958

After Mawdudi had unveiled the Jama'at-ı Islami's political objectives ın Pakıstan for the first time ın July 1947,[1] he collected hıs troops and moved to Lahore
on a truck, escorted by units of the Pakıstan army His first contact with the
leaders of the new state took place soon after through the Muslim League
mınıstry ın Punjab. While he was still livıng ın a tent ın Islamıyah Park, Mawdudi
met with the Muslim League chıef mınıster of the province, Nawwab Iftikhar
Husaın of Mamdot.[2] In that meeting Mawdudi asked for permıssıon to begın
work among the refugees, and he discussed the future of Kashmır.[3] Mawdudi
ımpressed upon the nawwab Pakıstan's obligation ımmediately to take the
offensıve ın Kashmır and secure control of strategıc locations there, and asked
the chıef mınıster to relay a message to that effect to Prıme Mınıster Lıaqat 'Ali
Khan.

The Nawwab of Mamdot was a powerful member of the landed gentry of
Punjab and was at the time embroiled ın a struggle with Lıaqat 'Ali Khan and
hıs chıef ally ın Punjab, Mian Mumtaz Daultana, over the control of that
province.[4] The chıef mınıster was eager to enlist the support of Islamıc groups
such as the Jama'at to stave off Daultana's challenge.[5] Mamdot, therefore, not
only welcomed the Jama'at's offer to assist with relief work among the refugees,
but ınvited Mawdudi to deliver a series of talks on Radio Pakıstan.[6] All unwit-
ting, Mawdudi had walked ınto the mıdst of a tug-of-war ın Pakıstanı politics
that was to determıne relations between the Jama'at and the central government.

Mawdudi quıckly learned that, gıven the balance of power ın Pakıstanı
politics, the Islamıc parties were bound to play the role of power brokers. Muslim
League leaders, concluded Mawdudi, were not as ınımıcal to sacralization of
politics as theır postindependence rhetorıc may have ındicated. In fact, as the
central government ın Karachı faced difficulties ın exertıng control over the new
country's wayward provınces durıng 1947–1948 and the crısıs before the state
grew, the legitimating role of Islam and the power of its spokesmen became more

evident. Politicians who otherwise decried the political role of religion were under the circumstances not altogether indifferent to the entry of Islamic groups into the fray The example set by Mamdot was followed elsewhere, in Lahore as well as in other provincial capitals. The relations between the Muslim League and the Jama'at during the prepartition years were now expanded to encompass the relations between Islam and the state of Pakistan. The holy community found great strength in acting as a party

Pakistan was founded in the name of Islam, but it had little else in the way of common national or cultural values around which to unite. Besieged with the threats posed by separatism and ethnic tensions—which were compounded by the problem of integrating autonomous princely states, such as Kalat and Bhawalpur, into Pakistan—and in the absence of a widely shared notion of nationhood, Islam became the only viable foundation on which to build unity Although many Pakistani political leaders did not like it, faced with the gravity of the situation few could resist the temptation of appealing to Islam. It was the only course open for leaders who discouraged mass politics, failed to adopt meaningful political platforms, and avoided elections. In the words of one observer, "'an Islamic State,' [became] a political motto to be used by the Muslims and, more particularly, by the Muslim League to continue indefinitely their predominant position in Pakistan politics."[7] The tendency to Islamize the national political discourse became even stronger when the League grew concerned over Communist activity The Communist threat was taken seriously, especially after a plot with the backing of the left was uncovered in the army in 1951, which came to be known as the Rawalpindi conspiracy case.[8] The alleged military plot was hatched in the Pakistan army by officers who favored a resumption of hostilities with India over Kashmir. It took its name from the garrison where the army headquarters were located. There is evidence that it may have had Communist backing and aimed at restructuring the political order of the country, especially after the leftist poet Faiz Ahmad Faiz was arrested for his part in the conspiracy, which led Liaqat 'Ali Khan to tell the parliament that the objective of the coup was to install a Communist government.[9] Islam, it was thought, was the one force capable of averting a Communist future for the country [10]

The appeal of Islam to a wide spectrum of Pakistani leaders was proof of the deeply entrenched loyalty Pakistanis had to Islam and their acceptance of its relevance to their concerns. Islam could not, however, be manipulated for political ends without the intercession and ultimately the interference of the Islamic parties, and herein lay the dilemma of waving the Islamic banner for political ends. Factors which also made Islam appealing to politicians, by making it easy for Islamic parties to go into politics, limited the ability of the same politicians to manage successfully the role of Islam in politics.

The conclusion the Jama'at had reached from the Muslim League's attempt to design a role for Islam in the future constitution of Pakistan in Lucknow in 1940 is instructive. The task of drawing up a constitution for Pakistan had begun there, in a session presided over by ulama, in which Mawdudi also participated, all at the behest of the Muslim League. In the Jama'at's eyes the Lucknow session was proof that Pakistan could not exist divorced from Islam. The Muslim League's role in convening the session suggested to Mawdudi that even Jinnah and his lieutenants were aware of that fact. For the Jama'at's leaders little had changed in this regard since partition. Islam could not be divorced from Pakistani politics, just as it could not have been divorced from partition politics. To the chagrin of many in the Muslim League, the party was therefore caught in a situation where first it emphasized Pakistan's Islamicity and then ridiculed and undermined those leaders and parties whose political fortunes were predicated upon Islamization.[11] As early as 1948 the Muslim League began to appeal to Islamic symbols, though at the same time it still viewed parties such as the Jama'at as inherently opposed to its vision of Pakistan.

The Jama'at did little to assuage the Muslim League's doubts. Not only was the party's rhetoric and confrontational style generally unpalatable to the League, but also the Jama'at reached its modus vivendi with the Pakistan state after a number of direct, although unsuccessful, challenges to it. Conflict between the Jama'at and the Muslim League–controlled government predated the party's decision to accept the legitimacy of the state and to participate in the political process.

In December 1947 the Jama'at had already begun to demand greater Islamization with the specific objective of highlighting the duplicity of the Muslim League in their appeals to Islam.[12] Amin Ahsan Islahi stated rather cavalierly that "Pakistan will deserve its name only if it becomes an Islamic state."[13] The Jama'at felt that the League's conception of Pakistan was merely territorial, opening the door for maneuvering by the "rear guard." The Jama'at, just as it had expected to lead the Pakistan movement, now saw its rise to power in the state to be imminent. Mawdudi saw the Jama'at in its "Meccan" era, and expected it to enter a "Medinan" one shortly after partition,[14] a reference to the flowering of the Islamic community following the Prophet's migration from Mecca to Medina. Mawdudi believed that Pakistan was built for the sole purpose of "demonstrating the efficacy of the Islamic way of life."[15] Using Jinnah's metaphor of the "mosque," Mawdudi asked, "Will the architects who are well-versed in building bars and cinemas spend their energies in erecting a mosque? If the answer is in the affirmative, it will indeed be a unique experiment of its kind in human history; godlessness fostering godliness to dethrone itself!"[16]

Soon these sporadic outbursts gave way to an organized campaign. On January 6 and February 19, 1948, Mawdudi presented two lectures at the Law College in Lahore.[17] In them he presented a coherent plan for the Islamization of Pakistan and set guidelines for drawing up an Islamic constitution. He emphasized the viability of such a constitution, to put pressure on members of the Constituent Assembly and to expose their "true intent." Was Pakistan made in the name of Islam or not? And were they going to establish an Islamic state or not? After Mawdudi delivered these talks, he was challenged by Faiz Ahmad Faiz, the renowned Pakistani literary figure, and by Muslim League leaders such as Raja Ghazanfar 'Ali that his schemes were incongruous and inoperable. Mawdudi thenceforth was careful to emphasize the feasibility and practicality of his ideas.[18]

The Lahore lectures were followed by a lecture tour of Pakistan in April and May 1948, during which Mawdudi continued to harp on the same themes. During this tour he made overtures to the ulama, hinting of a grand Islamic alliance, a suggestion the Muslim League viewed with considerable concern. In March, Mawdudi sent an emissary to Karachi to contact a number of Constituent Assembly members and press upon them the Jama'at's demands; he was to encourage them to pass a resolution which would confirm that Pakistan was an "ideological state."[19] The emissary failed to solicit the resolution. 'Umar Hayat Malik, then the vice-chancellor of the University of Punjab, a man sympathetic to the Jama'at's position, advised Mawdudi to act directly He argued that while members of the Constituent Assembly were not prepared to pass a resolution, they were not necessarily opposed to it either. They simply did not want to take a stand before the electorate.[20] If the Jama'at succeeded in mobilizing public opinion in favor of it, argued Malik, they would be more favorably disposed.[21] Mawdudi took the advice, and the Jama'at began a concerted public campaign for an Islamic constitution. Pakistani politicians did not take kindly to his attempt to force their hand, especially since his rhetoric was pleasing to the Muhajirs who also served as the Muslim League's base of support. Muslim League leaders were particularly perturbed by Mawdudi's threats that Islamization could not be left to the League and required direct action by devout Muslims themselves.[22] Jama'at members believe that as early as 1947 members of the cabinet had demanded action against their party Jinnah had, however, opposed clamping down on the Jama'at, or so Jama'at leaders were told by Chaudhri Muhammad 'Ali. With Jinnah out of the picture the cabinet debated the idea of placing restraints on the Jama'at's activities, and subsequently leading party members were placed under surveillance. The grant of a school in Lahore to Mawdudi in compensation for property he had lost in India was revoked on the direct orders of Liaqat 'Ali Khan.[23] The Jama'at's political naïveté and maverick style in the following months only further strained the Muslim League's tolerance.

The 1947 Independence Act had stipulated that until a new constitution was promulgated Pakistan would remain a British domain, and oaths of allegiance by all government employees from the governor-general on down would be made in accordance with the provisions of the India Act of 1935 Early in 1948, Mawdudi was asked about swearing an oath of allegiance to the British Crown. In a private letter to the questioner, Mawdudi declared that such an oath would be "sinful," arguing that a Muslim can, in clear conscience, swear his allegiance only to God. The letter soon found its way into the press, causing much consternation among the authorities, even in Punjab, where Nawwab of Mamdot's ministry was favorably disposed to Mawdudi.

Soon thereafter the Jama'at became embroiled in yet another controversy In April 1948 India and Pakistan had reached an interim cease-fire agreement over who controlled Kashmir, the provisions of which among other things provided that the government of each country would desist from hostilities against the other and that the press in each country would refrain from publishing incendiary articles. Pakistan, however, had continued to struggle for the freedom of Kashmir, now mainly through covert means. In a letter to Mawlana Shabbir Ahmad 'Uthmani, the doyen of Pakistani ulama at the time, Mawdudi argued that regardless of the merits of this agreement, now that it had been signed by the government its terms were binding on all Pakistani citizens. A Muslim government, and its citizenry were compelled by the shari'ah to abide by the terms of agreements to which they were a party Covert operations, it could be surmised from Mawdudi's letter, for so long as the India-Pakistan agreement was standing, would be in violation of the shari'ah and as such could attest to the "un-Islamic" nature of the Pakistani state.[24]

Rumors regarding the contents of Mawdudi's letter to 'Uthmani began to circulate, and the letter was interpreted as a religious decree (*fatwa*) against jihad in Kashmir. In May 1948, during a speech in Peshawar, a province in which many of the volunteer Pathan tribal forces fighting the covert war in Kashmir were recruited, Mawdudi was asked by the director of information of Pakistan's provisional Kashmir government to explain his position on the jihad. Mawdudi responded that so long as the government of Pakistan was bound by the terms of its cease-fire agreement with India, it could not declare a jihad in Kashmir, lest it violate the shari'ah's injunctions to abide by the terms of the agreement. Since jihad had to be declared by a proper governmental body, added Mawdudi, there was no possibility that any other source could declare one. Therefore Pakistanis could not wage jihad in Kashmir as long as their government was officially observing a cease-fire.

Mawdudi had thus tied the question of Kashmir to the Islamicity of the state. An Islamic state could not engage in covert operations, nor wage jihad through proxy, and since Pakistan could not forego Kashmir, it was best in Mawdudi's opinion to resume hostilities against India, which is what Mawdudi had recommended to Mamdot in 1947 Mawdudi's explanation only further complicated the matter for Pakistani authorities. The force of his argument was sufficiently provocative to bring the wrath of the government upon the Jama'at. India, however, would provide even a better pretext for that.

The Srinagar and Kabul radio stations broadcast reports of Mawdudi's challenge to the Pakistan government as a "decree against" war in Kashmir, hoping to dampen the resolve of Pakistan's "freedom fighters." The Pakistan government was not only incensed but also found the Jama'at sufficiently liable on the charges of sedition being circulated by the authorities, along with tales of Mawdudi's disloyalty to the Pakistan movement, to effectively silence this most outspoken of the Islamic parties. Undaunted, Mawdudi issued his rebuttals, while restating his arguments in simpler terms, all to his own detriment. The government, understandably, was not assuaged by Mawdudi's remark that "it was sheer hypocrisy to sanction a jihad, stealthily declared, while Pakistan told the whole world that it was in a state of cease-fire with India";[25] Pakistan should either desist from jihad or, preferably, go to war. The government understood Mawdudi to be saying that only an Islamic government could declare jihad, which they believed to be more seditious than the argument that there could be no jihad during the cease-fire.[26]

Unable satisfactorily to explain its ostensibly "unpatriotic" casuistry to Pakistanis, and especially to the all-important Muhajir community, which was then subject to "Indophobia" and obsessed with Kashmir, by August 1948 Mawdudi was compelled to alter his stand. Debating the logic of jihad in Kashmir gave way to solemn oaths of allegiance to Pakistan, denunciation of Indian policy in Kashmir, and declarations of support for Pakistan's claims over Kashmir.[27] He now argued that while the cease-fire agreement was binding on the government volunteers could still participate in the freedom movement in Kashmir. When in September the Pakistan government officially admitted to its involvement in the conflict in Kashmir, eager to demonstrate the logic of his position, Mawdudi lost no time in supporting a jihad.[28] It was with the same thought in mind that in 1989, when Kashmir erupted in turmoil, the Jama'at took the lead in the "jihad in Kashmir" campaign in Pakistan. But the party's intellectualized approach to politics had overestimated the power of Islamic dicta and underestimated the appeal of nationalist and patriotic sentiments. The stand seriously damaged its image, and it never fully recovered.

The Kashmir episode had not yet fully died down when Mawdudi's high-handed style landed the Jama'at in yet another controversy In August 1948, Mawdudi was again asked about the issue of swearing allegiance to the state. In an unnecessarily detailed response Mawdudi said again that the allegiance of a Muslim was to God alone, and therefore until Pakistan became an Islamic state ruled by the writ of the shari'ah, a Muslim was forbidden to declare allegiance to it and, more to the point, to serve in a "non-Muslim," i.e., the Pakistan, army [29] Undermining the army was not a trifling matter. Mawdudi's attitude was increasingly seen to be deliberately subversive and dangerous. The editor of the pro–Muslim League newspaper, *Nawa'-ı Waqt*, Hamıd Nizamı, began a series of articles in which Mawdudi was depicted as an Indian agent, a supporter of the Jami'at-ı Ulama-ı Hind, and a Congressite.[30] Muslim League leaders, especially those in the civil service and the armed forces, who were generally less inclined to be religious, successfully argued that the Jama'at's menace had clearly outstripped its political utility;[31] the party was doing more to undermine the state than to support it. This group, led by the senior Muslim Leaguer, Raja Ghazanfar 'Ali, defense secretary General Iskandar Mirza, and possibly the ranking general and later commander-in-chief of the armed forces, General Muhammad Ayub Khan, prevailed upon Liaqat 'Ali Khan to clamp down on the Jama'at. In October 1948, the Jama'at's publications, *Tarjumanu'l-Qur'an, Kawthar, Tasnım,* and *Chıragh-ı Rah* were closed down, and Mawdudi, Islahı, Mian Tufayl, and editors of some of the Jama'at's newspapers were apprehended.[32] The minister of the interior declared the Jama'at to be a seditious party on a par with the Communists and proceeded to extend the civil service code that barred bureaucrats from joining Communist organizations to membership in the Jama'at.

It then lost no time in strictly enforcing the code to eliminate the Jama'at's influence from the civil service.[33] Twenty-five Jama'at members and sympathizers were forced to resign from the civil service in October and November 1948.[34] In December another ordinance was issued by the prime minister, this time forbidding government employees from reading Mawdudi's works and Jama'at literature. Between 1949 and 1951, the government further clamped down on the Jama'at by arresting more of its leaders and by either closing more of its magazines or demanding new forbidding security deposits for allowing them to operate.[35]

The Jama'at was stunned by these developments. Mawdudi had never thought of his challenges to the legitimacy of the state as seditious or disloyal; "enjoining the good and forbidding the reprehensible" was after all incumbent on the holy community He failed to appreciate the gravity with which the government had viewed his religious decrees. His first reaction had been to rejoice in the prominence the confrontation gave to the party [36] However, once in the Lyallpur (later Faisalabad) jail, he saw matters differently He still saw no fault in himself, but decided the matter tested the government's commitment to democracy He concluded that the government had moved against the Jama'at with such force only because Jinnah was no longer a restraining influence on the authority of Muslim League leaders. The Jama'at now began to appreciate Jinnah for abiding by the promise he had given Qamaru'ddin Khan in Delhi to allow the Jama'at to work toward Islamizing Pakistan and for his unbending adherence to principles of individual freedom and due process of law In 1948, Mawdudi praised him for his democratic spirit.[37] The Jama'at has since then repeatedly appealed to Jinnah's memory, more emphatically each time it has been persecuted under the provisions of the Public Safety Act or the Defense of Pakistan Rules. Mawdudi's experiences gave the Jama'at's political thinking an acute awareness of the importance of civil liberties and thenceforth fused its clamor for Islamicity with demands for constitutional rights.

Mawdudi interpreted the government's actions as a ruse to guarantee the secular nature of the state at a time when the constitutional debates were reaching a climax. The Jama'at was silenced and Mawdudi was stowed away, relieving the Constituent Assembly of their constant pressure.[38] The government, by casting the party in an unsavory light, had encouraged its radicalization. Its members, however, balked at the prospect of being a subversive party, a truly revolutionary force. Instead, Mawdudi chose to desist from questioning the legitimacy of the state and to concentrate on ensuring the virtue, efficacy, and Islamicity of its governments. The distinction between Pakistan and the Muslim League was once again emphasized. Opposition to the League was tantamount to questioning the authority of the state, and Mawdudi set out to do all in his power to reverse the impression that that was what he was doing. The demand for an Islamic state was redirected into a demand for an Islamic constitution. This way Islamicity could be combined with the party's newly found dedication to constitutional rights and the Pakistan state.[39]

From his prison cell, Mawdudi pushed for the resumption of the campaign for Islamization, but this time with the objective of confirming the Jama'at's commitment to the state. The government had failed to silence the Jama'at, but it had compelled it to do away with its romantic idealism. The Jama'at now reentered the fray, not as a distant observer—a "rear guard" waiting to benefit from the Muslim League's failure—but as a participant in the political process. Although it still viewed itself as a holy community, its posture became that of a political party Unable to interact directly with the government or as yet to mobilize the masses effectively, Mawdudi and the Jama'at turned to the ulama as a convenient vehicle for realizing their aims.

The ulama at that time did not possess a clear agenda of their own, nor a clear idea of what their objectives in Pakistan were. However, under the leadership of Mawlana Shabbir Ahmad 'Uthmani, a token convert to the Muslim League from the ranks of the eminent Deobandi ulama, they had a great deal of leverage with the government. Aware of their power, Mawdudi sent two Jama'at leaders, 'Abdu'l-Jabbar Ghazi and 'Abdu'l-Ghaffar Hasan, to contact some of them, and especially 'Uthmani, with a view to creating a united religious front against the government. The two were themselves members of the ulama, and were also serving as the Jama'at's provisional amirs while Mawdudi was in jail. The immediate aim of these contacts was to influence the content of the Objectives

Resolution which the prime minister was going to present to the Constituent Assembly as a statement of the government's intentions with regard to drafting of the constitution, and which was approved in March 1949 Ghazi and Hasan worked diligently to bring the various ulama groups into an alliance and were especially successful in influencing Mawlana 'Uthmani, who was then a member of the Constituent Assembly and showed an interest in Mawdudi's ideas, which were relayed to him from prison through Ghazi.

Mawdudi's efforts from behind bars proved fruitful, and the alliance with ulama augured well for the Jama'at. The demands he had voiced through 'Uthmani did appear in the Objectives Resolution, and the ulama would be an effective medium for political action in the campaign for an Islamic constitution.[40] The alliance also confronted the government with a new dilemma: their efforts to sideline the Jama'at had instead resulted in a more formidable alliance for the cause of Islam. Breaking up this alliance would became a major concern of the government in the years to come.

The Jama'at was quick to proclaim victory following the passage of the Objectives Resolution, letting its hand show through 'Uthmani's sleeve. Mawdudi's own reaction was more guarded. For him this was not yet victory; the battle had just begun. The government should not be allowed to think that it had mollified the Islamic parties, nor should the ulama be allowed to relax their vigil. His first public statement on the passage of the resolution was therefore, to everyone's surprise, far from enthusiastic: "This is a strange rain, before which there were no clouds rising, and after which no growth is visible."[41] He ordered the Jama'at to begin educating the masses on the contents of the Objectives Resolution, lest the government manipulate their ignorance and interpret the resolution into extinction.[42] The government retaliated by extending Mawdudi's sentence.

Officially the party did not forego its moment of glory and declared the Objectives Resolution a victory for Islam and for the Jama'at and a statement of the government's good intentions. It was a commitment by the government to Islamization. This simultaneously gave the political order a new face and permitted the Jama'at to accept its legitimacy Mian Tufayl recollects that the resolution was described by the Jama'at as a Muslim testimony of faith by an unbeliever, a symbolic but consequential act of conversion.[43]

The Jama'at's stand was also, in part, motivated by the deterioration of the relations between Karachi and Dhaka. Throughout 1949 public opinion in East Pakistan had voiced its opposition to the policy directives from Karachi and the hegemony of the Punjabi and Muhajir elite. East Pakistan was threatening rebellion. The Jama'at viewed the challenge to the authority of the central government with grave concern, and consequently sided with the state against East Pakistan, which provided the party with a pretext for gaining entry into the political system without compromising doctrine. The Bengali challenge to Pakistan's federal arrangement may also have softened the state's resolve to eliminate the Jama'at, creating a climate that would be conducive to the Jama'at's political enfranchisement. With Mawdudi still in prison the Jama'at's shura' declared that the party would participate in the Punjab provincial elections scheduled for March 1951, thereby consolidating the Jama'at's new orientation.[44]

For the Jama'at, accepting the state's legitimacy after its promulgation of the Objectives Resolution meant that the task of Islamization would be carried out from within rather than from without, but even more important that it would be carried out. The resolution ensured that Pakistan had to evolve into an Islamic state if the government was compelled to carry through its promise as reflected in the resolution. Hence, in July 1950, the Jama'at began its campaign in Punjab, using the election to disseminate its ideas, to "Islamize" the campaign, and to influence the composition of the future Punjab Assembly Meanwhile, aware of the rapidly changing political environment and the need personally to oversee the Jama'at's transition to its new political existence, Mawdudi demanded his release. He had been imprisoned in October 1948 under the provisions of the Public Safety Act but had not been officially charged with any crime. Hence, soon after his jail term was extended, Mawdudi wrote to the chief secretary of the Punjab government, arguing that the government should either bring charges against him or release him. He quoted at length from Jinnah's criticisms of the Public Safety Act before the central assembly of India in 1935 to make his point.[45] The Jama'at, meanwhile, organized a letter-writing campaign to the press and the government, lamenting the unconstitutional persecution of Mawdudi for "the crime of loyalty to God" at a time when the government itself had passed the Objective Resolution which placed national sovereignty in God.[46]

The tactics were effective, but the fate of Mawdudi still rested with the judiciary, which has time and again defied the state to give the Jama'at a new lease on life. In an earlier ruling, the Lahore High Court had declared that the terms of those jailed under the Public Safety Act could be extended only twice. Mawdudi's jail term had already been extended on two occasions. Since he could no longer be held under the Public Safety Act, the court ordered his release in May 1950.[47] Mawdudi was impressed by the independence of the judiciary, which was later reflected in his ideas of how the Islamic state should function.

No sooner had he taken off his prison garb than he launched a fresh campaign for the Islamic state, setting a new tone for the Jama'at's bid for power. He reiterated his declaration of prepartition days that the ruling establishment— whom he now referred to derisively as the "innovators" (ahl-i bid'at)—were incapable of realizing the aims of the Objectives Resolution. Only those firmly rooted in Islamic learning, the followers of tradition (ahl-i sunnat), could be entrusted with realizing the task set before the state.[48] This distinction had the added advantage of drawing a line between the government and the religious alliance as a whole; for a silent war between the Jama'at and the government over the loyalty of the ulama was already afoot. As it began to act more like a party, the Jama'at's campaign against Liaqat 'Ali Khan's administration extended ever farther. The party would no longer challenge the government only over Islam alone, but over a range of issues that it deemed politic. For example, the Jama'at opposed Liaqat 'Ali Khan's plans for a land-reform bill on the grounds that Islam protected the right to private property,[49] although the Muhajir community which the Jama'at was also courting at the time favored land reform.[50] More frequently, however, the government came under fire for its autocracy, an attack that soon found a life of its own.

In October 1950, the Basic Principles Committee of the Constituent Assembly presented its interim report on the distribution of power in the future legislature. The Jama'at criticized the report for its autocratic bent and unequal distribution of power among the provinces. Mawdudi especially objected to powers the report had vested in the presidency He depicted the report, uncharitably, as a reiteration of the Government of India Act of 1935, and in violation of the spirit of the Objectives Resolution.[51] Its government design was thoroughly secular, argued Mawdudi, and had no basis in the Islamic doctrines of governance and statecraft. The government, ever more sensitive to the Jama'at's carping, once again closed the party's publications, *Kawthar, Tasnim, Qasid* and *Jahan-i Naw*, and jailed the editors of the first two.[52]

The committee report had also come under fire from other quarters for its distribution of power between the provinces and the center. It was rejected by Bengalis of all political hues, creating the first serious crack in the edifice of the Pakistan state. The Jama'at, true to its legitimating role, scurried to the support of the state, reiterating the preeminence of Islam and Urdu in the scheme for a united Muslim state.[53] Bolstering the position of the state was not, however, tantamount to a vote of confidence for the government. Mawdudi astutely combined his support for the unity of Pakistan with his demand for a truly Islamic constitution, which, he argued, would underscore the two guarantors of the unity of Pakistan: Islam and an equitable distribution of power in a just and constitutional arrangement. The interim report, Mawdudi argued, was deficient on both counts.

The government, unable to withstand criticism from both the Bengalis and the Islamic parties, was compelled to withdraw the interim report, and it challenged the religious divines to present a viable substitute. The Jama'at responded by initiating negotiations with leading Jami'at-i Ulama-i Islam (Society of Ulama of Islam) leaders, Mawlanas Zafar Ahmad Thanwi, Ihtishamu'l-Haq Thanwi ('Uthmani's successor), and Mufti Muhammad Shafi', to devise a new report that would keep Islamization moving. These contacts eventually culminated in a major gathering of thirty-one ulama in Karachi in January 1951, under the aegis of the eminent divine Sayyid Sulaiman Nadwi, which demanded an Islamic state and proposed twenty-two principles to be submitted to the Constituent Assembly for consideration.[54] Mawdudi's imprint on this report was evident in its emphasis on an independent judiciary The ulama convention, to the government's chagrin, was yet another display of the alliance between the ulama and the Jama'at, of which Mawdudi was openly proud. It was perhaps the success of this ulama convention that prompted the government to organize an anti-Jama'at campaign in Indian religious circles in 1951. Numerous books, pamphlets, and religious decrees denouncing Mawdudi and his ideas were published, all with the hope of driving a wedge between the self-styled religious maverick and the conservative divines. The anti-Jama'at campaign soon overflowed into Pakistan. It was spearheaded by Mawdudi's old rivals in the Jami'at-i Ulama-i Hind, Brailwi ulama in both India and Pakistan, and those among the Indian ulama who had always viewed Mawdudi's ideas as religiously suspect. It was supported by such prominent ulama as Husain Ahmad Madani and 'Abdu'l-Majid Daryabadi. The scope of the campaign soon spread to all schools of Islamic thought in Pakistan. It remained focused on religious issues and sought to undermine Mawdudi's claim to religious leadership. It accused Mawdudi of religious innovation, violating the sanctity of immutable religious doctrines and practices, messianic tendencies, and insulting the memory of the Prophet and his companions. Since much of the attacks were put forth in the form of religious decrees, they greatly damaged the Jama'at's popular standing and religious prestige. Moreover, in its own propaganda the government continuously associated the Jama'at with the Jami'at-i Ulama-i Hind, hoping to provoke the Jama'at into a renewed attack on the Jami'at-i Ulama-i Hind and thereby create trouble between the Jama'at and the Deobandi establishment in Pakistan.[55]

After the campaign against the interim report, the Jama'at's promotion of Islamization was intertwined with an effort to safeguard the constitutional rights and civil liberties of Pakistanis, which was tantamount to an "Islamic constitutionalist" platform. What began as a tactical consideration to protect the Jama'at's rights in a polity dominated by secular forces bent on consolidating power in the executive increasingly became doctrine. Constitutionalism presented the Jama'at with a useful slogan and a political program with which to appeal to educated people. As politically opportune as this platform may have seemed, however, it was more than a mere ploy It had its roots in Mawdudi's experience with the Public Safety Act and the independent spirit of the Pakistani judiciary on the one hand and the desire to placate the secular opposition to Karachi's policies on the other.

The Jama'at's political platform and role as a party were put to the test in the Punjab provincial elections of March 1951. The Jama'at was not contesting any tickets; instead it took upon itself the role of judging the moral caliber and Islamicity of the candidates. It would assist those candidates whom it found morally upright, religiously committed, and favorably disposed to the intent and aims of the Objectives Resolution. This peculiar approach to elections reflected its continued adherence to the idea that it was still essentially a holy community and its cautious approach to party politics. Although the Jama'at did not officially endorse any party, it is safe to assume that few, if any, of the candidates supported by Mian Mumtaz Daultana, the "progressive" chief minister of Punjab, were found virtuous (salih), and that many of the candidates put forth by Nawwab of Mamdot's Jinnah Awami League (Jinnah People's League) and Husain Shahid Suhrawardi's Awami League, who had forged an electoral alliance, received the Jama'at's blessing and support. Mamdot had courted Mawdudi after he was ousted as chief minister of Punjab by Daultana. Mawdudi was receptive to those advances in part because Liaqat 'Ali Khan and Daultana had also increased pressure on the Jama'at. Suhrawardi, then leader of the Awami League, had made overtures to the Jama'at in 1950 to form a joint front to defend Mamdot against the Liaqat-Daultana axis. Mawdudi's initial response was favorable, and hence, on January 12, 1951, the Jama'at participated in the Awami League and Azad Pakistan (Free Pakistan) party conference in Rawalpindi to object to Daultana's strong-arm tactics in the election campaign. The cooperation between Suhrawardi and the Jama'at continued until 1952, when Suhrawardi became prime minister.[56] The Jama'at began by organizing 1,390 voter councils (panchayat) in thirty-seven electoral districts across Punjab to determine the moral caliber of the various candidates,[57] and ended up supporting fifty-two candidates in the race for the 192 seats of the Punjab Assembly

Despite the Jama'at's efforts, however, the chosen candidates did not do well in the elections. The eight months and the Rs. 127,000 the party spent on the campaign had yielded only 50,000 signatures supporting its Islamization proposals and 217,859 votes for its chosen candidates out of the estimated total of 4,500,000 votes cast (24 percent of the province's total population of 18,816,000 at the time).[58] It had secured the election of only one "virtuous" candidate (see table 7).[59]

This poor showing was due in part to the campaign having run afoul of Daultana's ministry, which, along with the government in Karachi, had clamped down on the Jama'at and greatly diminished its ability to wage an effective campaign. Mawdudi had come under attack by a flurry of religious decrees from the progovernment ulama; the Jama'at's newspapers in Punjab, Kawthar, Tasnim, and Qasid, were closed down, and the pro–Muslim League press attacked the Jama'at and, as was usually was the case, had "exposed" its "anti-Pakistan" background. Government machinations also worked against the Jama'at sufficiently to compel the disappointed and exhausted party not to participate in the

Table 7 Results of the 1951 Punjab Provincial Elections

	Seats Won	% of Vote
Muslim League	143	51.1
Jinnah Awami League / Awami League	32	22.7
Independents	16	23.7
Azad Pakistan Party	1	2.0
Islam League	0	0.4
Communists	0	0.1
Total	192[a]	100.0

Source: Radio Pakistan News, quoted in U.S. Consulate General, Lahore, desp. #136, 4/9/1951, 790D.00/4-951, NA.

[a] There were also five special minorities seats, which bring the total size of the assembly to 197

North-West Frontier Province provincial elections scheduled for later that year, for Daultana's strong-arm tactics would pale before those of the North-West Frontier Province chief minister, 'Abdu'l-Qayyum Khan, who had always shown a penchant for outdoing the central government when it came to clamping down on religious activists. The Jama'at initially put forward five candidates in those elections; after the papers of three were rejected, it decided to withdraw from the race.[60]

The balance in relations between the Jama'at and the government, however, changed significantly in October 1951 when Liaqat 'Ali Khan was assassinated. The prime minister's death made Khwaja Nazimu'ddin, the Bengali Muslim League leader and the governor-general at the time, prime minister. He was known to be a pious man, as were a number of men he chose as his ministers: Mawdudi's personal friend Chaudhri Muhammad 'Ali became the minister of finance, and the pro-Jama'at Ishtiaq Husain Quraishi was appointed minister of state for refugees and overseer of the ministry of information. Meanwhile, the consummate bureaucrat, Ghulam Muhammad, was appointed to the office of governor-general. Known for his secular ways, Ghulam Muhammad's elevation was of less comfort to the Jama'at.

Nazimu'ddin's administration greatly encouraged religious activism because it led various Islamic parties to expect better returns for their activism. Mawdudi took advantage of the situation to formalize the party's increasingly politicized agenda and to push for fundamental changes in the government apparatus. By 1952 his speeches had become centered on the virtues of democracy seasoned with Islamic precepts.[61] In January, Mawdudi began to criticize severely the Public Safety Act—under the provisions of which he had been imprisoned—and the Public Representatives Disqualification Act. The latter act had originally been devised to discourage abuse of office among elected representatives by disqualifying those found guilty of corruption or illegal acts. It had, however, been widely used by Muslim Leaguers to control the provincial legislatures and to keep the opposition in line. The Jama'at's promotion of civil rights became so open that the American envoy in Lahore included Mawdudi in "the usual array of leftist talent" active in civil rights campaigns in his report to his superiors on the leadership of Pakistan's Civil Liberties Union.[62]

In May, in a speech in Karachi, Mawdudi presented his most lucid formulation yet of Islamic constitutionalism, intermeshing Islamization with a demand for a democratic constitution. In the following months this theme was repeated across Pakistan. Expecting a new report from the Basic Principles Committee that would set the agenda for the debates on the constitution, the Jama'at's activities on behalf of an Islamic constitution reached a fever pitch. The party celebrated a "constitution week" in November 1952, organizing demonstrations, the largest of them in Karachi, and dedicating an entire issue of the *Tarjumanu'l-Qur'an* to discussing the details of the Islamic constitution of Mawdudi, all in the hope of preventing the committee report from sidelining the idea.[63] The committee, having caught a glimpse of the reaction which it could expect from the report, postponed its presentation, arguing that there was need for further consultation. It was not presented until December 22, 1952.

The final draft of the committee's report made several concessions to the Islamic parties, which were duly acknowledged by Mawdudi, who attributed them to the efficacy of the Jama'at's organizational activity. Having smelled victory and sensed weakness in the government, Mawdudi now raised the stakes. He demanded that Pakistan be called the "Islamic Republic of Pakistan," that the shari'ah be made the supreme law in the land, and that ulama boards be set up to oversee the passage of laws in the country.[64] In addition, he called for the further streamlining of electoral procedures, to be supervised by the supreme court of Pakistan, which would limit the government's ability to manipulate future elections to the Jama'at's disadvantage. Finally, he demanded that Pakistan follow a nonaligned foreign policy—that is, maintain a greater distance from the West—which was then becoming an article of faith among Islamic groups across the Muslim world. His incessant demands backed by his Islamic constitutional platform and the increasingly rambunctious party activism on the streets were closely monitored by the government, especially the bureaucracy and the army, which determined their decisions regarding the fate of the Jama'at after the government and Islamic parties became locked in combat yet again in 1953–1954.

The Jama'at's activism in the 1948–1953 period anchored the constitutional debate in Islam and introduced Islamic concepts to the national political discourse. The Jama'at's propaganda and maneuvering and Mawdudi's untiring campaign for Islamization foiled the attempts both of Muslim Leaguers such as Raja Ghazanfar 'Ali to extricate Islam from politics and of the government to manipulate Islam for its own ends. The Jama'at mobilized the ulama and the masses, set the terms of the debate, and defined the role of Islam in the state. Throughout this period, the party supported the unity of Pakistan by underlining the primacy of Islam and Urdu in the national culture. At the same time, it was at odds with the government over virtually every issue, from war in Kashmir to the refugee problem to any center-province standoff, and the constitution. Conflict continued in relations between the two, even as the inseparable entanglement of Islam and Pakistan continued to keep the Jama'at and the government in an uneasy symbiosis.

The Jama'at itself also underwent change during this period. Opposition to the state was supplanted by maneuverings within the state system, and the party's ideological proclamations and idealistic approach to politics gave way to an Islamic constitutionalist platform. Yet the Jama'at's political enfranchisement, as significant as it was in institutionalizing its ideological zeal, did not resolve the discord between the party and the government in Lahore and Karachi. Nor did it ease the tensions within the party between those who viewed it as a holy community and those who saw it as a political party Although the Jama'at made giant strides in transforming itself into a full-fledged party, just as it did in the 1940–1947 period, its use of Islam to gain political advantage deepened its commitment to the holy community

The Anti-Ahmadi Controversy, 1952–1954

The status of minorities in Pakistan had long been of major concern to a number of the Islamic parties and to the ulama. Mawdudi, however, had never given much attention to what their place should be, believing that the question would be automatically resolved within the overall framework of an Islamic constitution. The other Islamic parties did not agree, particularly when it came to the Ahmadis, a sect which had emerged at the turn of the century in Punjab. The Ahmadis follow the teachings of Mirza Ghulam Ahmad (d. 1908), who claimed he had experienced divine revelation. The orthodox believe that the Ahmadis, also known as Qadiyanis or Mirza'is, stand outside the boundaries of Islam despite the Ahmadis' insistence that they are Muslims. For Ghulam Ahmad's claims are incompatible with the Muslim belief that Prophet Muhammad was the last of the prophets. The opposition of the ulama to the Ahmadis predated the partition, and the Deobandis had campaigned against them as early as the 1920s. Mawlana 'Uthmani had written a book in refutation of the claims of Mirza Ghulam Ahmad in 1924.

The Ahmadi issue had been the favorite of the Majlis-i Ahrar-i Islam (Society of Free Muslims), a populist Islamic party created in 1930 that grew out of the Khilafat movement and that was best known for the impassioned style of its speakers. The Ahrar had vacillated between supporting the Congress and the Muslim League before partition and did not declare its allegiance to Pakistan until 1949 The one constant throughout its existence, aside from its socialism, had been its vehement opposition to the Ahmadis. The Ahrar had first expressed this opposition in 1934, when Shah 'Ata'u'llah Bukhari, the party's leader, had demanded the official exclusion of the Ahmadis from Islam and the dismissal of Sir Zafaru'llah Khan—the Ahmadi Muslim League leader and later Pakistan's foreign minister—from the viceroy's council.[65] Following partition, the erstwhile pro-Congress Ahrar moved to Pakistan, and after losing a significant portion of its membership between 1947 and 1950, its new leader, Taju'ddin Ansari, joined hands with Daultana's faction of the Muslim League in Punjab.

With the passage of the Objectives Resolution, the Ahrar decided to utilize the state's professed loyalty to Islam to elicit a ruling on the Ahmadis. Throughout 1949 it incited passions in Punjab against them (they had meanwhile established their Pakistan headquarters in Rabwah, not far from Lahore). The Ahrar were once again demanding the ouster of Zafaru'llah Khan, this time from the cabinet, and to weaken his position went so far as to argue that two of the defendants in the Rawalpindi conspiracy case were Ahmadis.[66] The anti-Ahmadi campaign soon found support among the ulama, and served as the foundation for a religious alliance comparable to the one forged earlier between the Jama'at and the ulama.

The Ahrar found an unexpected ally in the putatively "progressive" chief minister of the Punjab, Mian Mumtaz Daultana, who had found the obstreperous Islamic party and the emerging anti-Ahmadi alliance a useful counterbalance to Mamdot and the Jama'at in the election campaign. Mamdot had defected from the Muslim League earlier in that year and had formed the Jinnah Awami League. The resignation of the former chief minister had greatly damaged the Muslim League's standing in Punjab, all the more so as Mamdot's electoral strategy—forming alliances with the Awami League and the Jama'at—was threatening Daultana's position. Mamdot had been particularly effective in depicting Daultana and his allies in Karachi as "un-Islamic."[67] The struggling Muslim League, also aware of challenges by the Jama'at on its right and Mian Iftikharu'ddin's Azad Pakistan party on its left could hardly withstand charges of secularism. Daultana therefore decided to mobilize the Ahrar to shore up the religious legitimacy of his ministry

The Punjab elections became a platform for the Ahrar's anti-Ahmadi propaganda. Daultana, bogged down in the election campaign and eager to build a base of support among the religious electorate, turned a blind eye to these activities. Nor did he show any signs of discomfort with the Ahrar following his victory in the elections. The continued pressures exerted on the Muslim League by Mamdot, Suhrawardi, Mawdudi, and Mian Iftikharu'ddin made the Ahrar an indispensable asset. Further emboldened by Daultana's sweep of Punjab, the Ahrar set out to turn the Ahmadi issue into a national debate.

The dire economic conditions in Punjab at the time—a rise in food prices and famine precipitated by the landowners—meanwhile provided fertile ground for the Ahrar's agitations.[68] The Islam League (formerly Tahrik-i Khaksar) had already done much to translate popular discontent into an Islamic movement. Throughout the summer of 1952, when food prices and the grain shortage reached their peak, Mawlana Mashriqi organized numerous anti-Muslim League demonstrations, demanding the amelioration of suffering and a greater Islamization of government. The economic situation in Punjab no doubt made local politics susceptible to religious activism. As social unrest spread, demonstrations led by religious activists in general and the Islam League in particular turned into riots. The Islam League's penchant for violence convinced the government of the dangers of allowing the continued sacralization of politics and eventually led to Mashriqi's arrest.

The Jama'at had also tried to take advantage of popular discontent. It organized the February 24, 1952, demonstration at Machi Gate of Lahore to protest the hike in the price of wheat flour, a protest that soon turned into a riot, which was forcibly quelled by the police. Although the Islam League and the Communists were implicated by the authorities as the main culprits, the role of the Jama'at in the whole affair did not go unnoticed.[69] It was, however, the Ahrar, with its socialist leanings, that assumed the role of the Islam League after Mashriqi was arrested. The Ahrar continued to articulate economic grievances in Islamic terms, but with a new twist; it tied the demand for economic justice to the Islamicity of the state by questioning the status of the Ahmadis. Every harangue against government policy and demand for greater Islamicity were accompanied by complaints about the discrepancy between the wealth of the Ahmadi community and the poverty of the struggling Muslim masses: in the homeland of Muslims, it was the Ahmadis who reaped the benefits and the Muslims who suffered hunger and hardship. This strategy was by and large successful, though it was the Ahmadis themselves who set off the final conflict. Zafaru'llah Khan played directly into the Ahrar's hands. On May 17, 1952, the foreign minister turned down Prime Minister Nazimu'ddin's pleas of caution and addressed a public Ahmadi session in Karachi. By openly admitting his religion, Zafaru'llah Khan gave credence to the charge made by the Ahrar that the government was "controlled" by the Ahmadis. For the other Islamic groups and the ulama, who viewed the Ahmadis with opprobrium, the very presence of an Ahmadi minister in the cabinet was proof of the un-Islamicity of the state. The Ahrar and the ulama, infuriated by the foreign minister's action, organized a protest march; the marchers clashed with the Ahmadis, and there was a riot.

On May 18, Sayyid Sulaiman Nadwi, Pakistan's new spiritual leader, convened an ulama board to formulate an official policy Shaikh Sultan Ahmad represented the Jama'at on the board. The board demanded that the Ahmadis be declared a non-Muslim minority, that Zafaru'llah Khan be removed from his cabinet post, and that all key government jobs be cleansed of Ahmadis. The board also elected a majlis-i 'amal (council of action) to implement its recommendations. Amin Ahsan Islahi became the vice-president of this majlis, and Malik Nasru'llah Khan 'Aziz one of its members.

The Jama'at's shura' considered the unfolding events: a number of the Jama'at leaders, including Sultan Ahmad, Islahi, and Nasru'llah Khan 'Aziz, favored the party's wholehearted participation in the agitations as a policy natural for the holy community to support; Mawdudi, who was keen on formalizing the Jama'at's political role, was reluctant to approve. He argued that the Ahmadi issue would be resolved automatically once the country was Islamized and that in the meantime riots would only tarnish the image of the Islamic groups, lessen the appeal of an Islamic constitution, and, by playing into the hands of the opponents of Islamization, was bound to derail the whole campaign for an Islamic state. The holy community's choice of policy could not be premised on religious considerations alone; it had to be examined in light of the party's political aims. Mawdudi was, moreover, not keen on alliance with the Ahrar built around the Ahmadi issue or any other cause. He never subscribed to the kind of impassioned denunciations which characterized the ulama or the Ahrar's encounters with them. Mawdudi had always believed that proper Islamization would "reconvert" the Ahmadis to Islam, and the Islamic state would find a political solution to their place in society [70] However, even among the Jama'at's members there was support for the riots. It was clear that they could open up contacts with the Punjabi masses, whose politics had thus far been dominated by landowners and pirs. Until then the Muhajirs had served as the Islamic parties' main constituency; now the Islam League, Ahrar, and the anti-Ahmadi riots had opened Punjabi politics to the Islamic groups. Given its political objectives, the Jama'at could not ignore the opportunity The desire to sustain the momentum for an Islamic constitution had to be balanced against the opportunities the agitations presented.

The shura', therefore, would not give its wholehearted endorsement to the majlis-i 'amal, then dominated by the Ahrar; but in recognition of the preeminence of the Ahmadi issue, it incorporated the demands of the majlis-i 'amal into its own constitutional proposals. The August 1952 issue of the Tarjumanu'l-Qur'an carried a lengthy denunciation of the Ahmadis written by Mawdudi, and promised to include the demand for their exclusion from Islam into the Jama'at's proposals for an Islamic constitution. The Jama'at members who sat on the majlis-i 'amal, in keeping with Mawdudi's views, sought to temper the Ahrar's violence, but when they failed, the Jamaʻat officially dissociated itself from the *majlis-ı ʻamal* on February 26, 1953 [71]

Between July 1952 and January 1953, Mawdudi had lobbied the ulama against the agitations, hoping instead to keep their attention on the Islamic constitution and to preserve the alliance which had produced the Objectives Resolution, repeating the argument that the Islamic constitution would provide a solution to the Ahmadi issue along with a host of other problems. Mawdudi was increasingly worried about what effect the riots were having on the government of Nazimu'ddin, which the Jamaʻat regarded as an asset, and about the distraction they presented from the constitutional cause. In June 1952, when the Ahrar were busy with their campaign against the Ahmadis, the Jamaʻat launched a nationwide drive to collect signatures in support of the Islamic constitution. In July, as the agitations grew worse, the Jamaʻat demanded that the government reveal the contents of the Basic Principles Committee report before the assembly convened in order to ascertain its Islamicity There followed a joint declaration of the Jamaʻat and other ulama parties to hold a "Constitution Day" in Karachi on December 19, 1952, which the American envoy called "the only effort in Karachi on behalf of the constitution."[72] Finally, in January 1953, when the Ahrar were engaged in fine-tuning their anti-Ahmadi campaign, the Jamaʻat joined the Jinnah Awami League, the Awami League, and the Azad Pakistan party in opposing the Muslim League by objecting to the committee's report.[73] The Jamaʻat, however, failed to redirect national attention away from the Ahmadi issue. The *majlis-ı ʻamal,* dominated by the Ahrar, and nudged along by Daultana and the Punjab Muslim League,[74] proved a more decisive force in determining the position of the ulama than Mawdudi's cautions.

In July 1952 the Punjab government imposed Section 144 of the Criminal Procedure Code restricting public gatherings. On July 19 the Ahrar organized a large demonstration in Multan which culminated in clashes with the police and the deaths of six people. Fearful of further escalation, Daultana sought to reign the Ahrar in, though his approach remained conciliatory On July 21, after securing from the Ahrar a promise to help restore order, the Punjab government lifted the Section 144 restrictions and the ban on the Ahrar's paper, *Azad.* A week later, in a gesture of conciliation, upon the insistence of Daultana[75] "the council of Punjab Muslim League   adopted a resolution by a vote of 264 against eight in support of the anti-Ahmediya agitation."[76] Given the Punjab government's response, the Ahrar found more reason to push for a showdown. On July 27, despite the Muslim League's endorsement of the Ahrar's position, it demonstrated against the League in Punjab and assaulted its councilmen.[77] Daultana ordered the arrest of some 137 people and put Punjab under heavy police protection.[78] The breakdown in the constitutional effort, which Mawdudi had feared, soon followed.

After a brief lull in January 1953, the Ahrar resumed its campaign in full force, and by arguing that the Muslim League resolution was not definitive enough again mobilized the ulama. Sacrificing their greater interests in the Islamization of Pakistan, the ulama, including the Jama'at leader, Sultan Ahmad, gave Nazimu'ddin an ultimatum: either sack Zafaru'llah Khan and declare the Ahmadis a non-Muslim minority within a month or face "direct action"—a euphemism for widescale riots.[79]

Nazimu'ddin had initially tried to win over the agitators by expressing sympathy for the anti-Ahmadi cause. But he had refused to ask for Zafaru'llah Khan's resignation, because in his view such a move would have upset the United States—which regarded Zafaru'llah Khan as an ally—and jeopardized the grain aid, which, given the gravity of food shortages in Punjab, was a risk he could not take.[80] On August 14 he issued a decree which forbade those holding public office from proselytizing, an open reference to the Ahmadis and Zafaru'llah Khan, but this too failed to subdue the agitations, and he soon came under pressure to take a tougher stand. At this point he changed his strategy completely He initiated a virulent attack against the ulama in the press that, given his reputation for piety, was a bolt out of the blue for the majlis-i 'amal and a cause for remorse for Mawdudi. When his trip to Lahore on February 16 was marked by strikes and black-flag demonstrations and the agitators threatened to carry their protest to Karachi on the occasion of Zafaru'llah Khan's return from abroad, the government reacted swiftly; on February 27 it ordered a number of ulama and Ahrar leaders to be rounded up and placed in protective custody

Mawdudi was no longer able to remain aloof. The constitutional debates were set aside. The government and the Islamic parties were now clearly on opposite sides, and the loyalties of the Jama'at naturally lay with the latter. The Ahrar's meteoric rise to prominence and the direction public opinion was taking led the Jama'at to reassess its own approach to the crisis. Mawdudi and Sultan Ahmad participated in an all-Muslim parties convention in January 1953, where they approved the declaration of the session which demanded the resignation of Nazimu'ddin.[81] Mawdudi then joined the majlis-i 'amal, but quickly withdrew [82] Mawdudi and the Jama'at became entangled in the agitations, which between February and March spread throughout Punjab. On March 5, 1953, Mawdudi published the most systematic denunciation of the Ahmadis since the beginning of the crisis: Qadiyani Mas'alah (The Ahmadi Problem). It was designed to establish his primacy in the religious circles, to confirm his religious credentials before the ulama who had chastised him for not supporting the agitations, and to upstage the Ahrar. In doing so, the book placed Mawdudi squarely at the center of the controversy [83] True to form, Mawdudi, who was opposed to the agitations, now became their leading figure.

The federal cabinet, although disturbed by Daultana's machinations, continued to vacillate. General Iskandar Mirza—the doyen of the bureaucracy and the defense secretary—was, however, sufficiently alarmed by the rising tide of agitations in Punjab, and especially by the Punjab government's decision to endorse openly the demands of the agitators to act. On March 6, the Punjab government, in its capacity as the representative of the people of Punjab, dispatched a provincial minister to Karachi to put before the central government the demands of the agitators and push for the dismissal of Zafaru'llah Khan.[84] Viewing Nazimu'ddin's indecision and Daultana's "flirtations with the mullahs as yet another example of the ineptitude and destructive potential of the politicians," on March 6 General Mirza ordered General A'zam Khan to place Punjab under martial law.[85] Soon thereafter Daultana resigned, and Mawdudi, along with Mawlana 'Abdu'ssattar Niyazi (the minister for religious affairs from 1990 to 1993) and a number of Ahrar leaders, was arrested.

Mawdudi was charged with violating martial-law regulations and "promoting feelings of enmity and hatred between different groups in Pakistan" by publishing the *Qadiyani Mas'alah*, as well as inflammatory articles in *Tasnim*.[86] Some twelve Jama'at leaders, including Islahi and Mian Tufayl, and twenty-eight workers, including the publisher of the *Qadiyani Mas'alah*, were also held on these charges; and Jama'at's newspapers, *Kawthar* and *Tasnim*, were closed down.[87] The Jama'at's headquarters were raided, and its papers and funds were confiscated. Mawdudi, the editor of *Tasnim*, and the publisher of *Qadiyani Mas'alah*, would be tried on charges of sedition in May

The anti-Ahmadi agitations, as Mawdudi had feared, proved to be the undoing of Nazimu'ddin, and a major setback for the Islamic constitution. With martial law in place in Punjab, and a climate of uncertainty and crisis reigning in the country, the governor-general, Ghulam Muhammad, found ample room for maneuvering and summarily dismissed Nazimu'ddin on April 17, 1953 In this he was backed by leaders such as General Mirza who had already taken issue with Nazimu'ddin's "flirtations with the mullahs" and placed the entire responsibility for the crisis in Punjab on his shoulders.[88]

The pious Nazimu'ddin was replaced by the more secular Muhammad 'Ali Bugra. The change was immediately reflected in the constitutional debates. The Constituent Assembly played down the Islamic provisions of the Basic Principles Committee report, and the interim constitutional proposals of June 1953 did not even mention the hitherto agreed-upon provisions regarding the place of Islam in the constitution.[89] A special court of inquiry was set up under the supervision of Muhammad Munir, the chief justice of the supreme court of Pakistan, to look into the roots of the agitation in Punjab and to roll back the gains made by Islamic groups. The power of religious activists was effectively reduced by the adroit Justice Munir, who depicted them as incompetent judges of how to run a modern state. The inability of the ulama and the lay religious activists to produce a unanimous response to such axiomatic queries as "the meaning of a Muslim" led to the conclusion that no such definition of Islam, let alone of an Islamic constitution, existed and that the religious experts were best advised to leave the constitution-making process alone and concentrate on putting their own house in order.

Munir's incisive inquiry, known popularly as the "Munir Report," was later singled out as the most celebrated "modernist" expression of backlash against Islamic activism and an indictment of religious activism, an act of bravado allowed by the change in the balance between the government and the Islamic parties. Munir's inquiry continues to cast its shadow over the activities of the sundry Islamic parties in Pakistan to this day

By blaming Pakistan's developmental crisis on the "perfidious" meddling of the Islamic parties in politics, the Munir Report turned the central question before the Pakistan state on its head. Islam was depicted as an unwelcome intruder into the political arena and an impediment to national development. What the Munir Report failed to realize was that, as deficient as the program of the Islamic groups may have been, in the absence of representative institutions, national elections, national parties with a strong organizational apparatus and a meaningful political platform, and shared national values Islam was all Pakistanis had in the way of a cohesive force, and that was the very reason why politicians had continued to appeal to it. In a society with arrested political development and state formation and deeply divided along ethnic, linguistic, and sectarian lines, Islam had become the intermediary between state and society, the more so as the former had faltered and the latter grown unruly Islam could not be selectively appealed to and then successfully manipulated. Forays into the domain of the ulama and the Islamic groups by politicians and the resultant sacralization of the political discourse could generate uncontrollable and undesirable outcomes. Costs and responsibilities had to be shouldered by Jinnah, Liaqat 'Ali Khan, Nazimu'ddin, and Daultana, to name only a few of Pakistan's political leaders of the time, as well as by those whom the Munir Report sought to implicate.[90] By inviting Islam into the political arena, it was the politicians, and not the Islamic activists, who confirmed the centrality of Islam to the national political discourse.

The same motives that governed the politicians' appealing to Islam now conditioned the role of Islam in the politics of the masses. Just as the politicians had opened the door to political activism by the Islamic parties, so had the masses. With no national elections in which to express their demands, nor any national parties to represent their interests rather than those of the elite, the masses, whose commitment to Islamization until that point was by no means certain, turned to Islamic slogans and Islamic parties to express their political demands and vent their frustrations. But as the Punjab crisis indicated, neither the ruling elite nor the masses were capable of controlling the flow of Islam into politics or the sacralization of the national political discourse. Munir had really focused on the symptoms rather than the causes of that sacralization. The lesson of the Punjab crisis might have eluded Munir but not the military and bureaucratic elite. From it they concluded that secularism was the handmaiden of political stability, and, moreover, only an apolitical polity could help bring about a secular society

Politicians and Islamic activists alike agreed that what happened in Punjab was a testament to the emotive power of Islamic symbols. The ulama and Mawdudi may be ridiculed, but in the absence of nationally shared values or a viable state ideology they were bound to rise again. The Munir Report was the last attempt to extricate Islam from Pakistan's politics; neither Munir nor Ghulam Muhammad, nor in later years, Ayub Khan, however, could find a substitute for its role. Islam held the state together. Whenever Pakistan fell into crisis in the years to follow, politicians and people alike appealed to Islam's symbols and loyalties to construct political programs and social movements, thereby expanding the wedge through which Islamic groups entered the political arena. As Justice Munir was busy systematically rolling back the gains made by the Islamic parties, Nuru'l-Amin, the chief minister of East Pakistan, told Prime Minister Bugra that "Islam was the League's one hope of warding off defeat in east Bengal"[91] and keeping the wayward province under Karachi's control. He then assured the public that the Muslim League was determined "to give the country a full-fledged Islamic Constitution within six months."[92]

Changes in the political climate in 1953 also proved to be a problem in the Jama'at's legal battles. In May the military tribunal convened to determine the fate of those arrested in Punjab. After a brief trial, on May 8 the tribunal found Mawlana 'Abdu'ssattar Niyazi and on May 11, Mawdudi, guilty of sedition; both were sentenced to death. Many among Pakistan's leaders were convinced that India was behind the Punjab disturbances, which made Mawdudi and Niyazi guilty not only of sedition but also of treason.[93] This, however, does not explain why the harshest sentences were reserved for only these two religious leaders. The tribunal also sentenced the publishers of *Tasnim* and *Qadiyani Mas'alah* to three and nine years in jail, respectively The sentences were unexpectedly harsh, and in the case of Mawdudi was thought by many to be incommensurate to his role in the entire affair, which was limited to having published the *Qadiyani Mas'alah,* and even that book had been published the day before martial law was declared. In effect, Mawdudi had been arrested for violating a martial law ordinance that had not yet existed when the book was published. Mawdudi's writings were hardly as inflammatory as those of the Ahrar leaders, none of whom received as severe a punishment. Even more perplexing, the most active of the Jama'at's leaders, Sultan Ahmad, had not even been arrested, and Mawdudi had received the same sentence as Niyazi, whose incendiary speeches had directly incited violence and on one occasion had led to the murder of a policeman outside of the mosque where Niyazi was preaching. The American consul-general in Lahore reported that the chief of the intelligence directorate of Punjab told him that "there is no evidence 'as yet' that Jamaat-i-Islami *as a party* was involved in the riots. He stated the arrests had been made of individuals against whom there was some evidence of participation in the riots.   He was sure a good case would be made" (emphasis in the original).[94]

The government was fully aware that the public regarded its case against Mawdudi to be weak. It had been hard-pressed even to explain his arrest. Four days before Mawdudi's sentencing, Justice Munir told the consul that "he [had] already been getting many informal petitions and letters challenging the legal validity of actions taken under Martial Law and especially of cases tried under Courts Martial which in many cases meted out severe sentences."[95] If the army, Justice Munir, or the secularist elite had thought they could cleanse the politics of Islamic parties this way, they were wrong. Nazimu'ddin criticized the sentence, and even offered to sign a petition for mercy for Mawdudi.[96] Prime Minister Bugra, too, was surprised with the sentence and remarked that Mawdudi could appeal, and should he do so would get a most sympathetic hearing.[97] Martial law and the persecution of religious groups proved to be highly unpopular enterprises, which only made heroes of the accused.[98] On May 13, Mawdudi's sentence was reduced to fourteen years.

The Jama'at, however, was not assuaged and continued to clamor for justice. On May 21 four Jama'at leaders were arrested for protesting Mawdudi's fourteen-year sentence, but they continued their campaign for his release and complained of government vindictiveness and strong-arm tactics toward their party On June 18, 1954, for instance, Sultan Ahmad, the provisional amir of the Jama'at, declared that Mawdudi's arrest and sentence had nothing to do with the anti-Ahmadi agitations, and everything to do with his constitutional proposals.[99] Echoing a general sentiment among the Islamic parties, Sultan Ahmad stated that the government's reaction to the agitations was merely a pretext for eliminating stumbling blocks to the passage of a secular constitution.[100] Justice Munir's probing into the politics of Islamic activists under the pretext of determining the causes of the Punjab agitations had only added to their suspicions. Many religious leaders, including those in the Jama'at, charged that the court of inquiry was better advised to look for the cause of agitation in economic injustice and the political maneuverings of Daultana.

Some in the military and the bureaucracy saw the Punjab agitations and the five-year campaign for an Islamic constitution as interrelated, and therefore believed that Mawdudi's crime extended beyond his role in the Punjab agitations. Zafaru'llah Khan and Iskandar Mirza claimed that Mawdudi was "one of the most dangerous men in Pakistan,"[101] guilty of generating a national crisis. Munir himself believed that the Jama'at had as "its objective the replacement of the present form of Government by a Government of the Jamaat's conception,"[102] a point that was hardly new since the Jama'at had openly advocated the establishment of a government to its liking since setting foot in Pakistan. But now the Jama'at's campaign for Islamization was depicted as a seditious undertaking whose result was the Punjab crisis. It followed that there existed no difference between Mawdudi's apparently academic activities and Niyazi's manipulation of the mob.

Mawdudi himself remained unapologetic. While he may have received assurances regarding the outcome of his case from Muslim League leaders,[103] he forbade his followers from seeking clemency on his behalf. They did, however, stage a number of strikes and street demonstrations decrying the "injustice." To the government's dismay, Mawdudi was gradually becoming a hero.

Reacting to pressures from within, reluctant to carry out the sentences against Mawdudi and Niyazi,[104] and dismayed by the Jama'at's success in arguing its case before the public, the government grew conciliatory Mian Muhammad Sharif, a judge of the supreme court, was appointed by the government to review the tribunal's judgment. Sharif recommended that the martial law administration commute the sentences. By the end of 1953 most of the Jama'at's workers had been freed, and in March 1954 Islahi was released. Mawdudi, however, was to be kept away for as long as the government could manage. The court, however, once again proved to be a boon for the Jama'at. Following the ruling of the federal court on a petition of habeas corpus for two defendants in the Rawalpindi conspiracy case, Mawdudi and Niyazi filed a habeas corpus petition before the Lahore High Court in April. However, before the court could render a verdict, the government remitted Mawdudi and Niyazi's sentences. After two years in prison, Mawdudi was released on April 29, 1955 Already a hero, he quickly became the spokesman for a religious alliance whose zeal he was determined to rekindle.[105]

The Constitution of 1956

The Jama'at's experience with martial law in Punjab and its dismay at the ouster of Nazimu'ddin had only increased the party's dedication to the preservation and promotion of civil liberties. In July 1953 the Jama'at celebrated "Islamic Constitution Day " In November of the same year it ordered its workers to join various civil liberties unions across Pakistan, and it contemplated forming a central civil liberties association.[106] The Jama'at's Islamic constitution and its civil rights cause were given a boost when the secularist governor-general Ghulam Muhammad, in an attempt to resolve the political stalemate in Karachi, summarily dismissed the Constituent Assembly on October 24, 1954. With no constitution in place, the governor-general was theoretically responsible only to the British Crown. Although Mawdudi was then still in prison and conceivably at the mercy of Ghulam Muhammad's good will, the party quickly organized demonstrations against the governor-general's decision and in support of the petition challenging the dismissal filed before the Sind High Court by the speaker of the dismissed assembly, Maulvi Tamizu'ddin, on November 7, 1954.[107] The Sind High Court ruled against the governor-general's action. Ghulam Muhammad appealed the ruling before the Supreme Court, where Justice Munir reversed the Sind High Court.

The case presented not only a suitable cause célèbre around which to organize and to reinvigorate the languishing religious alliance, but an occasion to challenge both Ghulam Muhammad and Justice Munir. The dismissal of the assembly had also removed the only institutional avenue open to the religious alliance for influencing the constitutional process, which now lay fully in the hands of secularist leaders. The restoration of the assembly was, therefore, a matter of life and death for the Islamic constitution, and yet another proof that the fate of Islam was enmeshed with that of democracy in Pakistan. Under political pressure the government restored the assembly in May 1955 In August both Ghulam Muhammad and Bugra left office, to be replaced by General Iskandar Mirza and Chaudhri Muhammad 'Ali, respectively Given the resumption of constitutional debates, the Jama'at redoubled its efforts on behalf of the Islamic constitution, though rather less zealously It did not, for instance, put forth candidates to contest the elections to the Constituent Assembly of June 21, 1955 In light of the Munir Report's debilitating criticisms and the government's dismissal of the Constituent Assembly, the party now felt that it should avoid issues of substance and concentrate on obtaining any constitution at all. The pious Muslim Leaguer and civil servant Chaudhri Muhammad 'Ali, whom Mawdudi had known since the 1930s, meanwhile received Mawdudi's endorsement for the renewed constitution-making process after he relaxed government pressure on the Jama'at and protected Mawdudi from further harassment. For instance, Muhammad 'Ali personally intervened on Mawdudi's behalf when the government had decided to prosecute him once again for his role in the anti-Ahmadi crisis by using a legal technicality [108] Pressure was brought to bear on the government to arrest Mawdudi and other martial law prisoners. The charges against Mawdudi and his codefendants were officially dropped eight days later.[109]

The government took steps to bring the Jama'at into the constitution-making process by pushing for greater Islamization.[110] Thirty-four members of the Constituent Assembly signed a declaration at the Jama'at's behest in May 1955, pledging to retain in the new constitutional draft the Islamic and democratic provisions adopted by the old constituent assembly Meanwhile, Sardar 'Abdu'r-rabb Nishtar, president of the Muslim League, and Mahmud Husain, minister of education, pressed to include in the Basic Principles Committee report a recommendation to establish an ulama board to advise the legislature.[111]

On February 29, 1956, the Constituent Assembly formally ratified the draft constitution proposed by Muhammad 'Ali. It was approved by the governor-general on March 2 and took effect on March 23 The constitution recognized some token demands of the Islamic parties—naming the state the "Islamic Republic" of Pakistan and subjecting all legislative undertakings to the veto of the "repugnancy clause." This clause (number 205), argued that no laws could be passed that were repugnant to the teachings of the Qur'an and the hadith and that all laws passed to date could be examined in light of the religious authorities and, if need be, repealed. But none of the concessions were substantive ones. The recommendations made by the Board of Ta'limat-i Islamiyah (Board of Islamic Teachings), the Objectives Resolution, and the reports of the Basic Principles Committee found no place in the constitution. Islam was not declared the official religion of Pakistan, nor was it stipulated that the speaker of the National Assembly, who could become president under special circumstances, must be a Muslim. Furthermore, the constitution of 1956 closely paralleled the India Act of 1935 and, hence, despite its prima facie adherence to the Westminster model, gave broad powers to the president to which the Jama'at was opposed. The constitution had retained all those features of the earlier interim committee reports which Mawdudi had most vehemently denounced as authoritarian.

Mawdudi and the Jama'at, however, quickly accepted the constitution as an "Islamic" constitution. The only serious criticism lodged by Mawdudi was to the "preventive detention" clause of the constitution, which given his recent experiences with the heavy-handed policies of the government, was derided as outright authoritarian.[112] This decision was doctrinally suspect but politically prudent. Mawdudi no doubt wanted to support Chaudhri Muhammad 'Ali and to make the best of a bad situation. Bengali discontent with Karachi's political intrigues had increased markedly after 1954, when the Muslim League had been routed in East Pakistan's provincial elections. Pakistan, Mawdudi decided, needed a working constitution, and debating over what it should be could only further divide the country The political maneuverings of General Mirza, who was no less a threat to the Jama'at's interests than Ghulam Muhammad, added to the party's anxiety Since October 1954, when Ghulam Muhammad had dismissed the Constituent Assembly and forced Prime Minister Bugra to admit generals Mirza and Ayub Khan into the cabinet, the military had taken a more direct role in managing the affairs of the country A prolonged constitutional deadlock could only have benefited General Mirza and his allies in the bureaucracy and the armed forces, who were impatient with Pakistani politics and were predisposed to dispense with the entire process. Chaudhri Muhammad 'Ali, who generally sought to minimize resistance to the constitution, had no doubt been instrumental in helping Mawdudi come to these conclusions.[113] So had the ransacking by the police of the party's offices eleven days earlier and its promise to continue such harassment.[114]

In addition, unless quickly promulgated, Muhammad 'Ali's constitutional draft was likely to be challenged by more secular versions. In 1955 the law minister, Isma'il Ibrahim Chundrigar, had drafted a constitution with the help of Britain's parliamentary counsel, Sir John Rowlatt.[115] The "Chundrigar constitution," as it was dubbed by a British diplomat, did not envision Pakistan as an "Islamic" Republic, and provided for no parliamentary body to determine whether or not legislation was repugnant to Islam. It referred to Islam only twice—when it stipulated the religion required of the president and when it suggested that oaths should be taken in the name of Allah.[116] Chundrigar viewed Islamic legislation as a restriction on the sovereignty of the parliament and wished to do away with it. It is clear that the law minister's initiative would have been particularly damaging to the Jama'at's cause. The party agreed to forego the hope of a constitution to its liking and to accept Muhammad 'Ali's formulation.

Soon thereafter, Muhammad 'Ali's power began to wane. Mawdudi's efforts to mobilize support failed, and the architect of Pakistan's first constitution was removed from office on September 12, 1956. He was replaced by the veteran Bengali politician Husain Shahid Suhrawardi, whose mix of Bengali nationalism and populism did not sit well with West Pakistan's landed and bureaucratic elite. The Jama'at did not approve of his secular outlook and populist inclinations. Once Suhrawardi, an ally of Mamdot, had taken over the Jinnah Awami League and secured a base in Punjab, he had moved steadily to the left and toward the Bengali nationalists, forming the United Front to expand his base of support in East Pakistan. Given all this, the Jama'at was certain to resume its antigovernment agitations. The new government's interpretation of the constitution would soon provide the necessary pretext.

The constitution of 1956 had left the question of the division of the electorates unresolved. Most West Pakistanis favored categorizing Muslims and non-Muslims as separate electorates. Suhrawardi and the East Pakistan Assembly had already voted in favor of joint electorates.[117] Soon after Suhrawardi took office, the Jama'at moved to oppose Suhrawardi over the joint electorate issue[118] and launched a campaign which placed the issue at the center of Pakistani politics.[119] The party argued that joint electorates would make a mockery of the state's claims to be Islamic and open the elections to machinations by the "anti-Pakistan" Hindu voters who were still numerous in East Pakistan. The party found itself in the same camp with many of its erstwhile enemies and rivals—the Muslim League and the Republican party leaders, and the bureaucratic and military elite who opposed Suhrawardi and the Awami League on the electorates issue.[120] The issue was largely symbolic, revealing the continued communalist outlook of the Pakistanis. Before the partition they had fought for separate electorates in India to establish their communal identity and protect the special interests of the Muslim minority The force of their arguments was still echoing in Pakistan; they still reacted to the issue as if they represented a religious minority They felt threatened by the Hindu electorate, whom they believed would use the joint electorates to promote Bengali nationalism at the expense of the Islamic, and by implication Pakistani, cause. The Jama'at was motivated by anti-Hindu sentiments, since Hindus were the main beneficiaries of joint electorates in East Pakistan. The party's idea of social organization was based on the Muslim/non-Muslim (*zimmi*) dichotomy and the overriding role of Islam in Pakistan's politics. In this case the interests of many Pakistani leaders and the religious sensibilities of the Jama'at had converged. The electorates issue was only the first of many examples of cooperation between the Muslim League and the Jama'at. For instance, when in March 1958 the prime minister, Malik Firuz Khan Noon, severely criticized Western powers for abandoning Pakistan on Kashmir, and called for Pakistan to steer away from overreliance on the West, none welcomed his initiative more than the Jama'at.

Hence once Suhrawardi and the Awami League were replaced by a Muslim League government, the Jama'at found itself markedly closer to the government.[121] Between 1957 and 1958, as the clamor for provincial autonomy among Bengalis came to dominate Pakistani politics, strikes and demands for economic justice grew, and as the hand of General Mirza in steering Pakistan toward military rule became more apparent, the Jama'at joined in the political process more actively.[122] To counter General Mirza's growing strength, the government was compelled to woo the Islamic parties. When Prime Minister Noon called an "all-parties conference" in 1958, the Jama'at was invited to attend,[123] a move the Jama'at regarded as propitious. The Jama'at had concluded that the electorates issue, which threatened to destabilize the political order, would be decisive in any future general election. Believing that most Pakistanis shared the party's enthusiasm for separate electorates, it expected to benefit in the anticipated elections from the anti–joint electorate tide. During a preelection rally in East Pakistan, Mawdudi declared rather cavalierly that "99% of West Pakistan's population and 80 to 90% of East Pakistani Muslims are against the system of joint electorates."[124]

On April 28, 1958, the party contested twenty-three seats in the Karachi municipal elections and won nineteen of them. The elections to the ninety-six seats of the city corporation, ninety-one of which were open to Muslims, were closely contested and stirred great popular interest.[125] The elections were used by most parties as a trial run for the general elections to gauge the popularity of the various parties.[126] Although the Karachi electorate was by no means typical of Pakistan as a whole, the Jama'at's victory still gave it a considerable boost. The U.S. embassy reported to the secretary of state that the Jama'at had done surprisingly well in the elections, "the most striking aspect of the election results."[127] The party had won a large proportion of the seats it had contested, coming second after the Muslim League with sixty-one seats.[128] Taking the results as a sign of greater victories to follow, the Jama'at began preparing for the national elections, to that end forging an alliance with Chaudhri Muhammad 'Ali's newly formed Nizam-i Islam (Islamic Order) party Preparations ended abruptly when on October 7, 1958, generals Iskandar Mirza and Muhammad Ayub Khan staged a military coup, dismissed the civilian government, and shelved the constitution of 1956.

Between 1948 and 1958 the Jama'at found its place in Pakistani politics. Following an uncertain start, and periodic confrontations with the government, it utilized its campaign for an Islamic constitution to replace its original ideological orientation with greater pragmatism, to articulate a political program, and generally to move along the path of becoming a full-fledged political party It found a clear-cut political platform by amending its Islamic vision to include a commitment to democracy and constitutional rights. In the process it infused the political discourse with religious references and ideas whose language and symbols have left such an indelible mark on Pakistani politics. The Islamic parties came to constitute a distinct interest group with specific demands on the state. Although these parties, and the Jama'at most notably among them, continued to fight the state, the symbiosis between Islam and the state was, nevertheless, strengthened.

7 The Secular State, 1958–1971

The coup engineered by generals Iskandar Mirza and Muhammad Ayub Khan was a blow to the cause of Islamic constitutionalism and the Jama'at-i Islami's plans for the national elections. Its members were convinced that the generals had staged the coup to destroy the Islamic constitution of 1956, and eliminate the possibility of an electoral victory by Islamic parties. The military's intentions were especially suspect as it lost no time in preparing a new constitution, setting up a committee for that purpose in December 1958. The Jama'at's performance in the Karachi municipal elections—winning eighteen of twenty-three contested seats—must have caused consternation among the supporters of secularism.[1] The coup, Mawdudi argued, was staged specifically to stop the Jama'at and its allies from getting any closer to power. If General Mirza's own memoirs are any indication, the Jama'at's conclusions were not that far off the mark:

> On 8th January 1956, the draft of the proposed constitution was published. I was very doubtful about two of its features. I was opposed to inserting Islamic provisions into the machinery of government. We have seen how Liaqat Ali Khan's "Objectives Resolution" gave a handle to the Ulama, and allowed them to go and almost destroy Pakistan in 1953. But the Muslim League never learnt anything from past experience. Despite my repeated warnings, Muhammad Ali deliberately created an "Islamic Republic" for Pakistan, giving the Ulama another invitation to interfere. Maulana Maudoodi and his party were given a heaven-sent opportunity to mess up the state.[2]

Iskandar Mirza singled out the Jama'at, although in the preceding three years the biggest challenge to his authority had come from Suhrawardi, and the most formidable problems before the polity had been the feud between the Muslim League and the neophyte Republican party, the debate over consolidating West

Pakistan provinces into a single unit, and the worsening economic situation. Iskandar Mirza also took seriously the possibility that either Noon or Suhrawardi would take control of the legislature and thereby challenge him for the presidency, a fact which may also explain why he delayed the general elections.[3] In justifying his preoccupation with the Jama'at despite the more formidable challenges to his authority, General Mirza said the politicians were able neither to withstand the temptation of "flirting with the mullahs" nor to avert or contain the political crisis that resulted.[4] The progress of the country depended on purging Islam from the political process; secularism could be guaranteed only through martial rule.[5] The coup had been staged not only to arrest the decline of the country's political institutions and to resolve the crisis of governability, but also to foil the "insidious" plans of the Islamic parties—the Jama'at in particular—to manipulate the political process.[6]

The generals had done away with the fruits of a decade of Islamic activism and, at least according to the Jama'at, had stolen the elections from them.[7] The party's hostility toward General Mirza and, after his dismissal and exile later in 1958, toward General Ayub Khan is not surprising. Only the restoration of the constitution and the democratic order could bring the party to power. The alliance between secularism and martial rule reinforced the party's commitment to Islamic constitutionalism, which would be the means for restoring the Jama'at's political fortunes.

The new secular composition of Pakistani politics led some in the Jama'at to favor returning to the isolation and moral high ground of the holy community, but others, Mawdudi among them, believed that the Jama'at could best fight the government by remaining in the fray as a political party, and over time this latter view gained the upper hand. As the generals sought to depoliticize the political process, the Jama'at became more and more politicized but did not radicalize, a development which stands in clear contrast to revivalist movements in Pahlavi Iran and Nasser's Egypt. The Jama'at confronted a political and administrative establishment less willing to yield to pressure and more willing to exert it. The opposition also labored under the disadvantage that martial law at this stage enjoyed a certain popularity The coup had brought a modicum of stability to a fractious polity The new regime's anticorruption, price-control, and economic readjustment policies, although not popular with business, were certainly welcomed by many Pakistanis, who had grown weary of food shortages and financial crises.[8] As a result, opposition to the new regime at first had little effect. Given the mood of the country at the time, even arguments for a constitution failed to rally the masses. The party was therefore compelled to look for another political program.

The Jama'at's problems were compounded by the changes in national politics which followed the coup. The generals instituted a new political system that sidelined the politicians, the power brokers who had the greatest need to appeal to religious symbols and slogans. They replaced them with the most anglicized, and hence least religiously inclined, Pakistani leadership from among the civil service and the military [9] By suspending the democratic process, the coup immunized the power structure against political activism of any sort. The architects of the coup then set about changing the focus of the constitutional debates from "why Pakistan was created" to "where Pakistan is heading," that is, from ideological to developmental concerns. The Bureau of National Reconstruction, established in January 1959 and directed by a military man, was charged with the task of devising a new outlook that would be both a secularizing and unifying force.[10] This agenda was supported by the national press[11] and had the blessings of the leftists, who could expect to benefit from the cleansing of Pakistani politics of its Islamic elements so the national political discourse could focus on socioeconomic concerns.[12]

This shift away from the symbiosis between Islam and Pakistan stretched the ties that bound the Jama'at to the state to the point of rupture, but somehow the party remained within bounds. Faced with government hostility and the secularization of politics during the Ayub era, the Jama'at resisted the temptation to withdraw from the political process. Mawdudi wanted above all to avoid the fate of Egypt's Muslim Brotherhood under Nasser and to that end steered the Jama'at clear of radical solutions to the challenges posed by the Ayub regime.[13] This was an arduous task which tested the limits of Mawdudi's hold over the Jama'at. "We put up with Ayub," Mawdudi wrote, "with the patience of Ayub [Job]."[14]

The Jama'at's restraint during this period is all the more amazing when one realizes how radical Pakistani politics became during the 1958–1969 period. Modernization and industrialization, combined with the secularization of society in those years, divided Pakistani society into a secular and Westernized ruling class and the mass of people living according to time-honored Indo-Islamic traditions. Each adhered to its own cultural, social, and political outlook, which resulted in alienation between the rulers and the masses. Had the regime remained in power, such a cleavage could have eventually culminated in revolution and the collapse of the social order. To this extent the Jama'at was more sensitive to the changes in the structure of Pakistani society than the government and did more to avert the polarization of the country

Throughout the Ayub era, the Jama'at continued to campaign for Islamic constitutionalism, with its mixture of Islam and democracy At times Islam was even thoroughly overshadowed by democracy This simultaneous appeal to tradition and modernity proved to be a way to bridge the widening political and cultural gap between the traditional and the modern and helped preserve the Pakistani state when the policies of the ruling establishment were pushing it increasingly to the brink of crisis.

Efforts to Eliminate the Jama'at, 1958–1965

No sooner had martial law been declared than the new regime began to squeeze the Islamic parties out, both to eliminate religion from politics and to justify suspending the 1956 constitution. But given the nature of the Pakistan state and the complexities of Islam's relation to it, such a radical measure proved not to be viable. The government turned to less drastic measures. It toned down its secular rhetoric, and pursued its agenda under the guise of religious modernism, hoping to negotiate a new role in society for Islam. Islam, it was apparent to the new regime, could not immediately be sidelined but it could be reformed, modernized, depoliticized, and eventually eased out of politics. In a surprise move, on May 3, 1959, Ayub Khan addressed a gathering of the ulama from both East and West Pakistan. He devoted his speech to exhorting the divines to do away with obscurantism and interpret religion in ways that were more relevant to the country's developmental agenda and that would fight communism.[15]

The general's speech set the tone for subsequent relations between the military regime and the Islamic groups. Thenceforth, the government sought to take the monopoly of interpreting Islam away from Islamic parties to control the nature and scope of religion's interaction with society and politics. The national concern for "Islamicity" in literary and political circles quickly gave way to lip service to the "principles of Islam," a change that in effect undermined the religiopolitical platform of parties such as the Jama'at. The government sought to limit the scope of their activities and demands, exclude them from the political process, and subject them to state control. To accomplish this, Ayub Khan turned to state-sponsored institutions that could appropriate the right to interpret Islam and control its flow into politics.

This job was given to two ministries, interior and education, and information and broadcasting. Together they launched a propaganda campaign questioning the loyalty to Pakistan of the self-styled spokesmen of Islam, their knowledge of modern statecraft, and even their moral and ethical standing. Under the provisions of the Waqf (endowment) Properties Ordinance of 1959, religious endowments were nationalized, and the government took over the management of shrines and mosques. Then it formulated its own conception of Islam, and its own religiopolitical platform, thereby entering the domain of the ulama with the goal of appropriating for the state the right to interpret Islam and implement its teachings. The government's synthesis was essentially modernist, premised on reforming Islamic law and interpreting its tenets liberally in light of the needs of the government's developmental objectives. Qazi Shahabu'ddin, the minister of education, information, and broadcasting, was particularly vocal in furthering the government's cause, and his pronouncements on a host of religious issues soon incensed the ulama.

The actual task of devising a new vision of Islam was delegated to the Institute of Islamic Culture (Idarah-ı Thıqafat-ı Islam) of Lahore, headed by Khalifah 'Abdu'l-Hakım (d. 1959), and, more significantly, to the Islamic Research Institute of Karachı, headed by Fazlur Rahman (d. 1988), a confidant of Ayub Khan. The two institutions outlined the government's strategy against the ulama and Islamic parties, providing an intellectual rationale for the essentially political campaign against the religious forces. The polarity between traditionalists and innovators (*ahl-ı sunnat* and *ahl-ı bıd'at*), identified by Mawdudi in earlier times, had now taken shape in earnest. However, while the government's attempts to appropriate Islamic symbols in politics undermined the Islamic parties, it also attested to the government's inability to do away with religion altogether. Secularism had to be presented with a veneer of Islamization. Using this wedge, the Islamic parties soon regained their momentum and were able to find new links between religion and politics which provided them with additional strategies by which to gain entry into the political process.

The campaign against the ulama and the Islamic parties unraveled when the secular opposition found common grounds for cooperation with the Islamic parties. In December 1959, Ayub Khan introduced his Basic Democracy scheme, a system of political representation based on voter councils at various levels which officially did away with parties and ended political pluralism in Pakistan. Two months later he was elected president of Pakistan with the vote of the "basic democrats." Soon thereafter he commissioned the chief justice of the supreme court Muhammad Shahabu'ddin to look into the causes of the "failure" of the 1956 constitution with a view to preparing a new one. The Jama'at, aware that Islam would most likely be singled out as a negative influence to be excluded from constitution making, began to mobilize the dormant religious coalition. A meeting of ulama and Jama'at leaders was convened in May 1960 in Lahore to present a set of proposals for future constitutional debates and to demand the abrogation of the marriage of convenience between "bureaucracy and autocracy" that Basic Democracy represented. They enjoined the government to hold national elections open to all. The government reacted by summoning Mawdudi to appear before the authorities in Lahore, where he was chastised for violating martial law regulations that prohibited political activities.[16] By and large, however, the government took little notice of this effort to revive the religious alliance and continued with its reform measures.

The government's team of religious reformers drew up plans for a new family law, which was introduced as the Family Laws Ordinance of March 1961.[17] It was the first in a series of legal and social reform measures designed to hasten Pakistan's development. The ordinance and the "fundamental changes" in Islamic laws governing marriage, divorce, and inheritance laws which it entailed suggested that government policy was no longer solely directed at limiting the influence of Islamic parties but was also beginning to encroach on the ulama's domain. The Jama'at took the lead in organizing street demonstrations and publishing pamphlets to inform the public of the government's transgression.[18] The government, unwilling to compromise, set out to silence the opposition. Mian Tufayl Muhammad, who had published the *fatwas* of fourteen eminent ulama denouncing the ordinance, along with a number of Jama'at workers, was put in prison.[19] For the Islamic parties, ending the government's effort to loosen the hold of the ulama over the life and thought of Pakistanis was a question of survival. The lines of battle were drawn, and the ordinance served as the first test.

The draft constitution was introduced on March 1, 1962. It made some references to Islam: it was to be the official religion of Pakistan, and the "repugnancy clause" and other Islamic provisions of the 1956 constitution were kept intact. Their implementation, however, was no longer mandatory and was to be overseen by the Advisory Council of Islamic Ideology, which was to be controlled by the president. The constitution substituted specific references to the Qur'an and religious traditions (*sunnah*) with the word "Islam," which made the sources of Islamic law much vaguer. Most procedural matters were also reformed to discourage the intrusion of religious forces into the constitutional process. To underscore the intent of the constitution, "Islamic" was dropped from the nation's official name, which became merely "Republic of Pakistan."

The new constitution represented a blow to the party's fundamental interests; it was certainly a setback for the cause of Islam in Pakistan, one which, if allowed to stand, would be the end of the Jama'at. In a decision that reflected its determination to survive, the Jama'at decided not to respond until June when the new legislature was to meet and martial law to be lifted.[20]

After the Political Parties Act of July 17, 1962, the Jama'at began to act. In August the shura' prepared a resolution which called for the restoration of democracy and denounced both the new constitution and the Basic Democracy system. Thenceforth, Mawdudi systematically fused democracy and Islam in its campaign against the Ayub regime. Convinced that democracy alone could safeguard the interests of Islam before Ayub's autocratic secularization policies, the party harped on the theme throughout Ayub Khan's term of office. It was a curious feature of the Ayub Khan era that religious modernism went hand in hand with martial rule, while the fortunes of revivalism became intertwined with those of democracy

The challenge of the authoritarian government and its determination to inculcate a modernist interpretation of Islam in Pakistan were too important to be tackled by the religious alliance alone. In October 1962, through the interme- diary of Chaudhri Muhammad 'Ali, the Jama'at began negotiating with the secular political opposition to Ayub Khan, then led by Suhrawardi under the umbrella of the National Democratic Front. The rank and file of the Jama'at did not approve of associating with this proponent of joint electorates, a man whom the Jama'at had once attacked with the same fervor that it now used to challenge Ayub Khan.[21] The Jama'at, however, had few other choices, and in the first of a series of rulings, Mawdudi argued that the dangers posed to Islam by Ayub Khan warranted compromise. The Jama'at had to act as a party, making compromises that would not have been possible for a holy community

After martial law was lifted, the Jama'at intensified its activism. Initially a minor irritant, the party quickly became a thorn in the side of the government. Mawdudi pressed the government to amend the new constitution to add "Islamic" to Pakistan's official name, demanded greater guarantees for fundamental individual rights, and excoriated the government's overtly pro-Western foreign policy [22] More disturbing to the government was that the Jama'at emerged from the martial law period intact and, by 1962, was the most organized and robust of the Pakistani political parties. Generally concerned with controlling political activism in Pakistan, the government became particularly sensitive to the Jama'at's politics and began to look for a solution.

The government commissioned the Ministry of Information to conduct a study of the Jama'at and to propose a course of action for containing its activities. A report presented to the cabinet in 1961–1962 argued that the Jama'at was essentially a seditious and invidious force with the potential to become "yet another Muslim Brotherhood,"[23] and recommended measures similar to those taken by Nasser against the brotherhood in Egypt. The cabinet did not endorse this line of action, partly because although the report focused on the Jama'at it had been vague in distinguishing between it and other Islamic parties the government was not willing to attack. The solution was also too drastic for the government to take seriously Some in Ayub Khan's coterie of advisers, such as Hakim Muhammad Sa'id (the minister of health), Allahbakhsh K. Brohi (the minister of law), and Afzal Chimah (the speaker of the legislature), who were also religiously inclined, began to defend the Jama'at.[24] Chimah advised Ayub Khan to mollify, and thereby co-opt, the party, a plan Ayub Khan favored. During a trip to Lahore in 1962 he invited Mawdudi to the governor's mansion and suggested that he leave politics to the politicians and dedicate himself to religious studies instead. For encouragement he offered Mawdudi the post of vice-chancellor of the Bhawalpur Islamic University In no mood to be appeased, Mawdudi rejected both the offer and the counsel, but he continued to keep the Jama'at's radical tendencies in check. When, soon after this meeting, he was pressed by his followers to take more militant measures, in a tone reminiscent of medieval Islamic political thinking, Mawdudi declared that he had no intention of creating "a chaotic situation in which forces inimical to the interests of Islam find an opportunity to capture power."[25]

After their meeting, Ayub Khan kept a close watch on the Jama'at. By 1963 it had become apparent that Suhrawardi's national coalition had broken down, providing the government with an opportunity to finish off the opposition by attacking, one by one, the constituent parties of the National Democratic Front. The Jama'at topped the government's list of targets, especially so after September 1963, when in a defiant mood, Mawdudi had announced that "even if Convention Muslim League [Ayub Khan's party] nominated an angel [in the future elections], the Jama'at would oppose him."[26]

When the Jama'at submitted a request to hold an open meeting in Lahore in October 1963, the government first stalled, then refused them a permit to use loudspeakers. The Jama'at petitioned the Lahore High Court for a ruling, but to no avail. The party held its meeting without loudspeakers. Halfway through the opening session, Mawdudi's speech was interrupted by hecklers; then a gun was aimed at Mawdudi, and during the ensuing commotion, a Jama'at worker was shot dead.[27] The Jama'at criticized these tactics as undemocratic, but the campaign had only begun. Habibu'llah Khan, the minister of the interior, followed the Lahore clash with a highly publicized literary campaign against the Jama'at, which within a year produced some seventy-two books and pamphlets against the party and its ideas.[28] The government now seriously contemplated liquidating the Jama'at and looked for the appropriate excuse.

Earlier in 1963, during a trip to Mecca, Mawdudi had met with Ayatollah Sayyid Ruhu'llah Khumayni.[29] Soon thereafter Khalil Ahmadu'l-Hamidi, the director of the Arabic Translation Bureau, wrote an article in Tarjumanu'l-Qur'an in which he severely criticized the Shah of Iran's regime and its secularizing policies.[30] The Iranian consulate in Karachi complained, and the government accused the Jama'at of sabotaging Pakistan's foreign policy and closed down Tarjumanu'l-Qur'an. In January 1964, backed by a lengthy charge-sheet which accused the Jama'at of anti-Pakistan activities, the government halted the party's operations. Mawdudi, Mian Tufayl, the entire shura', and forty-four other members were arrested and put in jail.[31]

The Jama'at challenged the government's action before the provincial high courts of East and West Pakistan. It won its case in the East Pakistan High Court and lost in the West Pakistan High Court. The government appealed the first ruling, and the Jama'at the second. The cases went before the Supreme Court, which declared the banning of the Jama'at to have been illegal and ordered the party restored. Mawdudi and other Jama'at leaders were freed from prison in October. The relations between the Jama'at and the government were now visibly deteriorating.

While the Jama'at's leaders were incarcerated, Pakistan was gearing up for a presidential election, scheduled for January 1, 1965 The opposition parties, including the Jama'at, had formed the Combined Opposition Parties, an electoral coalition which was led by such Muslim League leaders as Chaudhri Muhammad 'Ali and Daultana. Once again the Jama'at saw itself in an alliance of convenience with an erstwhile enemy, and this time the Jama'at's politically motivated compromises went even farther. In Mawdudi's absence, the coalition's leaders had agreed that Fatimah Jinnah—Muhammad 'Ali Jinnah's sister and a popular Muhajir leader—would be the opposition's presidential candidate.[32] Chaudhri Muhammad 'Ali was sent by the coalition to secure Mawdudi's agreement to this unpalatable choice.[33] Muhammad 'Ali met with Mawdudi in prison, and by playing on his increasing apprehension over the course the Ayub regime was taking, convinced Mawdudi of the urgency of the situation and the necessity of giving Fatimah Jinnah unwavering support. Mawdudi acceded to the coalition's demand, partly because Jinnah was popular among Muhajirs, who then constituted the Jama'at's base of support. The decision opened Mawdudi to a barrage of criticism and provided the government with the opportunity to divide the Islamic parties and embarrass and paralyze the Jama'at. The government appealed to conservative ulama for support in defeating a woman's bid to rule Pakistan and received it; in the process it weakened both the Jama'at and the Combined Opposition Parties. Numerous religious decrees were issued by the government's newfound allies among the ulama, denouncing Mawdudi and his religiously dubious justification for supporting a woman's candidacy

The controversy was then used by the government to engineer a split in the ranks of the party by instigating Kawthar Niyazi to challenge Mawdudi's authority in the party.[34] In this the government failed. Mawdudi retained control over the Jama'at and undaunted by the *fatwa* campaign pushed the Jama'at to the forefront of the opposition coalition's campaign. Mawdudi himself toured Pakistan, denouncing Ayub Khan for his dictatorship and secularism, and demanded a restoration of democracy as the first step toward the establishment of the Islamic state. In his zeal to dethrone Ayub Khan, Mawdudi increasingly appealed to democracy and less to Islam. He reorganized the Jama'at to match the government's campaign operations. Despite his efforts and the hopes and aspirations of the Combined Opposition Parties, however, Miss Jinnah failed to unseat Ayub Khan, a defeat that was particularly ominous for the Jama'at. Victory in the presidential elections gave Ayub Khan confidence and bestowed some legitimacy on his government, and with them the opportunity to hound the Jama'at more effectively. That party, which following the elections had braced itself for renewed government pressure, was spared by the reemergence of problems in Kashmir and the resumption of war with India.

The End of Ayub Khan's Rule

Throughout the presidential campaign, Ayub Khan and his foreign minister Zulfiqar 'Ali Bhutto had sought to divert attention from democracy and Islamicity by rekindling passions over Pakistan's irredentist claims to Kashmir. Having whipped up passions over Kashmir to generate demands for action, the general then led Pakistan down the path to war. Eager to consolidate his hold over the country, soon after the presidential election Ayub Khan decided to resolve the Kashmir issue once and for all and in the process redeem Pakistan's strategic and national interests in the region. The subsequent escalation of conflict in Kashmir led to a costly war between Pakistan and India in September 1965

War put a hold on the conflict between the government and the opposition parties. On September 6, 1965, Ayub Khan invited Mawdudi along with opposition leaders Chaudhri Muhammad 'Ali, Chaudhri Ghulam 'Abbas, and Nawwabzadah Nasru'llah Khan to a meeting in Islamabad, where they preached to him about his duties and obligations, none more than Mawdudi. Eager to secure their cooperation, and especially to get the Jama'at's blessing, the general chose to regard the meeting as a boost for his regime. A photograph of Ayub Khan talking with Mawdudi while surrounded by the other opposition leaders adorned the front page of Pakistani newspapers the following day

Anxious to assist the state in this moment of crisis and to erase the memory of his stand on the jihad in Kashmir in 1948, Mawdudi declared a jihad to liberate Kashmir from India.[35] He was again invited to meet with Ayub Khan in September, this time alone, where he lectured the president on the virtues of the Islamic state. Ayub Khan talked Mawdudi into publicizing his declaration of jihad, this time on Radio Pakistan,[36] a clear indication of the Jama'at's importance and the government's need to appeal to Islam to bolster its rule, the very notion which for seven years it had diligently worked to erase from the political scene.

Mawdudi was pleased with the government's overtures and basked in his newfound status as senior statesman. Ayub Khan's attentions had not only given him political prominence but had also attested to the continued salience of Islam, and hence the Jama'at, in the political life of Pakistan. After the cease-fire between India and Pakistan was declared on September 23, 1965, Mawdudi again appeared on Radio Pakistan, this time to speak on jihad in peacetime.[37] The Jama'at meanwhile focused its attention on relief work in the war-ravaged areas of Punjab[38] and pushed the government to agree to the cease-fire if it led to a plebiscite in Kashmir over the future of that territory[39]

The Jama'at did not intend to become religious window dressing for the government, nor to be restricted to religious affairs. Mawdudi used the thaw in the Jama'at's relations with the government to underscore his belief that the fate of Pakistan as a state was meshed with the Muslim reality of the country He called upon the government to move toward the greater Islamization of Pakistan to strengthen the state and to realign Pakistan's foreign policy by bringing the country closer to the rest of the Muslim world.[40] Mawdudi's argument was not welcomed by the government, which, with the war at an end, no longer felt the need to placate its opposition. Moreover, the government saw Mawdudi's proclamations as a criticism of its seven-year rule and as unsolicited interference with its management of the affairs of the country Just as in the 1950s, the political benefits of Islamic symbols for the government were matched by their costs. Islam bolstered the stability of the state and legitimated the government's rule, but it also sanctioned greater religious activism and led to the interference of Islamic parties in political matters, all of which bore consequences that the government, short of using force, was unable to control.

The Tashkent agreement of January 1966, which marked the cessation of hostilities, proved to be unpopular. It fell far short of the expectations of the Muhajir community and the Punjabis, who had borne the brunt of the Indian offensive and wanted a favorable resolution to the dispute over Kashmir. Discontent first manifested itself in student demonstrations in Lahore[41] and soon extended beyond the Tashkent agreement to encompass a whole gamut of complaints. The country became the scene of large-scale leftist agitation which manifested pent-up socioeconomic frustrations. The Jama'at was taken unawares and for the first time began to view socialism with greater alarm than the secular modernism of the regime.[42] On January 16, Mawdudi, who hoped to become the opposition leader, convened a meeting of the opposition at his house in Lahore, where he criticized the Tashkent agreement for sidestepping the future of Kashmir and for its tacit acceptance of a "no-war" arrangement with India.[43]

Despite their opposition to the government, it soon became apparent that Mawdudi and his supporters would be unable to successfully ride the tide of discontent. They, too, narrowly looked at Pakistani politics solely as a struggle for Islam and democracy and were oblivious to the significance of the socioeconomic changes that Pakistan had undergone in the meantime. Although the Jama'at's position supported the interests of the Muhajirs who were opposed to Ayub Khan, Bhutto and the Awami League, and favored Islamization, it failed to note the extent to which socioeconomic imperatives were propelling the mounting antigovernment agitations, regarding them instead as resulting from frustrations over Kashmir or Indian intrigues supported by atheists and unpatriotic Pakistanis. The realization of the depth and breadth of socioeconomic discontent which led Zulfiqar 'Ali Bhutto to leave the cabinet and form the Pakistan People's Party completely eluded the Combined Opposition Parties, still cast in the mold of the early 1960s and free of populism. In addition, emphasizing the role of Islam in Pakistan had committed the party to the unity of the state, therefore making it unsympathetic to ethnic and linguistic sentiments, which were now ineluctably predicated upon socioeconomic cleavages. The Awami League, and especially its left wing, led by Mawlana 'Abdu'l-Hamid Khan Bhashani, was a bulwark of leftist agitation. Mawdudi was opposed to the left. That

Shaikh Mujibu'l-Rahman, the leader of the Awami League, and Bhashani were behind the agitations was enough to prompt him to reaction. In the February gathering of the opposition parties, Mawdudi criticized the left and engaged Mujib in a bitter altercation over the Awami League's controversial six-point plan for provincial autonomy [44] This altercation also marked a major turning point in the Jama'at's ideological unfolding. Mawdudi's discourse ceased to be preoccupied with the West, but became anchored in defense of Islam against socialism and communism. Many projects were abandoned to focus the party's energies on preparing literature which could stem the rising tide of socialism in Pakistan.[45]

The Awami League's politics were also interfering with the Jama'at's designs. Having gained prominence in the Combined Opposition Parties, the Jama'at now had a vested interest in an orderly transfer of power from Ayub Khan to the opposition coalition, which Mawdudi hoped to lead. Opposition to the left combined with political self-interest blinded the Jama'at to the grievances that underlay leftist agitation. Mawdudi kept the Jama'at in the coalition and continued to demand Islam and democracy, while fighting to cleanse Pakistani politics of the menace of the left. The Jama'at was particularly disturbed by the growing popularity of Maoism in Punjab, the fruit of China's assistance to Pakistan during the war, as well as by Bhutto's populism and "Islamic socialism."

Confrontations were still largely restricted to polemical exchanges, however. In 1967, Muhammad Safdar Mir published a series of articles in the *Pakistan Times* criticizing Mawdudi for supporting capitalism and feudalism.[46] The articles soon generated a debate between the Jama'at and the left, serving as a prelude to the more open hostilities that were soon to break out in Punjab, Sind, and East Pakistan.

In the meantime, relations between the government and the Jama'at also continued to strain. Ayub Khan, as perturbed as he was with leftist agitations, proved to be equally impatient with the opposition coalition's campaign, and especially with the Jama'at's activities. The main issue was, once again, the government's intrusions into the jealously guarded domain of the ulama and the Islamic groups. In May 1966, Fazlur Rahman, director of Islamic Research Institute, declared that religious tax (*zakat*) rates should be increased to add to the state's financial resources, and usury (*riba'*) should not be equated with interest but with the real rate of interest only, permitting the normal functioning of banks. The Jama'at severely criticized the government's "misguided tampering with Islam."[47] Fazlur Rahman reciprocated by advising Ayub Khan that Mawdudi's religiously controversial book, *Khilafat'u Mulukiyat* (Caliphate and Monarchy), published in June 1966, was a direct attack on his government.[48] The dispute culminated in another showdown between the government and the

Jama'at in January 1967, when Mawdudi and a number of ulama rejected the "scientifically" determined observation of the moon by the government—which is traditionally observed by the ulama to mark the end of the holy month of Ramazan.[49] The religious divines had again rebelled against the government's attempt to interfere in their affairs and were once more jailed. Mawdudi remained in prison from January 29 until March 15, 1967, when the High Court of West Pakistan rejected the legality of the invocation of the Defense of Pakistan Rules under the provisions of which he had been jailed. The controversy, however, came to an end only when Ayub Khan agreed to dismiss Fazlur Rahman in September 1968.[50]

The Jama'at attempted to use the entire episode to reinvigorate its campaign for an Islamic constitution, but to no avail. For while the Jama'at had been deadlocked with the government over Fazlur Rahman, the Awami League had unabashedly escalated its agitations, further radicalizing Pakistani politics. Mawdudi had sought to diffuse the situation to the Jama'at's advantage by challenging Bhashani and Mujib in his speeches, demanding changes in the constitution of 1962, restoration of democracy, and redress for the political grievances of the East Pakistanis. The focus of the Jama'at's activism, however, had been shifting to street clashes with the Awami League in East Pakistan and with leftist groups in West Pakistan.

The main force behind this campaign was the Islami Jami'at-i Tulabah, which since 1962 had successfully organized students to protest a number of antigovernment causes, usually unpopular educational reforms.[51] The government, already apprehensive about the Jama'at's activities, had tried to halt student unrest by restricting the IJT and arresting and incarcerating numerous IJT leaders. This served only to politicize and radicalize the student organization still further.

Given the Jama'at's antagonism to the left and that the party had arrogated the role of defender of Pakistan's territorial unity, the student organization could not remain immune to provocations from the left, especially in East Pakistan. In the 1962–1967 period, the IJT developed into an antileft force, with the tacit encouragement of the government. The government actively encouraged the IJT in its clashes with the leftist National Student Federation in East Pakistan and with labor union activists in West Pakistan.[52] Its success in attracting new recruits from among the ranks of religiously conscious students in Punjab, and anti-Bengali Muhajirs in Karachi and Dhaka, further encouraged its antileft activities and showdowns with the left and Bengali nationalists. Opposition to the Tashkent agreement, however, continued to give the IJT its much needed antigovernment image, which helped consolidate the organization's base of support on campuses. This two-tiered policy of simultaneous opposition to the left and to the government gradually disappeared as the student organization sublimated its opposition to Ayub Khan in favor of a crusade against the left, especially in East Pakistan. From 1965 onward, the IJT became increasingly embroiled in confrontations with Bengali nationalist and leftist forces in East Pakistan, first at Dhaka University, and later in pitched battles in the streets.

In May 1967 the Combined Opposition Parties, including the Awami League, formed a new coalition, the Pakistan Democratic Movement. In its first resolution, the new coalition demanded the reinstatement of the 1956 constitution, the restoration of democracy in Pakistan, the resolution of the Kashmir crisis, the adoption of a nonaligned foreign policy, and greater regional autonomy for East Pakistan. Mawdudi interpreted the resolution as a new call for an Islamic constitution and in his subsequent elaboration of the resolution throughout 1967 and 1968 launched into tirades against the Awami League's six-point plan and Mawlana Bhashani's homegrown version of Maoism. Mawdudi's rhetoric combined with the IJT's clashes with the Awami League in East Pakistan greatly weakened the Pakistan Democratic Movement, and the alliance finally collapsed when, implicated in an antigovernment conspiracy case, the Awami League withdrew from its fold. The movement was replaced by a new multiparty arrangement called the Democratic Action Committee.

The new coalition demanded the lifting of the state of emergency and the rescinding of the criminal law amendment which had been invoked to arrest Mujib for participation in the same conspiracy These were both tools the government was using to deal with the worsening political situation and which the Jama'at and the Awami League both wanted eliminated so they could pursue their political objectives more freely Faced with Mujib's rising popularity following his arrest, the government responded by lifting the emergency and abrogating the amendment. It was a Pyrrhic victory for the opposition. To begin with, it did away with the demands that the Jama'at and the Awami League had shared and which had fostered a working arrangement between them. Instead, tensions between them escalated in East Pakistan following the government's conciliatory overtures. It also removed the rationale for democratic demands from the political agenda and focused attention instead on provincial demands in East Pakistan and populist demands in West Pakistan. Consequently, Mawdudi's efforts to revive interest in the Islamic constitution came to naught. The Jama'at's political agenda became completely divorced from the critical political issues in the country

In August 1968 Mawdudi was taken ill and was compelled to leave Pakistan for medical treatment in England. During the months he was gone the Jama'at's affairs were overseen by Mian Tufayl. Mawdudi's absence reduced both the Jama'at's prominence in the Democratic Action Committee and reduced the party's flexibility Mian Tufayl did not provide new strategies for confronting either the more rambunctious Awami League or the new force in Pakistani politics, the People's Party and was unable to control the IJT, which soon became a force unto itself, drawing the Jama'at into the quagmire of East Pakistani politics.

Mawdudi returned before the Round Table Conference between Ayub Khan and the Democratic Action Committee, which convened in March 1969 to reform the constitution of 1962 with a view to accommodating the Awami League's demands for autonomy No mention was made of the socioeconomic grievances which Mujib and Bhutto were manipulating so successfully Mawdudi's address to the conference was totally removed from the realities of Pakistani politics. He placed the entire blame for the crisis on the government's intransigence over the demand for Islamization, which, he argued, was the only policy that could keep Pakistan united.[53] The conference not only left the committee more vulnerable than ever to the populist challenges of Mujib and Bhutto but also made clear the chasm that separated Jama'at's political outlook from that of the rest of Pakistan. The committee and the Jama'at were only shadows of the Combined Opposition Parties in 1965 The real force in the polity was now the Awami League and the People's Party

This was not lost on the Jama'at. Soon after the conference, the party stopped attacking the government and directed its invective more squarely against Bhutto, Bhashani, and Mujib, accusing them of encouraging violence and acting undemocratically and in violation of Islamic dicta. Mawdudi still resisted populism, however, and regarded with contempt Islamic thinkers such as Bhashani and Ghulam Ahmad Parwez who mixed Islam with leftist ideas, a course of action which distinguished the Jama'at from Shi'i revolutionaries in Iran.

On March 25, 1969, General Ayub Khan resigned. Mawdudi declared the move a victory for the Round Table Conference that would now allow the establishment of the Islamic order which he believed democracy would bring. In a display of political naïveté, he exhorted Bhutto and Mujib to demobilize their forces. To his dismay, however, he soon learned that democracy and Islam were for the moment irrelevant. With no political platform to lure the masses, the Jama'at had to accept the martial rule of General Muhammad Yahya Khan and to follow the IJT into the streets against the Awami League and the People's Party

The Regime of Yahya Khan, 1969–1971

After Ayub Khan's resignation, power was not transferred to the Democratic Action Committee, who had negotiated with the government in the Round Table Conference, but to a military government. The Jama'at's first reaction was to negotiate with the government rather than to appeal to the masses, who were clamoring for economic justice and provincial autonomy When Yahya Khan assumed power, the Jama'at quickly renewed its demands for the restoration of democracy and Islamization and for the reinstatement of the constitution of 1956 as the only satisfactory framework for putting the state on the road to Islam and democracy [54] Although Yahya Khan, a Shi'i with a reputation for heavy drinking, was by no means a favorite of the Jama'at, the party once again acceded to an alliance of convenience. Both were opposed to the left and looked upon Bengali nationalism with suspicion. With no political manifesto to recapture popular support, the Jama'at was compelled to cast its lot with the central government, hoping that the system could be democratized after the left had been routed. Without the left to turn to, the people would cast their vote for the Jama'at in the elections. The party assumed that the investiture of Yahya Khan meant the army was going to crush both the Awami League and the People's Party, because Yahya Khan had often declared that no party opposed to the "ideology of Pakistan"—by which the Jama'at understood he meant Islam— would be acceptable to his government. The Jama'at could only rejoice at the prospect and lend support to the regime and its promise of a democracy cleansed of the left.

These impressions were strengthened in personal contacts between the Jama'at's leaders and members of Yahya Khan's circle of advisers, including Nawwabzadah Shair 'Ali Khan, the minister of information, who was the main architect of the new regime's political strategy,[55] through whom they lobbied to become the party that would inherit the reins of power. On March 23, 1969, Mawdudi and Mian Tufayl met with Yahya Khan in Lahore; they came back convinced that Yahya Khan was going to turn Pakistan over to them after the left and the Bengali nationalists had been dealt with. Mian Tufayl lauded Yahya Khan as a "champion of Islam" and declared that the basis for the general's future constitution—the Legal Framework Order—not yet unveiled, would be "Islamic."[56] Political exigency had led Islamic constitutionalism into an unholy alliance with the very regime it had fought against. Democracy, the *condicio sine qua non* of Islamization, for the duration of the Yahya Khan regime was replaced by martial rule. The Jama'at's shift, however, was not doctrinal; martial rule was merely to be the midwife of an "Islamic democracy " This new strategy meant that all efforts to formulate a new political platform in place of Islamic constitutionalism were shelved, and the party's energies became concentrated on combating the Awami League and the People's Party Fighting communism became a substitute for a sound and efficacious political platform, as the Jama'at tried to alter the political climate rather than adapt to it.

In West Pakistan, Mawdudi launched a crusade against Bhutto and his economic policies, arguing that only Islam would remedy the socioeconomic grievances that Bhutto's "Islamic socialism" falsely claimed to be able to solve. the Jama'at's attacks prompted Safdar Mir to resume his criticisms of Mawdudi and the Jama'at in *Nusrat*, a pro–People's Party monthly published in Lahore, but

Bhutto, from his prison cell, ordered the articles stopped. Although the leftists in the People's Party regarded the Jama'at as the enemy, Bhutto hoped to mollify the party,[57] hopes that were soon dashed when violence broke out in Lahore, Multan, and Karachi.

In East Pakistan the Jama'at launched a propaganda campaign to convince the Bengalis that their loyalties lay first with Islam and Pakistan, not with their ethnic, linguistic, cultural, and provincial roots. In the violent clashes with the Awami League that followed, an IJT worker was killed on the campus of Dhaka University, giving the party its first martyr in the battle against the left.[58] Mawdudi demanded that the IJT cleanse Pakistani universities of the left. Yahya Khan's offer to hold elections in December 1970 only added fervor to the Jama'at's campaign to bring the party closer to Yahya Khan's regime,[59] although it also continued to demand the reinstatement of the 1956 constitution to retain a semblance of an oppositional role vis-à-vis the government.

In December 1969 the Jama'at published its election manifesto, with minor variations a reiteration of its Islamic constitutionalist platform and a testimony to the party's obliviousness to sociopolitical issues. Forty years of drawing-room politics had left them without the means properly to interpret politics, much less turn popular demands into a plan of action. Its slow development into a party had denied it any mechanism for formulating policy positions the electorate could relate to. Pakistan's economy had undergone a great many changes during the Ayub Khan era. The country had gained an industrial infrastructure and had made significant strides in developing its economy This development had been accomplished at great social and political costs, however.[60] Rapid industrialization and growth through the "functional utility of greed" openly advocated by the regime and its host of foreign advisers had arrived hand in hand with a notable increase in poverty in both urban and rural areas, as well as a widening of the gap between rich and poor, giving rise to greater class consciousness.[61] Between 1963 and 1967, when opposition to Ayub Khan gained momentum, the percentage of the poor—those whose incomes were below Rs. 300 per month— had somewhat declined in both the rural and the urban areas, from 60.5 percent to 59.7 percent and from 54.8 percent to 25 percent, respectively,[62] but the disparity in the distribution of wealth between the provinces and between the propertied classes and the masses had increased.[63] According to Mahbub ul-Haq, "By 1968 22 families controlled 2/3 of Pakistan's industrial assets; 80% of banking; 70% of insurance."[64] Economic growth had favored the industrial sector at the cost of the traditional economy, the cities at the cost of the hinterland, and Punjab and West Pakistan at the cost of East Pakistan. The business elite had amassed great fortunes, as had senior civil servants and high-ranking members of the armed forces, while the middle class and the poor had lost ground. Corruption, which by 1967 had infested the country, had only further discredited the government's promise of economic progress in the eyes of those who had not shared in its fruits. Agricultural policy had caused large-scale migration to the cities, while industrialization had generated grievances among the labor force, whose numbers had risen threefold in the 1960s. These statistics and their reflection in the political mood of the country explain, in good measure, the popularity of Mujib's six-point program and Bhutto's "clothing, bread, and shelter" (kapra, roti, awr makan) motto.

The Jama'at's manifesto made only token references to economic grievances; they were by and large left to the Islamic state to solve. It attacked feudalism and capitalism, promised to limit land ownership to two hundred acres, and proposed a minimum wage of Rs. 150–Rs. 200 and better working conditions, but these promises were divorced from any concerted political attack on the ruling classes and buried among demands for Islamization, greater democratization, and opposition to the idea of "sons of the soil," a reference to Bengali and Sindhi nationalist sentiments. This treatment of socioeconomic issues in the manifesto therefore fell far short of attracting support from the Pakistani electorate.

The manifesto bore the unmistakable imprint of Mawdudi's thinking. It posed three questions, the answers to which Mawdudi assumed were self-evident to Pakistanis, since he was convinced that they were more concerned with Islam and patriotism than socioeconomic issues. The questions were (1) Should Pakistan retain its Islamic foundations?[65] (2) Should Pakistan remain united? and (3) Is not the Jama'at the only party running in the elections which is capable of maintaining the primacy of Islam while fostering national unity? Mawdudi believed that once the Pakistani electorate had confronted these questions squarely, they would vote for Islam, national unity, and the Jama'at. His campaign was therefore designed to place these three questions at the center of the national political debate.

That the strategy would not work became apparent first in East Pakistan. The party's campaign there came to an abrupt end when Mawdudi was prevented by Awami League supporters from reaching a Jama'at rally in Dhaka. Clashes followed which led to the death of three Jama'at workers.[66] After that there were bloody confrontations between Jama'at workers and Mawlana Bhashani's supporters in East Pakistan and Punjab. In West Pakistan the Jama'at had more room to maneuver. There it launched a campaign against the People's Party's platform, the watershed of which was the Glory of Islam Day (Yawm-i Shawkat-i Islam), on May 30, 1970. The Jama'at organized rallies, marches, speeches, and political meetings across West Pakistan to bring Islam back into the center stage of Pakistani politics.[67] Convinced the celebration was a great success and had popularized the party's election manifesto,[68] the Jama'at decided to field 151 candidates for National Assembly seats, challenging nearly every seat the People's Party was contesting.

In fact, however, the Glory of Islam celebrations had not improved the Jama'at's support and had done nothing to derail the electoral campaigns of either the People's Party or the Awami League. They had produced one unexpected side effect, however. They caused a serious rupture in the religious alliance, which since 1958 the Jama'at had led by awakening the heretofore dormant Jami'at-ı Ulama-ı Islam and Jami'at-ı Ulama-ı Pakistan and bringing them into the political arena. The Jama'at believes that this development resulted from the machinations of the People's Party, KGB, or the CIA.[69] The two parties were apparently convinced by the Glory of Islam celebration that a religious platform was politically viable. The ulama, since 1947 willing to cooperate with the Jama'at in politics, were not prepared to submit to Mawdudi in religious matters. As the anti-Mawdudi *fatwa* campaign of 1951 and the clamor against Mawdudi's book *Khilafat'u Mulukıyat* in 1965–1966 indicate, they were not pleased with Mawdudi's religious views. They decided that the Glory of Islam celebration represented a concerted effort by Mawdudi to monopolize religious thought and become the cynosure of the religious establishment. To the ulama this was a danger much greater than any posed to Islam by the Awami League or the People's Party The Jami'at-ı Ulama-ı Islam's Mawlanas Mufti Mahmud and Hazarwı thereafter criticized the celebration, and the Jami'at-ı Ulama-ı Pakistan proceeded to field forty-two candidates for National Assembly seats in competition with Jama'at's candidates. These moves divided the religious and anti–People's Party vote and took seats away from the Jama'at. This division accounts in part for the success of the People's Party and the Jama'at's defeat. In eighty-two electoral constituencies in Punjab, where the People's Party was strongest, 260 candidates from right-of-center parties and another 114 independent rightist candidates divided the vote. Four parties had the demand for an Islamic constitution on their election manifestos, and another four favored it.[70]

The Elections of 1970 and Their Aftermath

Between May and December 1970 the Jama'at campaigned frantically Competition with the Awami League and clashes with Bhashani's supporters escalated tensions in East Pakistan and Punjab, and clashes with the People's Party tied down the Jama'at in West Pakistan. These conflicts, combined with the challenge from the party's religious flank, taxed the Jama'at's energies. Despite untiring efforts, it won only four of the 151 National Assembly seats which it contested, all in West Pakistan, and only four of the 331 provincial assembly seats it had aimed for, one in each province except Baluchistan (see tables 8–11). It trailed far behind the Awami League and the People's Party in the final tally of seats and to its dismay and embarrassment finished behind the Jami'at-ı Ulama-ı Islam and Jami'at-ı Ulama-ı Pakistan. The Jami'at-ı Ulama-ı Islam even gained enough seats to serve as a partner to the National Awami party (National People's Party)

Table 8. Votes Cast for the Islamic Parties in the 1970 National
Assembly Elections

	East Pakistan	Punjab	Sind	NWFP	Baluchistan	Total
Jama'at-i Islami	1,044,137	515,564	321,471	103,958	4,331	1,989,461
	(6.07%)	(4.74%)	(10.31%)	(7.22%)	(1.16%)	(6.03%)
Jami'at-i Ulama-i	158,058	564,601	151,284	366,477	74,651	1,315,071
Islam, West	(0.92%)	(5.19%)	(4.85%)	(25.45%)	(20%)	(3.98%)
Pakistan						
Jami'at-i Ulama-i	485,774	28,246	0	7,744	0	521,764
Islam / Jami'at-i	(2.83%)	(0.26%)		(0.54%)		(1.58%)
Ahl-i Hadith						
Jami'at-i Ulama-i	0	1,083,196	216,418	244	0	1,299,858
Pakistan		(9.96%)	(6.94%)	(0.02%)		(3.94%)

Source: Report on the General Elections, Pakistan 1970–71 (Islamabad, n.d.) 2:68–69.

Table 9 National Assembly Seats Contested and Won by the Islamic
Parties in the 1970 Elections

	East Pakistan	Punjab	Sind	NWFP	Baluchistan	Total
Jama'at-i Islami						
Seats contested	71	44	19	15	2	151
Seats won	0	1	2	1	0	4
Jami'at-i Ulama-i Islam,						
West Pakistan						
Seats contested	15	46	21	19	4	105
Seats won	0	0	0	6	1	7
Jami'at-i Ulama-i Islam/						
Jami'at-i Ahl-i Hadith						
Seats contested	49	3	0	2	0	54
Seats won	0	0	0	0	0	0
Jami'at-i Ulama-i Pakistan						
Seats contested	0	41	8	1	0	50
Seats won	0	4	3	0	0	7
Total seats contested	781	460	170	143	25	1579
Total seats won	162	82	27	25	4	300

Source: Report on the General Elections, Pakistan 1970–71 (Islamabad, n.d.) 2:70–99, 100–21.

Table 10. Votes Cast for the Islamic Parties in the 1970 Provincial Assembly Elections

	East Pakistan	Punjab	Sind	NWFP	Baluchistan	Total
Jama'at-i Islami	678,159	161,62	89,245	37,387	8,609	975,027
	(4.5%)	(1.61%)	(2.93%)	(2.58%)	(2.07%)	(3.25%)
Jami'at-i Ulama-i Islam, West Pakistan	76,735	313,684	37 418	201,030	45,609	674,416
	(0.51%)	(3.13%)	(1.23%)	(13.89%)	(10.96%)	(2.25%)
Jami'at-i Ulama-i Islam/ Jami'at-i Ahl-i Hadith	223,634	2,262	14,702	691	0	241,289
	(1.48%)	(0.02%)	(0.48%)	(0.05%)		(0.8%)
Jami'at-i Ulama-i Pakistan	0	448,008	184,151	0	0	632,159
		(4.47%)	(6.06%)			(2.11%)

Source: Report on the General Elections, Pakistan 1970–71 (Islamabad, n.d.) 2:268–69.

Table 11. Provincial Assembly Seats Contested and Won by the Islamic Parties in the 1970 Elections

	East Pakistan	Punjab	Sind	NWFP	Baluchistan	Total
Jama'at-i Islami						
Seats contested	174	80	37	28	12	331
Seats won	1	1	1	1	0	4
Jami'at-i Ulama-i Islam, West Pakistan						
Seats contested	23	72	23	35	14	167
Seats won	0	2	0	4	3	9
Jami'at-i Ulama-i Islam/ Jami'at-i Ahl-i Hadith						
Seats contested	63	4	5	2	0	74
Seats won	1	0	0	0	0	1
Jami'at-i Ulama-i Pakistan						
Seats contested	0	73	15	0	0	88
Seats won	0	4	7	0	0	11
Total seats contested	1,850	1,323	579	319	164	4,235
Total seats won	300	180	60	40	20	600

Source: Report on the General Elections, Pakistan 1970–71 (Islamabad, n.d.) 2:270–355.

in forming provincial governments in Baluchistan and North-West Frontier Province. To the Jama'at's surprise the two ulama parties did better than the Jama'at, although they had contested fewer seats and received a lower percentage of votes cast. In elections to the National Assembly, the Jama'at's share of the total vote was at 6.03 percent, as opposed to the Jami'at-i Ulama-i Islam's 3.98 percent and the Jami'at-i Ulama-i Pakistan's 3.94 percent. Where the Jama'at had won only four seats (and none in East Pakistan, where its share of the total votes cast was 6.07 percent) the ulama parties had won seven seats each. In provincial elections the Jama'at received 3.25 percent of the votes cast, the Jami'at-i Ulama-i Islam 2.25 percent, and the Jami'at-i Ulama-i Pakistan 2.11 percent. In contrast with the Jama'at's four provincial seats, the Jami'at-i Ulama-i Islam had won nine and the Jami'at-i Ulama-i Pakistan eleven. The Jama'at's 6.03 percent of the votes cast in National Assembly elections had yielded only 1.3 percent of the seats, and its 3.25 percent share of the vote in provincial elections a mere 0.67 percent of the seats. The results turned the Jama'at into an ardent advocate of proportional representation for Pakistan. Finally, partly because they had competed with one another, the Islamic parties taken together did poorly in both parts of Pakistan. This limited the political power of Islam and further constricted the Jama'at.

The election results dealt a severe blow to the morale of Jama'at members. Mawdudi's leadership was questioned, as was the party's time-honored reliance on Islamic symbols and the putative Islamic loyalties of Pakistanis. The election results, moreover, effectively eliminated the Jama'at as a power broker. The Jama'at quickly regrouped, however, this time to defend Pakistan against the polarization of the country between the Awami League and the People's Party The Jama'at leaders encouraged Yahya Khan not to discriminate against the Awami League and to allow Mujib to form a government.[71] When Yahya Khan refused, the party broke with him, accusing him of unfair partiality toward the People's Party, which the Jama'at was convinced would have disastrous consequences for Pakistan. Meanwhile, the Jama'at excoriated the People's Party for lobbying with the generals to deny the Awami League the fruit of its victory

The Jama'at's argument did not endear it to the Awami League; Mawdudi's attacks on Bhashani and Mujib, the former for his religious views and the latter for his rapacious political ambition, had continued with his criticisms of Yahya Khan and Bhutto. Its pro-Pakistan and anti–Awami League propaganda had increased the violence between IJT supporters and Bengali nationalists following the elections. As the situation in East Pakistan deteriorated throughout 1971, the Jama'at members became convinced of a Communist-Hindu plot to dismember Pakistan. Driven by its dedication to Pakistan's unity and unable to counter the challenge of the Awami League, the Jama'at abandoned its role as intermediary and formed an unholy alliance with the Pakistan army, which had been sent to Dhaka to crush the Bengali nationalists.

After a meeting with General Tikka Khan, the head of the army in East Pakistan, in April 1971, Ghulam A'zam, the amir of East Pakistan, gave full support to the army's actions against "enemies of Islam." Meanwhile, a group of Jama'at members went to Europe to explain Pakistan's cause and defend what the army was doing in East Pakistan; another group was sent to the Arab world, where the Jama'at drew upon its considerable influence to gain support.[72] In September 1971 the alliance between the Jama'at and the army was made official when four members of the Jama'at-i Islami of East Pakistan joined the military government of the province.[73] Both sides saw gains to be made from their alliance. The army would receive religious sanction for its increasingly brutal campaign, and the Jama'at would gain prominence. Its position was, in good measure, the result of decisions made by the Jama'at-i Islami of East Pakistan, then led by Ghulam A'zam and Khurram Jah Murad. This branch of the Jama'at, faced with annihilation, was thoroughly radicalized, and acted with increasing independence in doing the bidding of the military regime in Dhaka. The Lahore secretariat often merely approved the lead taken by the Jama'at and the IJT in Dhaka. Nowhere was this development more evident than in the IJT's contribution to the ill-fated al-Badr and al-Shams counterinsurgency operations.

In the civil war, two thousand Jama'at and IJT members, workers, and sympathizers were killed and upward of twelve thousand held in prison camps.[74] The East Pakistan war also had its bright side insofar as the nationalist credentials of the party, which had repeatedly been accused of being "anti-Pakistan," could no longer be questioned. As one Jama'at leader put it, "While the Muslim League youth took refuge in their opulent homes, it was the Jami'at [IJT] which gave its blood to save Pakistan."[75] The party, which had been routed at the polls only a year earlier, now found a new measure of confidence that facilitated its return to the political arena.

8 The Bhutto Years, 1971–1977

The rise of Zulfiqar 'Ali Bhutto and the Pakistan People's Party to power between 1969 and 1971 promised to bring fundamental changes to the country, but they did not produce what Pakistan had hoped for. The People's Party never managed to institutionalize the charismatic appeal of its leader, and his regime fell back into the mold of the country's time-honored patrimonial politics. The advent of a populist government in Pakistan shaped the Jama'at's outlook on politics as well as the pace of its organizational change, but it was still unable to take advantage of the opportunities presented by Bhutto's assault against the traditional power structure (1971–1973) and later the decline of his power (1973–1977).

The People's Party rose to power as the movement which took most of the credit for ousting both Ayub Khan and Yahya Khan. It took over the reigns of power after the dismemberment of Pakistan, when Dhaka had fallen to Indian troops. This, combined with the impact of the new regime's populist political and economic agenda, led to greater participation by various social strata in the political process, which the government was able neither to harness nor suppress. The problems of the new regime were further aggravated by Bhutto's autocratic style and his unwillingness to use the army's moment of weakness to strengthen both his party and civilian rule. As a result, the People's Party bogged down in political disputes and lost sight of its agenda.

No sooner had Bhutto assumed power than the anti–People's Party constituency became apparent. Between 1971 and 1977 it grew and became more powerful. As part of this opposition the Jama'at channeled its efforts into a successful campaign of political agitation that eventually brought down the government.

The failure of Ayub Khan's regime had unleashed the Islamic opposition in the political arena. The Bhutto government initially tried to control the activities of the Islamic parties by following the example of its predecessors, but given the gradual rise in the popularity of Islam, the weakening of the state following the civil war, and the mistakes made by the ruling party, it failed and the Islamic parties continued to press the state for greater representation. This led to a further decline in the government's authority as the Islamic parties grew stronger. By the end of the Bhutto era, they were in a position to make a direct bid for controlling the state.

The inability of Islam to keep the two halves of the country united had not diminished the appeal of religion either to politicians or the people. Oddly enough it even increased it. The precariousness of Pakistan's unity led Pakistanis to reaffirm their Islamic roots. Even the avowedly secularist and left-of-center People's Party government did not remain immune and talked of "re-Islamizing" the country The People's Party government, much as Ayub Khan's regime, sought to both manipulate Islam and marginalize its principal spokesmen, but did not succeed. Efforts to woo the religious vote provided the government with a mechanism for support, but also made it susceptible to criticism from religious quarters. By sanctioning the sacralization of politics, the People's Party created the kind of political climate in which parties such as the Jama'at had a clear advantage. Although not the main force behind the return of Islam, the Jama'at proved to be its main beneficiary For, given the prevailing climate, its views on an array of national issues were for once in tune with those of a larger number of Pakistanis. Its growing influence in the army, the most secular and anglicized of state institutions, was indicative of this trend.

Since the beginning of the East Pakistan crisis, Mawdudi had claimed that the problem before the country was the product of lackluster adherence to Islam. He in fact blamed the loss of East Pakistan on Yahya Khan's womanizing and drinking.[1] The IJT echoed Mawdudi's sentiments: its answer to "What broke up the country?" was "wine" (*sharab*). Some in the army apparently agreed. In 1972–1973, the military high command uncovered a conspiracy, later dubbed the Attock conspiracy, hatched by a group junior officers, led by Brigadier F. B. 'Ali, most of them veterans of the civil war of 1971.[2] The officers were charged with sedition and brought to trial. S. M. Zafar, who defended the officers in court, recollects that they believed East Pakistan had been lost because of the government's "un-Islamic" ways and Yahya Khan's drinking in particular.[3] This concern for Islamicity in the army was the result of the officer corps having opened its ranks to cadets from the lower-middle classes after 1965, which made it markedly more subject to the influence of traditional Islamic values.[4] The Attock conspiracy certainly shows that the armed forces—dominated by Punjabi and Pathan officers, and the staunch defender of the unity of Pakistan and the integrity of the state—were no longer a bastion of secularism and were gradually turning to religion.

This trend was reinforced in the subsequent years thanks in part to Bhutto's choosing General Muhammad Zia ul-Haq as the army's chief of staff. Zia had long been sympathetic to the Jama'at. He had been greatly impressed with Mawdudi's works, and following his investiture as chief of staff, used the powers vested in his office to distribute the party's literature among his soldiers and officers. When in July 1976 Zia gave copies of Mawdudi's *Tafhimu'l-Qur'an* (Understanding the Qur'an) as "prizes" to soldiers who had won a debate arranged by the Army Education School, and subsequently proposed to include the book in the examination "for promotion of Captains and Majors," Bhutto was greatly dismayed.[5] Finally, on November 24, 1976, Bhutto summoned the general before the cabinet to explain his actions.[6] Later during his trial before the supreme court, Bhutto was to remark, "I appointed a Chief of Staff belonging to the Jamaat-i-Islami and the result is before all of us."[7] His statement underscores the Jama'at's increasing influence in the armed forces and the party's role in bringing down his regime.

The revival of the Islamic dimension in Pakistani politics extended beyond the army, however. The People's Party's credo from its inception had been "Islamic Socialism"; Bhutto had said "Islam is our faith, democracy is our polity, socialism is our economy," but under the pressures of Islamization, as he lost his grip over the hearts and minds of the people and with growing ties with the Persian Gulf states, he had to forego the second two in favor of the first.[8] The constitution of 1973, promulgated under the aegis of the People's Party, reinstated "Islamic" as part of the official name of the state. But because Bhutto had been a protégé of General Mirza, and one of the most antireligious of Ayub Khan's lieutenants, he was still regarded as a rabid secularist, and his gestures toward Islam were not thought to be genuine by those he sought to appease.[9] For instance, the People's Party government named Kawthar Niyazi, who had gained prominence while a member of the Jama'at, as its minister for religious affairs, a concession to the Islamic parties. Niyazi, however, was not held in high esteem either by the ulama or by the Jama'at, since he had left the party in 1964, and the appointment was not popular with either of them.

The ulama, the Jama'at, and religiously conscious Pakistanis were also greatly disturbed with the open flouting of religious values and mores by the prime minister and his coterie of friends and associates which belied their claim to promote Islam. This image of moral corruption was compounded by the widely held belief in religious circles that Bhutto enjoyed the financial and organizational backing of Pakistan's Ahmadi community, rumors of which had been circulating since 1969 The government could do little to stop these charges or to allay the suspicions of the Islamic parties.[10] By 1974 the Ahmadi connection had become sufficiently damaging to the government to compel Bhutto to declare the Ahmadis to be a non-Muslim minority, but despite this concession the

People's Party government never managed to develop a following among the religiously inclined Pakistanis. It was caught in a situation of sacralizing the national political discourse, while it was unable effectively to appeal to Islam. In fact, given Bhutto's policies and style, the re-Islamization of national politics would not favor him or his party The un-Islamic ways of the People's Party's leaders never ceased to be a political issue. When, in 1976, the Jama'at demanded the enforcement of the shari'ah in public affairs it unexpectedly attracted some fifteen thousand new affiliates to its ranks.[11]

The confrontations between the People's Party government and the Islamic parties soon extended beyond purely religious issues to other political and socioeconomic concerns, attracting others to the opposition. The result was the Nizam-i Mustafa, the opposition coalition that eventually toppled Bhutto's government.

The People's Party's weakness was rooted in the very program of action which had brought it to office. Populism defined both the People's Party's base of support and that of its opposition. Throughout the 1970s the People's Party ignored its supporters in favor of placating its opponents, substituting the party's program for a balancing act between various Pakistani interest groups. Bhutto was compelled to eviscerate his agenda of its substantive content, purge his party of its left-of-center workers, and push the People's Party in the direction of patrimonial politics. By the mid-1970s the People's Party—populist by claim and leaning to the right in practice—was paralyzed. Discrepancies between ideals and reality spelled disaster for the party The left wing and its network in the labor unions, who had played a pivotal role in bringing Bhutto to power, were purged in favor of the landed and industrial elite who had begun to join the ranks of the People's Party from 1973 onward, in reaction to the growing strength of the Islamic parties. Rather than developing a reliable party machine, Bhutto placed his faith in the army, civil service, and the newly found Federal Security Forces. The government's suppression of labor unrest in Karachi in 1973 alienated labor from the government, broke the monopoly of the left over its politics, and opened the workers up to the Jama'at's influence.

The People's Party did implement new policies in the economy, but it failed to manage the changes it had initiated. As a result, the very policies which were designed to respond to the demands of the masses and thereby consolidate the People's Party's support became its undoing. Failing to harness the popular enthusiasm it had generated, the People's Party's rhetoric and socioeconomic policies instead coalesced the opposition.

The nationalization of industries and the use of the public sector to foster greater economic equity, which followed the People's Party's rise to power, had benefited the bureaucracy and the state bourgeoisie, whose powers had been increased to allow them to oversee the new state-run industries, more than it had the labor force. With the influx of its erstwhile enemies—landed gentry and business leaders—into the ranks of the People's Party following its ascension to power, Bhutto's populist agenda was turned on its head. The party was transformed into a patronage machine to benefit those with political clout rather than the poor. Bhutto's appeal to Islamic symbols and to the support of the traditional elite and interest groups and his strong-arm tactics in dealing with the left disheartened loyal party workers and eroded the People's Party's base of support among the modern social sector, whose expectations had remained unfulfilled. As a result, in 1977, although labor union members and the urban, educated middle class, both of which were by this time far more numerous than in 1969, did not participate in the agitations that brought the Bhutto government down, more significantly, they also did little to save it. By abandoning ideological politics, the People's Party government handed it over to the opposition, which mobilized Islam to wage all-out war against the government.

The opposition also found ample ammunition in People's Party nationalization and land-reform measures. The propertied elite and the Islamic parties—the first motivated by its economic and business interests and the second by its belief in the sanctity of property—joined forces to denounce the government's economic policies. Their opposition manifested itself in a host of anti–People's Party issues. The government's efforts at land reform in 1972, and the nationalization of agribusinesses—cotton-ginning and rice-husking mills—in 1976 (shortly before national elections) allied the landed gentry, small landowners, rural politicians, shopkeepers, and merchants who saw their economic interests threatened. This alliance, however, did not focus its attention on economic issues alone. Religious and political arguments were thought to provide a more effective basis for a social movement and had the added advantage of taking the debates beyond individual policies to challenge the legitimacy of the government as a whole. The alliance between the state and the bourgeoisie, which was the People's Party's avowed aim, produced a more significant alliance between the rural people and the landed classes. Bhutto responded with efforts to find his own base of support in the rural areas, but in line with the People's Party's dilemma of meeting the demands of diverse interest groups, the move was interpreted by city dwellers as having an "anti-urban bias" and further pushed the middle and lower-middle classes into the fold of the anti–People's Party alliance.

The government confronted similar problems in its dealings with the bureaucracy. The civil service of Pakistan was used to having power under Ayub Khan and did not fare well under the rule of a politician. Bhutto's power, although unleashed against the interests of the propertied elite, found its targets, for the most part, among the bureaucrats, the only group in Ayub Khan's regime to be unaffected by the events of 1969–1971. In 1973 the civil service was formally abolished and was replaced by a national grade structure which permitted the lateral entry of political appointees into the bureaucracy This move and Bhutto's deliberate humiliation of senior bureaucrats were greatly resented and pushed the bureaucracy into the anti–People's Party alliance. When Altaf Gauhar, one of Ayub Khan's trusted lieutenants and a senior civil servant in the 1960s, was imprisoned in 1972–1973 on Bhutto's orders, significantly he chose to use his time in jail to translate Mawdudi's *Tafhimu'l-Qur'an* into English. The text was serialized in the Karachi daily *Dawn*.[12] Although alienated by the regime, the bureaucracy benefited from the nationalization of the industries which extended its activities. The gradual empowerment of the bureaucracy combined with its embittered attitude toward the People's Party was a source of great concern to Bhutto. The People's Party's failure to evolve into a well-organized party eventually left Bhutto with no means to counter the power of the bureaucracy and placed him at its mercy

The anti–People's Party alliance also found an ethnic and provincial base of support. Bhutto's open courting of the Sindhis, his use of the army to suppress dissent, and his conciliatory policy toward both India and Bangladesh were quite unpopular with the Muhajirs and the Punjabis. Throughout the electoral campaign of 1970, Bhutto had openly assailed the Muhajirs and promised the Sindhis a greater share of power in Sind as well as in the central government. Once in power, Bhutto delivered on his promises by distributing coveted bureaucratic and political positions to Sindhis without regard for bureaucratic procedures or merit. In addition, he closely allied the People's Party with the secessionist Jiya Sind (Long Live Sind) party and emboldened the Sindhis by allowing vitriolic anti-Muhajir passages in the People's Party newspaper, *Hilal-i Pakistan*.[13] The Muhajirs, who already blamed Bhutto's intransigence for the loss of East Pakistan, did not take kindly to the new prime minister's pro-Sindhi policies. In July 1972 the Sind provincial assembly, controlled by the People's Party, passed the Teaching, Promotion, and Use of Sindhi Language Bill, which declared Sindhi the official language of the province, made its teaching in public schools mandatory, and made its use by civil servants obligatory The assembly also passed a resolution stipulating that all provincial government employees—most of whom were Muhajirs and Punjabis—learn Sindhi in three months or be dismissed. The Muhajirs rose up in protest.[14] There were riots in Karachi, and Muhajirs and a good segment of Punjabi public opinion regarded this challenge to the primacy of Urdu as treasonous. For the Muhajirs and Punjabis, Bhutto was increasingly sounding like Shaikh Mujibu'l-Rahman in the 1960s.

Bhutto's suppression of dissent in Baluchistan added to his problem. In February 1973 he summarily dismissed the Jami'at-i Ulama-i Islam–National Awami Party coalition government in that province, whereupon the Jami'at-i Ulama-i Islam–National Awami Party government of North-West Frontier Province resigned in protest. The Baluchis resisted, and a brutal guerrilla war broke out which by the December of 1974 pitched the Baluchi tribes against the Pakistani army For the Jama'at and its constituency the parallels between Baluchistan and the civil war in East Pakistan were uncomfortably close, and the Baluchistan debacle was yet another proof that the People's Party must be defeated. The crisis compelled Bhutto to appeal to Islamic symbols to bolster the state to avoid yet another secessionist movement.

Also of concern to the already apprehensive Muhajir and Punjabi communities was Pakistan's decision to recognize Bangladesh. In June 1972, Bhutto met with Indira Gandhi in Simla to discuss the geopolitical order in South Asia following the division of Pakistan. Although the meeting was a positive step in creating a framework for improving the relations between Pakistan and India, the agreements reached were not popular in all quarters in Pakistan. Two groups who had both fought to prevent the creation of Bangladesh, the Indophobic Muhajir community, many of whose members had suffered greatly at the hands of Bengali nationalists, and the Punjabis, who boasted the greatest numbers in the Pakistan armed forces, were vehemently opposed to recognizing the independence of Pakistan's erstwhile province. The nonrecognition of Bangladesh campaign (Bangladesh *namanzur*), was spearheaded by the IJT and was concentrated in Lahore, Karachi, and Hyderabad; it found great support among Muhajirs and Punjabis. The Muhajir-Punjabi-Sindhi standoff in Sind, the Baluchistan imbroglio, and the dispute over the recognition of Bangladesh made the Muhajir community and a sizable portion of Punjabi public opinion—which had sent most of the People's Party's elected representatives to the National Assembly in 1970—a strong base of support for the anti–People's Party alliance. The participation of religiously inclined groups in the anti–People's Party coalition was guaranteed by its Islamic coloring. The government's failure to attract mass support, combined with its disregard for the public's religious sensibilities, provided the opposition with an open field for political action. The emergence of this discernible anti–People's Party coalition provoked the government to resort to undemocratic measures which in turn further fueled the fire and emboldened the opposition.

Bhutto, confined by the realities of Pakistani politics and beguiled by the popular enthusiasm that brought him into office, missed an opportunity in 1972–1973 to transform his movement into a strong party; the Jama'at fell into the same trap. The party grew in strength throughout the Bhutto era, when Islam was reintroduced into the political process and a constellation of dissident political forces and social groups formed the core of the anti–People's Party alliance, but it failed to unite these forces and effectively manipulate and direct their political action and to develop a coherent sociopolitical program which could attract a base of support beyond mere opposition to the government. Even the Islamic constitution was shelved in favor of political action. The Jama'at remained content to agitate against single issues such as Bhutto's language policy in Sind, the nonrecognition of Bangladesh, and declaring the Ahmadis to be a non-Muslim minority The party basked in the momentary glory of its leadership and failed to consolidate its position. The alliance of convenience between the Jama'at and other anti–People's Party forces remained transitory

The Formation of the Opposition

Hostility between the Jama'at and the People's Party dated back to Yahya Khan's regime. After the elections of 1970, the Jama'at had pressed Yahya Khan to call on Shaikh Mujibu'l-Rahman to form an Awami League government and had berated Bhutto for betraying Pakistan's interests by lobbying with the army to keep the Awami League out of office. This attitude led many in the People's Party, especially in the party's left wing led by Mi'raj Muhammad, to encourage Bhutto to suppress the Jama'at,[15] but others including Bhutto himself favored mollifying it.[16] The Jama'at, meanwhile, having championed the cause of democracy for the preceding two decades, was compelled to recognize the People's Party's electoral mandate, albeit grudgingly The government may have understood the Jama'at's move to be a sign of conciliation, but conflict continued to loom. On December 20, 1971, the Jama'at announced its opposition by ridiculing Bhutto for assuming the title of chief martial law administrator, and demanded the formal abrogation of martial rule as the precondition for the start of the constitutional debate.[17]

Meanwhile the People's Party and the IJT were fighting things out on the nation's campuses. The IJT had proved to be a thorn in the side of the People's Party since 1969, when it had begun soundly defeating People's Party candidates in campus elections in Karachi and Punjab. The People's Party was particularly unhappy with the IJT's success at the University of Punjab in Lahore, a People's Party stronghold. The IJT's victory on Punjabi campuses not only shattered the myth of the People's Party's invincibility but also turned the IJT into an opposition party, the only political organization willing and able to challenge the People's Party electorally As a result, the IJT confronted the People's Party on issues beyond campus politics. In January 1972 at a national educational conference in Islamabad, IJT students got a resolution passed which demanded the Islamization of the educational system in Pakistan.[18] Shortly after, IJT students disrupted the convocation ceremonies at Karachi University to keep the governor of Sind from addressing the gathering.[19] Convocation ceremonies thenceforth became an occasion for asserting student power; for instance, not until 1990 was a senior government official—on this occasion President Ghulam Ishaq Khan—again permitted to preside over the convocation ceremonies at the IJT-controlled campus of the University of Punjab in Lahore.

The episode at Karachi University showed that the IJT would be more than just a political inconvenience to the People's Party While the parent party advocated Islamic constitutionalism, the IJT demanded Islamic revolution. Victory at the polls at the University of Punjab had greatly boosted the morale of the student organization, whose growing radicalism continued to guide its politics. The tales of the heroism of the al-Badr and al-Shams counterinsurgency units in defense of East Pakistan, a project in which the Jama'at had no direct role, had filled the IJT with revolutionary zeal. It was therefore not long before the IJT was able to exert a certain amount of control over the Jama'at and the direction of its politics, and it was the students who pushed the party to adopt more unbending positions. In February 1972 the Jama'at launched a countrywide campaign demanding the convening of the National Assembly, and in March it demanded an official investigation into the roles of Yahya Khan and Bhutto in the loss of East Pakistan.[20] The party stepped up its campaign against the continuation of martial law to revive its Islamic constitutionalist platform, which it had abandoned during the Yahya Khan period.

The National Assembly was convened in late April of 1972, altering the political climate of Pakistan once again. The Jama'at welcomed the measure, abandoned its demand for the restitution of the 1956 constitution, and prepared itself for participation in the drafting of a new constitution. The government again understood the Jama'at's move as a sign of conciliation. There was reason for the government's conclusion; Mawdudi had interceded to break the boycott by the opposition coalition, the United Democratic Front, of the constitutional debates in parliament.[21] But then the government, in what the Jama'at regarded as a breach of faith, sent security agents, disguised as People's Student Federation activists, to the University of Punjab to control campus elections in April and steal them from the IJT, using guns and other strong-arm tactics.[22] In the end, ballot boxes were confiscated, and the events created much bitterness toward the government among the IJT's rank and file.[23]

In August 1972 the IJT took it upon itself to secure the release of two girls who had been abducted by the People's Party governor of Punjab, Ghulam Mustafa Khar, for illicit purposes. The IJT rally in Lahore, which was well attended, secured the release of the abducted girls and embarrassed the government by revealing the extent of arbitrary rule and immorality in the ruling circles. Although the government's immediate reaction was to disrupt an IJT session in Karachi in September, generally it sought to mollify the students. In late September, an IJT leader, Javid Hashmi, by now a national political figure, was invited to meet with Bhutto at the governor's mansion in Lahore, and later with Mumtaz Bhutto, the People's Party chief minister of Sind in Karachi.[24] The meetings attested to the IJT's growing prominence, but the truce that resulted lasted only until December.

In the National Assembly, meanwhile, the Jama'at had strongly opposed

Bhutto's pro-Sindhi policy as well as his handling of opposition to it, and had pressed the government to reveal its dealings with India over Bangladesh and the extent of its commitment to socialism. Its members were tenacious opponents and presented an obstacle to Bhutto's monopoly on the constitutional process. Frustrated with the Jama'at, the People's Party resorted to force. On June 8, 1972, Nazir Ahmad, one of the Jama'at's most vociferous National Assembly representatives, was assassinated in his home constituency of Darah Ghazi Khan in Punjab.[25] Never before had any Pakistani government gone so far to silence its opposition. Although Mawdudi preached caution to the Jama'at, and especially to the IJT, the assassination of Nazir Ahmad marked the beginning of the rapid radicalization of the IJT.

A month later Bhutto invited leaders of various Pakistani parties to Murree to report on his meeting with Indira Gandhi in Simla. The Jama'at was represented by Mian Tufayl, who warned Bhutto against recognizing Bangladesh and "selling out Pakistan's interests to India."[26] Events in Sind soon thereafter provided the party with the means for precipitating a crisis over the issue. Muhajirs and Sindhis began fighting in July over the question of what was to be the official language of the Sind government. Emboldened by Bhutto's rhetoric and enjoying the patronage of the People's Party ministry in Sind, the Sindhis asserted their power at the expense of the Muhajirs. Bhutto was alarmed by the extent of discontent among the Muhajirs and by the fact that they could become supporters of the opposition, especially after the Jama'at used the government's decision to recognize Bangladesh as a way to mobilize them. Although the campaign for the nonrecognition of Bangladesh later found great support in Punjab as well, the Muhajirs represented its original base of support.

On September 25, 1972, Bhutto invited Mawdudi to a meeting at the governor's mansion in Lahore to discuss recognizing Bangladesh, but no apparent understanding on the issue emerged from the meeting. The two made more headway in their discussion of the future role of the left in the People's Party, which also featured prominently in that session. Mawdudi was adamant in his opposition to the left and, sensing Bhutto's ambivalence, encouraged him to distance himself from them: "If they [the left] challenge you, we will support you."[27] Mawdudi's promise played an important part in Bhutto's decision to downplay socialist themes in the constitutional debate and later to purge the left from the People's Party Leftist activists confirm this, claiming that the People's Party gave the IJT free reign on Pakistani campuses to uproot the left in the universities.[28] In return, Bhutto got Mawdudi's support for his constitution, although not before agreeing to call the state the "Islamic Republic" of Pakistan, and stipulating in the constitution that the president and prime minister must both be Muslim, and laws passed under the constitution would be compatible with Islamic law [29]

During the meeting, Mawdudi also pressed Bhutto to adhere to his own democratic principles and said that fair play was the *condicio sine qua non* for any rapprochement between the Jama'at and the government:

> We have no policy of confrontation with anyone. In the remaining Pakistan [i.e., after the secession of East Pakistan] as long as your party enjoys a majority, we recognise your party's right to rule the country constitutionally, democratically and with justice and fair play We shall not exert to remove you by undemocratic and violent means. But you should also concede that we have a right to perform the role of the opposition in a peaceful and democratic manner. And this is our constitutional and democratic right, that we should point out and criticize the wrong policies of the government. If the ruling party and the opposition were to act within their limits, there would be no danger of confrontation between them.[30]

Given that the meeting took place soon after the assassination of Nazir Ahmad, Mawdudi's proposals were conciliatory The proceedings, moreover, revealed the extent of his own, if not the Jama'at's, commitment to the political process. It was also paradoxical that the leader of a putatively autocratic Islamic party lectured the leader of the avowedly democratic People's Party on his constitutional duties. Relations between the two were thenceforth in good measure typified by Bhutto's undemocratic ways and the Jama'at's demands that he abide by the country's constitution. Neither side, however, viewed the exchanges in this meeting as binding, and soon thereafter they were at odds again. The government barred the Jama'at from contesting by-elections in Swat and Darah Ghazi Khan; the Jama'at reciprocated by intensifying its opposition to the recognition of Bangladesh.[31]

In October, Mawdudi, in his last political undertaking as amir, prepared a detailed case against the Simla agreement and the recognition of Bangladesh's independence. The new amir, Mian Tufayl, continued the campaign through numerous meetings and gatherings across Pakistan.[32] The government reacted by arresting and jailing scores of IJT activists.[33] With Mawdudi no longer at the helm, the Jama'at was unable to control the IJT, which became further enmeshed in violence and agitation with each bout of government repression. Its popularity only increased as it withstood arrest and imprisonment, and the repressive measures by the Federal Security Forces. By 1974 the IJT was winning campus elections at an increasing number of colleges across Punjab, North-West Frontier Province, and Karachi and Hyderabad in Sind, with larger margins than before. The Jama'at gave the IJT its full support.

Throughout 1973 the Jama'at expanded the purview of its anti government activities. The dismissal of the provincial government in Baluchistan in February

1973 gave the Jama'at the opportunity once again to put Bhutto's record during the East Pakistan crisis on trial. The Jama'at lambasted the government's increasingly "fascist" tendencies, stated that "Pakistan is not the fief of Mr. Bhutto," and demanded that the ruling establishment abide by the constitution in its dealings with the provinces and opposition parties.[34] On February 18, 1973, Mian Tufayl was arrested and jailed for his criticism of the government's policies in Baluchistan and his participation in the campaign for the nonrecognition of Bangladesh.[35] He remained in jail for a month, where he was badly mistreated by the Federal Security Forces. The Jama'at's leaders had not been strangers to Pakistani prisons, but never before had they suffered as they did during the Bhutto period.[36] Although in 1977 Bhutto formally apologized to Mian Tufayl for his poor treatment and blamed the wrongdoing on Khar,[37] Mian Tufayl remained bitter toward the People's Party, which may in part explain why he supported General Zia in demanding Bhutto's execution in 1979

The government was finally able to resolve the Bangladesh controversy by convening an Islamic summit in Lahore in 1974. The full force of the support of Muslim heads of state silenced its critics and finally allowed Pakistan to recognize Bangladesh. In the same year, the Jama'at had pressed Bhutto to convene the National Assembly and had participated in its proceedings when he finally did. But once there its representatives suddenly made an about-face and declared the assembly illegal because it was based on the elections of 1970, and the majority of the seats belonging to East Pakistan were never occupied. It therefore never had a quorum to operate and the 1973 constitution was thus not valid.[38] This pronouncement was followed by a flurry of criticisms against Bhutto's economic policies, the moral laxity of the ruling elite, demands for a more aggressive posture toward India over Kashmir, and greater adherence to Islamic values, in the constitution as well as in the conduct of government affairs. The Jama'at probably sensed the government's weakness and the potential for mobilizing a political movement around Islamic symbols. The government must have reached the same conclusion, as it became noticeably more attentive to the demands of Islamic parties, thoroughly purged itself of its socialist trappings, and itself sought to ride the rising tide of religious fervor.

A renewed anti-Ahmadi campaign, under the banner of Finality of Prophethood (Khatm-i Nubuwwat), began on May 22, 1974, when a train carrying 170 IJT students en route to Lahore from Multan stopped in Rabwah, an Ahmadi town in Punjab.[39] Ahmadi missionaries boarded the train and distributed pamphlets and books among the passengers. The students reacted by staging an anti-Ahmadi demonstration at the station. A week later, on May 29, another group of Ahmadis boarded the train, which was carrying the same IJT contingent back to Multan and, in an ill-conceived move, attacked the students. Three days later the nazim-i a'la of the IJT, delivered a tirade against the Ahmadis and revived the demand to declare them a non-Muslim minority As in 1953–1954, the movement quickly gained momentum in Punjab. The Jama'at was not initially in favor of pursuing the matter but since Mawdudi was away from Pakistan for medical treatment the party proved unable to influence the IJT, and quickly fell in line in order to retain control over the IJT and the flow of events.[40] 'Abdu'l-Ghafur Ahmad took up the issue in the National Assembly and Mian Tufayl met Bhutto regarding the unfolding events.[41] The leadership of the campaign remained with the IJT, which confirmed the student organization's emergence as a semiautonomous organization. The anti-Ahmadi campaign also brought the IJT closer to a host of other Islamic groups, especially the rural and small-town-based Brailwis who have a special attachment to the memory of the Prophet and are therefore vehemently anti-Ahmadi. This alliance served as the basis for the IJT's hold over the religious vote on university campuses well into the 1980s.

Thanks to its part in the anti-Ahmadi agitation, the IJT's membership grew considerably, and it won nine consecutive student elections on various Peshawar and Karachi campuses.[42] The government approached IJT leaders, hoping to persuade them to desist from pursuing its campaign, but they flatly refused, and in fact on June 26 began to escalate the conflict. The ensuing 102 days produced 8,797 meetings and 147 processions, and despite the arrest of some 834 IJT leaders and workers, the government proved unable to stem the tide.[43] On September 7, 1974, the government capitulated, declaring the Ahmadis a non-Muslim minority The polity, which only five years earlier had been overwhelmingly in support of populism and socialist idealism, had once again exposed itself to manipulation by Islamic symbols. The return of Islam to center stage was now complete. The fact that all this happened under the aegis of Pakistan's most popular government to date, one which had a strong ideological basis of its own, only attested to the incomparable influence of Islam on the life and thought of Pakistanis. The seemingly implausible resurgence of Islam in lieu of socialism during the Bhutto era meant total victory for Islam and confirmed its central role in Pakistani politics. As populism lost its momentum to Islam, the fate of Bhutto's government was sealed, long before Islam actually pulled down the People's Party and its populist government.

The Pakistan National Alliance and the Nizam-i Mustafa Movement

After the constitution of 1973 had been promulgated, a parliamentary opposition coalition, the United Democratic Front, emerged in the National Assembly The Jama'at was a member and used it as a forum for propagating its views on the government's handling of politics, economics, and religious issues. Between 1974 and 1975 the Jama'at registered 283 complaints against the government and the

People's Party for harassment and the closing of its paper *Jasarat*.[44] The Front proved to be an effective tool for dissent because its appeal to the constitution and use of parliamentary procedures emphasized how the government was abusing its power. For instance, in February 1975, following the banning of the National Awami Party and the arrest of Wali Khan, the Front's members walked out of the National Assembly, damaging the democratic image of the government. Consequently, on October 21, 1975, opposition leaders decided to strengthen the United Democratic Front as an anti–People's Party coalition. In a move indicative of the increasingly central role which Islam was playing, Mufti Mahmud of the Jami'at-i Ulama-i Islam was made its leader.

While the composition of the Front already pointed to the Islamization of dissent, a number of government policy initiatives in 1976 accelerated this trend. In the summer of that year the government appointed the attorney general, Yahya Bakhtiyar, to head a committee charged with drawing up a legislative proposal for a women's rights bill. The committee's report was presented to the government in July The Islamic parties immediately moved to oppose it, and Bhutto's initiative was nipped in the bud. He was losing his grip over national politics and saw that his only course was to call for fresh elections. He appointed his minister of religious affairs, Kawthar Niyazi, to oversee the People's Party's press and public relations during the election campaign.[45]

The government announced that national elections would be held on March 7 The opposition immediately sprang into action. The United Democratic Front was disbanded and was replaced by the Pakistan National Alliance (PNA), which eventually incorporated nine parties.[46] The alliance adopted a religiously in-spired platform, popularly known as Nizam-i Mustafa (Order of the Prophet), which favored the Islamic parties. The PNA gave the Jama'at thirty-two national tickets and seventy-eight provincial ones.[47] The party took the possibility of an electoral victory seriously, even wooing the Shi'i vote to break up the alliance between the People's Party and the Shi'i community Mian Tufayl and 'Abdu'l-Ghafur Ahmad personally courted a number of Shi'i politicians.

The PNA decided to contest Bhutto in his hometown constituency of Larkana in Sind. When Bhutto went to Larkana to declare his candidacy, the PNA announced that Jan Muhammad 'Abbasi, amir of the Jama'at-i Islami of Sind and a native of Larkana, would challenge him. 'Abbasi was, however, kidnapped by Bhutto's supporters on January 18, thereby preventing him from filing his papers on time and thus permitting the government to declare that Bhutto was uncon-tested in his bid for the Larkana seat.[48] In spite of these strong-arm tactics, the PNA's campaign was sufficiently effective to compel the People's Party to resort to rigging the elections in order to guarantee its victory

Of thirty-one seats contested (18 percent of the PNA's total of 168) in the National Assembly, the Jama'at won nine (25 percent of the PNA's total of

Table 12. Results of the 1977 Elections for the Jama'at-ı Islamı

	Punjab	NWFP	Sind	Total
Votes received by the Jama'at	789,743	133,362	290,411	1,213,516
Seats contested by the Jama'at	20	5	6	31
Seats won by the Jama'at	2	3	4	9
Seats won by the PNA	8	17	11	36

Source: Election Bureau of the Jama'at-ı Islamı.

thirty-six seats) (see table 12).[49] The Jama'at did surprisingly well, winning two seats ın Punjab (Multan and Muzaffargarh), three ın North-West Frontier Province (Swat, Malakand, and Dir), and four ın Sind (one ın Hyderabad and three ın Karachi). If the results of the rigged elections were any indication, the Jama'at had been headed for ıts best electoral showings to date, dominatıng the PNA ın the process. By July 1977, as a result of the PNA's postelection agitatıonal campaign, the Jama'at's popularıty had rısen still farther, enough so to suggest that ıt would have done even better if new elections were held. The government's interference with the election secured it 155 of the total of 191 seats contested (77.5 percent of the Natıonal Assembly of 200 seats) (see table 13).[50]

The PNA lost no time ın denouncıng the election, declarıng the results fraudulent and unacceptable to the opposition. The PNA partıes called for Bhutto's resignation, boycotted the provincial elections scheduled for March 10, demanded new national elections, and called for a national strike on March 11. Mian Tufayl claimed that Bhutto had not only stolen the elections but had also deprıved the Jama'at of ıts best chance yet to assume power. Disturbances over the election results broke out ın Karachi and quıckly spread across Pakıstan.

In a defiant mood Bhutto denıed any wrongdoıng, whıch only fanned the flames of the opposition. On March 18, 'Abdu'l-Ghafur Ahmad, then the secretary-general of the PNA, Chaudhrı Rahmat Ilahı, and Mahmud A'zam Faruqı of the Jama'at, all of whom would become PNA mınısters ın 1978, were arrested along with other PNA leaders. On March 25, Mian Tufayl Muhammad and Sayyıd Munawwar Hasan and, ın early April, Mawlana Gulzar Mazahırı and Jan Muhammad 'Abbası were also apprehended.[51] Civil disobedience, street demonstratıons, and clashes with the government organızed ın good part by the Jama'at and the IJT, meanwhile, increased, deepenıng the cleavage between the government and the opposition. Demand for constitutıonal and democratic rights were ın the process transformed ınto an Islamıc social movement under the banner of the demand for Nizam-ı Mustafa.

With all of the Jama'at's leaders behınd bars, Mawdudi returned to center stage to lead the party On April 2 he ıssued a statement ınvıtıng the government to negotıatıons with the PNA based on a set of precondıtıons: the release of all

Table 13   Seats Won in the 1977 Elections

	Punjab	Sind	NWFP	Baluchistan	Islamabad	Tribal Areas	Total
Pakistan People s Party	107 (93%)	32 (74%)	8 (31%)	7 (100%)	1 (100%)	0	115 (77.5%)
PNA	8 (7%)	11 (26%)	17 (65%)	0	0	0	36 (18%)
Independent	0	0	1 (4%)	0	0	8 (100%)	9 (4.5%)
Total	115	43	26	7	1	8	200

Source: Overseas Weekly Dawn (March 13. 1977). reprinted in Shahid Javed Burki. Pakistan under Bhutto. 1971–1977 (London. 1980). 196.

arrested PNA leaders and workers; the lifting of Section 144 and the abrogation of the Defense of Pakistan Rules, both of which authorized the government crackdown; trying in civilian courts all those cases which were referred to special tribunals by the government for violation of Section 144; and a declaration by the government to the effect that it would be open to amending the constitution through negotiations.[52] When the government did not respond, Mawdudi declared it illegal.[53]

Bhutto had all along regarded Mawdudi as a major force behind the PNA.[54] With the government's options rapidly narrowing, he decided to break the impasse by dealing with Mawdudi directly On the evening of April 16, 1977, under the pretext of "wishing to solicit the advice and good offices of an elder statesman,"[55] he went to Mawdudi's house in Lahore. The news of Bhutto's visit spread throughout the country, raising expectations for a break in the impasse. Many anti–People's Party politicians and scores of PNA leaders pleaded with the Mawlana not to meet with Bhutto.[56] A crowd of IJT workers congregated outside Mawdudi's house and began shouting slogans against Bhutto and Mawdudi. Mawdudi responded that he had not asked for the meeting, but common courtesy (adab) did not permit him to turn away a visitor.[57] The meeting, which lasted for forty minutes, did not bear the results Bhutto wished. Mawdudi counseled him to resign and allow a provisional government to take over while new elections were held.[58]

To stay in power Bhutto was compelled to devise a new strategy He actively championed Islamization in the hope of co-opting a part of the opposition. Two days after his meeting with Mawdudi, he announced that in recognition of the demands of the Nizam-i Mustafa, casinos and nightclubs would be closed down, sale of alcoholic drinks and gambling would be banned, and generally activities proscribed by Islam would be against the law In addition, he would reconvene the Council of Islamic Ideology under the supervision of Mufti Mahmud, the leader of the Jami'at-i Ulama-i Islam and the PNA, so it could oversee the implementation of government-sponsored Islamization. The other two members of the council were to be Mawlanas Shah Ahmad Nurani of the Jami'at-i Ulama-i Pakistan and Ihtishamu'l-Haq of the Jami'at-i Ulama-i Islam; no member of the Jama'at was included in the council. The Islamic parties rejected this idea and again demanded new elections.

Unable to stem the rising tide of PNA's agitational campaign, Bhutto resorted to more repressive measures. On May 17, Mawdudi's house was surrounded by police, and an attempt was made to arrest him.[59] The PNA issued a statement warning the government that the arrest of Mawdudi would start a rebellion.[60] With no way out of the impasse, Saudi Arabia intervened, using its financial leverage on both sides to end the stalemate. Negotiations began again on June 3 'Abdu'l-Ghafur Ahmad of the Jama'at served as a member of the PNA's three-man team in the negotiations.[61]

The PNA contingent was careful to keep negotiations focused on the elections of 1977, the legitimacy of the government, and new elections. Islam and the Nizam-i Mustafa, on which Bhutto was willing to make substantial concessions, did not figure prominently Bhutto now tried to divert attention from the negotiations by rallying Pakistanis around a nationalist and anti-imperialist platform. In a speech before the parliament on April 28 he declared, "The elephant [the United States government] is annoyed with me."[62] His charge was that the PNA and the Jama'at were being led by American agents who had been ordered to debunk the government because of its socialist and Third World leanings and because Pakistan's nuclear program ran counter to American interests in the region.[63] No one was persuaded by Bhutto's theory, and the accusation brought a sharp rebuke from Mawdudi.[64]

Negotiations went on for a month. During this period, Bhutto's resolve gradually waned, and he became increasingly amenable to new elections. It is not certain whether the government and the PNA actually reached an agreement or not.[65] All sides, however, concur that the delay in reaching a final agreement during the last hours before the coup owed much to General Zia's counsel to Bhutto. The general had warned him against entering into an agreement with the PNA based on preliminary understandings reached in the negotiations because the army would not accept its requirement of leaving Baluchistan in two months and releasing from custody National Awami Party leaders who had fought the army in that province. Bhutto's indecision augured ill for the stability of the country On July 5, 1977, the Pakistan army led by Zia staged a military coup, removed the government, arrested political leaders from both sides to the conflict, and imposed martial law

The Bhutto years saw the apogee of the Jama'at's political activism. The party contributed to the repression of socialism and the reinstitution of Islam in national politics, which brought it to the verge of political victory The Bhutto years, however, proved to be a short-lived aberration. For the success of agitational politics and the gains made by the resurgence of Islam diverted the party's attention from the importance of opening its ranks to greater numbers and establishing more lasting relations with new groups in the society that the People's Party's economic policies and ill-conceived political measures had produced. When the coup of July 5 changed the political map of Pakistan, the alliance of convenience based on opposition to the government dissolved, leaving the Jama'at once again at odds with popular politics. The Bhutto regime and the vicissitudes of the antigovernment agitational campaign also compromised the Jama'at and the IJT's moral resolve and initiated an irreversible trend toward a political activism that would become their vocation.

9 Accommodation and Opposition, 1977–1988

Opposition to Bhutto had not only made the party popular and presented it with its first opportunity to further its political standing in Pakistan but it had also coalesced Islam and democracy into one political platform. The alliance between Islam and democracy quickly became antagonism between the two, however, when Zia came to power.

The Zia Regime

The military coup, dubbed Operation Fair Play, that toppled Bhutto in July 1977 caught the country's political parties off guard and threw them into a state of confusion. In one fell swoop the coup had removed the opposition's raison d'être. The government had been removed too quickly and by the armed forces rather than by the PNA, leaving the opposition with no immediate plan of action.

This confusion was compounded by the Islamic veneer of the new regime. For the first time in its history it appeared that Islamic parties would operate in a hospitable political environment and enjoy a certain amount of government patronage. Their ideological rapport produced what one party source called "a mother-daughter relationship" with Zia's regime.[1] The general had hoped to restore state authority by controlling the Islamic parties by including them in his regime. What he offered was similar to what elsewhere has been termed inclusionary corporatism.[2] He had incorporated the demands of the Islamic parties into state ideology, thereby offering the Islamic parties a power-sharing arrangement in which the state would act as the senior partner, but the Islamic forces would gain from state patronage and enjoy a modicum of political activity This strategy had short-run success because it appealed to the ideological sensibilities of the Islamic parties, but in the long run it failed as it ran counter to their fundamental political interests. The general's mixture of Islam and autocracy

generated corresponding tensions between the Jama'at's commitment to Islamization and its avowed democratic objectives.

The Jama'at and its allies in the PNA were not pleased with Zia's coup. For
one thing the general had canceled the elections, though he emphasized the fact
that Bhutto had never intended to abide by his agreement to hold elections and
had himself planned to unleash the army against the opposition.[3] Therefore, had
the army not acted with alacrity, according to the general, Pakistan would have
been immersed in a blood bath and the alliance parties would have been
thoroughly routed. Having removed the obdurate People's Party government,
Zia would now pave the way for the realization of the PNA's demands for a
democratic order. Zia also made full use of his reputation as an observant
Muslim to gain the sympathy of the Islamic parties and quickly adopted the
Nizam-i Mustafa, thereby adding to the PNA's confusion over what political
strategy to adopt. Zia also had a humble demeanor which, in contrast to the
arrogant Bhutto, went a long way to impress the PNA leaders and also allay their
fears.[4]

The Jama'at was by no means immune to Zia's manipulations. It had performed rather well in the elections of 1977, better than most of its allies in the
PNA. If the campaign which followed the disputed elections of 1977 was any
indication, the political fortunes of the party both within the PNA and nationally
had subsequently soared even higher. The alliance had expected to inherit the
government from the People's Party, and the Jama'at had anticipated ruling the
coalition government that was to succeed Bhutto. Encouraged by the Islamic
facade of Zia's regime, the party therefore tried to salvage its fortunes by
lobbying with Zia for early elections. Elections and Islamization thereby became
the bait which Zia used to co-opt the Jama'at. Between 1977 and 1979 the Jama'at
was increasingly drawn into his regime. Zia announced the first of a series of
promised election dates for October 1, 1977 He referred to the house arrest of
the anti-Bhutto politicians as "an enforced rest   [to] rejuvenate themselves for
the coming General Elections."[5] He promised the Jama'at that after the elections
a civilian government would be allowed to take over.[6] Eager to maintain
stability, the Jama'at went to great lengths to promote cooperation between Zia
and the PNA, eventually acting as the broker between the two. Zia's avowed
commitment to the Jama'at's ideological position and the fact that he and Mian
Tufayl both belonged to the Ara'in clan (*biradri*) and were from Jullundar in East
Punjab helped strengthen the entente.

Mawdudi enthusiastically endorsed Zia's initiatives in implementing the
Nizam-i Mustafa movement, hailing his efforts as the "renewal of the covenant"
between the government and Islam.[7] As a result, the harmony between the
Jama'at's ideological position and its political aims was lost. By appealing to the
ideological sensibilities of the Jama'at, Zia was able to turn the party's attention

from its political interests. Between 1977 and 1979, Zia adroitly manipulated the fate of Bhutto and his party—to whom government propaganda had given apocalyptic significance—to postpone the elections while still keeping the Islamic parties in check. He thought that once Bhutto was executed the anti-Bhutto alliance would fall apart, giving more breathing room to his regime.[8] He argued that elections were in the interests of neither the alliance nor of the country, if they were to serve as the means for resuscitating the People's Party Bhutto, he added, could be prevented from returning only if he was made accountable for the abuses which were committed while he was in office.

The prospect of Bhutto's return was disconcerting to the opposition especially after it had been convinced that the gallows had awaited them all in July 1977 had Zia not intervened.[9] When Bhutto, temporarily released from prison, was received in Lahore on August 8, 1977, by a large and cheering crowd, the Jama'at quickly fell in line with the government and raised the banner of "retribution first, elections next!"[10] The enthusiasm shown for Bhutto by Lahoris made the impending elections seem less promising than they had seemed earlier.[11] There was no point in pushing for elections unless the Jama'at and the PNA would win them. With the memory of the anti-Bhutto agitations of the summer of 1977 waning, the Jama'at and its allies now looked to the government and the judicial system to thwart any attempt at a comeback by the People's Party by trying Bhutto for abuse of power. With the Jama'at's and the PNA's support, Bhutto was implicated in an assassination attempt on one of his opponents; the intended victim survived but his father died, and Bhutto was charged with murder.

The quest for justice soon shifted to thinly disguised vindictiveness. Once the courts had convicted Bhutto on the charge of murder, the Jama'at's demand for his execution was loud. "Mr. Bhutto has not been punished as a political convict. The Court has sentenced him for involvement in a murder case. Being a moral criminal and murderer, any demand for commutation of his sentence would be tantamount to interference in judicial verdicts," was how Mawdudi rationalized their stand.[12] So central was the Jama'at's support for Bhutto's execution that Zia deemed it politic to meet with Mian Tufayl for an hour and a half the night before the former prime minister's hanging.[13] The Jama'at also provided Zia with support in suppressing the remaining pockets of People's Party resistance. Mawdudi argued that if the People's Party were allowed to run in the elections the debacle of East Pakistan would be repeated in Baluchistan or Sind;[14] this provided Zia with a convenient pretext for institutionalizing the martial-law regime and repeatedly postponing elections.

The Jama'at's effort to bring the elections about became the focus of the party's relations with the government. Zia now argued that elections could not be held by a martial-law regime—a civilian government was required to oversee an orderly electoral process and, if necessary, the transfer of power. After months of negotiations between the PNA and the Zia regime, on August 21, 1978, an agreement was reached whereby the PNA would form a government which would oversee the national elections. The two sides agreed that the PNA would appoint two-thirds of the cabinet ministers and the general one-third. The Jama'at joined the new government as part of both the PNA's quota and General Zia's team. As part of the PNA's quota of ministers the Jama'at received the portfolios of production and industry; petroleum, minerals, water, and power; and information and broadcasting.[15] Khurshid Ahmad was appointed to be minister of planning as part of Zia's quota of ministers. After thirty years of political activity in Pakistan, for the first time in its history the Jama'at had become part of the ruling establishment.[16]

The PNA's arrangement with Zia, however, did not last for long. On April 21, 1979, to prepare for national elections, the PNA dissolved the government. Zia appealed to the Jama'at to stay in the cabinet, but the party, hoping to control the postelection civilian government, turned down the general's offer and decided to stay with the PNA.[17] To create some distance with the martial-law regime in preparation for elections, the Jama'at also began to criticize Zia, especially his economic policy. Soon after Khurshid Ahmad left the cabinet, he criticized the government's proposed budget as un-Islamic and as harmful to the interests of Pakistan as Bhutto's policies.[18] The maneuver paid off. On October 7, Zia reached an agreement with the PNA, which committed the regime to elections on November 17, 1979.[19]

They took Zia at his word. Mawdudi declared that elections would soon bring the Jama'at to power and that no additional extraconstitutional activities were therefore needed to hasten the advent of the Islamic state.[20] The party's enthusiasm for an electoral victory soared even more when the Jama'at participated in municipal elections in September 1979[21] and won 57 of the 160 seats contested in the elections to the Karachi municipal corporation (city council).[22] The 35 percent margin of victory was sufficient to assure the Jama'at's domination over the corporation and, by implication, the politics of the Muhajir community, at least for the time being. The elections had been boycotted by some PNA parties and had been held on a nonparty basis. The Jama'at nonetheless saw any election better than none and, viewing the vote as a positive sign, formed the Ukhuwwat (Brotherhood) group, a surrogate for the Jama'at in the election campaign. The Jama'at's tally of seats in the corporation was sufficient to secure the mayoralty of Karachi for the party; the office was held by 'Abdu'ssattar Afghani until 1986.[23]

The results from elsewhere in Sind were not as promising. Of the province's thirteen district councils, eleven were won by pro–People's Party candidates, two by those close to the Muslim League and one by the Jama'at.[24] In Punjab the Jama'at did not do well either. In the Punjab district council elections, of the 500 seats contested, pro—People's Party candidates received 212, independents 135, and the Jama'at 35 seats. The Jama'at may have come in a distant third, but it did better than the Muslim League with 28, the Jami'at-i Ulama-i Islam with 13, and the Jami'at-i Ulama-i Pakistan with 6 seats each. In corporation and municipal elections in Punjab, pro—People's Party candidates got 527, independents 390, and the Jama'at's candidates 93 seats. Overall, in Punjab the Jama'at got one district council vice-chairman, five municipal committee chairmen, six municipal committee vice-chairmen, five town committee chairmen, and four town committee vice-chairmen.

In North-West Frontier Province of the 360 district council seats, the Jama'at got 32, but came in second behind pro—People's Party candidates, who won 52 seats. The Jama'at again defeated the Muslim League and the Jami'at-i Ulama-i Islam. The Jama'at did better in the elections than the other participating PNA parties and was defeated only by the cluster of pro—People's Party candidates. Zia, however, would not have allowed Bhutto's party to run in the national elections, which led the Jama'at's leaders to believe that they would sweep the polls in November 1979 This, however, also meant that the Jama'at would render more support to Zia just to make sure that the People's Party would be kept out of the elections. The Jama'at became even more sanguine about its electoral prospects when, after Mawdudi died in September 1979, his funeral procession in Lahore later that month, less than a month before the promised November 17 national elections, drew a large crowd.

The municipal councils were the first openly elected bodies to be put in place since the advent of martial law, which, given the Jama'at's full participation in them, intensified the party's rivalry with the Zia regime for the control of Pakistan. Zia found the Jama'at's good showing useful in that for the time being the party could be relied upon to control Karachi and contain the pockets of pro-People's Party sentiments in Pakistan's largest city, which was critical to the stability of the military regime. The Jama'at's ability to manipulate a nonparty election, however, did not go unnoticed by Zia.

The Ruling Islamic Alliance

Although throughout the 1977—1979 period the Jama'at's activities were directed toward national elections and capitalizing on its popularity during the anti-Bhutto agitations, Zia's use of Islamization to silence the party continued to dampen its resolve. Zia's manipulation of the Jama'at's ideological platform had a certain appeal for the party's leaders and rank-and-file members.[25]

The rapport between the Jama'at and the martial-law regime had been established by Mawdudi two years before he died. By 1977 he was at odds with the more pragmatic leadership that had succeeded him. He no longer had any official standing, but he nonetheless publicly endorsed the Islamization initiatives of Zia.

In March and April 1978 in talks on Radio Pakistan, he hailed Zia's efforts as welcome first steps in applying Islamic principles to Pakistan's judicial and political system.[26] While Mawdudi's objective was to claim that this greater visibility of Islam in the political process was all his party's doing, he ipso facto made Islam a major issue in the alliance between the new regime and the PNA—a prerogative which the Jama'at had denied Bhutto in 1977—at a time when the two sides were locked in debate over the formation of the PNA government.

The Jama'at's leaders, taking their cue from Mawdudi, wholeheartedly assisted Zia in preparing a comprehensive Islamization program. It was introduced to the public on February 10, 1979, with the promulgation of Islamic edicts concerning taxation and *hudud* punishments (punishments for practices proscribed in religious texts). The Jama'at claimed the new measures to be the fruits of its decades-long struggle to introduce Islamic law to Pakistan. Islamization, however, proved to be a problem: while it created concord between the Jama'at and the Zia regime in principle, in practice it promoted conflict between the two over what the content of the Islamization program should be.

The Jama'at had endorsed Zia's Islamization measures, assuming it would then dominate the process. Zia, having received the party's blessings, decided that it was not politic to restrict its patronage to one Islamic party and began cultivating stronger ties with the Jami'at-i Ulama-i Islam and the Jami'at-i Ulama-i Pakistan, the ulama and Sufi leaders (*mashayakh*), and a host of other Islamic organizations, a policy which the Jama'at ridiculed as religiously suspect and politically motivated. As one Jama'at leader put it, "We were interested in the *siratu'l-nabi* [path of the Prophet], while Zia was content with the *miladu'l-nabi* [the popular celebration of the birthday of the Prophet, a custom of Sunni folk religion in Pakistan]."[27] The Jama'at surmised from Zia's "divide and rule" that he was not sincere about Islamization and would not be easily manipulated by the Jama'at.

Zia's motives in diversifying the religious basis of his regime were not entirely Machiavellian. The general had been an admirer of Mawdudi and the Jama'at for a long time, and he had looked to the Jama'at as an intellectual force which could serve the same function in his regime as the left had done in the People's Party The fact that the Jama'at had been the main ideological adversary of the left since the 1960s and had always claimed to have a blueprint for the Islamization of the state led Zia to draw parallels between the Jama'at and Pakistan's leftist intelligentsia. That is why the Jama'at leaders were given cabinet portfolios and invited to serve on such prominent state-sponsored bodies as the Council of Islamic Ideology A number of pro-Jama'at thinkers, writers, and journalists were also inducted into the inner circle of Zia's advisers, to help him lay the foundations for the Islamic state.

Zia's expectations, however, came to naught. The Jama'at proved unable to deliver on the claims it had made. Aside from abstract notions about the shape and working of the ideal Islamic state, the party had little to offer in the way of suggestions for managing its machinery Its notions about the working of Islamic dicta in economic and political operations provided Zia with no coherent plan of action. Just as the Jama'at became disappointed with the politics of Zia's regime, so the general became disillusioned with the practical relevance of the Jama'at's ideas.

After the execution of Bhutto on October 17, Zia suspended the November 1979 elections. The Jama'at had taken his promise of elections seriously and had mobilized its resources in anticipation of them. It also sensed that after two years the memory of the excesses of the Bhutto government had begun to fade, and the paramount political issue before the country would now be martial law, opposition to which had by 1979 become the rallying point for the prodemocracy forces to which the Jama'at claimed to belong. The solid showing of pro—People's Party candidates in the national municipal elections was sufficient proof that opposition was mounting. The tightening of martial law following the cancellation of the November elections was only likely to damage Zia's political standing further. The Jama'at saw its popularity dwindle in tandem with the waning hopes for elections. The party's association with the ruling order, which had been designed to bring about elections and secure a political victory for the party, was rapidly becoming a liability

Zia's postponement of the November elections led Mian Tufayl, the general's most ardent supporter among the Jama'at's leaders, to warn Zia about the consequences of his policy [28] In October 1980 the Jama'at issued a statement critical of martial law and encouraging Zia to restore civilian order and the rule of law, end censorship, and hold elections.[29] This was the first sign of an open breach, but it brought no reaction from the general. The Jama'at's shura' sessions reassessed the party's policy and issued strong denunciations of martial law, tampering with the constitution, and strong-arm tactics in dealing with the opposition.[30] The pace and breadth of the attacks against the government increased between 1980 and 1985 as it became apparent that the martial-law regime had in good measure dissipated Islam's political appeal and diminished the ability of religion to legitimate political action and authority Zia's triumph had proved to be a Pyrrhic victory for Islam.

The Jama'at to its own detriment did not distance itself from the martial-law regime swiftly enough to put an end to its political hemorrhaging. Mian Tufayl, who was close to Zia and particularly bitter toward the Bhutto regime, dampened the party's zeal for resuming agitational politics by pointing out that the last time the Jama'at had opted for such a course, in Ayub Khan's time, the ultimate beneficiary was not the Jama'at but the left.[31] As evil as martial law might turn out to be, he argued, the People's Party remained Pakistan's greatest scourge. Under Mian Tufayl's leadership, the Jama'at was reduced to inaction, though it was compensated for its political losses with gains of another kind. The party's status was bolstered by the regime. It dealt with Mawdudi as a senior statesman and a religious sage. He was invited to give talks on Radio Pakistan, his advice was solicited by Zia, and his words began to adorn the front page of national newspapers. This new prestige opened government to the Jama'at's influence to an unprecedented extent. The Jama'at now began to infiltrate into the armed forces, the bureaucracy, and important national research and educational institutions.

Nowhere are the nature and extent of recompense for cooperation with the Zia regime clearer than in the Jama'at's role in the Afghan war. The Jama'at had been privy to the government's Afghan policy since 1977, when, following Nur Muhammad Taraki's coup in Afghanistan, generals Zia and Fazl-i Haq had met with Mawdudi, Mian Tufayl and Qazi Husain Ahmad to explore a role for the Jama'at in Pakistan's Afghan policy.[32] The party had played a major role in marshaling Pakistani public opinion in favor of an Islamic crusade against the Soviet Union. Soon after the Soviet invasion of Afghanistan, Zia brought the Jama'at into his Afghan policy, using its religious stature to legitimate his depiction of the war as a jihad. This arrangement was mutually beneficial, especially to the Jama'at. The Afghan war encouraged close ties between the Jama'at and the Pakistani army and security forces, opened the inner sanctum of government to the party, involved it in the flow of funds and arms to the Mujahidin, and provided Jama'at and IJT members with valuable military training.

Contact with the Afghan Mujahidin and refugees opened them to the Jama'at's political and religious influence. The party's intellectual sway over segments of the Afghan refugee community, in turn, boosted its image in Islamic revivalist circles across the Muslim world and gave it a pan-Islamic image.[33] The jihad had served Zia as a useful means of harnessing the Jama'at's energies and diverting them away from domestic politics and was no doubt instrumental in the Jama'at's decision to retain its close ties to the Zia regime despite the opposition of many of its members. The Jama'at construed these gains as beneficial because they increased the party's power, but they were no substitute for winning elections. It eventually became clear that the party had exhausted the utility of these compensations and would have to reevaluate its role.

By 1984, after seven years of "Islamic autocracy," the Jama'at began to distance itself from the regime; the IJT forced the party's hand. A formidable political force in its own right, it too had supported Zia until he banned student activity. Then relations deteriorated. This allowed the multiparty coalition, the Movement for Restoration of Democracy (MRD), organized by the People's Party

Table 14. Votes Cast for Jama'at-ı Islamı Candidates ın the
1985 Elections

	Votes Received	Total Votes Cast	% of Total
Punjab			
Lahore (1)	26,258	81,814	32
Lahore (2)	17,896	56,071	32
Lahore (3)	18,895	44,796	42
NWFP			
Mardan	14,063	50,031	28
Swat	20,568	54,090	38
Malakand	29,950	57,615	52
Dir	31,166	59,871	52
Sind			
Karachı (1)	23,961	66,910	36
Karachı (2)	20,647	49,264	42
Baluchıstan			
Turbat	16,169	32,845	49

Source: Report on the General Elections, 1985 (Islamabad, n.d.).

ın 1981, to make overtures to the IJT, begınnıng ın March 1984.[34] Mian Tufayl ıntervened wıth IJT leaders,[35] but rather than responding to the demands of ıts student wıng, he trıed to get them under hıs control, whıch was what the martıal-law regıme wanted. In defiance the students contınued to agıtate.

Mian Tufayl then appealed to Zia to defuse the sıtuatıon by liftıng the ban on student actıvitıes, usıng the Jama'at's endorsement of the referendum Zia was pushıng to legıtımate hıs policıes ın the name of Islam as hıs reward for liftıng the ban and promısıng that the future Natıonal Assembly would be sovereıgn.[36] Zia accepted both condıtıons, only to renege on the first after the referendum was conducted and the second when he dismıssed the Muslim League government and dissolved the assemblies ın May 1988. These breaches of faıth greatly under-mıned Mian Tufayl's posıtıon. He had promısed to deliver on the IJT's demands through hıs personal tıes with the regıme; now members decıded that nothıng further could be gaıned from cooperatıon with Zia.

The Electıons of 1985

After the referendum the Jama'at's politıcal fortunes plummeted, and the na-tıonal electıons, when they were finally held ın 1985, proved that the popularıty of the 1977–1979 perıod had vanıshed. Debate over the Jama'at's relatıons to Zia and the possibility of cooperatıon with the MRD only prolonged the party's ınability to act. In the electıons of 1985 the Jama'at won 10 of the 68 seats it contested for the Natıonal Assembly (compared with 9 out of 31 ın 1977, and 4

Table 15 Votes Received and Seats Won by the Jama'at-i Islami in the
1985 Elections

	Punjab	*NWFP*	*Sind*	*Baluchistan*	*Total*
National Assembly					
Seats contested	37	13	15	3	68
Seats won	3	4	2	1	10
Total votes received	625,848	196,585	238,228	30,527	1,091,188
Average votes per					
candidate	16,914	15,121	15,881	10,175	16,046
Provincial Assembly					
Seats contested	53	22	24	3	102
Seats won	2	5	5	1	13
Total votes received	377,790	114,131	160,056	13,916	665,893
Average votes per					
candidate	7,128	5,187	6,669	4,638	6,528

Source: Election Bureau of the Jama'at-i Islami.

out of 151 in 1970),[37] and 13 of the total of 102 contested for various provincial assemblies (compared with 4 out of 331 in 1970) (see tables 14–15). These results showed Zia that the Jama'at had lost its power, and he turned to the Muslim League and an array of ethnic parties for support. The elections, as all Pakistanis knew, had been boycotted by the left and centrist parties and were an easy prey for the Islamic and right-of-center parties. Consequently, the Jama'at did better in these elections than it had in its previous electoral showings. It won three of Dir's five provincial assembly seats, and for the first time won a seat in the Baluchistan provincial assembly But these modest gains paled before those of the other right-of-center parties, especially in Punjab and Sind. The political damage caused by associating with Zia was reflected in the fact that Jama'at candidates who were PNA ministers were not elected.

The gradual dissipation of the PNA's base of political support; the relative success of the MRD after 1981, the ban on labor unions, political parties, and, finally, student unions; and the results of the elections of 1985 had all acted to create doubts in the minds of many Jama'at members regarding the wisdom of their close ties to Zia. If the public's apathy over the referendum of 1984 was any indication, after seven years of martial rule Islamization had lost much of its appeal. To the extent to which Islamization measures still held sway over the masses, it was Zia and not the Jama'at who benefited. Ghafur Ahmad, the head of the Jama'at's parliamentary contingent in the 1970s and the secretary-general of the PNA, was the first in the Jama'at to show his opposition to Mian Tufayl's alliance with Zia by not running in the elections of 1985 at all. Dissent soon spread to the Jama'at's rank and file.

Mian Tufayl continued to argue that Zia's Islamization scheme was in accordance with the Jama'at's agenda and at odds with the spirit of the MRD, which the amir had dubbed the "movement for the restoration of the People's Party "[38] He pointed to the dangers that the Soviet presence in Afghanistan and the activities of the pro–People's Party clandestine organization, Al-Zulfiqar, posed to the interests of Pakistan. This argument collapsed when, soon after the elections, civilian rule returned to Pakistan, not under the aegis of the Jama'at, but in the form of a Muslim League government.

A contingent began to form in the Jama'at which sought to restore pragmatic politics to its rightful place in the party The anti-Zia faction was centered in Karachi and led by Ghafur Ahmad. The Karachi Group, as they were called, argued that if the Jama'at was to survive it would have to cultivate support, and that meant moving away from the purely ideological concerns which Mian Tufayl was using to keep the Jama'at in Zia's camp. The party had to find a recipe for success, one which was rooted less in ideology and more in pragmatic considerations. The Jama'at, argued the Karachi Group, had no choice but to adopt a populist platform demanding democracy and socioeconomic justice.[39] They recognized the limits to Islam's appeal in the face of socioeconomic, ethnic, and democratic demands. Islam could no longer undergird a successful political campaign. Religious politics had begun to ebb.

The size of the religious vote had increased in Zia's time, but so had the number of parties which depended on it. While the Islamic vote was divided many-fold, the MRD, and later the Muhajir Qaumi Mahaz, were left to monopolize the relatively neglected secular constituency The political fortunes of the Jama'at, argued the Karachi Group, could be salvaged only if the party broke completely with the Zia regime, joined the MRD, and established contact with the People's Party, the undisputed party of populism. The Jama'at had always thrived on dissent, and therefore such a strategy had a certain appeal for a party which had for most of its existence been in the opposition. For some, democracy was as much a basis of the Jama'at's message as Islamization, and neither could satisfactorily exist without the other.[40]

The new approach provided a way of shifting ground without openly denouncing the ideological basis of the Jama'at. It began now to preach that martial law was a worse evil than socialism, modernism, or the People's Party [41] The abrupt shift was not entirely convincing and opened the Jama'at to the charge of inconsistency, but the reorientation was real.

Karachi was particularly receptive to these new ideas. The city has the largest concentration of Jama'at members. In 1990 there were 1,100 members and 7,000 workers in Karachi.[42] They are ideologically the least rigid, the most clearly driven by the desire for success, and therefore the most willing to experiment with a pragmatic approach to politics, with which they have had considerable practice since they controlled the municipal government at the time. As opposition to Zia gained momentum, the Jama'at's leaders became more receptive to the views of the party's Karachi members, especially as they were echoed by IJT students and workers across Pakistan. As a result, Mian Tufayl finally agreed to split with Zia and demand the restoration of the 1973 constitution—which the Jama'at now accepted in the interests of denying Zia the opportunity to bog down the political process in lengthy constitutional debates—and the holding of party-based elections.[43]

The Karachi Group demanded more radical action. Contacts between the Jama'at and the MRD had gone on since 1981, when one of the alliance's founders, Sardar 'Abdu'l-Qayyum, had invited the party to join its ranks and had been rebuffed by Mian Tufayl.[44] Three more meetings had taken place; they had had no tangible results, in large measure because of Mian Tufayl's intransigence.[45]

The debate grew more intense when, after the elections, Zia turned over the government to the Muslim League, to replace the Jama'at as the main pillar of his regime. The Jama'at became an opposition party and was once again locked in rivalry with the League.

The Muslim League government was secular and wary of criticism from the religious quarter; it was also aware of the mischief that the Jama'at and the IJT were capable of. The Jama'at, the League believed, was Zia's last line of defense against any challenges to his authority—the "B-team of the martial law" as the Pir Pagaro, the president of the Muslim League at the time, put it. The League hoped eventually to inherit power from Zia and to that end embarked upon a policy that involved putting civilian rule into place and asserting its autonomy from Zia. This was a bold strategy, which Zia would not take lightly, but before launching any campaign against Zia, the Muslim League had to neutralize the Jama'at. It began by putting up its own student union, the Muslim Student Federation, against the IJT and undermining Jama'at's power base in Karachi, a city crucial to any successful antigovernment campaign.[46] In February 1987 the Sind ministry dissolved the Karachi municipal corporation, arresting Afghani and 101 other Jama'at councilmen, and called for new municipal elections, which brought the MQM into power in that city The MQM won the mayoralty of Karachi in January 1988.[47] But most damaging were the League's propaganda attacks on the party The Jama'at was identified with the martial-law regime and as Zia's most important ally just when it had decided to abandon both. The Pir Pagaro's "B-team" showed the isolation that proximity to the Zia regime could produce and that the Karachi Group had warned against.

The Loss of Muhajir Support

The Muslim League's anti-Jama'at campaign was compounded by a more devastating development—the loss of the Karachi, Hyderabad, and the Muhajir vote to the MQM. The MQM had been founded by former members and affiliates of the IJT, and it initially drew support from the Jama'at's constituency among the Muhajirs. The Jama'at's leaders believed its meteoric rise to power could not have occurred without the approval of the armed forces,[48] and realized that Zia had engineered it to destroy their base in Sind.

Since the beginning of his rule, Zia had remained wary of rural Sind, where Bhutto still enjoyed a considerable following and which had shown little enthusiasm for Zia's coup. He had sought to placate Sindhi landlords and ethnic parties by catering to their interests, which were often at odds with the demands of the Muhajirs. For instance, the controversial quota system in Sind put in place by Bhutto, which reserved prized bureaucratic positions for Sindhis to the detriment of the Muhajirs, was kept intact by Zia. Nor did the general do anything about the worsening social conditions in Karachi, which by 1986 had reduced many Muhajir neighborhoods to squalor. The Zia regime encouraged the rise in power of the Punjabi and Pathan communities of Karachi, in the form of the Punjabi-Pakhtun Ittihad (Punjabi-Pathan Alliance) party, which the Muhajirs also resented. Zia had turned a blind eye to the Pathans' trade in contraband and narcotics, brought to Karachi from Afghanistan for export.[49] The Muhajirs' frustrations erupted in the form of the anti-Pathan riots of 1986, which culminated in a protracted conflict between the MQM and the Punjabi-Pakhtun Ittihad, waged in Karachi well into 1990. Between 1979 and 1986, Zia had relied on Islamization and anti–People's Party propaganda to keep the Muhajir community in check and had deputized the Jama'at—with the help of the Punjabi-Pakhtun Ittihad in Punjabi and Pathan areas—to maintain order in Karachi. Not surprisingly, the Muhajirs grew resentful of the "Islamic" regime and its allies. The rise of Muhajir ethnic consciousness ended the Jama'at's control of Karachi politics and for the first time brought to light the grievances of the Muhajirs against the Zia regime.

Zia concluded that he needed a new political order in Karachi and other cities in Sind to supplant the Jama'at and harness the political energies of the Muhajirs to his benefit. The organization of the MRD in 1981 had generated concern among Pakistan's military leaders. While Sindhi landowners and the ethnic parties could be relied upon to keep the MRD out of rural Sind, the situation in Karachi was more complex. Wali Khan, the Pathan leader of the Awami National Party and a MRD stalwart who was opposed to the Afghan war and the Zia regime, was popular among Karachi's sizable Pathan community The inroads he made had led the People's Party, which could also benefit from the restlessness of the Muhajir community, to action. When the 1985 elections proved that the Jama'at no longer had the political power to keep the MRD out of Karachi and had developed doubts of its own about the Zia regime, the general decided that the Karachi-based MQM was a better choice for his support. Jama'at leaders in fact claim that the army and the Sind ministry not only encouraged the MQM but also armed it.[50] Although it too had been organized by people with grievances against the Zia regime, it was still more hostile to the People's Party and preoccupied as well with defeating its rivals—the Jama'at, the Punjabi-Pakhtun Ittihad, and the MRD. The Muhajir-Pathan clashes in 1986 greatly benefited Zia as they pitted the Pathan supporters of Wali Khan and the MRD against the Muhajirs. What Zia did not realize was that the advent of the MQM gave the Jama'at and the People's Party a common cause. As the IJT was squeezed out of the campuses in Sind and the Jama'at lost its base of support in Karachi, both found a natural ally in the People's Party, which was also trying to make inroads into the MQM's territory [51]

The Reorientation of the Jama'at

Mian Tufayl decided not to seek another term as amir of the Jama'at-i Islami, and in October 1987 the party elected Qazi Husain in his stead. Qazi Husain was a populist who appealed to the pro-Zia faction, although he belonged to the Karachi Group. He had maintained close contacts with the Zia regime as the Jama'at's liaison with the army in the Afghan war, but more important, he had advocated joining the MRD as early as 1983. His election therefore indicated that the majority of Jama'at members favored populism, democracy, and the break with Zia.

Following his election mandate, Qazi Husain lost no time in attacking feudalism and capitalism, demanding rights for the impoverished many, and pointing to the obligations of the wealthy few The party's activities were extended into the rural areas and among the urban underclass.[52] Qazi Husain's populist agenda kept pace with the demands of the Karachi Group, which was greatly encouraged by the words and actions of their new leader, and it also provided a basis on which to approach the People's Party

Qazi Husain was openly against Zia, arguing that neither Islamization nor the Afghan war justified the abrogation of democracy in Pakistan.[53] He asserted that Zia's Islamization measures paid lip service to Islam but Islamized none of the country's judicial, bureaucratic, or political structures. Pakistan's political predicament could be solved only by ending martial rule, not by promulgating the shari'at bill,[54] which had taken effect on June 15, 1988, replacing most of the existing legal code with injunctions from the shari'ah. Zia's persistence in using Islam to justify martial rule had hurt the cause of Islam in Pakistan.[55] The Jama'at therefore had refused even to participate in the discussions on either the shari'at bill before it was passed, or the eighth amendment to the constitution, which would vest greater powers in the president. On June 16, 1988, a day after the bill took effect, the Jama'at's secretariat issued a statement in Lahore signed by nine of the Jama'at's senior leaders, which criticized the bill for paying superficial lip service to Islam and deplored Zia's use of Islam for political ends.[56]

Although the final draft of the shari'at bill was similar to Jama'at's own earlier proposals and the party had originally favored it, it rejected the bill outright on the grounds that it did not address popular concerns and was meaningless so long as the anglicized legal system remained the same.[57] Nor was criticism of the shari'at bill limited to Qazi Husain and the leaders of the Karachi Group; it was also voiced by many Jama'at leaders in Punjab, including Mian Tufayl.

Qazi Husain then attacked the military regime at its foundations. Fear of Soviet encroachment in South Asia and the jihad that was mounted to counter it had been critical to Zia's survival. Aware of all this, Qazi Husain claimed that Pakistan's Afghan policy had originally been conceived by Bhutto.[58] He also claimed that the Jama'at was open to cooperation with all political forces and particularly wished to end its "cold war" with the People's Party.[59] He had himself laid the foundations for discussions with the People's Party in two meetings with the MRD emissary, Faruq Laghari. During those meetings the MRD had invited the Jama'at to join its ranks, and Qazi Husain had favored accepting that invitation. Despite pressures exerted by the Karachi Group, whose views were aired through the editorials of the Jama'at daily *Jasarat*, Mian Tufayl had barred the party from contemplating such a move. After 1987, with Mian Tufayl out of the way and the greater possibility of elections in 1988, the Karachi Group and the new amir made another bid for joining the MRD. The new initiative was prompted by the dismissal of Prime Minister Muhammad Khan Junejo and the dissolution of the assemblies on May 29, 1988, which the Karachi Group interpreted as the recrudescence of martial rule.

The People's Party was eager to secure the Jama'at's support. Elections were expected, and it was deemed important for the MRD to represent as wide a spectrum of parties as possible. Moreover, the Jama'at had been the People's Party's staunchest opponent throughout the 1970s and was closely associated with Zia. Winning over the Jama'at, therefore, had symbolic significance for the MRD. The People's Party was also aware of the Jama'at's street power and wished to neutralize the party's potential opposition to the MRD's own campaign and possibly to solicit the Jama'at's help in mounting a more effective one.[60]

In June 1988, Benazir Bhutto, the leader of the MRD, met with Ghafur Ahmad of the Jama'at in Karachi. This meeting resulted in an understanding between the MRD and the Jama'at and was followed by a second more formal meeting. The purpose of this second meeting was to agree that the next elections would be party-based, held within ninety days, and governed by the People's Party–PNA agreement of July 1977,[61] which incorporated a plan to conduct elections without the Registrations Law and provided for an autonomous election commission to oversee them. The three-point agreement was to serve as the basis for a common electoral platform which would induct the Jama'at into the MRD. Some say that the negotiations also involved a discussion of the distribution of candidates, with the Jama'at asking for 30 percent of the MRD's slate.

The Benazir-Ghafur meetings were followed by two meetings between Qazi Husain and Laghari in Lahore, the second of which occurred in September 1988. Meanwhile, Ghafur Ahmad asked the shura' for a ruling which would convert the agreements reached by him into political directives. The shura', whose members were mainly from Punjab and North-West Frontier Province, was not eager to cooperate with the MRD, especially since it was led by a woman. Nor had they been as antagonistic toward Zia. Despite the intercession of the amir, the members deadlocked. The Jama'at put forth a new condition for continuing association with the MRD· its political platform had to include a demand for the "creation of an Islamic order."

Senior Jama'at leaders led by Mian Tufayl now began to lobby against joining the MRD, assisted by a host of right-of-center writers, statesmen, and intellectuals, none of whom were Jama'at members and many of whom were affiliates of the Muslim League, who though they had always denounced the Jama'at's ideological convictions, suddenly began to complain that it had forsaken them. An array of publications began to pressure the Jama'at to revert to its ideological fervor and forego the agreement with the MRD. Although they were foes of the People's Party, Zia was not altogether uninvolved in encouraging this sudden concern for the Jama'at's ideological fidelity Leading those criticizing the Jama'at was the pro-Jama'at journalist and close adviser to Zia, Muhammad Salahu'ddin, through whom Zia managed to encourage a split in the party [62] Salahu'ddin, an opponent of the People's Party, was particularly vociferous in his criticism of Ghafur Ahmad and the Jama'at's new policy Possibly prompted by Zia, he reminded the party's leaders of the excesses of the Bhutto government, of the People's Party's secular approach to politics, and of the suffering the Jama'at and the IJT had endured under that party's rule.[63] Citing Mawdudi's often-quoted statement that the "Jama'at-i Islami is not only a political party, but also an ideological one,"[64] Salahu'ddin also told Jama'at leaders that their political instincts were drowning out their religious sensibilities and that the party was turning its back on its ideological heritage. An alliance with the MRD, warned Salahu'ddin, would turn the Jama'at into a party with no principles and no ideological mainstay; it would be the end of the Jama'at.

Takbir, Salahu'ddin's magazine, has always been popular and influential with Jama'at members and supporters across Pakistan as the party's semiofficial but independent organ and a forum for the Jama'at and other right-of-center groups. It is an important part of the Jama'at's propaganda machine and, until the People's Party alliance, had never been openly at odds with the party's leaders. Salahu'ddin's editorials were therefore particularly effective in casting doubts among rank-and-file members regarding the propriety of the Jama'at's new strategy, and they undermined its leaders both in Karachi, which was initially in favor of Ghafur Ahmad's position, and in Punjab, where Zia enjoyed a good following among Jama'at members. *Takbir's* campaign was particularly influential because the shura' had postponed any decision on what action to take until a poll of the rank-and-file members had been tallied. In Karachi, pro–Ghafur Jama'at workers responded to Salahu'ddin's criticism by demonstrating outside the offices of *Takbir*, where they burned copies of the magazine. In Lahore the party's publications bureau reprimanded Salahu'ddin, to show the Jama'at's annoyance at his interference with party authority

Although the Lahore Group agreed with Salahu'ddin, it was compelled to close ranks with the Karachi Group lest the Jama'at's internal disputes become public. The Jama'at's secretariat defended Ghafur Ahmad, arguing that he had met Benazir Bhutto as an emissary of the amir and as part of the Jama'at's routine contacts with the leaders of various political parties. The Jama'at was, however, clearly on the defensive, not only because the general public had been alerted to its rapprochement with the erstwhile enemy but also because Salahu'ddin had cast the new changes in an unsavory light. The implications of the charge of inconsistency and the propaganda war that surrounded it were serious, especially in North-West Frontier Province and Punjab, where followers of the Jama'at are from small towns and rural areas and are more ideologically oriented. Radical change, especially in light of *Takbir's* successful propaganda campaign, was no longer possible. The turn of events, moreover, had proved to the Jama'at that it could not switch gears too radically without jeopardizing its traditional base of support. It had to chart its course more judiciously

The attempts of the Jama'at, and the Karachi Group in particular, to provide a more balanced mix of ideology and pragmatism and to replace commitment to Islamization with greater populism had been effectively checked. While some continued to press for joining the MRD, the Lahore Group resisted it. The Jama'at began to renege on its agreements with the MRD. Discipline within the Jama'at had grown lax, opening up the internal debates of the party to public scrutiny Qazi Husain sought to restore party unity by denouncing Zia for undermining the People's Party–PNA talks, for his excessive reliance on the United States, for promoting corruption in Pakistan, for creating ethnic dissension in Sind, and for sowing discord among Pakistani political parties.[65] *Jasarat* elaborated further on these themes and, taking its cue from Qazi Husain, stepped up its anti-Zia rhetoric throughout the summer of 1988. Zia was criticized for killing demonstrators in Karachi in 1986, for his anti-Shi'ism, and for his sleight of hand in using the shari'at bill to oust Junejo from office. He had used the excuse that Junejo had been reluctant to promulgate a shari'at bill to dismiss the government, and then proceeded to promulgate a shari'at bill of his own to obfuscate his constitutionally suspect ouster of the prime minister. "Nothing good came of the rule of the anglicized army officer, whose Islamic convictions were skin deep," Qazi Husain remarked.[66]

This escalation of attacks against Zia went hand in hand with distancing the Jama'at from the MRD. After three tumultuous meetings, the Jama'at's shura' finally rejected the MRD option.[67] Faced with this decision, the party reaffirmed its ideological priorities and established limits to how much it could compromise on issues of principle. It would adopt a more cautious approach to pragmatic politics. Discord, however, continued to reign in the party

Zia died in a plane crash on August 17, 1988, and this event abruptly altered the political scene. The subsequent democratization of Pakistani politics opened new vistas to the party and posed new questions to its leaders. Martial rule ceased to exist, but its departure only highlighted the fundamental problems of the Jama'at's religiopolitical agenda. Once Pakistani politics found new life in the post-Zia period, the same considerations that had compelled the party's move to populism reappeared. Political expedience forced the party to search once more for an acceptable and politically meaningful equilibrium between commitment to Islamization and pursuit of political interests, which would at the same time retain the support of the religiously conscious electorate and permit the party to expand its base.

10 The Rebirth of Democracy, 1988–1993

With Zia, and a number of army leaders who were also killed in the crash, out of the picture, the armed forces were thrown into confusion. The balance of power shifted to the People's Party, which counted on the elections, scheduled for November 1988, to allow it to take over the government. It therefore saw no further need for the MRD and dissolved the alliance. It would contest the elections alone. This made any debate about joining the MRD moot: "The final decision to keep the Jama'at out of MRD was taken not by the shura', but by the People's Party "[1]

The dissolution of the MRD did not, however, end the Jama'at's trouble because the party was clearly unprepared to contest any elections on its own. Since 1970 the Jama'at had participated in national elections only as part of a larger coalition, which had allowed it to project its power more effectively than would otherwise have been possible. It had lost its Muhajir support, and its popularity had plummeted as a result of its association with Zia. It was ill-equipped to stand on its own, all the more so as it soon became apparent that the elections of 1988 would pit the People's Party against a cluster of pro-Zia candidates.

The solution was found in the Islami Jumhuri Ittihad (IJI, Islamic Democratic Alliance), a coalition put together soon after Zia's death at the behest of the armed forces and the Inter-Services Intelligence, which had managed the Afghan war since the early years of the Zia regime. The IJI consisted of right-of-center and Islamic parties, the most important of which was the Muslim League. They had in common a hostility to the People's Party and a vested interest in the policies of the Zia regime. The military and intelligence establishments had their own reasons for wishing to keep the People's Party out of power, including protecting the power they had gained under Zia, a vested interest in the continuation of the Afghan war, and apprehension over Benazir Bhutto's vengeance for the execution of her father. Only a strong national coalition rooted in Islam and support for Zia could challenge the People's Party The Jama'at had strong Islamic credentials and was an obvious addition to such an alliance. Considerable pressure was brought to bear on it to join up. Qazi Husain opposed joining the IJI until he was approached by the Inter-Services Intelligence; then with no counteroffers forthcoming from the People's Party he capitulated. The matter was put before the shura'

There were several issues at stake in the decision. Many among the Karachi Group were not willing to join an alliance with the Muslim League, a party of landowners and the propertied elite, the very groups Qazi Husain had vowed to topple. The memory of repression by the People's Party in the 1970s was by then far less compelling than more recent battles with the League governments in Karachi and Islamabad. It was unlikely that the League had grown more friendly; it was likely to continue harassing the Jama'at despite any alliance. Qazi Husain and his circle argued that joining the IJI would in the end prove to be a setback for their long-run political objectives. As convincing as their argument may have been, they could not produce a viable alternative other than not contesting the elections at all, which the Jama'at was not willing to countenance—or contesting them alone, which meant humiliating defeat.[2] Meanwhile, the intelligence service's anti–People's Party propaganda campaign, stirring up memories of Bhutto's "reign of terror" in the 1970s and exhorting Islamic groups to defend the gains made under Zia and the Afghan war, had struck a receptive chord, especially as the People's Party failed to bury the hatchet with the Islamic parties.

Zia had become a far more popular figure dead than he had been alive. The sympathy and admiration that emerged for him among the right-wing voters in the country was politically compelling. Even the Karachi Group, which was eager to distance the Jama'at from Zia, saw that joining an alliance to continue Zia's legacy was not an impolitic option. The rank and file had also begun to pressure their leaders to join the alliance. As a result, the position of Qazi Husain and the Karachi Group was undermined, and they agreed to join the IJI.

The Jama'at now had to figure out how to enter into an alliance supporting Zia's legacy after having spent the preceding three months denouncing it and him. They solved the problem by talking about the Afghan war instead, and about the common goals which the Jama'at and the armed forces shared regarding its conduct. By justifying its entry into the IJI solely in terms of defending the war in Afghanistan, the Jama'at hoped it would avoid the embarrassment of openly going back on its words,[3] though it gradually referred more frequently to Zia's Islamization measures as the basis for its continued participation in the IJI. Anti–People's Party propaganda was also increased, so it could argue that it was choosing the lesser of two evils.

Mian Nawaz Sharif played a major role in the decision to join the IJI. He had

Table 16. Results of the 1988 National Assembly Elections for the Jama'at-ı Islamı

	Punjab	NWFP	Sind	Baluchıstan	Total
Seats contested	14	4	8	0	26
Seats won	5	2	0	0	7
Special women s seats	1	0	0	0	1
Total seats	6	2	0	0	8
Total votes received	620,952	88,840	100,520	0	810,312
Average votes per candidate	44,354	22,210	12,565	0	31,165

Source: Election Bureau of the Jama'at-ı Islamı.

Table 17 Votes Received by the Jama'at-ı Islamı ın the 1988 National Assembly Elections

	Votes Received	Total Votes Cast	Votes Received by Closest Rival	Party of Closest Rival
NWFP				
Swat	16,639	67,669	16,149	Not stated
Dir	35,288	74,643	28,974	Pakistan People s Party (PPP)
Punjab				
Rawalpındı	61,188	139,142	39,294	Independent
Sargodha	65,210	125,581	57,351	PPP
Gujrat	32,827	86,465	31,125	PPP
Lahore	51,764	108,382	47,908	PPP
Darah Ghazı Khan	60,297	120,234	45,590	PPP

Source: Tarıq Isma'il, *Election '88* (Lahore, 1989).

been a prominent Muslim Leaguer and chief minister of Punjab during the Zia period, a position he held until he became prime minister in 1990. He had been a close ally of Zia and defended him even when the general dismissed the Muslim League government in 1988. The Inter-Services Intelligence had managed to broker a truce between Sharif and his fellow Muslim Leaguers, who had broken with him over his support of Zia, but his position in the League remained shaky Challenged by Junejo and his allies in Punjab, Sharif turned to the Jama'at for support. The same pro-Jama'at writers, political analysts, and journalists who had served as Zia's advisers—Muhammad Salahu'ddin, Altaf Hasan Quraishı, and Mujibu'l-Rahman Shamı—were now inducted into Sharif's inner circle, as were a number of erstwhile IJT votaries, the most notable of whom was Husain

Table 18. Results of the 1988 Provincial Assembly Elections for the Jama'at-ı Islamı

	Punjab	NWFP	Sind	Baluchistan	Total
Seats contested	20	14	9	1	44
Seats won	5	6	0	0	11
Special women s seats	1	1	0	0	2
Total seats	6	7	0	0	13
Total votes received	327,617	93,826	36,537	1,185	459,165
Average votes per candidate	16,380	6,700	4,059	1,185	10,435

Source: Election Bureau of Jama'at-ı Islamı.

Table 19 Votes Received by the Jama'at-ı Islamı ın the 1988 Provincial Assembly Elections

	Votes Received	Total Votes Cast	Votes Received by Closest Rival	Party of Closest Rival
NWFP				
Swat	7,649	24,592	5,284	Independent
Swat	5,542	18,448	2,856	Awamı National Party (ANP)
Dir	7,098	14,334	5,852	Independent
Dir	11,324	24,049	11,067	Pakıstan People's Party (PPP)
Dir	6,767	16,317	5,930	ANP
Dir	9,363	23,034	4,156	Independent
Punjab				
Rawalpındi	27 452	67,149	23,559	PPP
Khushab	32,452	64,632	24,580	PPP
Faısalabad	22,836	48,069	22,549	PPP
Lahore	26,729	59,424	25,864	PPP
Lıyah	26,438	67,832	14,940	Independent

Source: Tarıq Isma'il, *Election '88* (Lahore, 1989).

Haqqanı. Jama'at members viewed Sharif as a breed apart from other Muslim Leaguers because he had been personally close to Zia and reached an understanding with hım, and he was known to be devout.[4]

As a result of the negotiations which organized the IJI, Ghafur Ahmad became the alliance's secretary-general, and the Jama'at was given twenty-sıx national tıckets and forty-four provincial ones. The Jama'at won eıght National Assembly seats, one of whıch was reserved for women only; and thırteen provincial assembly seats, two of whıch were reserved for women (see tables 16–19). These seats, fixed ın number, are distributed after the elections based on the vote of the assemblies. The Jama'at had won only 26.9 percent of the National Assembly seats and 25 percent of provincial seats it contested, the weakest showing of the IJI parties.

The elections tilted the advantage within the party in favor of the pro-IJI Lahore Group. With the MQM's total victory in Karachi, all of the party's national and provincial seats came from the pro-Zia and pro-IJI North-West Frontier Province and Punjab. Meanwhile, with the blessing of the Inter-Services Intelligence, Sharif, who was able to retain control of Punjab despite the People's Party's solid electoral showings, became the leader of the IJI.

The People's Party Government

After the elections, the People's Party took over the central government and the ministries of the North-West Frontier Province and Sind, and the IJI took over the ministry of Punjab. Since neither the People's Party nor the IJI had stable majorities, parliamentary intrigues directed at toppling both the central government and the various provincial ministries soon followed. The resulting intrigues replaced the time-honored agitational style of dissent in Pakistan and took politics off the streets—where the Jama'at was most effective—and into the national and provincial assemblies, where it was weakest. The party therefore found itself increasingly marginalized and irrelevant. Consequently, there was concern over the party's future once again as the Jama'at began to ponder ways to break out of this impasse.

In the long run, the Jama'at had to become better represented in parliament to improve its political standing; in the short run it had to find a way to project its power sufficiently to remain influential. Obviously the IJI would not be useful for this, and in any case not all the members were reconciled to their membership in the IJI because the Muslim League dominated the alliance.[5] Their connection with it was restricted to Nawaz Sharif, whose own position in Punjab in 1988–89 was by no means certain. He was under attack from the People's Party, which was trying to engineer a vote of no confidence against him in the Punjab assembly, and from Muslim League leaders, who were controlled by Junejo and favored a break with the Jama'at. Meanwhile, attacks by the Muslim Student Federation on the IJT escalated, and the unchecked rivalry between the two became a source of grave concern for IJI leaders.[6]

As eager as it may have been to find a viable alternative, the Jama'at could not easily break with the IJI. The posthumous popularity of Zia which was manifest at the commemoration of the first anniversary of his death on August 17, 1989, in Islamabad restricted its maneuverability, especially since the Jama'at's own members displayed the same sentiments. During the speeches of the Jama'at's leaders at their open convention in Lahore in November 1989, for example, the crowd continually interrupted the speakers, to their annoyance, by chants of "*mard-ı haq,* Zia ul-Haq (man of truth, Zia ul-Haq)." The party therefore began to equivocate, criticizing the IJI but at the same time supporting Nawaz Sharif.[7]

The relations between the Jama'at and the IJI worsened in October 1989 when the MQM, which had formed an alliance with the People's Party after the elections, decided to go its own way Eager to add the fourteen MQM National Assembly votes to the opposition, and in the process, to secure a base in Karachi, the IJI began to woo the MQM. After securing considerable concessions from Nawaz Sharif, in November 1989 the MQM threw in its lot with the opposition, anticipating that it could topple the People's Party government through a vote of no confidence in the National Assembly Cooperation with the MQM, which now played the role of the IJI's representative in Sind, brought relations between the IJI and the Jama'at to the brink of collapse. The Jama'at-ı Islamı of Karachi was offended because the IJI-MQM negotiations had been conducted without consulting them and without securing from the MQM any concessions that would benefit the Jama'at.[8]

The IJI-MQM alliance signaled to the Jama'at that Nawaz Sharif was following in Zia's footsteps and building a power base detrimental to the Jama'at's interests. Nawaz Sharif, they decided, had merely been paying lip service to Islam; he was really looking for a coalition between the Muslim League's landed elite and the provincial and ethnic parties, to sustain his power. The Jama'at would then be sidelined by the MQM and the other parties. The more the IJI consolidated its relations with its ethnic and provincial partners, the more the Jama'at would become estranged from the alliance.

The Jama'at's disaffection with the IJI first manifested itself in November 1989, when Benazır Bhutto's government set out to secure the Jama'at's cooperation and thereby deny Nawaz Sharif his street power and political workers, especially in Punjab. To that end, she was considering calling for elections; and for a government preoccupied with averting a vote of no confidence, the Jama'at's eight votes in the National Assembly could be useful. The Jama'at could also provide the government with much-needed Islamic legitimacy, which would in turn weaken the seemingly unified pro-Zia political camp.

Early in November the Jama'at's old foe, Ghulam Mustafa Khar, along with a veteran of the IJT-People's Student Federation clashes of the late 1960s, Jahangır Badr—both People's Party stalwarts—met separately with Qazı Husain and Liaqat Baluch in Lahore. They said that Benazır Bhutto was making headway in winning over key leaders of the Muslim League of Punjab, and if she succeeded, Nawaz Sharif would fall. It would be to the Jama'at's benefit to reach an agreement with the People's Party while the party still had a good bargaining position; otherwise, "it would be buried along with Nawaz Sharif."[9] The Jama'at considered the People's Party's offer seriously, especially after the government survived a vote of no confidence and appeared to be gaining strength; and it asked for concrete proposals from the People's Party

On February 1, 1990, Qazi Husain met with N. D. Khan, the deputy secretary-general of the People's Party On February 18 Khan met with Ghafur Ahmad, who gave him messages of advice for Benazir Bhutto and the People's Party chief minister of Sind, Qa'im 'Ali Shah, regarding the deteriorating law and order in Sind.[10] Khan and Ahmad reached no agreement. The Jama'at did acknowledge that in principle it might cooperate with the People's Party, but it then stipulated conditions for cooperation which the People's Party could not possibly agree to. It also made the conditions public: the People's Party had to change its policy in Sind, alter its foreign policy, agree to calling Pakistan an Islamic state, establish an Islamic order, and change its leadership by eliminating Benazir Bhutto, Begum Nusrat Bhutto, Ghulam Mustafa Khar, and Mukhtar A'wan, the first two because they were women—although the Jama'at had supported the candidacy of Fatimah Jinnah in her bid for the presidency—and the second two "for their atrocities against the Jama'at and the Jami'at."[11] Their candidates to replace Benazir Bhutto were Mi'raj Khalid, Faruq Laghari, or Amin Fahim.[12] Khalid was the speaker of the National Assembly and the other two were cabinet members. Not surprisingly, these conditions ended any possibility of serious negotiations for the moment.

The possibility reappeared in March 1990 when the IJI, having failed to unseat Benazir Bhutto, encouraged the army to overthrow the government. A shura' meeting in the first week of March passed a resolution criticizing the move and advising the amir to pull the party out of the IJI.[13] On March 6, Qazi Husain announced that the Jama'at was in full agreement with Benazir Bhutto's policy of defending the independence movement in Kashmir. If the Afghan war permitted the Jama'at to join the IJI without losing face, the Kashmir crisis allowed it to back out again with its dignity intact.

The warming between the Jama'at and the People's Party, however, came to naught. The government was being accused of corruption and mismanagement by the IJI and began to lose popular support. Little could be gained from siding with it. The Jama'at, therefore, found it prudent to wait. The government was ousted on August 6 when the president, Ghulam Ishaq Khan, citing rampant corruption and mismanagement in government circles, instability in Sind, and the deleterious effects of horse-trading—whereby parliament representatives would switch party allegiances for financial compensation—dissolved the national and provincial assemblies, dismissed the People's Party government, and called for fresh elections in October 1990.

The Elections of 1990 and the IJI Government

When it became obvious that Benazir Bhutto would not be returned to office, the Jama'at decided to remain with the IJI, which was expected to form the next

Table 20. Seats Contested and Won by the Jama'at-ı Islamı ın the 1990
Elections

	Punjab	NWFP	Sind	Baluchıstan	Total
National Assembly seats contested	7	4	6	1	18
National Assembly seats won	7[a]	1[b]	0	0	8
Provıncıal Assembly seats contested	14	12	11	0	37
Provıncıal Assembly seats won	12[c]	8[d]	0	0	20

Source: Electıon Bureau of the Jama'at-ı Islamı.

[a] The Jama'at's Natıonal Assembly seats were won ın Rawalpındı. Lahore (2). Sargodha. Sahıwal. Shaikhapura. and Sialkot.

[b] The Jama'at's Provıncıal Assembly seats were won ın Rawalpındı (2). Lahore (3). Faısalabad. Sargodha. Gujranwala. Lıyah. Bhawalpur. and Gujrat.

[c] The Jama'at won ıts Natıonal Assembly seat ın Swat.

[d] The Jama'at's Provıncıal Assembly seats were won ın Swat (2). Chıtral. and Dir (5).

government. Overnıght ıt once more became a dedicated member of the IJI and enthusıastıcally rejoıned the alliance. Between August and October the Jama'at provıded the IJI wıth workers and polıtıcal support and whıpped up popular passions agaınst the People's Party and ıts maın source of foreign support, the Unıted States. The Jama'at was not welcomed back to the IJI's fold wıth much enthusıasm. It was gıven eıghteen Natıonal Assembly tıckets, eıght fewer than ın 1988, and thırty-seven provıncıal tıckets, seven fewer than ın 1988. Islam did not play a central role ın determınıng the outcome of the elections, another mark of the Jama'at's dimınıshıng value for the IJI. The Jama'at had ınsisted on challengıng the MQM ın Sind. The IJI was reluctant to oblige, for theoretıcally such a move would pit pro-IJI candidates agaınst one another to the advantage of the People's Party, but the Jama'at persısted and finally receıved sıx of ıts natıonal tıckets and eleven of ıts provıncıal ones ın Sind,[14] all of whıch were lost to the MQM. The rout of the Jama at ın Sind, whıch showed the power of ethnıc over Islamıc sentıments, justıfied the IJI's turn to ethnıc and provıncıal partıes to bolster ıts power base.

The Jama'at won only 3 percent of the popular vote (640,000) ın the elections to the Natıonal Assembly, and 4 percent, 3 percent, and 0.8 percent of the vote ın the provıncıal assembly elections ın the North-West Frontıer Provınce, Punjab, and Sind, respectıvely [15] Although runnıng for fewer seats, the Jama'at did better ın these elections than ın 1988 (see table 20). It won eıght out of eıghteen contested natıonal seats (as opposed to seven out of twenty-sıx ın 1988), and twenty out of thırty-seven contested provıncıal seats (as opposed to eleven out of forty-four ın 1988). The Jama'at's ratıo of elected members to tıckets contested was ımproved to 44 percent and 54 percent for the Natıonal and Provıncıal Assembly races respectıvely The Jama'at did especıally well ın Punjab, where ıt won all of the seven National Assembly seats it contested, and twelve of the fourteen provincial tickets it was assigned. Although the improvement was a result of the IJI's soaring popularity, it nonetheless boosted Jama'at's morale.

Despite its wholehearted support for the alliance with the IJI during the elections, the Jama'at declined to participate in Nawaz Sharif's cabinet.[16] Nawaz Sharif's government was Islamic, but increasingly relied upon ethnic and provincial bases of power. It now openly turned to the MQM in Sind and the Awami National Party in the North-West Frontier Province to control those provinces and to keep the People's Party at bay The Jama'at was particularly disturbed by the IJI's close affinity with the MQM, which continued to dominate Karachi to the exclusion of the Jama'at.[17] It perpetuated that party's control over the politics of the Muhajir community and desacralized the political discourse in that province as well as in Pakistan as a whole, all to the detriment of the Jama'at. The MQM's onslaught against the remaining pockets of Jama'at power in Karachi did not help the situation, and it set the Jama'at at odds with the IJI. The Jama'at began openly to criticize the government for its lackluster performance on religious issues, joining the swelling chorus demanding greater Islamization. The Jama'at hoped both to expose the government's spurious allegiance to Islamic causes, thereby compelling Nawaz Sharif to reorient his politics, and to salvage Islam's political fortunes before the rise in importance of ethnic and provincial parties.

The Jama'at's posture against the government soon found a suitable issue in the Persian Gulf war. The Jama'at, against the official policy of the IJI government, supported Iraq and opposed the Persian Gulf monarchies and emirates, which were the party's financial patrons and political allies. This stand had several explanations. To begin with, the Jama'at was reacting to the United States' cut-off of aid in October 1990 in response to Pakistan's refusal to abandon its nuclear arms program. The IJI's electoral success has in part been attributed to its adroit manipulation of anti-Americanism, and no doubt this was not lost on the Jama'at. It also objected to the United States' de-escalating the war in Afghanistan in 1989 and the lack of American support for the Muslim cause in Kashmir, not to mention the Palestinians.[18] It claimed that the United States' argument that it had to liberate Kuwait was part of a "Zionist plot" by the United States to weaken the Muslim world and the Middle East and guarantee the security of Israel.[19] Khurshid Ahmad called American policy a "trap," designed to "entangle Iraq in war so that it could provide the United States with a chance to interfere and advance its sinister designs—to give an edge to Israel in the region and to control the Muslim oil."[20] The war thereby became a battle between Islam and its "enemies." There could be no observers, and it was clear where the Jama'at's loyalties lay

The Jama'at concluded from what had come to pass that the days of Persian

Gulf monarchies were numbered. If they did not fall before the onslaught of their northern neighbor, they would be pulled down by their own people. Saddam Hussein's rhetoric about the rich Persian Gulf states and the poor Arab and Muslim brethren elsewhere, along with the belief that the United States' presence in the region would deliver the kiss of death to the monarchies, had convinced the Jama'at that it was time to side with the future power brokers in the region.

There was a surprising amount of support for Iraq in Pakistan in November 1990; the party, which had since 1988 been trying to find a popular cause, now decided to take up "this cause of the masses" and ride the tide of resurgent Islamic feelings which it believed would once again sweep across Pakistan. Initially, the Jama'at had been critical of Saddam Hussein and had viewed the plight of Pakistani refugees from Kuwait with alarm. It wanted a viable settlement that called on Iraq to withdraw from Kuwait, above all else to prevent the United States from gaining a foothold in the Muslim "holy land." Qazi Husain even led a prominent delegation to several Middle East capitals to convince them of this. As war became imminent and soldiers from Western countries dug in their heels in Saudi Arabia, attitudes toward the crisis began to change in Pakistan, and Saddam Hussein found a base of support there.

Conscious of the changing tide of public opinion and somehow convinced of the ultimate victory of Saddam Hussein, after January 17 the Jama'at abandoned any pretense of following a via media and openly supported Iraq throughout the remainder of the conflict, denouncing the methodical destruction of that country under massive air bombardment. Again it found itself allied with some strange bedfellows, all of whom had also come to believe that the United States was headed for defeat and that Saddam Hussein was the horse to bet on. The armed forces, led by General Mirza Aslam Beig, who regarded to the war as a repeat of Karbala, the People's Party activists, and the left joined in denouncing American imperialism and quickly became allies of the Jama'at. Pictures of Qazi Husain sharing intimate moments with leftist poets and politicians began to adorn the pages of newspapers and magazines. On the international level, the Jama'at joined the ranks of the Tahrik-i Islami (Islamic Movement), a multinational Islamic umbrella organization which coordinates the activities of a number of revivalist groups across the Muslim world, including support for Iraq during the war. In Pakistan, the Jama'at organized fifty-seven "jihad rallies" and two dozen "coffin-clad" rallies to emphasize that its workers were ready for martyrdom in the jihad against the anti-Islamic forces of the West;[21] the IJT reinforced the Jama'at's protest by organizing 338 public rallies and demonstrations during the same period.[22]

As popular as the Jama'at's new policy was, not all members agreed with it. Many were critical of supporting Iraq and were ill at ease with Qazi Husain's blasts against the Persian Gulf monarchies. Mian Tufayl argued that, as unwelcome as the American assault on Iraq may have been, the only culprit in the entire ordeal was Saddam Hussein;[23] the Jama'at could not by any stretch of imagination justify defending such a ruthless enemy of Islam. Salahu'ddin, who had long enjoyed the patronage of Saudi Arabia, pointed out that "populism and demagogy did not befit an Islamic movement."[24] He derided the Jama'at's anti-Saudi rhetoric and suggested that inveighing against its long-time patrons and endorsing the actions of a secular dictator were perilously close to chicanery If the Jama'at believed that the kingdom was an "undemocratic lackey of imperialism," it should return the money it had received over the years from the Saudi government.[25]

Salahu'ddin's charges of "irresponsible," "irrational," and "opportunistic" behavior on the Jama'at's part were quickly reiterated by other pro-Jama'at periodicals and dailies, which also chided the party for sacrificing its principles to the demands of the mob. Many of the Jama'at's members and sympathizers had close ties in the Persian Gulf monarchies and were, as a result, greatly disturbed by the suggestion that they, their friends, or their families had earned their livelihood in the service of the enemies of Islam. The Jama'at could hardly reconcile its long-standing financial and political alliance with Saudi Arabia with its new rhetoric against it, and was thus placed on the defensive. Discontent in the party was widespread enough to prompt Qazi Husain to tour Pakistan in March 1991 to try to explain the logic of the party's policy on the Persian Gulf crisis to its workers and supporters.[26]

At the cost of losing its Saudi financial support and compromising its ethical and ideological principles, the Jama'at had taken up Saddam Hussein's cause because it was popular. It had hoped that its support for Iraq against "American imperialism and its stooges" would separate the Jama'at's position from that of the government and breathe new life into the party Instead it opened itself up to charges of duplicity which continued to exact a price. The pro-Iraq campaign had popularized Islamic issues, which no doubt benefited the Jama'at. With the Islamic forces on the move and the very basis of the IJI shaken over its support of Iraq, Sharif was compelled to mend fences with his religious right. When Qazi Husain publicly censured the foreign minister Sahibzadah Ya'qub Khan for "pursuing American interests," Sharif dismissed him,[27] and hastily pushed a modified version of the shari'at bill through the parliament.[28] The Jama'at then attacked the bill as mere window-dressing, an attack it renewed periodically Mian Tufayl, who had initially supported the IJI, even declared the bill "heretical."[29] The Jama'at also criticized the government for succumbing to American pressure to reach a compromise over Afghanistan, and for its "soft" stand on Kashmir.

The IJI was unable to accommodate the Jama'at's new populist ideas. Far from an Islamic coalition government, which the Jama'at believed would serve as a vehicle for the realization of its aims, the IJI proved to be a collection of the Jama'at's staunchest enemies—the Muslim League, the Awami National Party, and especially the MQM. Although the enmity between the Jama'at and the Muslim League and the Awami National Party was longstanding, the MQM presented the greater challenge. It had already defeated the Jama'at in Sind and was still busily eliminating the party from that province; it was also making inroads into the party's base of support elsewhere in Pakistan. In 1990, the MQM considered changing its name from Muhajir Qaumi Mahaz (Muhajir National Front) to Mutahhidah Qaumi Movement (United National Front), turning it into a national and not just a Muhajir party, to eliminate the handicap of its narrow group focus.[30] The Jama'at concluded that the MQM was positioning itself to compete with its national standing. In the spring of 1991, MQM activists killed two IJT workers and set the offices of *Takbir* ablaze; Qazi Husain openly threatened to leave the IJI,[31] especially as the coalition was losing ground. The IJI was being charged with corruption and mismanagement just as its predecessor had been, and it had become apparent that it was unlikely to remain popular for long, so the Jama'at found it easy to criticize. In November, it gave support to the opposition, led by the People's Party, to demand the removal of the prime minister pending an investigation of corruption charges.[32]

The prime minister could not afford a break in the IJI's putatively united ranks, particularly a break with its principal Islamic party He hoped that the promise of yet another shari'at bill would assuage the Jama'at. In July Ghafur Ahmad resigned from his position as secretary-general of the IJI, and in August Qazi Husain gave the government a two-month ultimatum to accommodate the Jama'at's demands or the party would leave the IJI.[33] Personal lobbying by Nawaz Sharif kept the Jama'at within the IJI's fold for a while longer. The relations between the two, however, remained strained, and closer cooperation did not appear likely The Jama'at set the price for its greater cooperation with the government as the control of the ministries of education, information and broadcasting, finance, and foreign affairs,[34] knowing full well that, given its modest parliamentary representation, the IJI would not oblige. The Jama'at in effect stipulated demands which ensured its exclusion from the cabinet.

The tensions between the government and the Jama'at rose further when the Najibu'llah government in Kabul fell. The government decided to accept a settlement to the Afghan war at the expense of the Mujahidin, whom the Jama'at favored. The Jama'at objected to the change of policy on Afghanistan. This and what the Jama'at depicted as the IJI's lackluster interest in Islamization provided the party with the pretext for breaking with the IJI on May 5, 1992. Qazi Husain announced that the government was infested with the "American virus," and no longer worthy of the Jama'at's loyalty The mounting anti-Americanism that had swept the country during the Gulf War gave reason to believe that defection would cost the party no support. It expanded its criticism of the government's Islamization and Afghan policies to include a host of other policy issues and the government's record in office.[35] The government responded by excoriating Qazi Husain for taking the Jama'at out of the IJI,[36] hoping to undermine his position in the party on the eve of his bid for re-election as amir. In September 1992, Mian Tufayl, leader of the Lahore Group during the Zia regime, resigned from the Jama'at's shura' in protest at the direction the party had taken;[37] but Qazi Husain was re-elected amir of Jama'at-i Islami. The debate over the Jama'at's choice of alliance, which had led to the stand-off between the Lahore and Karachi groups, appeared for now to have been resolved.

In the same month the army was sent to Sind to restore law and order, which had collapsed following the resumption of Muhajir-Sindhi clashes. The MQM offices were raided, and the party's leaders went underground. The MQM withdrew from the government. By July, it was clear that sending the army to Sind had greatly weakened Nawaz Sharif, who borrowed a move from General Zia and turned to Islamization to bolster the IJI's position. The government thus began openly to woo the Jama'at. The party, however, showed no inclination to rejoin the IJI after its enemy's departure. The leader of the Jama'at's parliamentary delegation, Liaqat Baluch, instead announced that the Jama'at and the People's Party ought to form an alliance.[38]

The extent of the estrangement between the Jama'at and the IJI became evident during the constitutional crisis which followed the stand-off between the president and the prime minister in the first half of 1993 Throughout the sordid affair, which culminated in the dismissal of the National Assembly and the government on April 18, their subsequent restoration by the Supreme Court on May 26, and finally the simultaneous resignations of the president and prime minister on July 18, the Jama'at remained cool toward the IJI. The party strongly condemned Ghulam Ishaq Khan's actions, accusing him of serving America's interests,[39] but it preferred to stay away from Nawaz Sharif and to work toward an alliance with other Islamic parties.

The return of democracy to Pakistan has pushed the Jama'at to search more rigorously for a proper mix of ideological commitment and pragmatic considerations, so as to develop a popular base. This has led the party to appeal more directly to popular sentiments and to put them above purely ideological considerations in formulating its policies. As a result, despite internal tensions, since 1988 the Jama'at has steadily moved away from the constellation of Islamic and right-of-center forces which supported Zia and formed the IJI, to find a more popular platform. The Jama'at continues to be an advocate of Islamization, but its political agenda is moving toward a vision of state and society that is inspired by Islam but is not limited to Islamization.

11   Islamic Revivalism in the Political Process

Throughout its history in Pakistan, the Jama'at-i Islami added to the national political discourse concerns for Islamic ideals, but the party's success in the intellectual and ideological domains found no reflection in politics. It has influenced politics but has failed to control them. The Jama'at proved capable of forming sociopolitical alliances predicated upon an Islamic political program but not of entering into the fundamental political debates in the country, and hence it found no means to secure power for the party

In the short run at least, success in Islamic revivalism can be directly correlated with the way the state reacts to it. The Iranian revolution owed its success to the inability or unwillingness of the Shah to respond effectively to Ayatollah Khumayni's challenge. Alternatively, the Syrian and Algerian examples prove that decisive state action can check revivalism's bid to control power. In Pakistan on some occasions the government sought to contend with Islamic revivalism by eliminating the Jama'at, as was the case during Liaqat 'Ali Khan's and the early period of Ayub Khan's rule, and then by challenging its religious position, a tactic that failed and emboldened Islamic revivalism. In 1958 and 1977 the party's drive for power was checked by decisive state action, and after 1977 the state sought to control Islamic revivalism by involving it in the political process more directly As the Jama'at's politics since the advent of the Zia regime indicate, there are limitations to this strategy for keeping Islamic revivalism in check.

Wherever Islamic revivalism has been successful, it has taken the political process unawares, capitalizing on a moment of enthusiasm to translate general sociopolitical discontent into a mass movement. As the Jama'at's case proves, protracted involvement in the political process, while it elicits certain concessions in the form of new laws and restrictions from the society, also creates barriers to the growth of revivalism and immunizes the political process to its challenge. It requires replacing a purely ideological orientation with an accommodation of pragmatic politics. This leads to compromise, and that transforms revivalist movements into political institutions tied to the system. Ultimately, democracy serves as the best check to the growth of revivalism. For democracy diversifies the scope of political debate and provides for exactly the kind of protracted involvement in the political process which is likely to constrict Islamic activism. Since 1989, for instance, the Jami'at-i Ulama-i Islam and the Jami'at-i Ulama-i Pakistan, the two dominant ulama parties of Pakistan, have both split into factions over policy

Democracy involves education to which revivalism cannot remain immune. In this regard revivalism's approach to and problems with democracy are not so very different from those which led to the evolution of Eurocommunism. New imperatives require fundamental changes, which lead to the adoption of new values. Since 1947, for instance, the Jama'at has become increasingly committed to democracy and the constitutional process—manifesting the party's modernization of Islamic thought. Although the party has not been thoroughly acculturated into a democratic mind-set, its commitment to democracy should not be dismissed. It emerged in the Jama'at's thinking, first as a political ploy, but increasingly as the mark of a new orientation. In a country which has spent twenty-five of its forty-six years of independence under military rule, and another five under the heavy hand of an autocratic civilian ruler, the fate of an oppositional expression of Islam, which had already passed on the option of revolution, would inevitably be intertwined with that of democracy It was this process which made Islam the bulwark of two national democratic movements, in the 1960s and again in the 1970s. Political exigency therefore plays an important role in determining Islam's attitude toward democracy, a fact which is of great importance to understanding the process of democratization in societies where religion remains a dominant force.[1] In the process, democracy transforms revivalist ideology and its plan of action. The often-asked question "What are the dangers of revivalism to democracy?" should be turned on its head: we should ask, "What are the dangers of democracy to revivalism?"

The Jama'at politicized Islam in Pakistan, but failed to reap any benefits from it. The size of the religious vote has increased markedly since 1947, but not the Jama'at's share of it. The Jama'at proved the efficacy of Islam as a political force, but it had no means to prevent others from exploiting religion for political gain. This is the second danger of democracy to revivalism. Democracy engenders a diversification of Muslim political expression, lures the spectrum of Islamic groups into the political arena, and strips revivalism of the means to manipulate the religious vote and to exercise effective political control over the Islamic vote bank. Instructive in this regard is the Jami'at-i Ulama-i Islam and Jami'at-i Ulama-i Pakistan's rivalry with the Jama'at in the elections of 1970. In those elections the Jama'at had launched an extensive electoral campaign to challenge the People's Party in West Pakistan and the Awami League in East Pakistan. The Jama'at had expected that its campaign would glorify Islam to undermine the left and the ethnic forces. It had not anticipated that its efforts would mobilize other religious forces and invite them into the elections, all at the Jama'at's expense.

The Jama'at was initially conceived of as a "holy community," in which high standards and ideological commitment limited membership; it was a vanguard party, an "organizational weapon." This allowed the party to project power far beyond its numbers and kept it alive through adversity While it was by no means unique in propagating a revivalist agenda in South Asia, no other revivalist movement has matched its staying power or political influence. Other self-styled Islamic parties, which either like the Jama'at emerged during the interwar period in India, the Khaksar or the Ahrar being the most notable, or those that made their debut later in Pakistan, such as the Nizam-i Islam or Tulu'-i Islam (Dawn Of Islam), although they also addressed the same concerns as the Jama'at and appealed to the same political constituency, were eventually overwhelmed by the vicissitudes of Pakistani politics and merged into larger parties. In fact, the Jama'at is perhaps the only Islamic religiopolitical organization in South Asia which has continued effectively beyond the life span of its founder.

On the other hand, it cannot be denied that the Jama'at's organization is not designed to run the political program to which the party has committed itself. The notion of a "holy community" is ill suited for operating as a party Similarly, the party's ideology is at odds with its political program. It continues to harp on the theme of Islamic revolution, although it operates within the bounds of the political process. In addition, it views revolution as a top-down process, whereby Islamization and its concomitant sociopolitical change will follow the education of the political elite in the teachings of Islam. Revolution is not a means of articulating popular demands but of defining a political struggle against the secular state. Islamic revolution in the Jama'at's rhetoric is not the battle cry of the masses but an elitist crusade aimed at appropriating the state. As a result, the Jama'at has adopted a pedantic and literary style and ignored populist themes. The party even continues to respect the right to private property and has avoided challenging the existing economic structure of Pakistan.

Its revolutionary rhetoric is also at odds with its support of the federal unit. Having joined the political process, it has in practice abandoned even a semblance of opposition to the current makeup of the state. Its rhetoric, however, continues to imply a revolutionary stand. Support for the state, the avowed homeland of Indian Muslims, has meant opposition to ethnic politics. The party, for instance, is rooted in Urdu, which has little following among the masses, who speak in local vernaculars such as Pakhtun, Punjabi, or Sindhi. The chasm between the Jama'at and the poor brought about by its obliviousness to socioeconomic concerns has reinforced its antiethnic attitudes.

In short, the Jama'at has failed to convert revivalism as ideology into revivalism as a social movement. It has failed to mobilize the masses for collective action for any sustained period of time under an Islamic banner. The two successful mass movements in Pakistan's history, those of Bhutto and the People's Party in the late 1960s and of the MQM in the 1980s, owed their success to a political platform which effectively combined populism with a radical antiestablishment platform and appeal to ethnic sentiments. Bhutto adopted a populist rhetoric, opposed the established order, and successfully manipulated tensions between Sindhis, Muhajirs, and Punjabis on the one hand and Punjabis and Bengalis on the other. The MQM similarly combined opposition to the established order with socioeconomic demands, while manipulating tensions between Muhajirs and Sindhis, Punjabis and Pathans. The Jama'at's political platform has lacked all three ingredients. The political fortunes of revivalism, as the case of Iran also shows, hinge on mobilizing more than just Islamic sentiments. To succeed, an Islamic revolution must effectively appeal to political sensibilities and satisfy socioeconomic demands.

The shortcomings of the Jama'at's program have been evident and to no one more than the party itself. Since the mid-1980s its leaders have been debating organizational reform and opening up its ranks. To date, however, no significant changes have been evident. With the election of Qazi Husain Ahmad to the office of amir the party did adopt a more populist rhetoric, but it was then forced to mute it when it joined up with the landowner-dominated Muslim League and the industrial magnate Nawaz Sharif to form the IJI. On the question of playing a role as the radical opposition and adopting a more ethnic outlook, it has been unyielding. Not unexpectedly, therefore, its political fortunes are little changed.

The party has sought to court the masses by making concessions to their religious sensibilities, which has brought the Jama'at somewhat closer to traditional Islam in South Asia and its practice of veneration of saints—which closely resembles North African maraboutism. Qazi Husain began his nationwide mass contact tour, the "caravan of invitation and benevolence" (karavan-i da'wat'u muhabbat), with a controversial visit to the shrine of Sayyid 'Ali Hujwiri (Data Ganjbakhsh) in Lahore, thus engaging in a religious activity that revivalism has always characterized as obscurantist and has strongly opposed—visiting a saint's shrine. Similarly since the mid-1980s the IJT has held annual conferences on Hujwiri to appeal to Brailwi students, especially from rural areas and small towns. This ideological compromise was necessitated by the Jama'at and IJT's efforts to expand their base of support, especially since the advent of democracy, and further underlines the danger of democracy to revivalism.

Compromises of this sort are a poor substitute for meaningful organizational and ideological reform and, by stirring up controversy, can even adversely affect the process of change. Some have been sufficiently contentious to cause defection in the ranks, but have not been drastic enough to cultivate new sources of support for the party The result has dampened the Jama'at's enthusiasm for undertaking major changes, for fear of losing the support the party already has. Change has as a result become a contentious issue that has inspired more controversy than action.

All this, however, is a continuing saga. Pakistan is changing, and so is the Jama'at. The political fortunes of the party may yet improve; only time will tell. It is obvious now, however, that operating in the political process, especially in a democracy, will require the party associated with the rise of contemporary Islamic revivalism and which has viewed itself as the "vanguard of the Islamic revolution" to embark upon changes that will inevitably diminish its commitment to its original ideology if it is to succeed.

Notes

1. THE QUEST FOR A HOLY COMMUNITY

1. The Jama'at-i Islami has not been much studied. A number of accounts of its ideology exist, which have, by and large, focused on the place of its program in, and its implications for, contemporary Islamic thought. See, for instance, SAAM, vol. 1, Erwin I.J. Rosenthal, *Islam in the Modern Nation State* (Cambridge, 1965); Aziz Ahmad, *Islamic Modernism in India and Pakistan, 1857–1964* (London, 1967); Hamid Enayat, *Modern Islamic Political Thought* (Austin, 1982); Charles J. Adams, "Mawdudi and the Islamic State," in John L. Esposito, ed., *Voices of Resurgent Islam* (New York, 1983), 99–133; Mumtaz Ahmad, "Islamic Fundamentalism in South Asia: The Jamaat-i-Islami and the Tablighi Jamaat," in Martin E. Marty and R. Scott Appleby, eds., *Fundamentalisms Observed* (Chicago, 1991), 457–530; and Kalim Bahadur, *The Jama'at-i Islami of Pakistan* (New Delhi, 1977). Bahadur's study addresses the political dimensions of the Jama'at's history, but remains focused on the ideological orientation of the party. Also of significance in this regard is Leonard Binder, *Religion and Politics in Pakistan* (Berkeley and Los Angeles, 1961). However, Binder's excellent study of the Jama'at's role in the constitutional debates following the creation of Pakistan is limited to the years 1947–1956.

2. For a more thorough discussion of Mawdudi's biography, see Seyyed Vali Reza Nasr, "The Politics of an Islamic Movement: The Jama'at-i Islami of Pakistan," Ph.D. dissertation, Massachusetts Institute of Technology, 1991.

3. Sayyid Abu'l-A'la Mawdudi, *Watha'iq-i Mawdudi* (Lahore, 1986).

4. In a eulogy which he wrote for Hyderabad in the TQ of September 1948, Mawdudi equated the collapse of nizam's state with the fall of Baghdad to the Mongols in 1258, the expulsion of the Moors from Spain in 1492, and the fall of the Mughal Empire in 1858.

5. On the significance of the fall of Hyderabad for South Asian Muslims, see Akbar S. Ahmed, *Discovering Islam: Making Sense of Muslim History and Society* (London, 1988), 143–71.

6. See, in this regard, *TQ* (October 1934). In a telegram to Shaikh Mujibur Rahman in March 1971, Mawdudi warned him against creating a debacle greater than the tragedy of "Islamic Spain", cited in Sarwat Saulat, *Maulana Maududi* (Karachi, 1979), 80. Elsewhere, Mawdudi referred to the eclipse of Islam from the centers of power in India as the "tragedy of Andalusia", see Sayyid Abu'l-A'la Mawdudi, *Tahrik-i Islami ka A'indah La'ihah-i 'Amal* (Lahore, 1986), 134. Ahmed, *Discovering Islam*, 2, has termed this anxiety about a Moorish fate the "Andalus Syndrome."

7 Francis Robinson, *Separatism among Indian Muslims: The Politics of United Provinces' Muslims, 1860–1923* (Cambridge, 1974), 320ff.

8. See for example, Maryam Jameelah, *Islam in Theory and Practice* (Lahore, 1973), 260–326.

9 On the Congress party's Muslim mass contact program, see Mushirul Hasan, "The Muslim Mass Contact Campaign: An Attempt at Political Mobilization," *Economic and Political Weekly* 21, 52 (December 27, 1986): 273–82. Mawdudi attacked the mass contact movement of the Congress severely in *TQ* (December 1937): 243–44, and in the following issue (January 1938), which served as the first installment of Mawdudi's famous book *Musalman awr Mawjudah Siyasi Kashmakash* (Lahore, 1938–1940).

10. Gail Minault, *The Khilafat Movement: Religious Symbolisms and Political Mobilization in India* (New York, 1982), 79–84, and Robinson, *Separatism among Indian Muslims*, 326–41, for the Jami'at-i Ulama-i Hind's relations with the Congress party, see Yohanan Friedmann, "The Attitude of the Jam'iyyat-i 'Ulama-i Hind to the Indian National Movement and the Establishment of Pakistan," in Gabriel Baer, ed., *The 'Ulama' in Modern History* (Jerusalem, 1971), 157–83.

11. For more on the history and politics of the Muslim League, see Stanley Wolpert, *Jinnah of Pakistan* (Oxford, 1984).

12. Sayyid Abu'l-A'la Mawdudi, *Tanqihat* (Lahore, 1989), 177ff.

13 On Mawdudi's version of this idea, see *TQ* (October–December 1938): 85–320, where Mawdudi presented a "two nation" scheme of his own. For more on this issue, see chapter 5

14. See David Gilmartin, *Empire and Islam: Punjab and the Making of Pakistan* (Berkeley and Los Angeles, 1988), 2–3 and 169–73, on Jinnah's advocacy of the Shariat Application Act of 1937; and Wolpert, *Jinnah*, 230, on the Muslim League's use of religious divines to undermine the Unionist Party Similar policies were also followed in Sind; see Sarah F.D. Ansari, *Sufi Saints and State Power: The Pirs of Sind, 1843–1947* (Cambridge, 1992), 117–28.

15 Interview with Mian Tufayl Muhammad.

16. Mawdudi's association with the Khilafat movement had made him particularly suspicious of Mustafa Kemal Ataturk, and he came to view Kemalism as a symbol of godless secularism posing danger to Muslim societies. Mas'ud 'Alam Nadwi, a leading Jama'at thinker, openly alluded to Muslim League members, in a derogatory fashion, as "Kemalists", cited in *RJI*, vol. 6, 175–77 For similar expressions of abhorrence of Kemalism, see Khurshid Ahmad, ed., *Adabiyat-i Mawdudi* (Lahore, 1972), 296–302; Mawdudi, *Tanqihat*, 96–110; Abad Shahpuri, *Tarikh-i Jama'at-i Islami* (Lahore, 1989), vol. 1, 297–98. Similar references also exist in the

Jama'at's literature regarding Pahlavi Iran; see *Kawthar* (February 21, 1948): 21, where Mawdudi specifies that Pakistan should not be modeled after Iran or Turkey

17 *RJI,* vol. 6, 180–95; and *Kawthar* (July 5, 1947): 1.

18. The word '*ibadah,* or "worship," was interpreted by Mawdudi to mean obedience to religious law; '*ibadah* in Arabic comes from '*abd,* which means "slave." Therefore, to worship in Islam meant to render unswerving obedience to God's will, an act that stripped Muslims of all volition. Most critics of Mawdudi had taken issue with equating worship with obedience, for it reduces religious spirituality to blind adherence to religious dictums. See, for instance, Sayyid Abu'l-Hasan 'Ali Nadwi, '*Asr-i Hazir Main Din Ki Tafhim'u Tashrih* (Karachi, n.d.).

19 See Nasr, "The Politics of an Islamic Movement," 272–353

20. *Short Proceedings of the 2nd Annual Conference, Jamaat-e-Islami, East Pakistan,* March 14–16, 1958, 2; enclosed with U.S. Consulate, Dacca, disp. #247, 4/3/1958, 790D.00/4–358, NA.

21. See for instance, *JIKUS,* 31.

22. S. Abul A'la Maududi, *The Process of Islamic Revolution* (Lahore, 1980), 17–18.

23. *JIKUS,* 32.

24. Shahpuri, *Tarikh,* vol. 1, 402–4.

25 Sayyid Abul A'la Maududi, *Islam Today* (Beirut, 1985), 12.

26. *Idem, The Islamic Way of Life* (Leicester, 1986), 16.

27 See *RJI,* vol. 5, 195, where the organization's missionary outlook is discussed.

28. Mujibu'l-Rahman Shami, "Karan Se Aftab Tak," in *HRZ,* 31.

29 Minault, *The Khilafat Movement,* 153.

30. Rahman Siddiqi, "Mawlana Azad Awr Mawlana Mawdudi ki Mabain ik Gumshudah Kari", *Nida* (February 7–13, 1990): 21.

31. For a thorough account of this movement, see Minault, *The Khilafat Movement.*

32. Sayyid Abu'l-A'la Mawdudi, "Khud Nivisht," in Muhammad Yusuf Buhtah, *Mawlana Mawdudi: Apni Awr Dusrun ki Nazar Main* (Lahore, 1984), 34–35

33. Following the creation of Pakistan in 1948, the Khaksar changed its name to the Islam League, and its uniformed wing became the Islam League Razakars (volunteers).

34. From a speech delivered by Jinnah to Muslim League members in Lucknow in October 1937; cited in Wolpert, *Jinnah,* 153–54.

35 While each Sufi order has its own set of rules, all follow the same organizational model. See Seyyed Hossein Nasr, *Sufi Essays* (London, 1972), 45–71.

36. On relations between the Sufi master and his disciples, see Mohammad Ajmal Khan, "A Note on *Adab* in the *Murshid-Murid* Relationship," in Barbara D. Metcalf, ed., *Moral Conduct and Authority: The Place of Adab in South Asian Islam* (Berkeley and Los Angeles, 1984), 241–51, and Margaret Malamud, "The Development of Organized Sufism in Nishapur and Baghdad from the Eleventh to the Thirteenth Century," Ph.D. dissertation, University of California, Berkeley, 1990.

37 The note is dated August 21, 1935, and is reprinted in Mawdudi, *Watha'iq,* 82.

38. Reprinted in 'Asim Nu'mani, ed., *Makatib-i Sayyid Abu'l-A'la Mawdudi* (Lahore, 1977), vol. 2, 8–10.

39 Nu'mani, *Makatib,* vol. 2, 14.

40. Interviews with Amin Ahsan Islahi and Abu'l-Hasan 'Ali Nadwi.

41. Adams suggests that while Mawdudi was not enamored by the ideas of fascism, he was impressed by the efficacy of its organizational methods; see Charles J. Adams, "The Ideology of Mawlana Mawdudi," in Donald E. Smith, ed., *South Asian Politics and Religion* (Princeton, 1966), 375 Others have viewed the Jama'at as modeled after communism; see Eran Lerman, "Mawdudi's Concept of Islam," *Middle Eastern Studies* 17, 4 (October 1981): 492–509 Evidence from the biography of Mawdudi tends to support the latter view.

42. Philip Selznick, in *The Organizational Weapon: A Study of Bolshevik Strategy and Tactics* (New York, 1952), utilizes this term in reference to Lenin's conception of "party"

43. Tony Smith, *Thinking Like a Communist: State and Legitimacy in the Soviet Union, China, and Cuba* (New York, 1987), 72–83.

44. Ibid., 83–84.

45 Selznick, *The Organizational Weapon*, 10–11.

46. Ibid., 9

47 For a detailed discussion of this theme, see Nasr, "The Politics of an Islamic Movement," 352–82.

48. See *JIKUS*, 18 and 21–22, and Mahiru'l-Qadri, "Chand Nuqush-i Zindagi," in Buhtah, *Mawlana Mawdudi*, 241–42.

49 Interview with Mian Tufayl Muhammad; the comment was made during the 1944–1947 period.

50. Interview with Na'im Siddiqi.

51. *TQ* (November 1934): 162.

52. Hamid Dabashi, "Symbiosis of Religious and Political Authorities in Islam," in Thomas Robbins and Ronald Robertson, eds., *Church-State Relations: Tensions and Transitions* (New Brunswick, 1987), 183–203.

53. Ayubi argues that in fact very little is said of the Medinan community in Islamic sources and that Muslims did not develop a clear notion of a "state" until modern times; Nazih Ayubi, *Political Islam: Religion and Politics in the Arab World* (New York, 1991), 6–8.

54. Farzana Shaikh, *Community and Consensus in Islam: Muslim Representation in Colonial India, 1860–1947* (Cambridge, 1989), 16.

55 Cited in *SAAM*, vol. 1, 215

56. For a discussion of the Daru'l-Islam project, see Nasr, "Politics of an Islamic Movement," 136–54.

57 *CRTIN*, 85–88, and Mawlana Muhammad Manzur Nu'mani, *Mawlana Mawdudi Miri Sath Rifaqat ki Sarguzasht Awr Ab Mira Mauqaf* (Lahore, 1980), 30–33.

58. These articles were eventually published in the form of the second and third volumes of *Musalman Awr Mawjudah Siyasi Kashmakash* but began to fully elaborate and espouse his notion of rule of religion (*iqamat-i din*).

59 Shahpuri, *Tarikh*, vol. 1, 448–49

60. Chaudhri 'Abdu'l-Rahman 'Abd, *Mufakkir-i Islam: Sayyid Abu'l-A'la Mawdudi* (Lahore, 1971), 152–64.

61. See the college's newspaper, *Crescent* (December 1939): 11.

62. Shahpuri, *Tarikh*, vol. 1, 356–57

63. See *Haftrozah Zindagi* (October 14–28, 1989): 38–39

64. The famous *'alim*, Sulaiman Nadwi, was ostensibly impressed with Mawdudi's *Tanqihat* (Lahore, 1989), while the famous Khilafat activist, 'Ubaidu'llah Sindhi, was approving of Mawdudi's articles in *TQ*; 'Abd, *Mufakkir-i Islam*, 96–97, and 156–57

65 *TQ* (May 1939): 2–13. Also see Sayyid Abu'l-A'la Mawdudi, "Ihya'-i Nizam-i Islami," in *Al-Furqan*, Shah Waliu'llah Number (1940): 18.

66. Reprinted in *Al-Ma'arif* 18, 2 (April–May 1985): 249–50. Zafaru'l-Hasan was then formulating plans of his own for a Muslim organization, to be called Shabbanu'l-Muslimin (Muslim Youth). Zafaru'l-Hasan's papers concerning this organization are kept in the archives of the Institute of Islamic Culture.

67 *Ibid.*, 249

68. *Ibid.*, 250.

69 See *TQ* (April 1941): 98.

70. Maududi, *The Process*, 18.

71. Sayyid Abu'l-Khayr Mawdudi writes that his younger brother viewed himself as a great leader of his community; see Sayyid Abu'l-Khayr Mawdudi, in *Nigar* (September 1963): 63. Mawdudi's career in later years further confirmed his ambitions; see, for instance, Amin Ahsan Islahi's critical letter to Mawdudi, dated January 16, 1958, reprinted in *Nida* (March 7, 1989): 28.

72. With no organization yet in the making, in August 1940, Mawdudi wrote to Abu'l-Hasan 'Ali Nadwi at the Nadwatu'l-'Ulama of Lucknow, requesting the services of an Arabist who could translate his writings on Islam into Arabic for the benefit of the Arab world. See Shahpuri, *Tarikh*, vol. 1, 466.

73. Across the board in Pakistan it is believed that Mawdudi was opposed to the Pakistan movement and the partition. This belief is the result of the anti-Jama'at propaganda campaigns by successive governments that tried to depict the Jama'at as unpatriotic. This view has also gained currency in academia. See, for instance, Aziz Ahmad, "Mawdudi and Orthodox Fundamentalism of Pakistan," *Middle East Journal* 21, 3 (Summer 1967): 369–80; Kalim Bahadur, *The Jama'at-i Islami of Pakistan* (New Delhi, 1977); or Freeland Abbott, *Islam and Pakistan* (Ithaca, 1968).

74. Nasr, "The Politics of an Islamic Movement," ch. 1.

75 *TQ* (December 1938): 304–5

76. Sayyid Abu'l-A'la Mawdudi, "Ham ne Tahrik-i Pakistan ke Sath Nehin Diya Tha," *Nawa'i Waqt* (August 15, 1975): 3.

77 Sayyid Abu'l-A'la Mawdudi, *Tahrik-i Pakistan Awr Jama'at-i Islami* (Multan, n.d.), 6.

78. Cited in Ja'far Qasmi, "Mujhe Yad Hey Sab Se Zara Zara,   " *Nida* (April 17, 1990): 32.

79 Shaikh, *Community and Consensus*, 209

80. *TQ* (February 1941): 66.

81. Mawdudi, *Tahrik-i Pakistan*, 7–8.

82. Peter Hardy, *The Muslims of British India* (Cambridge, 1972), 239

83. Mawdudi, *Tahrik-ı Pakıstan*, 7–8.

84. It ıs ımportant to note that Mawdudi was not alone among the self-styled Muslim leaders of the time to put forward such a claım. 'Allamah Mashrıqı, for ınstance, ın 1948 changed the name of Tahrik-ı Khaksar to the Islam League—closely paralleling the Muslim League's appellation, but underscorıng the greater religıous dedication of the Khaksar. The claım to beıng the "true League" was ımplicit ın Mashrıqi's maneuver.

85 *TQ* (April 1941): 90–101.

86. *SAAM*, vol. 1, 244.

87 *JIKUS*, 5, and Sayyıd Abul Ala Mawdudi, *The Islamıc Movement: Dynamıcs of Values, Power, and Change* (Leıcester, 1984), 6.

88. Interviews with Mian Tufayl Muhammad and Na'im Siddiqı.

89 *RJI*, vol. 1, 25

90. *Ibıd.*, 27–30.

91. Nu'manı, *Mawlana Mawdudi*, 32.

92. *Ibıd.*, 41–43

93. Islahı was not present at the first meeting of the Jama'at ın Lahore, but later Nu'manı persuaded hım to joın. His name was therefore cited among the organızation's founding members; ınterview with Amın Ahsan Islahı.

94. On thıs debate see *NGH*, 58.

95. Interviews with Nadwı and Malik Ghulam 'Ali.

96. 'Abd, *Mufakkır-ı Islam*, 175–76.

97 *Ibıd.*

98. Nu'manı, *Mawlana Mawdudi*, 40–43.

99 Na'im Siddiqı, *Al-Mawdudi* (Lahore, 1963), 35

100. Interview with 'Abdu'l-Rahım Ashraf.

101. Shahpurı, *Tarikh*, vol. 1, 525

102. Sayyıd As'ad Gilanı, "Jama'at-ı Islamı, 1941–1947," Ph.D. dissertation, Unıversity of Punjab, 1989–1990, 360–65

103. *Ibıd.*, 365

104. *JIKUS*, 47, and Nu'manı, *Mawlana Mawdudi*, 43–46.

105 *SAAM*, vol. 1, 256.

106. *RJI*, vol. 1, 60.

107 By 1946 the Jama'at had grown large enough to hold regıonal conventions and to organıze the Jama'at's finances locally; *RJI*, vol. 4, 115–18 and 124–26.

108. *RJI*, vol. 4, 41.

109 Cited ın *RJI*, vol. 5, 43.

110. *RJI*, vols. 4 and 5

111. *RJI*, vol. 5, 57–58.

112. Interview with Amın Ahsan Islahı.

113 Thıs book was written ın Hyderabad at the behest of the nızam's government and was used as a textbook ın that state's schools. It ıs Mawdudi's first and best known exposition on Islamıc revıvalism. The first work of Mawdudi to be translated ınto English (in 1947), by 1974 it had appeared ın twenty-sıx languages.

114. See Begum Mahmudah Mawdudi, "Mawlana Mawdudi Apne Ghar Main," in Buhtah, *Mawlana Mawdudi*, 263.

115 Nu'mani, *Mawlana Mawdudi*, 46–52.

116. *SAAM*, vol. 1, 256.

117 Nu'mani, *Mawlana Mawdudi*, 46–52.

118. In a letter to Nu'mani at a later time Mawdudi wrote: "If you were attracted to the Jama'at because of me, then you should never have joined; and if you were attracted to it because of its cause, then how can I prompt you to fall from a path you deemed to be in the interest of Islam?"; cited in Abu'l-Afaq, *Sayyid Abu'l-A'la Mawdudi: Sawanih, Afkar, Tahrik* (Lahore, 1971), 266–67

119 *SAAM*, vol. 1, 256.

120. *SAAM*, vol. 1, 256; and *RJI*, vol. 1, 71–76.

121. Nu'mani, *Mawlana Mawdudi*, 60–62.

122. As quoted in an interview with 'Abdu'l-Ghaffar Hasan.

123. *SAAM*, vol. 1, 284–85

124. Ibid., 297

125 Ibid.

126. *RJI*, vol. 5, 251ff., see chapter 5 for more on this issue.

127 *SAAM*, vol. 1, 297

128. *RJI*, vol. 1, 8ff.

129 Cited in Bahadur, *The Jama'at-i Islami*, 19 The 50 percent estimate is based on figures for membership for 1942 and 1946.

130. *RJI*, vol. 5, 58–59

131. *SAAM*, vol. 1, 297, and 318–21.

132. *Nida* (March 7, 1989): 23.

133 *RJI*, vol. 5, 94–106.

2. FROM HOLY COMMUNITY TO POLITICAL PARTY

1. Cited in *Mithaq* 39, 3 (March 1990): 52–53.

2. *SAAM*, vol. 1, 323

3. *SAAM*, vol. 1, 408–13.

4. Interview with Mawdudi in *Chatan* (January 24, 1951): 2.

5 *SAAM*, 419

6. Interview with 'Abdu'l-Rahim Ashraf.

7 See Mawdudi's interview reprinted in *A'in* (October 1989): 33–36, and his speech before the Jama'at's annual session of November 20–23, 1955, cited in *MMKT*, vol. 3, 139–56, wherein Mawdudi asserted that the Jama'at was not a party but a multidimensional organization. On Islahi's views see, for instance, his article in *TQ* (September 1956): 377–402.

8. Much of the following discussion unless otherwise stipulated is based on interviews with 'Abdu'l-Ghaffar Hasan, 'Abdu'l-Rahim Ashraf, Israr Ahmad, and Mustafa Sadiq.

9 *RJI*, vol. 2, 48–60 and 72ff.

10. NGH, 68–69

11. Israr Ahmad, Tahrik-ı Jama'at-ı Islamı: Ik Tahqıqı Mutala'ah (Lahore, 1966), 5

12. Cited in Ahmad, Tahrik-ı Jama'at-ı Islamı, 187–201.

13. NGH, 21.

14. Ibid., 22–24.

15 Interview with Amın Ahsan Islahı.

16. See, for instance, Gilani's later account of Machchı Goth in Sayyıd Asad Gilanı, Maududi: Thought and Movement (Lahore, 1984), 10.

17 For instance in a letter to Islahı after Machchı Goth, dated January 18, 1958, Mawdudi explains that he viewed the shura' session of November–December 1956 as the proof of emergence of factionalism in the Jama'at, which unless controlled there and then would destroy the party altogether. Since the factionalist tendency was unconstitutional and anti-Jama'at, no compromise with it, as was evident in the resolution that shura' session, was possible; and in the interests of preserving the Jama'at, Mawdudi was justified in using all means available to him. The letter is reprinted in Nida, March 7, 1989, 29–30.

18. Abd cites that even Islahı eulogized Mawdudi's sacrifices in prison, stating, "I spontaneously kissed his hands which Allah had endowed with the help of the pen to be testimony to the Truth"; cited in Abdur Rahman Abd, Sayyed Maududi Faces the Death Sentence (Lahore, 1978), 16–17

19 NGH, 31.

20. Ibid.

21. Ibid., 33–56.

22. Archival papers of Islamıc Studies Academy, Lahore.

23. Israr Ahmad argues that Mawdudi knew that his resignation was serious enough to create fears in the hearts of the party's members regarding the future of the Jama'at, thus influencing their choice; see NGH, 73–75

24. NGH, 82.

25. In a letter to Mawdudi in 1958, explaining his resignation, he denies harboring personal ambitions in the strongest terms. That letter is reprinted in Nida (March 14, 1989): 29

26. Mithaq 39, 3 (March 1990): 32. Israr Ahmad also reports that similar efforts were mounted by Jama'at members from all over Pakistan to prevail upon their leaders to resolve their differences; ibid., 50.

27 Since members of the review committee had never asked for Mawdudi's resignation, they were hard-pressed not to go along with Ghulam Muhammad's initiative. Sultan Ahmad did register a note of dissent regarding such manipulations of the shura' to Mawdudi's advantage. This note was excluded from circular no. 118–4–27 of January 19, 1957, which reported the proceedings of this shura' session to the members; see NGH, 80–81.

28. Ibid., 81.

29 Islahı names Tarjumanu'l-Qur'an and Tasnım as most significant in this regard; see Nida (March 14, 1989): 30.

30. Islahı had a following of his own in the party and was viewed as a more

serious scholar than Mawdudi by many outside the Jama'at. In later years a number of the Jama'at's rising intellectual leaders, notably among them, Javid Ahmadu'l-Ghamidi and Mustansir Mir, became impressed with Islahi's Qur'anic commentaries and left the Jama'at to study with him.

31. *NGH*, 75

32. *SAAM*, vol. 2, 8–10.

33. *Mithaq* 39, 3 (March 1990): 50–55

34. *Nida* (March 14, 1989): 30–31.

35 *Mithaq* 39, 3 (March 1990): 58. Elsewhere Israr Ahmad reports that 'Abdu'l-Rahim Ashraf had asked Chaudhri Ghulam Muhammad to guarantee adequate time for all views to be aired at Machchi Goth. Mawdudi turned down the request flatly, and Ghulam Muhammad complied; *Mithaq* 13, 2 (February 1967): 49

36. The speech was later published as *Tahrik-i Islami ka A'indah La'ihah-i 'Amal* (Lahore, 1986). This book is seen today as the most lucid exposition of Mawdudi's views on religion and politics, but it is often not examined within the context of the debate over the enfranchisement of the party which prompted its ideas.

37 Mawdudi, *Tahrik-i Islami*, 172–73.

38. *Mithaq* 39, 3 (March 1990): 58–68.

39 Hasan was also disturbed by what he saw as Mawdudi's innovative religious interpretation in an article in *TQ* (December 1956): 9–32. In that article, Mawdudi had responded to those who criticized his departures from his earlier position by arguing that Islam was a rational religion and it permitted choice between two evils when expediency necessitated such a choice; see *SAAM*, vol. 2, 59–60.

40. Of Islahi's disagreements with him and his departure from the Jama'at Mawdudi said deprecatingly, "Amin Ahsan sahab was scared off by his experience with prison" (referring to his incarceration following the anti-Ahmadi agitations); interview with Begum Mahmudah Mawdudi. On a more serious note, Mawdudi explained to Chaudhri Ghulam Muhammad that Islahi's temper, which had shown its full force throughout the Machchi Goth ordeal, was likely to be a source of trouble and had alienated many in the Jama'at from him, hinting that Mawdudi was not eager for Islahi to return to the Jama'at; *Nida* (March 7, 1989): 26.

41. Among those who left, the most noteworthy were Amin Ahsan Islahi (Jama'at's second highest ranking leader, provisional amir, 1954; and later an important scholar and commentator of the Qur'an); Sultan Ahmad (member of the shura', provisional amir, 1953–1954); 'Abdu'l-Jabbar Ghazi (member of the shura', provisional amir, 1948–1949); 'Abdu'l-Ghaffar Hasan (member of the shura' provisional amir, 1948–1949 and 1956); 'Abdu'l-Rahim Ashraf and Sardar Muhammad Ajmal Khan (both members of the shura'); Mawlana Abu'l-Haqq Jama'i (former amir of Bhawalpur); Sa'id Ahmad Malik (former amir of Punjab); Muhammad 'Asimu'l-Haddad (director of the Arabic Translation Bureau); Arshad Ahmad Haqqani (editor of *Tasnim*); and Israr Ahmad and Mustafa Sadiq (both of whom became notable political and religious figures in later years).

42. Sayyid Ma'ruf Shirazi, *Islami Inqilab ka Minhaj* (Chinarkut, 1989).

43. Mawdudi's letter is reproduced in *Nida* (March 27, 1989): 24–25

44. For instance, in preparation for the general elections of 1958, the Jama'at reiterated the four-point plan of action of 1951; see *Short Proceedings of the 2nd Annual Conference, Jamaat-e-Islami, East Pakistan* (March 14–16, 1958), 2; enclosed with U.S. Consulate, Dacca, disp. #247, 4/3/1958, 790D.00/4–358, NA.

45 Rana Sabir Nizami, *Jama'at-i Islami Pakistan; Nakamiyun ke Asbab ka 'Ilmi Tajziyah* (Lahore, 1988), 47, and 76–77

46. Some years previously, in the summer of 1950, the Jama'at had criticized a public appearance by Fatimah Jinnah, questioning the presence of a woman at such an occasion; see *TQ* (July–September 1950): 220.

47 Mawdudi explained the Jama'at's position in the following terms: "On one side is a man; other than his gender there is nothing good about him; on the other side is a woman; aside from her gender nothing is wrong about her." Cited in Israr Ahmad, *Islam Awr Pakistan: Tarikhi, Siyasi, 'Ilmi Awr Thiqafati Pasmanzar* (Lahore, 1983), 37

48. Interview with Kawthar Niyazi; also see Kawthar Niyazi, *Jama'at-i Islami 'Awami 'Adalat Main* (Lahore, 1973), 11–17

49 Niyazi, *Jama'at-i Islami,* 31–32.

50. Ibid., 38, and interview with Niyazi.

51. The Jama'at had become more adept at contending with internal dissent and had also became more sensitive to it over the years. While Niyazi was asked to resign, Mawlana Wasi Mazhar Nadwi, an elder of the Jama'at and the one-time amir of Sind, was expelled from the Jama'at in 1976 for divulging information about Mawdudi's disagreements with the shura' over the issue of the Jama'at's continued participation in elections (which is discussed later); correspondence between the author and Wasi Mazhar Nadwi, 1989–1990, and interview with Javid Ahmadu'l-Ghamidi.

52. The Machchi Goth affair was replayed in Bangladesh following the bloody Pakistan civil war of 1971. During the civil war the Jama'at of East Pakistan, which later became the Jama'at-i Islami of Bangladesh, was drawn into the conflict and was thoroughly politicized. The debacle of East Pakistan and the calamity which befell the Jama'at in Bangladesh after the war precipitated a major debate over the party's mission—religious work or political activity A schism followed when Mawlana 'Abdu'l-Rahim, amir of Jama'at-i Islami of East Pakistan during the war, left Jama'at-i Islami of Bangladesh to form a new organization which would embody the original idea of the Jama'at as a holy community, primarily immersed in religious work, and only indirectly interested in politics. See Mumtaz Ahmad, "Islamic Fundamentalism in South Asia: The Jamaat-i-Islami and the Tablighi Jamaat," in Martin E. Marty and R. Scott Appleby, eds., *Fundamentalisms Observed* (Chicago, 1991), 503. Similarly, a major internal conflict erupted in the Jama'at in 1988 over the party's relations with General Zia, which is discussed in chapter 9

53. See, for instance, *SAAM,* vol. 2, 310.

54. Ibid., 426–28.

55 Mawdudi's anguish was reflected in a letter to Wasi Mazhar Nadwi, wherein he discussed his disappointment with the Jama'at; cited in Nizami, *Jama'at-i Islami,* 101–2. Begum Mawdudi recollects that her husband was particularly perturbed

about the breakdown of ethical conduct in the Jama'at caused by the party's politicization, something he introduced to the party and could not later control; interview with Begum Mawdudi.

56. Interview with Begum Mawdudi.

57 Interview with Khwaja Amanu'llah.

58. Wasi Mazhar Nadwi, who had been present in that shura' session, later wrote to Mawdudi and asked the Mawlana to reiterate his views and confirm what Nadwi had understood him to say Mawdudi repeated his disdain for elections in a letter to Nadwi. Nadwi was subsequently expelled from the Jama'at for divulging information about the shura' session and Mawdudi's letter to those outside the party Correspondence with Wasi Mazhar Nadwi, 1989–1990; interview with Ghamidi; and *Mithaq* 39, 3 (March 1990): 11–12.

59 The Jama'at for instance no longer has a notable and widely respected religious thinker. While it does indulge in religious exegesis, its leaders are not at the forefront of revivalist thinking in Pakistan any longer. Mian Tufayl accedes to this conclusion: "the calibre of *Tarjumanu'l-Qur'an* despite its continued vitality has gone down since Mawlana Mawdudi's death", interview with Mian Tufayl Muhammad. However, he takes comfort in the fact that "Mawlana [Mawdudi] was such a paramount thinker that the Jama'at will not need one for another century"; interview with Mian Tufayl Muhammad in *Takbir* (November 16, 1989): 52.

60. Similarly, in India, Mawlana Wahidu'ddin Khan and in Bangladesh Mawlana 'Abdu'l-Rahim left the Jama'at to form more vital Islamic intellectual movements.

3   ORGANIZATION

1. *RJI*, vol. 1, 35–37 and 40. Also the Jama'at set up a tax division on August 31, 1941, again with a view to supporting the propaganda efforts.

2. Maryam Jameelah, *Islam in Theory and Practice* (Lahore, 1973), 336.

3. Cited in Mumtaz Ahmad, "Islamic Fundamentalism in South Asia: The Jamaat-i-Islami and the Tablighi Jamaat," in Martin E. Marty and R. Scott Appleby, eds., *Fundamentalisms Observed* (Chicago, 1991), 492.

4. *RJI*, vol. 1, 45–56; vol. 2, 16–28; vol. 3, 53–96; and vol. 4, 37–40.

5 Jameelah, *Islam in Theory*, 337

6. Ibid., 338–40.

7 During Mawdudi's tenure of office, on a number of occasions, other Jama'at leaders served as provisional amirs. While Mawdudi was in prison in 1948–1950, 'Abdu'l-Jabbar Ghazi and 'Abdu'l-Ghaffar Hasan were jointly provisional amirs. According to one account, Mas'ud 'Alam Nadwi also served briefly as amir during this period, between 1949 and 1950; see *RJI*, vol. 6, 144–45 In 1953–1955, when Mawdudi was again imprisoned, first Sultan Ahmad and, later, Amin Ahsan Islahi served as provisional amirs. In 1956, when Mawdudi was away on a tour of the Arab world, 'Abdu'l-Ghaffar Hasan served as the overseer of the party Finally, in 1969, when Mawdudi underwent medical treatment in England, Mian Tufayl Muhammad served as the acting amir.

8. The date of this meeting is cited in *A'in* (April 25, 1985): 6.

9 *TQ* (June–August 1971).

10. Mian Tufayl joined the Jama'at in 1941; he served as the secretary-general of the party from 1942 to 1972 and for a period was deputy amir and vice-amir.

11. Mawlana Muhammad Manzur Nu'mani, *Mawlana Mawdudi Miri Sath Rifaqat ki Sarguzasht Awr Ab Mira Mauqaf* (Lahore, 1980), 38.

12. *RJI*, vol. 6, 154.

13 *JIKUS*, 42.

14. *RJI*, vol. 6, 131–32.

15 *RJI*, vol. 7, 60.

16. *ISIT(2)*, 44.

17 Figure provided by the election commission.

18. *RJI*, vol. 1, 84. The figures are as cited in the sources and do not reflect changes in the value of the rupee compared to the dollar.

19 *Ibid.,* 77

20. *RJI*, vol. 5, 92; and vol. 6, 168.

21. U.S. Embassy, Karachi, disp. #61, 7/27/1956, 790D.00/7–2756, NA.

22. Between 1941 and 1945 the income of the Jama'at stood at Rs. 73,119, Rs. 42,573 of which came from the sale of books, Rs. 19,531 from outside help to the Jama'at, and Rs. 5,118 from *zakat* donations; see *RJI*, vol. 3, 50–52. The income from the sale of animal skins and hides collected during religious holidays when animals are sacrifices, in 1955 was Rs. 70,000; U.S. Embassy, Karachi, disp. #61, 7/27/1956, 790D.00/7–2756, NA.

23 Jama'at's ties with Saudi Arabia go as far back as the 1950s, when Mawdudi's Arabic translations gained him respect among Saudi Arabian ulama and with the country's rulers King Saud and King Faisal. The former personally funded Mawdudi's trip to Saudi Arabia in 1959–1960. In 1963 Mawdudi got permission from Saudi Arabian authorities to have the cloth covering the Ka'bah (the *kiswah*) made in Lahore rather than in Cairo, and in 1965 he became a founder and member of the board of governors of Medina University; *SAAM*, vol. 2, 77–79 Mawdudi was also honored with the prestigious and generous Faisal Award for his services to Islam, the proceeds of which funded the establishment of Jama'at's Islamic Studies Academy in Lahore.

24. The Islamic Foundation was in fact one of the initiators of the entire anti-Rushdie campaign in England, Pakistan, and Saudi Arabia. Following the publication of *The Satanic Verses,* the foundation circulated numerous photocopies of passages from Rushdie's book in England and distributed them far and wide across the Muslim world, and Jama'at's emissaries traveled to Saudi Arabia to secure funding for the anti-Rushdie campaign. Jama'at activists in England then utilized Saudi Arabia's support to galvanize the Muslim community of England and to alert Muslims across the world of their cause. It was following weeks-long agitations in England that Pakistan and later Iran joined the fray and converted the issue into a diplomatic imbroglio; interviews in London and Islamabad.

25 Sayyid Abu'l-A'la Mawdudi, *Tafhimat* (Lahore, 1965), vol. 2, 286. At that time student activism was rampant in northern India, and critical to the success of the

Pakistan movement; Ishtiaq Husain Qureshi, *Education in Pakistan: An Inquiry into Objectives and Achievements* (Karachi, 1975), 263–65

26. Interview with Zafaru'llah Khan in *JVNAT*, vol. 1, 11.

27 Ahmad Anas, "Jami'at ka Ta'sisi Pasmanzar," in *TT*, vol. 1, 113–14.

28. Interview with Khurram Jah Murad in *JVNAT*, vol. 1, 48.

29 Interviews with Khurshid Ahmad and Absar Ahmad in *JVNAT*, vol. 1, 144–45 and 153.

30. Interview with Khurshid Ahmad in *JVNAT*, vol. 1, 127–28.

31. Gilani, in fact, cites combating the left as a reason why the IJT was initially formed; see Sayyid Asad Gilani, *Maududi: Thought and Movement* (Lahore, 1984), 78.

32. Interview with Khurshid Ahmad.

33. Interview with Zafar Ishaq Ansari, an early leader of the IJT.

34. Interview with Israr Ahmad in *JVNAT*, vol. 1, 92–99

35 See Mawdudi's speeches of May 30, June 19, and October 30, 1955; cited in *MMKT*, vol. 3, 31–36, 51–54, and 108–17

36. On November 9, 1969, for instance, Mawdudi told a gathering of IJT members that the important task before them was to rid Pakistani universities of the left; cited in *SAAM*, vol. 2, 348–49

37 Salim Mansur Khalid, *Al-Badr* (Lahore, 1985); and K.M. Aminu'l-Haq, "Al-Badr Commander Bulta Hi," in *TT*, vol. 2, 326–54.

38. Interview with Muti'u'l-Rahman Nizami in *JVNAT*, vol. 2, 234–35

39 *The Annual Report of Islami Jami'at-i Tulabah* (Lahore, 1988), 4–10.

40. The extent of the IJT's activities have led to charges, often credible, that IJT workers receive stipends from the Jama'at, suggesting that furtive financial linkages do exist between the two organizations. One source cites that stipends of Rs. 150 to Rs. 1,000 per month are dispersed among IJT workers, depending on the level and function of the worker or member; *Friday Times* (September 14, 1989): 11.

41. 'Abdu'l-Shakur, "Jahan-i Tazah ki Takbirin," in *TT*, vol. 2, 71–72.

42. Javid Hashmi, "Ik Jur'at-i Rindanah," in *TT*, vol. 2, 51–52.

43. Hafiz Khan, "Zawq-i 'Amal," in *TT*, vol. 2, 23

44. U.S. Embassy, Islamabad, disp. #5303, 5/7/1979, DFTUSED, no. 45, 61.

45 Information was provided by offices of the Jama'at-i Islami of Sind, Karachi.

46. Cited in Zahid Hussain, "The Campus Mafias," *Herald* (October 1988), 52. Some thirty of those killed belonged to the IJT.

47 On the attack on the offices of the *Muslim* newspaper in Islamabad, see U.S. Embassy, Islamabad, disp. #7850, 7/12/1979, DFTUSED, no. 46, 1–2.

48. Muhammad Afzal, Zia's minister of education, negotiated with Khurshid Ahmad, Jama'at's overseer of the IJT, on the issue of student violence a number of times. The Jama'at resisted taking serious measures, in part due to its fear of being unable to control the IJT. The regime then decided to ban all student union activities as a way of clamping down on the IJT, interview with Muhammad Afzal.

49 Interview with Mian Tufayl.

50. *Friday Times* (September 14, 1989): 11.

51. *Hamqadam* (July and August 1965).

52. Information provided by the Office of Secretary-General of the IJT.

53. Kiren Aziz Chaudhry and Peter McDonough, "State, Society, and Sin: The Political Beliefs of University Students in Pakistan," *Economic Development and Cultural Change* 32, 1 (October 1983): 28.

54. Benedict Anderson, *Imagined Communities: Reflections on the Origins and Spread of Nationalism* (New York, 1991), 3.

55 The Jamaʻat-i Islami was officially divided into Indian and Pakistani organizations in February 1948. Of the organization's 625 members at the time 385 ended up in Pakistan and 240 remained in India; see *JIKUS*, 52.

56. The Jamaʻat-i Islami of Kashmir was formed in 1947 at the time of Partition. *RJI*, vol. 5, 61, which gives a list of Jamaʻat members in 1947, cites no members in Kashmir. It has, however, been argued that a number of Kashmiris had visited Daruʼl-Islam as early as 1937–1938. They set up the first Jamaʻat cell in Jamun in 1944 and in Kashmir in 1946; see ʻAshiq Kashmiri, *Tarikhi Tahrik-i Islami, Jamunʻu Kashmir* (Lahore, 1989), 212–99 The party in that province, however, continued to grow independently of its sister organization centered in Delhi and is today a major actor in the separatist movement in that province. According to Jamaʻat sources the Jamaʻat-i Islami of Kashmir runs over 1,000 schools in the vale of Kashmir; interview with Khurshid Ahmad.

57 Mumtaz Ahmad, "The Politics of War: Islamic Fundamentalisms in Pakistan," in James Piscatori, ed., *Islamic Fundamentalisms and the Gulf Crisis* (Chicago, 1991), 180.

58. As a result the Jamaʻat has influenced the development of revivalism across the Muslim world. On the Jamaʻat's influence in the West, the Arab World, Afghanistan, Iran, and Malaysia, see Larry Poston, *Islamic Daʻwah in the West: Muslim Missionary Activity and the Dynamics of Conversion to Islam* (New York, 1992), 64–93; Emmanuel Sivan, *Radical Islam: Medieval Theology and Modern Politics* (New Haven, 1985); John L. Esposito, *The Islamic Threat: Myth or Reality?* (New York, 1992), 154–55; Abdelwahab El-Affendi, "The Long March from Lahore to Khartoum: Beyond the 'Muslim Reformation,' " *British Society for Middle Eastern Studies Bulletin* 17, 2 (1990): 138–39; Abdel Azim Ramadan, "Fundamentalist Influence in Egypt: The Strategies of the Muslim Brotherhood and the Takfir Groups," in Martin E. Marty and R. Scott Appleby, eds., *Fundamentalisms and the State: Remaking Polities, Economies, and Militance* (Chicago, 1993), 156 and 161, Olivier Roy, *Islam and Resistance in Afghanistan* (New York, 1990), 68–70 and 80; Said Amir Arjomand, *The Turban for the Crown: The Islamic Revolution in Iran* (New York, 1988); and Zainah Anwar, *Islamic Fundamentalism in Malaysia* (Kualalampur, 1989).

59 Mawdudi's works were, for the main part, translated into Arabic by four of his followers: Masʻud ʻAlam Nadwi, Muhammad Kazim, ʻAsimuʼl-Haddad, and Khalil Ahmaduʼl-Hamidi. The four were all competent Arabists, of whom only Hamidi remains with the Jamaʻat today, as the director of the Arabic Translation Bureau. For an outline of the bureau's activities, see Khalil Ahmaduʼl-Hamidi, "Jamaʻat-i Islami ki Dasturi Jaddʻu Jahd," in *CRTIN*, 337–55

60. Mawdudi's works began to appear in Iran in the 1960s. They were translated into Persian from Arabic by Ayatollah Hadi Khusrawshahi and members of a translating team working with him. Articles on Mawdudi and excerpts from his

works also appeared in various issues of Khusrawshahi's journal *Maktab-ı Islam.* Following the revolution of 1978–1979, a number of Mawdudi's works were translated into Persian from Arabic by Ayatollah Sayyid Muhammad Khamana'i. Interestingly, the first Persian translation of a work of Mawdudi was done in Hyderabad, Deccan, by Mahmud Faruqı in 1946; *RJI*, vol. 4, 90. More recent translations of Mawdudi's works into Persian have occurred in Pakistan by the Jama'at, which target the Afghan community of Pakistan.

4. SOCIAL BASE

1. Leonard Binder, *Islamıc Liberalism: A Critique of Development Ideologies* (Chicago, 1988), 328–41; Abdallah Laroui, *L'ideologie arabe contemporaine* (Paris, 1967); Said Amır Arjomand, *The Turban for the Crown The Islamıc Revolution in Iran* (New York, 1988); Henry Munson, Jr., *Islam and Revolution in the Middle East* (New Haven, 1988), 98–104; Nazih Ayubi, *Political Islam Religion and Politics in the Arab World* (New York, 1991), 158–77; and Saad Eddin Ibrahım, "Anatomy of Egypt's Militant Islamıc Groups: Methodological Note and Preliminary Findings," *International Journal of Middle East Studies* 12, 4 (December 1980): 423–53.

2. The importance of this omission is underlined by the fact that the Muhajir community, the Jama'at's main base of support at the time, was also the strongest advocate of land reform and populist politics. It had pressed the Muslim League to advocate land reform as early as 1949; U.K. High Commission, Karachi, disp. #31, 8/3/1949, DO35/8948, PRO.

3. U.S. Embassy, Karachi, disp. #102, 7/13/1950, 790D.00/8–1150, 5, NA.

4. Nu'manı states that the *Tarjumanu'l-Qur'an* was read widely among the religious literati in the 1940s and did enjoy a certain following among them; see Muhammad Manzur Nu'manı, *Mawlana Mawdudi Mirı Sath Rifaqat kı Sarguzasht Awr Ab Mira Mauqaf* (Lahore, 1980), 31–33.

5 This was also true of members of other religious movements, some of which were opposed to Pakistan, and hence waned in power after 1947; see Freeland Abbott, "The Jama'at-ı-Islamı of Pakistan," *Middle East Journal* 11, 1 (Winter 1957): 41. The followers of these movements, again mainly from the lower-middle classes, saw the Jama'at as the only effective movement representing their sentiments and objectives, and hence they flocked to the Jama'at. Two notable lieutenants of Mawdudi, Aqa Shurısh Kashmırı—a close companion of Mawdudi—and Chaudhrı Ghulam Muhammad, a senior Jama'at leader, came from such a background. The former had belonged to the Majlis-ı Ahrar, and the latter to the Tahrik-ı Khaksar.

6. Ahmad reports that in 1990 of Jama'at's top fifteen leaders, nine held master of arts degrees, three had master of science degrees, one had earned a law degree (LL.B.), one had a bachelor of arts degree, and one had been educated in the traditional system. Of the fourteen, twelve had specialized in the humanities or the social sciences, and two in technical fields; Mumtaz Ahmad, "Islamıc Fundamentalism in South Asia: The Jamaat-ı-Islamı and the Tablighı Jamaat," in Martin E. Marty and R. Scott Appleby, eds., *Fundamentalisms Observed* (Chicago, 1991), 495

7 This observation is confirmed by the Jama'at's leaders themselves. In an

interview with this author, Chaudhri Aslam Salimi, the former secretary-general, stated that "the Jama'at is by and large lower-middle class." Binder, Ahmed, and Ahmad, too, confirm this finding in their studies on the party Binder identified the Jama'at's supporters in the 1950s as those "drawn from the traditional middle classes, the students, and those who have failed to enter into the modern middle class despite achieving a bachelor's degree;" Leonard Binder, *Religion and Politics in Pakistan* (Berkeley and Los Angeles, 1961), 8. Ahmed writes, "Jamaat-i-Islami's social base is located amongst small businessmen, small land-holders, and urban lower middle class strata of shopkeepers, teachers, clerks and petty government officials"; Ishtiaq Ahmed, *The Concept of an Islamic State: An Analysis of the Ideological Controversy in Pakistan* (New York, 1987), 112–13. Ahmad argues that the lower sections of the new middle classes and traditional petite bourgeoisie are the backbone of the Jama'at; Ahmad, "Islamic Fundamentalism," 496–500.

8. As a result of emphasis placed upon education in 1989, the Jama'at had a literacy rate of 85 percent while the literacy rate in Pakistan stood at 28 percent; figures provided by the office of secretary-general. The Jama'at did make some headway in attracting members of the Pakistan civil service, but these figures are not reflected in organizational records. Wary of government reaction, Mawdudi told his followers among the country's bureaucrats that in the interests of the party's long-run goal they should avoid official affiliation with the Jama'at and to clandestinely support it from whatever position they serve. In later years the same policy was adopted vis-à-vis the personnel of the armed forces.

9 Sayyid As'ad Gilani, *Maududi: Thought and Movement* (Lahore, 1984), 132.

10. Cited in Sayyid As'ad Gilani, *Qafilah-i Sakht Jan* (Sargodha, 1965), and Khurshid Ahmad, *Tazkirah-i Zindan* (Karachi, 1965), which contain information on members of the shura' arrested in 1963–1964.

11. *JIKUS*, 43.

12. *Ibid.*, 43–44.

13. Cited in Ahmad, "Islamic Fundamentalism," 495

14. Following its creation, the Jama'at made a concerted effort to translate Mawdudi's works into local Indian languages, from Malayalam to Sindhi; see *RJI*, vols. 1–5 However, the scope of these efforts never matched the weight of the party's efforts in Urdu, nor did it change the predominantly Urdu orientation of the movement.

15 According to the 1951 census, only 3.4 percent of Pakistanis identified themselves as Urdu speakers; cited in Rounaq Jahan, *Pakistan: Failure in National Integration* (New York, 1972), 12.

16. In 1955, for instance, with a view to expanding its base of support, the Jama'at launched a three-year plan to teach Urdu to twenty-five thousand people; cited in *RJI*, vol. 7, 244.

17 *Manifesto of Jama'at-i Islami of Pakistan* (Lahore, 1970), 4–5

18. In a gathering of Jama'at members in 1974, Mawdudi declared that the Jama'at's aim was not only gaining political success for itself but also, more important, preserving the unity of Pakistan. As such, he enjoined Jama'at's members not

to be distracted from the legitimating function which their party performs at the national level nor swayed by the lure of ethnic politics, and hence to maintain the organizational unity and all-Pakistan poise of the Jama'at; cited in *ISIT(1)*, 47–49

19 For instance, of the first thirteen *nazim-i 'alas* of the IJT, only three were born in Indian provinces inherited by Pakistan (one in Punjab and two in North-West Frontier Province). The other ten were born in areas which today rest within India, and all belonged to the Muhajir community See the biographical sketches of *JVNAT*, vols. 1–2.

20. 'Ali Ahmad Khan, *Jama'at-e-Islami of Pakistan*, Introduction Series, no. 2 (Lahore, 1954), 4–6.

21. Cited in Syed Riaz Ahmad, *Mawlana Mawdudi and the Islamic State* (Lahore, 1976), 176.

22. Syed Abul 'Ala Maudoodi, *Islamic Law and Constitution* (Karachi, 1955), 144–45

23. Cited in Shahid Javed Burki, *Pakistan: A Nation in the Making* (Boulder, 1986), 44.

24. Cited in *Herald* (August 1992): 151.

25 Mawdudi's speech was reprinted in *A'in* (April 25, 1985): 6.

26. Sayyid Abul Ala Maudoodi, "Muslim Women Must Participate in Islamic Movement," *Criterion* 5, 5 (Rajab-Sha'ban 1390/1970): 45 and 74.

27 *ISIT(2)*, 49

28. *Ibid.*

29 The motto defined Jama'at's new *khidmat-i khalq* (service to the masses) approach launched in 1972. See *Rudad-i Jama'at-i Islami, Pakistan, 1972* (Lahore, n.d.), 22–23

30. *Ibid.*, 48–50.

31. In January 1979 the Jama'at's shura' declared attracting new affiliates (*mutaf-fiq-sazi*) a major goal of the party, setting a goal of a 25 percent increase in their numbers, and directing the party to form committees and circles across Pakistan to accomplish this feat. Between March and May 1979 the drive brought 109,000 new affiliates to the Jama'at, 50,000 from North-West Frontier Province, 32,000 from Sind, 22,000 from Punjab, and 5,000 from Baluchistan; *ibid*, 32.

32. In 1988 elections the Jama'at won four and in 1990 five of Dir's six provincial assembly seats. For more on these elections see chapters 8–10.

33 In 1990, however, the Jama'at did better in Punjab than in North-West Frontier Province, at least in the contests for seats in the National Assembly Moreover, it did better in the larger cities of Punjab than it had in the elections of 1988. For details see chapter 10.

34. It should, however, be noted that Muhajirs still predominate in many of Jama'at's top offices. For instance, in 1992 of the five deputy amirs, three were Muhajirs.

35 Interview with Chaudhri Aslam Salimi.

36. See the text of Qazi Husain's speech to the "Jama'at's youth," printed in *Takbir* (October 12, 1989): 42–43, wherein he argues fervently for expanding Ja-

ma'at's reach into the masses of illiterate Pakistanis. Qazi Husain himself is of the opinion that while the Jama'at realized the importance of appealing to lower social strata after the 1970–1971 elections few structural changes were undertaken to reorient the politics of the Jama'at. He therefore sees such an undertaking as the central focus of his leadership of the party; interview with Qazi Husain Ahmad.

37 Khurram Badr, Qazi Husain Ahmad (Karachi, 1988), 95–108.

38. Interview with Qazi Husain Ahmad in Takbir (June 30, 1988): 14.

39 JIKUS, 32.

40. RJI, vol. 6, 26–27

41. SAAM, vol. 1, 384.

42. RJI, vol. 7, 244.

43. SAAM, vol. 2, 392–93.

44. Personal correspondence with Mawlana Wasi Mazhar Nadwi, 1989–1990.

45 The censure was published in Wifaq and Nawa'i-i Waqt in Lahore; also see Rana Sabir Nizami, Jama'at-i Islami Pakistan: Nakamiyun ke Asbab ka 'Ilmi Tajziyah (Lahore, 1988), 102.

46. This issue has been extensively debated between Javid Ahmadu'l-Ghamidi, Khurshid Ahmad, Ahmad Nadim, and Na'im Siddiqi in Ishraq throughout 1993.

47 Interview with Khurram Jah Murad in JVNAT, vol. 1, 78–79

48. Nizami, Jama'at-i Islami, 77–79

49 The most notable advocates of opening up the Jama'at in this category are 'Abdu'l-Ghafur Ahmad and Khurram Jah Murad, both Muhajir deputy amirs of the party; interviews with 'Abdu'l-Ghafur Ahmad and Khurram Jah Murad; also see interview with Khurram Jah Murad in Awaz-i Jahan (January 22, 1990): 10–14. In addition, journalists Altaf Hasan Quraishi, Muhammad Salahu'ddin, and Mujibu'l-Rahman Shami have become quite vocal on this issue. They are staunch supporters of the party but are not bound by the code of conduct which bars Jama'at members from public discussion of party issues. Moreover, as editors of magazines and journals with large followings in the party, these men have been able to disseminate ideas about change directly into the Jama'at, forcing the party to debate its future course of action.

5 PRELUDE TO PAKISTAN, 1941–1947

1. Sayyid Abu'l-A'la Mawdudi, Musalman Awr Mawjudah Siyasi Kashmakash (1938–1940), vol. 1, 317–20, and 327–28. Also see idem, Mas'alah-i Qaumiyat, reprint (Lahore 1982), 52–59, 63–64, and 70–72.

2. On elaboration of these charges and Mawdudi's attacks on Nehru's socialist inclinations, see Mawdudi, Musalman, vol. 1, 308–9, 457–58, and 464–68. Also see Abad Shahpuri, Tarikh-i Jama'at-i Islami (Lahore, 1989), vol. 1, 293–307

3 Cited in 'Abdu'l-Ghani Faruqi, "Hayat-i Javidan," HRZ, 27

4. Mawdudi, Musalman, vol. 3, 162–63.

5 Ibid., 127

6. Ishtiaq Husain Qureshi, Ulema in Politics: A Study Relating to the Political

Activities of the Ulema in South Asian Subcontinent from 1566–1947 (Karachi, 1974), 352.

7 Cited by Mian Muhammad Shafi' in *Iqdam* (June 9, 1963): 1. Shafi' had been Iqbal's private secretary

8. Interview with 'Abdu'l-Ghaffar Hasan.

9 Zafar Ahmad Ansari, "Tahrik-i Pakistan Awr 'Ulama," *Chiragh-i Rah* 14, 12 (December 1960): 233.

10. Interview with Malik Ghulam 'Ali, a former Muslim League worker, in *Awaz-i Jahan* (November 1989): 20–21.

11. Manzuru'l-Haq, "Mawlana Mawdudi, Hama Pahlu Shaksiyat," in Jalil Ahmad Rana and Salim Mansur Khalid, ed., *Tazkirah-i Sayyid Mawdudi* (Lahore, 1986), 113. The author was himself a Muslim League worker in Amritsar at the time.

12. Ansari, "Tahrik," 232.

13. See, for instance, the interview of Sayyid Sharifu'ddin Pirzadah, Jinnah's secretary, in *Jasarat* (Mawdudi Number 1973), 2, where the interviewee asserts that *Tarjumanu'l-Qur'an* was critical in galvanizing support for the Muslim League in such places as Aligarh.

14. Nawwab Sadiq 'Ali, *Bi Tiq Sipahi* (Karachi, 1971), 28. The Nawwab had been the supreme commander (*salar-i a'la*) of the Muslim League's national guard and, later, the secretary to Liaqat 'Ali Khan.

15 Sayyid Abu'l-A'la Mawdudi, *Tahrik-i Pakistan Awr Jama'at-i Islami* (Multan, n.d.), 2.

16. Interview with Malik Ghulam 'Ali.

17 See, for instance, Mawdudi's interview with Radio Pakistan of April 8, 1975, printed in *TQ* (October 1980): 17

18. *JIKUS*, 27

19 *TQ* (October 1980): 18.

20. Mawdudi, *Musalman*, vol. 3, 127

21. See interview with Sayyid Abu'l-Khayr Mawdudi in *Nigar* (September 1963): 63. Mawdudi was not alone in his opinion of Jinnah. The American envoy in Karachi writes of the reaction to naming Jinnah as the "Father of Pakistan" in the following terms: "Although the more ardent followers of the Muslim League rejoiced, there were numbers of others who were not so enthusiastic on the ground that Jinnah was not as orthodox a Muslim   and that he had been known to use alcoholic beverages"; U.S. Consulate, Karachi, disp. #41, 7/8/1947, 845F.00/8–1947, NA.

22. In a letter to Dr. Zafaru'l-Hasan, dated 23 Rabi'u'l-Thani 1356 (1938–1939), Mawdudi stated that Muslims were demanding an Islamic state and hence "cannot fully identify with the Muslim League", the letter is reprinted in *Al-Ma'arif* 18, 1–2 (April–May 1985): 249

23. Letter to Zafaru'l-Hasan in *Al-Ma'arif* 18, 1–2 (April–May 1985): 249–50; the term "rear guard" in reference to the Jama'at's strategy was also cited in *TQ* (December 1937): 301.

24. *TQ* (August 1948): 2–3

25 Interview with Malik Ghulam 'Ali.

26. *Kawthar* (October 28, 1945): 1.

27 Sayyıd Abu'l-A'la Mawdudi, "Ham ne Tahrik-ı Pakıstan ke Sath Nehın Diya Tha," *Nawa'-ı Waqt* (August 15, 1975): 3.

28. *TQ* (May 1939): 171.

29 *SAAM*, vol. 1, 256.

30. *TQ* (May 1939): 50–51.

31. *RJI*, vol. 5, 93.

32. Shahpurı, *Tarikh*, vol. 1, 474.

33. *CRTIN*, 299, and *JIKUS*, 23.

34. *TQ* (October–December 1938): 306.

35 *Ibıd.*, 85–320.

36. From Iqbal's presidential address to the Muslim League on December 29, 1930; cited ın Farzana Shaikh, *Community and Consensus ın Islam: Muslim Representation ın Colonıal India, 1860–1947* (Cambrıdge, 1989), 200.

37 *TQ* (October–December 1938): 317

38. *Ibıd.*, 318–20.

39 The text of the letter ın whıch Mawdudi responded to thıs question ıs cited ın Shahpurı, *Tarikh*, vol. 1, 396–97

40. In fact, Mawdudi's position ın thıs perıod led to a serıes of serıous criticisms agaınst hım ın *Al-Islah* by Amın Ahsan Islahı, who took exception to hıs vıews and accused Mawdudi of "Muslim nationalism" and of stealthily supporting the Muslim League; cited ın *NGH*, 58.

41. Cited ın *SAAM*, vol. 1, 138–39

42. Malik Ghulam 'Ali, "Professor Mawdudi ke Sath Sath Islamıyah College Se Zaildar Park Tak," *HRZ*, 119

43. Qaıd-ı A'zam Papers Seal, Paper Number 952, Mınıstry of Culture, Pakıstan. The book was sent to Jinnah ın January 1940.

44. Sarwat Saulat, *Maulana Maududi* (Karachı, 1979), 22–23.

45 The council was headed by Mawlana Azad Subhanı, and its findings were later published ın Mawlana Muhammad Ishaq Sindihlawı, *Islam ka Siyası Nizam* (A'zam-garh, n.d.).

46. The details of thıs meeting were narrated by Qamaru'ddin Khan ın *Thınker* (December 27, 1963): 10–12.

47 *TQ* (September–October 1945): 2–3.

48. *Kawthar* (January 13, 1947, June 13, 1947, and June 17, 1947).

49 *RJI*, vol. 5, 140–41.

50. Opponents of the Jama'at among Muslim League workers have often vıewed the Jama'at-ı Islamı and Jamı'at-ı Ulama-ı Hind as one and the same.

51. *RJI*, vol. 5, 257

52. *Ibıd.*, vol. 5, 170–77, and 253–62.

53. *Nawa'-ı Waqt* (April 30, 1947): 1.

54. *Kawthar* (June 21, 1947): 2 and (July 5, 1947): 1. However, Mawdudi qualified hıs decree by stipulating that a vote for Pakıstan was not a vote of confidence ın the Muslim League; *MMKT*, vol. 1, 285–88.

55 *Kawthar* (July 5, 1947): 1.

6. ENTERING THE POLITICAL PROCESS, 1947–1958

1. *Kawthar* (July 28, 1947): 3
2. Sarwat Saulat, *Maulana Maududi* (Karachi, 1979), 29
3. Saulat, *Maulana Maududi*, 29; and interview with Mian Tufayl Muhammad in *Takbir* (November 16, 1989): 56.
4. Syed Ahmad Nur, *From Martial Law to Martial Law: Politics in the Punjab, 1919–1958* (Boulder, 1985).
5 Interview with Mian Tufayl Muhammad.
6. These talks were delivered between January 6 and February 10, 1948. They were later published as *Islam ka Nizam-i Hayat*, and published in English in Sayyid Abu'l-A'la Mawdudi, *The Islamic Way of Life* (Leicester, 1986).
7 U.S. Embassy, Karachi, disp. #189, 4/28/1948, 845F.00/4–2848, NA.
8. For more details see Ayesha Jalal, *The State of Martial Rule: The Origins of Pakistan's Political Economy of Defence* (Cambridge, 1990), 119–24.
9 U.S. Embassy Karachi, disp. #1671, 5/29/1951, 790D.00/5–1651, and disp. #1394, 3/28/1950, 790D.00/3–2851, NA. The British envoy in Pakistan took a less drastic view of the Communist threat, and attributed the plot largely to frustrations over Kashmir. He explained Faiz's part in the affair as conjectural; see U.K. High Commissioner, Karachi, tel. #FL1018/18, 3/10/1951, FO371/92866, PRO.
10. See, for instance, *Civil and Military Gazette* (January 28, 1950): 2 and (June 6, 1951): 1. Similar sentiments were expressed by Liaqat 'Ali Khan; U.S. Consulate General, Lahore, disp. #33, 9/15/1950, 790D.001/9–650, NA. Also the IJT, for instance, as a bulwark against communism in Pakistan, received financial support from the Muslim League between 1949 and 1952; see interview with Khurram Jah Murad in *JVNAT*, vol. 1, 70.
11. Freeland Abbott, *Islam and Pakistan* (Ithaca, 1968), 193
12. See *Kawthar* (November 25, 1947): 7; (December 13, 1947): 2; (December 17, 1947): 1, (December 25, 1947): 4; and (January 25, 1948): 2.
13. *Ibid.* (March 5, 1948): 1.
14. See Rana Sabir Nizami, *Jama'at-i Islami Pakistan: Nakamiyun ke Asbab ka 'Ilmi Tajziyah* (Lahore, 1988), 44–45
15 This comment was made in February 1948 and was later printed in Syed Abul 'Ala Maudoodi, *Islamic Law and Constitution* (Karachi, 1955), 1.
16. *Ibid.*, 53.
17 These lectures were subsequently published in *Islamic Law and Constitution* (Karachi, 1955).
18. Interview with Mian Tufayl Muhammad in *Takbir* (November 16, 1989): 48.
19 Ahmad Ra'if, *Pakistan Awr Jama'at-i Islami* (Faisalabad, 1986), 26.
20. U.S. Embassy, Karachi, disp. #328, 7/26/1948, 845F.00/7–2648, NA.
21. Ra'if, *Pakistan*, 26.
22. For an example of such an assertion, see *Kawthar* (December 25, 1947): 4.
23. Interview with Begum Mawdudi.
24. Interviews with Mian Tufayl Muhammad, Sultan Ahmad, and 'Abdu'l-Ghaffar Hasan.

25 SAAM, vol. 1, 225

26. Report of the Court of Inquiry Constituted under Punjab Act 11 of 1953 to Enquire into the Punjab Disturbances of 1953 (Lahore, 1954), 226.

27 TQ (June 1948): 121–26.

28. Ibid., 357

29 SAAM, vol. 1, 359–60.

30. Nawa'-ı Waqt (September 2, 1948): 1; (September 3, 1948): 1; and (September 3, 1948): 4.

31. In the words of one observer, while Muslim League leaders may have never forgiven the Jama'at's opposition to their cause before the partition, many shared the party's social and moral concerns and were therefore generally more tolerant of the Jama'at. The high civil servants, such as Iskandar Mirza, Ghulam Ahmad, or 'Aziz Ahmad, in contrast, were far more secular in outlook than the politicians and by the same token less tolerant of the Jama'at; U.S. Embassy, Karachi, disp. #61, 7/27/1956, 790D.00/7–2756, NA.

32. RJI, vol. 6, 133–34 and 138–39 Between 1948 and 1951 additional Jama'at leaders were jailed for various periods; ibid., 133–35

33. On October 16, 1948, in the Division Classified Letter No. F 4/8/48 EST.(SE) the Jama'at was declared a subversive organization, the membership of which was prohibited for Pakistani government employees. Other organizations cited in this code were the Anjuman-ı Azad Khiyal Musaniffin (Society of Free-Thinking Writers) and the Punjabı Majlis (Punjabı Council), both of which were Communist bodies. The code is interestingly still in the statutes, and was cited in the latest edition of the Civil Service Code printed during the Zia years; see ESTA CODE: Civil Service Establishment Code (Islamabad, 1983), 317

34. RJI, vol. 6, 136–37

35 Ibid., 136–42.

36. SAAM, vol. 1, 360.

37 Sayyıd Abu'l-A'la Mawdudi, Shakhsıyat (Lahore, n.d.), 273–80.

38. RJI, vol. 6, 101–2, and JIKUS, 57–58.

39 For a detailed account of the constitutional debates, see Leonard Binder's excellent analysis in Religion and Politics in Pakistan (Berkeley and Los Angeles, 1961).

40. As an indication of the importance of the alliance with 'Uthmani, Mian Mumtaz Daultana observed at the time that the Objectives Resolution was a personal favor to 'Uthmani by Liaqat 'Ali Khan, in that the sovereignty of God was acknowledged in the resolution; see Afzal Iqbal, Islamization of Pakistan (Lahore, 1986), 41. In a similar vein 'Abdu'l-Ghaffar Hasan recollects that 'Uthmani personally interceded with the authorities on a number of occasions to obtain the release of Mawdudi from prison; interview with 'Abdu'l-Ghaffar Hasan.

41. RJI, vol. 6, 107–8.

42. Ibid., 110–11.

43. Interview with Mian Tufayl.

44. RJI, vol. 6, 115

45 *SAAM*, vol. 1, 365–66.

46. *Ibid.*, 370.

47 *Ibid.*, 244.

48. *MMKT*, vol. 2, 82–99, and Sayyid Abu'l-A'la Mawdudi, *Sunnat'u Bid'at ki Kashmakash* (Lahore, 1950).

49 *SAAM*, vol. 1, 373.

50. On the Muhajir's demands for land reform, which were first aired in 1949, see U.K. High Commission, Karachi, disp. #18, 5/3/1949, DO35/8948, and disp. #31, 9/3/1949, DO35/8948, PRO.

51. *MMKT*, vol. 2, 161–65

52. *RJI*, vol. 6, 138–39

53. *TQ* (June 1950): 360–65

54. *RJI*, vol. 6, 115; and Binder, *Religion and Politics*, 216–17

55 For a full discussion of this issue, see Seyyed Vali Reza Nasr, "The Politics of an Islamic Movement: The Jama'at-i Islami of Pakistan," Ph.D. dissertation, Massachusetts Institute of Technology, 1991, 410–21, and *RJI*, vol. 6, 140–42.

56. U.S. Consulate General, Lahore, disp. #49, 9/25/1950, 790D.00/9–2950; disp. #72, 11/3/1950, 790D.00/11–350; and disp. #84, 11/30/1950, NA.

57 *RJI*, vol. 6, 118.

58. U.S. Consulate General, Lahore, disp. #136, 1/31/1952, 790D.00/1–3152, NA.

59 *RJI*, vol. 6, 117–29

60. *Ibid.*, 121, and U.S. Embassy, Karachi, disp. #660, 12/11/1951, 790D.00/11–2851, NA.

61. For details of these speeches, see *MMKT*, vol. 2.

62. U.S. Consulate General, Lahore, disp. #189, 5/1/1952, 790D.00/5–152, NA.

63. *TQ* (November 1952).

64. *MMKT*, vol. 2, 385–432.

65 Yohanan Friedmann, *Prophecy Continuous: Aspects of Ahmadi Religious Thought and Its Medieval Background* (Berkeley and Los Angeles, 1989), 37

66. U.S. Embassy, Karachi, disp. #1882, 6/21/1951, 790D.00/6–2151, NA.

67 U.S. Embassy, Karachi, disp. #1103, 1/27/1951, 790D.001/1–2750, 2, NA.

68. Nur, *From Martial Law*, 315–16, and Jalal, *State of Martial Rule*, 144–51.

69 U.S. Consulate General Lahore, disp. #146, 2/27/1952, 790D.00/2–2752, NA.

70. Malik Ghulam 'Ali, "Professor Mawdudi ke Sath Sath Islamiyah College Se Zaildar Park Tak," in *HRZ*, 123–24.

71. *SAAM*, vol. 1, 441.

72. U.S. Embassy Karachi, disp. #59, 7/17/1952, 790D.00/7–1752, NA.

73. U.S. Consulate General, Lahore, disp. #3, 7/14/1952, 790D.00/6–1452; U.S. Embassy, Karachi, disp. #591, 12/11/1952, 790D.00/12/1152, NA.

74. Daultana's financial and logistical support for the Ahrar and his direct role in precipitating the crisis in Punjab are detailed in reports of U.S. and British

diplomats; see U.S. Consulate General, Lahore, disp. #41, 10/1/1953, 790D.00/10–153, and disp. #58, 11/19/1953, 790D.00/11–1953, NA, and U.K. Deputy High Commissioner, Lahore, disp. #23/53, 11/17/1953, DO35/5296, PRO.

75 U.S. Consulate General, Lahore, disp. #10, 7/28/1952, 790D.00/7–2852, NA.

76. Jalal, *State of Martial Rule*, 153.

77 U.S. Consulate General, Lahore, disp. #12, 7/31/1952, 790D.00/7–3152, NA.

78. U.S. Consulate General, Lahore, disp. #17, 8/4/1952, 790D.00/8–452, NA.

79 Binder, *Religion and Politics*, 294.

80. Mawlana Abu'l-Hasanat, the president of the *majlis-i 'amal*, told the Court of Inquiry of Justice Munir that Nazimu'ddin had intimated to the *majlis* that if Zafaru'l-lah Khan was dismissed "Pakistan would not get one grain of American wheat"; U.S. Consulate General, Lahore, disp. #41, 10/1/1953, 790D.00/10–153, NA. Similar views were also expressed by the Ahrar leader Taju'ddin Ansari, who said Nazimu'd-din had sympathized with their cause, but argued that Zafaru'llah Khan's presence in the cabinet was essential to receiving wheat from the United States. See U.K. Deputy High Commissioner, Lahore, disp. #20/53, 10/1953, DO35/5296, PRO. Sayyid Amjad 'Ali, who negotiated the wheat loan from the United States, recollects no such threat on the part of the United States; interview with Sayyid Amjad 'Ali.

81. *Report of Court*, 50.

82. The Jama'at's relations with the *majlis-i 'amal* were sufficiently ambivalent to implicate the Jama'at in later court proceedings; see *ibid.*, 69–71: "While Jama'at's criticism[s] of acts of violence by agitators were only indirect and veiled, Mawdudi was throughout emitting fire against the Government in a most harsh language."

83 The book was not rounded up by Martial Law authorities until March 23, and in eighteen days it sold fifty-seven thousand copies; *SAAM*, vol. 2, 32.

84. U.K. High Commissioner, Karachi, disp. #405, 3/6/1953, DO35/5326, PRO.

85 In his memoirs, unpublished in full to this date, General Mirza takes full responsibility for martial law in Punjab. See General Iskandar Mirza's "Memoirs," 52–54 (unpublished manuscript). General Mirza's claim is confirmed by reports of U.S. and British diplomats; see U.S. Embassy, Karachi, tel. #5258, 4/16/1953, 790D.00/4–1653, and tel. #1913, 4/7/1953, 790D.00/4–753; U.S. Consulate General, Lahore, disp. #71, 1/5/1954, 790D.00/1/454, NA. Also see U.K. High Commissioner, Karachi, disp. #56, 4/18/1953, DO35/5377, PRO.

Other sources detailing the course of events which led to the imposition of Section 92a in Punjab place greater emphasis on the role of the central government and Nazimu'ddin in the events leading to the declaration of martial law. Aware of Daultana's dealings with the Ahrar, and eager to prevent him from assuming the image of a martyr once the martial law was imposed, the army prevented his resignation. Daultana was forced to negotiate with Nazimu'ddin, and agreed to hand in a letter which explicitly endorsed and supported the army's direct action. The army even summoned Daultana's links with the Ahrar to Karachi, indicating that unless the chief minister cooperated in the termination of his political career a case would be made against him and he could face a trial at a later date. The final deal which led to Daultana's resignation also explains the fact that Justice Munir in his probe into the agitations glossed over the chief minister's role in the agitations, and then *in camera;* U.S. Consulate General, Lahore, disp. #159, 3/17/1953, 790D.00/3–1753, NA. Also see U.K. High Commissioner, Karachi, disp. #442, 3/11/1953, DO35/5326, PRO.

One British source has pointed to General A'zam Khan as the prime mover behind the coup, reporting that "General Azam, who had for the past two days been pressing for authority from Nazimu'ddin but had not been able to get any orders, had taken over (as I understood it), entirely on his own"; U.K. High Commissioner, Karachi, disp. #417, 3/7/1953, DO35/5326, PRO. In light of the foregoing and evidence to the contrary, it is unlikely that A'zam Khan acted independently The period March 4–6, during which A'zam Khan had demanded action, was likely used by General Mirza and Nazimu'ddin to elicit concessions from Daultana.

86. The articles were published in February 28 and March 7, 1953, editions of the magazine; see *HRZ,* 134.

87 *Ibid.*

88. Memoirs of General Mirza, 46–48.

89 Binder, *Religion and Politics,* 305

90. Even the uncompromisingly secularist Iskandar Mirza appealed to Islam to bolster his political standing and promote national unity For instance, during a tour of Pathan tribal areas in October 1957, he lectured the tribes on the importance of Islamic unity; U.S. Consulate General, Lahore, disp. #58, 10/10/1957, 790D.00/10–1057, NA.

91. Jalal, *State of Martial Rule,* 184.

92. Cited in U.K. High Commissioner, Karachi, savingram #199, 11/26/1953, DO35/5284, PRO.

93. *Civil and Military Gazette* (July 22, 1952): 1.

94. U.S. Consulate General, Lahore, disp. #169, 4/2/1953, 790D.00/4–253, NA.

95 U.S. Consulate General, Lahore, disp. #185, 5/7/1953, 790D.00/5–753, NA.

96. U.K. High Commissioner, Karachi, savingram #94, 5/13/1953, DO35/5284, PRO.

97 U.K. Deputy High Commissioner, Lahore, disp. #10/53, 5/19/1953, DO35/5296, PRO.

98. For instance, the Awami League, hardly a friend of the Jama'at at this time, announced its intention to hold a Mawdudi Day on May 22, 1953, and was thwarted in its efforts only by government pressure; U.S. Consulate, Dacca, disp. #99, 5/28/1953, 790D.00/5–2853; also see U.S. Consulate General, Lahore, disp. #192, 5/31/1953, 790D.00/5–2153, NA.

99 *Report of the Court,* 92, and Abdur Rahman Abd, *Sayyed Maududi Faces the Death Sentence* (Lahore, 1978), 14–15

100. See Na'im Siddiqi and Sa'id Ahmad Malik, *Tahqiqat-i 'Adalat ki Report Par Tabsarah* (Lahore, 1955).

101. U.S. Embassy, Karachi, tel. #1711, 5/12/1951, 790D.00/5–1253, NA. In an interesting exchange soon after the anti-Ahmadi agitations came to an end, the U.S. Consul reports that Malik Firuz Khan Noon, chief minister of Punjab, asked the

American consulate general not to give any money to the Jama'at should the party ask for it under the pretext of waging an anti-Communist crusade. The chief minister then explained that the consulate should be aware that the Jama'at was "very dangerous" and that the anti-Ahmadi alliance could be revived to "kill off the Muslim League." U.S. Consulate General, Lahore, disp. #103, 1/4/1955, 790D.00/1–455, NA.

102. Muhammad Munir, *From Jinnah to Zia* (Lahore, 1979), 55.

103. Abu'l-Khayr Mawdudi, who seems to have always taken pleasure in cutting his younger brother's ego to size, mentions that such Muslim League stalwarts as Mushtaq Ahmad Gurmani, Chaudhri Muhammad 'Ali, and the ousted premier, Nazimu'ddin, had told Mawdudi that he would not be harmed; cited in Ja'far Qasmi, "Mujhe Yad Hey Sab Se Zara Zara   " in *Nida* (April 17, 1990): 28–34. Also see Aziz Ahmad, "Mawdudi and Orthodox Fundamentalism in Pakistan," *Middle East Journal* 21, 3 (Summer 1967): 369–70, where the author argues that Nazimu'ddin and Chaudhri Muhammad 'Ali interceded on Mawdudi's behalf with the authorities, preventing his execution. King Saud of Saudi Arabia, too, intervened on Mawdudi's behalf with Governor-General Ghulam Muhammad; cited in Sayyid Asad Gilani, *Maududi: Thought and Movement* (Lahore, 1984), 103–4. After Mawdudi's sentence was commuted, the Muslim League of Punjab lobbied for his release from prison; U.K. High Commissioner, Karachi, disp. #INT.29/26/4, 5/1/1954, DO35/5405, PRO.

104. 'Abdu'ssattar Niyazi recollects that a section of the army was unhappy with the decision of the military tribunal in Mawdudi's and Niyazi's cases; interview with 'Abdu'ssattar Niyazi in *Herald* (January 1990): 272.

105 For instance, Hajj Amin al-Husayni, the former grand mufti of Palestine, congratulated Mawdudi, which appeared in the press; cited in U.K. Deputy High Commissioner, Lahore, disp. #16/55, 8/8/1955, DO35/5297, PRO.

106. Chaudhri Ghulam Muhammad, "Pakistan Main Jumhuri Iqdar ki Baqa Awr Furugh," *Chiragh-i Rah*, Tahrik-i Islami Number (November 1963): 211.

107 On the Jama'at's efforts to assist the petition, see Nawwabzadah Nasru'llah Khan, "Ham Unke, Vuh Hemarah Sath Rahe', in *HRZ*, 37

108. On May 22, 1955, the governor-general amended the Emergency Powers Ordinance of 1955 to validate the Constituent Assembly for Pakistan Act of 1949 (expanding and redistributing the seats of the Constituent Assembly). As a result, all acts passed by the Constituent Assembly after 1949, including the Martial Law Indemnity Act of 1953, could be argued to be valid. Prisoners arrested under the Indemnity Act such as Mawdudi had been released when the law had been declared invalid; U.K. High Commissioner, Karachi, disp. #203, 10/31/1955, DO35/5120, PRO.

109 U.S. Embassy, Karachi, disp. #767, 5/28/1955, 790D.00/5–2855, and disp. #776, 6/2/1955, 790D.00/6–255, NA.

110. Faruqi writes that Chaudhri Muhammad 'Ali maintained close contact with Mawdudi throughout 1956 and frequently consulted him over the constitutional draft; 'Abdu'l-Ghani Faruqi, "Hayat-i Javidan," *HRZ*, 29

111. U.K. High Commissioner, Karachi, disp. #56, 4/18/1953, DO35/5372, P.3, PRO.

112. *TQ* (January–February 1956): 2–8.

113. Nur, *From Martial Law*, 351–55

114. U.S. Consulate General, Lahore, disp. #159, 1/6/1956, 790D.001–656, NA.

115. Letter from I.I. Chundrigar to United Kingdom's high commissioner, Sir Alexander Symon, dated 1/9/1956, DO35/5119, PRO.

116. U.K. High Commissioner, Karachi, confidential memo to Commonwealth Relations Office, London, 10/22/1955, DO35/5119; U.K. High Commission, Karachi, internal memo, 11/30/1955, DO35/5119 Interestingly, although a few months earlier the British had turned down Iskandar Mirza's request for advice on constitutional matters, this time the high commissioner thought otherwise and sent Chundrigar's draft constitution to Rowlatt for consideration; letter from U.K. High Commission, Karachi, to Commonwealth Relations Office, London, 9/23/1955, DO35/5119, PRO.

117 The vote in the East Pakistan provincial assembly had been 159 to 1, U.K. High Commissioner, Karachi, tel. #1585, 10/2/1956, DO35/5107A, PRO.

118. Mawdudi went on a tour of East Pakistan to campaign against joint electorates, hoping to influence the East Pakistan provincial assembly's decision on the matter; *MMKT*, vol. 4, 31–32, 66–70, 77–80, 166–79, and 182–83.

119 U.S. Embassy, Karachi, disp. #61, 7/27/1956, 790D.00/7–2756, NA.

120. In fact, it was the Jama'at's successful anti–joint electorates campaign that gave Iskandar Mirza a handle in 1958 to keep Suhrawardi's challenges to him and the Noon government at bay; U.S. Embassy, Karachi, tel. #1890, 1/31/1958, 790D.00/1–3158, NA.

121. Suhrawardi left office on October 11, 1957 His successor, Isma'il Ibrahim Chundrigar, remained in office until December 16, 1957, and was replaced with Malik Firuz Khan Noon, whose tenure of office extended until October 7, 1958.

122. See Mawdudi's criticisms of General Mirza's policies in *MMKT*, vol. 4, 125–32.

123. Nasru'llah Khan, "Ham Unke," 37

124. Cited in U.S. Consulate, Dacca, disp. #247, 4/3/1958, 790D.00/4–358, NA.

125 U.S. Embassy, Karachi, disp. #678, 4/10/1958, 790D.00/4–1058, NA.

126. U.S. Embassy, Karachi, disp. #939, 4/11/1958, 790D.00/4–1158, NA.

127 U.S. Embassy, Karachi, tel. #2708, 5/1/1958, 790D.00/5–158, and disp. #1094, 790D.00/5–2958, NA.

128. The Jama'at, moreover, defeated the Awami League and the National Awami party (with one seat each), both of which were deemed far more powerful than the Jama'at. The U.S. Embassy attributed the Jama'at's success to its good rapport with the Muhajir community, owing to its long history of social work among that community, its good choice of candidates, and the efficiency of its campaign. The Jama'at, it is reported, spent a total of Rs. 40,000 on the campaign, an average of less than Rs. 2,000 per candidate; U.S. Embassy, Karachi, disp. #1094, 790D.00/5–2958, NA.

7 THE SECULAR STATE, 1958–1971

1. Interview with Mian Tufayl Muhammad in *Takbir* (November 16, 1989): 53.

2. General Iskandar Mirza's unpublished memoirs, 109–10.

3 U.S. Embassy Karachi, disp. #537, 12/20/1957, 790D.00/12–2057; tel. #1470, 12/20/1957, 790D.00/12–2057; and tel. #1471, 12/20/1957, 790D.00/12–2057, NA, and U.K. High Commissioner, Karachi, disp. #21, 4/14/1958, DO35/8936, 5–7, PRO.

4. General Mirza's unpublished memoirs, 110.

5 As early as 1953 General Mirza had hinted at changing the regime because of "a growing possibility that unprogressive and anti-Western Moslem religious elements might become dominant in Pakistan"; U.S. Embassy, Karachi, tel. #278, 11/2/1953, 790D.00/11–253, NA.

6. In December 1957 he accused the Jama'at of making Islam into an "elastic cloak for political power." Cited in U.S. Embassy Karachi, tel. #1549, 12/31/1957, 790D.00/12–3157, NA.

7 *TQ* (June 1962): 322.

8. Syed Ahmad Nur, *From Martial Law to Martial Law: Politics in the Punjab, 1919–1958* (Boulder, 1985), 405; also see U.K. High Commission, Karachi, preliminary report, 10/25/1958, 4–5, DO134/26; U.K. High Commissioner, Karachi, fortnightly summary, 10/29/1958, DO134/26; and U.K. High Commission, Dacca, report, 11/7/1958, DO134/26, PRO.

9 Altaf Gauhar, himself a high-ranking Pakistani civil servant during the Ayub Khan era, writes that since 1947 the civil bureaucracy, given its British traditions, had been the repository of the greatest animosity toward Mawdudi in Pakistan; Altaf Gauhar, "Pakistan, Ayub Khan, Awr Mawlana Mawdudi, *Tafhimu'l-Qur'an* Awr Main," *HRZ*, 41–42. The fact that following the coup the military did away with the ministerial position and appointed eleven civil servants to oversee various government operations, forming a quasi-cabinet under Ayub Khan, further strained relations between the Jama'at and the government.

10. U.K. High Commissioner, Karachi, disp. #INT.83/6/2, 3/10/1959, DO35/8949, PRO.

11. Noteworthy in this regard are the editorials of Z. A. Suleri in *Pakistan Times*, which articulated the government's position to a large number of Pakistanis. On Suleri's views, see Anwar Hussain Syed, *Pakistan: Islam, Politics, and National Solidarity* (New York, 1982), 109–11.

12. Quraishi claims that the left eagerly pushed Ayub Khan to clamp down on the Islamic groups, and especially the Jama'at. Leftist propaganda soon created a climate wherein any talk of religion was derided as "Jama'ati" and hence deemed as insidious; see Ishtiaq Husain Qureshi, *Education in Pakistan: An Inquiry into Objectives and Achievements* (Karachi, 1975), 268–69

13. Mawdudi, in fact, disapproved of the brotherhood's increasing radicalization; *TQ* (April 1956): 220–28.

14. Sayyid Asad Gilani, *Maududi: Thought and Movement* (Lahore, 1984), 135

15 The text of the speech is enclosed with U.K. High Commission, Karachi, disp. #INT.48/47/1, 5/25/1959, DO35/8962, PRO.

16. *SAAM*, vol. 2, 121.

17 The Commission on Marriage and Family Law was first set up in 1955 with a view to enhancing the legal status of women. The Family Law Ordinance began with the report of that earlier committee, which had been presented in 1956.

18. On March 14, 1961, ulama led by the Jama'at issued a statement in Lahore denouncing the ordinance; *SAAM*, vol. 2, 65, and Khurshid Ahmad, *Studies in the Family Law of Islam* (Karachi, 1961).

19 *SAAM*, vol. 2, 65–66. Also see Mian Tufayl Muhammad, ed. and trans., *Statement of 209 Ulema of Pakistan on the Muslim Family Law Ordinance* (Lahore, 1962).

20. *SAAM*, vol. 2, 58.

21. Kawthar Niyazi, *Jama'at-i Islami 'Awami 'Adalat Main* (Lahore, 1973), 19

22. *SAAM*, vol. 2, 128–34.

23. Interview with S.M. Zafar.

24. Interview with Hakim Muhammad Sa'id, and personal correspondence with Allahbakhsh K. Brohi, 1985–86.

25 Cited in Muhammad Saeed, *Lahore: A Memoir* (Lahore, 1989), 224–25

26. *SAAM*, vol. 2, 156–57 Ayub was particularly riled by Mawdudi's attacks on his person and decided to retaliate; interviews with Hakim Muhammad Sa'id and S.M. Zafar.

27 *SAAM*, vol. 2, 187

28. Sarwat Saulat, *Maulana Maududi* (Karachi, 1979), 59

29 In Mecca, Mawdudi had delivered a lecture about the duties of Muslim youth in contemporary times. Khumayni, who had attended the lecture, was impressed with Mawdudi, and stood up and praised him for his views. Later that evening, along with a companion, Khumayni went to Mawdudi's hotel, where the two men met and talked for half an hour, aided by Khalil Ahmadu'l-Hamidi, Mawdudi's Arabic translator. Khumayni described the outlines of his campaign against the Shah to Mawdudi during that meeting; interview with Khalil Ahmadu'l-Hamidi; and Bidar Bakht, "Jama'at-i Islami ka Paygham Puri Duniya Main Pahila Raha Hey," *Awaz-i Jahan* (November 1989): 33–34.

30. Khalil Ahmadu'l Hamidi, "Iran Main Din Awr La-Dini Main Kashmakash," *TQ* (October 1963): 49–62.

31. *SAAM*, vol. 2, 169–70; and *ISIT(1)*, 6–7

32. On the reasons for the Combined Opposition Parties' choice of Miss Jinnah, see Rounaq Jahan, *Pakistan: Failure in National Integration* (New York, 1972), 150–51.

33 Nawwabzadah Nasru'llah Khan, "Ham Unke, Vuh Hemarah Sath Rahe," *HRZ*, 39

34. Mushtaq Ahmad Gurmani, the senior statesman and governor of Punjab in 1953–1954 who later became a close friend of Mawdudi, had related to the Jama'at's leaders that Kawthar Niyazi had, since the 1950s, maintained close contacts with the Punjab government and was put up to challenging Mawdudi by the authorities; interviews.

35 MMKT, vol. 6, 63–67

36. Gauhar, "Pakistan," 43.

37 MMKT, vol. 6, 85–94.

38. ISIT(1), 8–9

39 MMKT, vol. 6, 78–79

40. Ibid., 97–102, and 138–43.

41. Salim Mansur Khalid, "Talabah Awr I'lan-ı Tashqand," TT, vol. 1, 216–23.

42. For instance, in 1967 the Jama'at journal Chiragh-ı Rah dedicated an entire issue to the study of socialism.

43. SAAM, vol. 2, 209

44. Chaudhrı 'Abdu'l-Rahman 'Abd, Mufakkır-ı Islam: Sayyıd Abu'l-A'la Mawdudi (Lahore, 1971), 361.

45 Interview with Na'im Siddiqı in Takbır (September 26, 1991): 28.

46. Mir's articles were later published as Muhammad Safdar Mir, Mawdudiyat Awr Mawjudah Siyası Kashmakash (Lahore, 1970).

47 MMKT, vol. 6, 279–82.

48. 'Abd, Mufakkır-ı Islam, 361–64.

49 Fazlur Rahman meanwhile declared that the government's position on the citation of the moon was binding on the religious divines, a position which only incensed the Jama'at and the ulama further; see Pakistan Times (January 16, 1967): 1.

50. The resignation followed wide-scale opposition, mounted by the Jama'at against Fazlur Rahman's book Islam (Chicago, 1966); see Israr Ahmad, Islam Awr Pakistan: Tarikhı, Siyası, 'Ilmı Awr Thıqafatı Pasmanzar (Lahore, 1983), 55–60.

51. Zia Shahıd, "Amıriyat, Talabah, Awr Garmı Guftar," TT, vol. 1, 180–82.

52. Interviews with Shaikh Mahbub 'Ali and Muti'u'l-Rahman Nizamı in JVNAT, vol. 2, 16–17 and 223–25, respectively

53 MMKT, vol. 8, 188–92; and S.M. Zafar, Through the Crisis (Lahore, 1970), 204–5

54. On demands put before the Yahya Khan regime, see ISIT(1), 15

55 On the minister's views on the notion of the "ideology of Pakistan," see Nawwabzadah Shaır 'Ali Khan, Al-Qisas (Lahore, 1974).

56. Cited by Sayyıd As'ad Gilanı in an interview in Nida (April 17, 1990): 14–15

57 Interview with Muhammad Safdar Mir.

58. SAAM, vol. 2, 328.

59 For instance, in the fall of 1969 the IJT entered into direct negotiations with the martial law administrator of the province, General Nur Khan, who hoped the IJT would be able to repeat its successful drive to control the University of Punjab in East Pakistan; see interview with Muhammad Kamal in JVNAT, vol. 2, 186–87

60. One observer has even challenged the veracity of the rates of economic growth cited for the Ayub era, arguing that they did not reflect indigenous economic activity but were bolstered by foreign aid. See Rashıd Amjad, Pakistan's Growth Experience: Objectives, Achievement, and Impact on Poverty, 1947–1977 (Lahore, 1978), 6.

61. Khalid B. Sayeed, Politics in Pakistan: The Nature and Direction of Change (New York, 1980), 54–83.

62. See S.M. Naseem, "Mass Poverty in Pakistan: Some Preliminary Findings," *Pakistan Development Review* 12, 4 (Winter 1973): 322–25

63. For a discussion of the impact of economic changes during Ayub Khan's rule on the distribution of wealth between the provinces, see Jahan, *Pakistan*, 51–107

64. Mahbub ul-Haq, *The Poverty Curtain: Choices for the Third World* (New York, 1976), 7–8.

65. *ISIT(1)*, 18–19

66. Ibid., 17

67 On the events of this day see ibid., 18.

68. *Pakistan Times* (December 7, 1970): 1 and 7

69 Interviews with Khurshid Ahmad and Sayyid Munawwar Hasan.

70. Sharif al Mujahid, "Pakistan's First General Elections," *Asian Survey* 11, 2 (February 1971): 170.

71. Mashriqi Pakistan Talib-i 'Ilm Rahnima, "Mashriqi Pakistan Akhri Lamhih," *TT*, vol. 1, 316.

72. Kalim Bahadur, *The Jama'at-i Islami of Pakistan* (New Delhi, 1977), 133.

73. The four portfolios given to the Jama'at's provincial ministers were revenue, education, commerce and industry, and local government; see *ISIT(1)*, 23.

74. Interview with Khurram Jah Murad. The interviewee, an overseer of the Jama'at-i Islami of East Pakistan at the time, was kept at a prison camp between 1971 and 1974. Also see interview with Tasnim 'Alam Manzar in *JVNAT*, vol. 2, 258, and *ISIT(1)*, 24. As in 1947, the Jama'at decided to divide in accordance with the new political reality The Jama'at-i Islami of Bangladesh was formed in 1971 and began to reorganize in 1972 under the leadership of Ghulam A'zam.

75. Interview with Khurram Jah Murad; a similar view was expressed by Liaqat Baluch (interview).

8. THE BHUTTO YEARS, 1971–1977

1. Cited in 'Abdu'l-Ghani Faruqi, "Hayat-i Javidan," *HRZ*, 31.

2. There was another Attock conspiracy case in 1984. The first coup attempt is therefore often referred to as the first Attock conspiracy case.

3. Interview with S.M. Zafar.

4. See Stephen P Cohen, *The Pakistan Army* (Berkeley and Los Angeles, 1984), 86–104.

5. See Stanley Wolpert, *Zulfi Bhutto of Pakistan: His Life and Times* (New York, 1993), 281.

6. Interview with 'Abdu'l-Hafiz Pirzadah.

7 Quoted in Khalid B. Sayeed, *Politics in Pakistan: The Nature and Direction of Change* (New York, 1980), 162. Similarly, Stanley Wolpert reports that when in 1977 the director of the Inter-Services Intelligence sent a secret report to Bhutto, informing him of the Jama'at's influence in the army's Multan barracks, the prime minister responded by saying that the Jama'at was dangerous to the army only because it

received General Zia's "*official blessings and respect.*" See Wolpert, *Zulfi Bhutto,*
280–81.

8. Shahid Javed Burki, *Pakistan under Bhutto, 1971–1977* (London, 1980), 53.

9 Muhammad Salahu'ddin, *Peoples Party: Maqasid Awr Hikmat-i 'Amali* (Karachi,
1982).

10. On the importance of this issue in the eventual fall of the Bhutto government,
see 'Abdu'l-Ghafur Ahmad, *Pher Martial Law A-Giya* (Lahore, 1988), 101.

11. *ISIT(2),* 17

12. Altaf Gauhar, "Pakistan, Ayub Khan Awr Mawlana Mawdudi, *Tafhimu'l-
Qur'an* Awr Main," *HRZ,* 42–44.

13 Tahir Amin, *Ethno-National Movements of Pakistan* (Islamabad, 1988), 144–48.

14. Sayeed, *Politics in Pakistan,* 154.

15 Mujibu'l-Rahman Shami, "Jama'at-i Islami Awr Peoples Party· Fasilah Awr
Rabitah, Ik Musalsal Kahani," *Qaumi Digest* 11, 2 (July 1988): 13.

16. Interview with Kawthar Niyazi.

17 *ISIT(1),* 25; and *Rudad-i Jama'at-i Islami Pakistan, 1972* (Lahore, n.d.), 1–2.

18. Interview with Tasnim 'Alam Manzur, in *JVNAT,* vol. 2, 297–98.

19 Zahid Hussain, "The Campus Mafias," *Herald* (October 1988): 56.

20. *Rudad,* 2–3.

21. Sarwat Saulat, *Maulana Maududi* (Karachi, 1979), 85

22. Liaqat Baluch, "Rushaniyun Ka Safar," *TT,* vol. 2, 220–21.

23. 'Abdu'l-Shakur, "Jahan-i Tazah ki Takbirin," *TT,* vol. 2, 71–72.

24. Javid Hashmi, "Ik Jur'at-i Rindanah," *TT,* vol. 2, 51–52.

25 *Rudad,* 5

26. Ibid., 6–7

27 Interview with Kawthar Niyazi.

28. Interviews with 'Azizu'ddin Ahmad and Khalid Mahmud.

29 Cited in Wolpert, *Zulfi Bhutto,* 206.

30. Cited in Saulat, *Maulana Maududi,* 83–84.

31. *Rudad,* 9–11.

32. Chaudhri Ghulam Gilani, "Ik Chatan," *TT,* vol. 2, 18–19; and Sajjad Mir,
"Wahid-i Shahid," *TT,* vol. 2, 60.

33 Hashmi, "Ik Jur'at-i Rindanah," 52–53.

34. *Rudad,* 19–20.

35 *ISIT(1),* 34.

36. On Mian Tufayl's experiences in prison, see Mian Tufayl Muhammad, "General Zia ul-Haq Shaheed," in *Shaheed ul-Islam: Muhammad Zia ul-Haq* (London, 1990),
50.

37 Ibid.

38. *ISIT(1),* 52, and Kausar Niazi, *Zulfiqar Ali Bhutto of Pakistan: The Last Days*
(New Delhi, 1992), 28–32.

39 Salim Mansur Khalid, "Talabah Awr Tahrik-i Khatm-i Nubuwwat," *TT,* vol.
2, 159–75

40. Abu Sufyan Muhammad Tufayl Rashidi, *Tahaffuz-i Khatm-i Nubuwwat Awr
Jama'at-i Islami* (Lahore, n.d.), 81–85

41. *ISIT(2),* 9–10.

42. Ibid., 10.

43. Ibid., 14.

44. Ibid., 15–16.

45 Niazı, *Zulfiqar Ali Bhutto,* 36–37

46. The nine parties were the Jamaʿat-ı Islamı, Jamiʿat-ı Ulama Islam, Jamiʿat-ı Ulama-ı Pakistan, Muslim League, Tahrik-ı Istiqlal (Freedom Movement), Pakistan Democratic Party, National Democratic Party, Tahrik-ı Khaksar, and the Muslim Conference.

47 *ISIT(2),* 25.

48. Ahmad, *Pher Martial Law,* 92–93; and Nizaı, *Zulfiqar Ali Bhutto,* 70–71.

49 Sharif al-Mujahıd, "The 1977 Pakistanı Elections: An Analysis," ın Manzooruddin Ahmed, ed., *Contemporary Pakistan: Politics, Economy, and Society* (Karachı, 1980), 73. The Jamaʿat was orıgınally given thırty-two tickets by the PNA, but it contested only thırty-one as Jan Muhammad ʿAbbasɪ was prevented by the government from runnıng ın Larkana, Sind.

50. The difference between the share of the popular vote between the two contenders was, however, less staggerıng. The People's Party won only 58 percent of the popular vote compared with PNA's 35 percent. For these figures see, Burkı, *Pakıstan,* 196. What was contentious was that given the success of the PNA, the People's Party was clearly less popular than ın 1970, yet both its percentage of national votes and seats won to the National Assembly ıncreased markedly, from 39.9 percent to 58 percent and from 81 to 155, respectively; see Mujahıd, "The 1977 Elections," 83–84.

51. Ahmad, *Pher Martial Law,* 122 and 140–52.

52. Saulat, *Maulana Maududi,* 96.

53. *SAAM,* vol. 2, 460–61.

54. For ınstance, ın a speech before the parliament on April 28 Bhutto had referred to "the person ınflamıng the country ın the name of Nizam-e-Mustafa, Maulana Maudoodi," thus attesting to Mawdudi's pıvotal role ın the crısıs, at least ın the People's Party's eyes; cited ın Niazı, *Zulfiqar Ali Bhutto,* 91.

55 Intervıew with Kawthar Niyazı.

56. Intervıew with Begum ʿAbıdah Gurmanı.

57 Ibıd.

58. Ahmad, *Pher Martial Law,* 152.

59 Ibıd., 182.

60. Saulat, *Maulana Maududi,* 98.

61. The government sıde consısted of Bhutto, ʿAbdu'l-Hafiz Pirzadah (mınıster of law), and Kawthar Niyazı (mınıster for religıous affaırs). The PNA was represented by Mufti Mahmud (Jamiʿat-ı Ulama-ı Islam), ʿAbdu'l-Ghafur Ahmad (Jamaʿat-ı Islami), and Nawwabzadah Nasru'llah Khan (Pakistan Democratic Party). For accounts of these meetings, see Kawthar Niyazı, *Awr Lıne Kat Gaʾi* (Lahore, 1987); ıdem, *Zulfiqar Ali Bhutto;* and Ahmad, *Pher Martial Law.*

62. Niazı, *Zulfiqar Ali Bhutto,* 89

63. Ibıd., 89–94; for other examples of thıs allegation see Wolpert, *Zulfi Bhutto,*

277–302. Pakistan's decision to embark on a nuclear weapons program had created tensions in the relations between the two countries; see, for instance, the alarmist report in U.S. Ambassador, Islamabad, tel. #4065, 4/26/1978, DFTUSED, no. 45, 19

64. Ahmad, Pher Martial Law, 194.

65 Most PNA leaders, along with Niyazi and Pirzadah, believe that an agreement was reached; whether or not it would have been signed by all PNA parties or by Bhutto remains open to speculation. Interviews with 'Abdu'l-Ghafur Ahmad, Sardar Shairbaz Khan Mazari, 'Abdu'l-Hafiz Pirzadah, Begum Nasim Wali Khan, and Kawthar Niyazi. Pirzadah argues that he and Mufti Mahmud finalized the agreement in the late hours of July 2 and Bhutto was to sign it on July 5 Niyazi too writes that a final accord was reached, and Bhutto had agreed to sign it; Niazi, Zulfiqar Ali Bhutto, 239–41. Begum Nasim Wali Khan argues that despite the enthusiasm of the negotiating team other PNA leaders had reservations about the agreement, and most were not likely to sign it. Absence of a formal agreement between the government and the PNA was used as an excuse by the armed forces to stage a coup in order to break the dangerous impasse. Those justifying the coup, therefore, argue that no agreement had been reached between the two sides. See, for instance, Lt. General Faiz Ali Chishti, Betrayals of Another Kind: Islam, Democracy, and the Army in Pakistan (Cincinnati, 1990), 66.

9 ACCOMMODATION AND OPPOSITION, 1977–1988

1. Chatan (November 15, 1989): 19

2. For a discussion of inclusionary corporatism, see Alfred Stephan, The State and Society: Peru in Comparative Perspective (Princeton, 1978), and Shahrough Akhavi, "Shi'ism, Corporatism, and Rentierism in the Iranian Revolution," in Juan R.I. Cole, ed., Comparing Muslim Societies: Knowledge and the State in a World Civilization (Ann Arbor, 1992), 261–93.

3. 'Abdu'l-Ghafur Ahmad, Pher Martial Law A-Giya (Lahore, 1988). General Chishti argues that as the government became desperate it turned to the military and that the coup was planned with Bhutto's knowledge. See Lt. General Faiz Ali Chishti, Betrayals of Another Kind: Islam, Democracy, and the Army in Pakistan (Cincinnati, 1990), 66–69 Kawthar Niyazi of the People's Party also says that by March Bhutto had begun to turn to the military for advice and support and a military crackdown had been discussed on numerous occasions; Kausar Niazi, Zulfiqar Ali Bhutto of Pakistan: The Last Days (New Delhi, 1992), 79–88, and 163–70. This view was also supported by Ghulam Mustafa Khar in interview

4. Interviews with Malik Ghulam 'Ali, 'Abdu'l-Ghafur Ahmad, and Mahmud A'zam Faruqi.

5 Chishti, Betrayals, 16.

6. Interview with Khurshid Ahmad.

7 Cited in Sarwat Saulat, Maulana Maududi (Karachi, 1979), 101.

8. U.S. Embassy, Islamabad, disp. #7789, 7/11/1979, DFTUSED, no. 45, 99–100.

9 Interview with 'Abdu'l-Ghafur Ahmad and Sardar Shairbaz Khan Mazari.

10. See Mian Tufayl Muhammad, "General Zia ul-Haq Shaheed," in *Shaheed ul-Islam: Muhammad Zia ul-Haq* (London, 1990), 46–47

11. The possibility of a strong showing by the People's Party in the elections was taken seriously Mufti Mahmud of the Jami'at-i Ulama-i Islam, for instance, went to great pains to attack the People's Party's record in office and to underline Islam's prohibition against rule by women in order to dampen enthusiasm for the People's Party, which was at this time led by Benazir Bhutto and Begum Nusrat Bhutto; U.S. Embassy, Islamabad, disp. #7502, 7/3/1979, DFTUSED, no. 45, 83–84.

12. Saulat, *Maulana Maududi*, 101.

13. Interview with Mian Tufayl Muhammad in *Takbir* (November 16, 1989): 55–56.

14. Interview with Mawdudi in *Asia* (September 4, 1977): 4–5

15 These posts were filled by Ghafur Ahmad, Chaudhri Rahmat Ilahi, and Mahmud A'zam Faruqi, respectively The first two were deputy amirs and the third was amir of Karachi at the time.

16. Mawdudi was, putatively, opposed to the Jama'at's joining the government, believing that the party would compromise its individuality; interview with Khwajah Amanu'llah.

17 Interview with Mian Tufayl in *Takbir* (November 16, 1989): 55

18. U.S. Embassy, Islamabad, disp. #8356, 7/25/1979, DFTUSED, no. 46, 15–19

19 The contents of this deal were discussed by Mufti Mahmud with U.S. Embassy officials; U.S. Embassy, Islamabad, disp. #1449, 10/14/1979, DFTUSED, no. 46, 80–82.

20. Cited in *Nawa'-i Waqt* (October 25, 1978): 1.

21. Zia had favored holding municipal elections before national elections, hoping to satiate the appetite for elections without paving the way for handing over power to civilians. The PNA had objected, arguing that the results could be used to postpone national elections; U.S. Embassy, Islamabad, disp. #5223/01–02, 5/7/1979, DFTUSED, no. 45, 56–59

22. *ISIT(2)*, 41.

23. In 1986 the Jama'at won in the Karachi municipal elections again. This time it won 36 percent (85 out of 232) of the seats, thus retaining hold over the mayoralty of the city

24. *ISIT(2)*, 41.

25 Interviews with Mian Tufayl, Chaudhri Rahmat Ilahi, Mahmud A'zam Faruqi, and 'Abdu'l-Ghafur Ahmad. Also see Siraj Munir, "Azadi ka Ik Nia Mur," *Urdu Digest* (August 1988): 211–17

26. These talks were given on March 8 and 10, and April 7 and 8, 1978. They were subsequently published as Sayyid Abu'l-A'la Mawdudi, *System of Government under the Holy Prophet* (Lahore, 1978).

27 Interview with Khurshid Ahmad.

28. *ISIT(2)*, 43–44.

29 *Ibid*, 47

30. *Ibid*, 76–77

31. Interviews with Mahmud A'zam Faruqi and Sayyid Munawwar Hasan.

32. Khurram Badr, Qazi Husain Ahmad (Karachi, 1988), 70–71.

33. The benefits from involvement in the Afghan jihad led the party to become directly involved in other Islamic causes. The Jama'at has actively aided separatist forces in Kashmir since 1989 and provided support to Muslim forces opposing the restoration of the Communist government in Tajikistan in 1993; see Herald (February 1993): 29

34. Amiru'l-'Azim, "Talabah Huquq Bihali ki Jadd'u Jahd," TT, vol. 2, 357–63.

35 Interview with Mian Tufayl.

36. Ibid.

37 The breakdown of these thirteen seats was as follows: two from Punjab (Sargodha and Liyah); five from North-West Frontier Province (Dir three, Mardan and Swat one); five from Sind (all in Karachi); and one from Baluchistan (Turbat); Report on General Elections, 1985 (Islamabad, n.d.), vol. 3.

38. Interview with Mian Tufayl.

39 Interview with Khurram Murad in Awaz-i Jahan (November 1989): 10.

40. Interview with Malik Ghulam 'Ali.

41. See, for instance, Jasarat (March 10, 1990): 6.

42. Information provided by the Jama'at-i Islami of Karachi.

43. Sayyid As'ad Gilani, a senior Jama'at leader, has gone so far as to refer to Zia as "one who sows discord among Muslims" (munafiq)—a title reserved for the enemies of the Prophet during the early years of Islam—and to chastise Mian Tufayl for his tendency to side with authoritarian regimes. See interview with Gilani in Nida (April 17, 1990): 14–15

44. Mujibu'l-Rahman Shami, "Jama'at-i Islami Awr Peoples Party· Fasilah Awr Rabitah, Ik Musalsal Kahani," Qaumi Digest 11, 2 (July, 1988): 22.

45. These meetings occurred in 1982 and again in 1984 between Qazi Husain Ahmad (the secretary-general of the Jama'at at the time) and Faruq Laghari (the secretary-general of the Pakistan People's Party) in Lahore, and between Ghafur Ahmad and Piar 'Ali Alana of the People's Party in Karachi, also in 1984; Takbir (July 14, 1988): 5

46. It was in this context, allege the Jama'at's leaders, that the chief minister of Sind, Ghaws 'Ali Shah, actively supported the MQM—if not actually creating it—to undermine the Jama'at; Takbir (July 7, 1988): 12–13.

47 The Jama'at won 20 out of the 232 seats on the Karachi Municipal Corporation, down to 8.6 percent from 36.6 percent in 1983. Figures provided by the Jama'at-i Islami of Karachi.

48. Badr, Qazi, 85–86; and Shami, "Jama'at-i Islami," 21.

49 Farida Shaheed, "The Pathan-Muhajir Conflict, 1985–1986: A National Perspective," in Veena Das, ed., Mirrors of Violence: Communities, Riots, and Survivors in South Asia (Delhi, 1990), 194–214.

50. Interviews with Ghafur Ahmad and Mahmud A'zam Faruqi.

51. Interview with Faruqi.

52. Chatan (November 15, 1989): 19

53. Interview with Ghafur Ahmad in Takbir (July 7, 1988): 15–19

54. *Ibid*, 16. The bill was designed to enforce the shari'at ordinance which had been promulgated earlier. For a discussion of debates surrounding the bill and the Jama'at's position in them, see Charles H. Kennedy, "Judicial Activism and Islamization after Zia: Toward the Prohibition of Riba," in Charles H. Kennedy, ed., *Pakistan 1992* (Boulder, 1993), 60–64.

55. Badr, *Qazi*, 81–84, and *Takbir* (July 7, 1988): 15–19

56. *Takbir* (June 30, 1988): 12.

57 Badr, *Qazi*, 97; Munir, "Azadi," 211–17 The Jama'at was, moreover, quick to point out that it would not look favorably upon the postponement of future elections on account of the shari'at bill; interview with Qazi Husain in *Takbir* (June 30, 1988): 11–14.

58. Badr, *Qazi*, 83.

59 *Ibid.*, 84–96.

60. Interview with Sardar Shairbaz. The interviewee was present at the first Ghafur-Benazir meetings.

61. Cited in *Takbir* (June 23, 1988): 24.

62. Both Mian Tufayl and Na'im Siddiqi hinted that Muhammad Salahu'ddin was prompted to criticize Ghafur Ahmad by General Zia; see *Takbir* (June 23, 1988): 24. Also see *Akhlaqi Jang* (March 29, 1990): 23.

63. *Takbir* (June 23, 1988; July 14, 1988; July 21, 1988).

64. *Takbir* (July 14, 1988): 7

65. Qazi Husain charged that Zia had encouraged Asghar Khan, the leader of Tahrik-i Istiqlal, to travel to Iran in 1977, where the Shah had persuaded the retired air marshal to part ways with the PNA, *Akhlaqi Jang* (March 29, 1990): 20–23, and *Jasarat* (June 18, 1988 and June 19, 1988).

66. *Jasarat* (June 3, 1988): 2 and (June 18, 1988; June 19, 1988): 4.

67 Interview with Khurshid Ahmad.

10. THE REBIRTH OF DEMOCRACY, 1988–1993

1. Interviews with Sayyid Munawwar Hasan and Mahmud A'zam Faruqi.

2. See Qazi Husain's interview in the *Herald* (June 1992): 50.

3. Interview with Siraj Munir.

4. Qazi Husain Ahmad told me in an interview that he did not view the IJI as a positive force, but merely as a means to end the hegemony of the People's Party However, there were benefits for the Jama'at in staying with Nawaz Sharif; for, as Qazi Husain put it, "he is the shadow prime minister"; the inability of the People's Party government to project power effectively went a long way to explain the solidarity of the IJI. Interview with Qazi Husain Ahmad.

5. Sayyid As'ad Gilani, for instance, accused the People's Party and the Muslim League of being secular and feudal. Interview with Sayyid As'ad Gilani in *Nida* (April 17, 1990): 14. Unhappiness with the League became more noted as antagonisms with Pir Pagaro and Junejo continued, as did clashes with Sharif's rivals in the Muslim League of Punjab, Mian Manzur Watu, Chaudhri Shuja'at, and Chaudhri Parwez Ilahi.

6. *Takbir* (September 28, 1989): 28–29

7 See the *Friday Times* (March 15–21, 1990): 1–2.

8. Interview with Mahmud A'zam Faruqi.

9 Interview with Ghulam Mustafa Khar.

10. *Nation* (February 2, 1990): 1, and (February 19, 1990): 8.

11. Interview with Chaudhri Aslam Salimi.

12. Interview with Qazi Husain in *Dawn* (February 9, 1990): 3.

13. Interview with Ghafur Ahmad in the *Friday Times* (March-8–14, 1990): 1.

14. *Herald* (October 1990): 62.

15 Election Bureau of Jama'at-i Islami, circular #19-A/5, October 21, 1991.

16. Interview with Qazi Husain in *Takbir* (January 31, 1991): 26. Although here Qazi Husain asserts that no concrete offers were forthcoming from the new government either.

17 See interview with Qazi Husain in *Takbir* (December 27, 1990): 26–27; (January 3, 1991): 35; and (January 31, 1991): 26–27

18. For a thorough discussion of the Jama'at's response to the war and these two considerations, see Mumtaz Ahmad, "The Politics of War: Islamic Fundamentalisms in Pakistan," in James Piscatori, ed., *Islamic Fundamentalisms and the Gulf Crisis* (Chicago, 1991), 155–85

19 See interview with Qazi Husain in *Herald* (February 1991): 24. Between September 12 and 15, 1990, the Jama'at participated in a pro-Iraq Islamic conference convened in Jordan, following which it demanded that the government recall its eleven thousand troops from Saudi Arabia. For greater details see the debate between the editor of *Takbir* and the Jama'at's leaders over this issue in *Takbir* (January 31, 1991): 5–57, and (February 14, 1991): 15–18.

20. Cited in Ahmad, "The Politics of War," 165

21. Ahmad, "The Politics of War," 167

22. *Ibid.*

23. *Takbir* (March 7, 1991): 7–8 and (June 6, 1991): 29–30.

24. *Takbir* (March 7, 1991): 7–8.

25. *Takbir* (January 31, 1991): 7; *Jang* (March 19, 1991): 4.

26. *Friday Times* (February 7–13, 1991): 7

27 Ahmad, "The Politics of War," 176.

28. For a discussion of Sharif's version of the shari'at bill, see Ann Elizabeth Mayer, "The Fundamentalist Impact on Law, Politics, and Constitutions in Iran, Pakistan, and the Sudan," in Martin E. Marty and R. Scott Appleby, eds., *Fundamentalisms and the State: Remaking Polities, Economies, and Militance* (Chicago, 1993), 131–32.

29 Cited in *Herald* (September 1991): 50.

30. *Takbir* (October 3, 1991): 9–10.

31. The Jama'at presented a formal complaint about the MQM's treatment of its workers in Karachi to the meeting of IJI parties on September 1991. Unable to secure any assurances from the government, Qazi Husain severely criticized the government soon after the meeting; *Newsline* (October 1991): 36.

32. *FBIS-NES* -91–217, November 8, 1991, 52.

33 *FBIS-NES* -91–147, and *Takbir* (August 8, 1991): 37–38 and (August 15, 1991): 11–13.

34. Interviews; also see *Newsline* (September 1991): 43

35 *Herald* (June 1992): 48.

36. *Takbir* (October 1, 1992): 9–10.

37 *Takbir* (September 17, 1992): 26–31.

38. *Takbir* (July 30, 1992): 6–8.

39 Examples of these allegations may be found in the *Jang* (May 16 and 19, 1993), *Nawa'-i Waqt* (May 10 and 14, 1993), and *Sharq* (May 9, 10 and 12, 1993).

11. ISLAMIC REVIVALISM IN THE POLITICAL PROCESS

1. For instance, in his seminal study of factors which bear on the democratization process, Huntington has alluded to the importance of changes in the Catholic church in promoting democratization in Spain, Portugal, Latin America, and the Philippines; see Samuel P Huntington, *The Third Wave: Democratization in the Late Twentieth Century* (Norman, OK, 1991), 75–85. The case of the Jama'at suggests that for Islamic movements to support democratization such prerequisite changes are not necessary Whether they will act democratically once in power is a different matter, one open to question as much as the commitment of many secular leaders of democratization movements.

Glossary

adab Manners, proper social behavior, and etiquette, an important aspect of the Muslim culture of South Asia.

ahl-i bid'at Innovators; the term has negative connotations, implying breaking with orthodoxy

ahl-i sunnat Those who follow tradition; the term stands for "orthodoxy"

'ālim Singular of *'ulamā'*, see below

amīr Military commander or leader; in the context of this study it means director or president.

'asabiyyah Kinship and tribal ties.

ashram Hindu place of worship.

'awām-parastī Bending to popular will.

bai'ah Oath of allegiance traditionally given to caliphs, and in Sufism to Sufi masters.

birādrī Lineage or extended family; in South Asia the term refers to tribal ties.

burqa' Face cover for women.

dars-i nizāmī A syllabus of religious education which was popular in South Asia in the eighteenth century and which continues to be taught to this day

dār'u'ulūm A place of advanced religious learning; seminary

da'wāh To call to Islam; religious missionary activity

dhimmī Non-Muslims whose religion is tolerated by Islam; they are protected under Muslim law and must submit a poll tax to Muslims.

dīn Literally, religion; used by Mawdudi to mean true faith, unwavering adherence to religious law *fājir* Sinful, dishonest.

fāsıq Corrupt.

fatwā A religious decree issued by an *'alim.*

hadīth The sayings of Prophet Muhammad.

haqq-parastī Defending the truth.

hudūd Punishments; plural of *hadd,* literally, limit. These are punishments for crimes clearly defined in the Qur'an and the *sunnah.*

hukūmat-ı ilāhıyyah Divine government.

i'anat Donation, contribution.

'ibādah Worship; performance of religious rituals and duties.

'īdu'l-azhā Commemoration of Abraham's sacrifice of his son, Ishmael.

ijmā' Consensus; a source of Islamic law

ijtihād Individual inquiry conducted by an *'alim* to determine the ruling of Islamic law

ijtimā'-ı 'ām Public meeting; open meeting.

ımārat The office of the *amır;* see above.

ıqāmat-ı dīn Establishing the rule of Islamic law

itā'at-ı nazm Obedience to authority

jāgīrdārī Hereditary right to the revenue of a piece of land given by the government in return for services; hereditary patronage system centered in control of rural land.

jā'izah Review

jamā'at Party, organization.

jihād Holy war; to strive in the path of God.

Karbala The battle during which the grandson of Prophet Muhammad, Husain ibn 'Ali, was martyred on the plains of Karbala (in what is now Iraq) in A.D. 682. Husain, along with 72 men, rose in rebellion against the formidable army of the corrupt Umayyad Caliph Yazid. In Sunni Islam Husain's cavalier actions are seen as a manifestation of the battle of good against evil—the struggle for justice and righteousness. In Shi'i Islam, where the tale of Karbala has fueled religious passions for centuries, Karbala occurred as Husain asserted his rightful claim to the caliphate.

khānaqāh The place where Sufis congregate and engage in meditation.

Khatm-i Nubuwwat Finality of Prophethood, the campaign to declare Ahmadis a non-Muslim minority in Pakistan in 1974.

khilāfat-i rabbānī Divine caliphate.

kiswah The cloth which covers the Ka'bah in Mecca.

kufr Blasphemy; disbelief; un-Islam.

madrasah A school which trains *'ulama*.

majlis-i 'amal Council of action.

majlis-i 'āmilah Executive council or assembly

majlis-i shūrā' Consultative assembly

markazī majlis-i shūrā' Central consultative assembly

mashāyakh Plural of *shaikh*; see below

maslahat-parastī Opportunism.

mīlādu'l-nabī Commemoration of the birthday of Prophet Muhammad.

muhājirūn Migrants; those who migrated with Prophet Muhammad from Mecca to Medina in A.D. 622.

muhāsibah Calculation; taking stock of accounts.

munāfiq One who sows discord among Muslims and brings disunity to the Muslim community

murīd Devotee; followers of a Sufi master.

murshid Sufi master.

mu'tamid-i a'lā' Supreme secretary (title of the secretary-general of IJT).

nā'ib amīr Deputy *amīr*; see above.

nāmanzūr Non-recognition.

nash'at-i naw Renaissance; new beginning.

nāzim-i 'alā' Supreme head or organizer (title of the overseer of the IJT).

panchāyat Rural councils, usually consisting of five elders; voter councils.

pīr Sufi master.

purdah Literally, curtain; the system through which men and women are segregated.

qa'id-i a'zam Supreme leader (Jinnah's title).

qā'im maqām-ı amır Vice-amır; see above.

qayyım Overseer (title of the secretary-general of the Jama'at).

ribā' Usury, which is banned by Islam.

rīyāsat dar rīyāsat State within a state.

salāt Muslim ritual prayer, performed five times a day

sālih Virtuous.

sālih qīyādat Virtuous leadership; the Jama'at's term for the kind of leadership it hopes to bring to power.

sarmāyadārī Capitalism.

sarsıpurdagī Literally, to submit one's head; in Sufi termınology it means to commit oneself to the Sufi master.

shahādah Muslim testimony of faith—"there is no god but God."

shaikh Sufi master.

sharī'ah The body of laws which govern Muslim personal and social life.

shırwānī Long overcoat traditionally worn by Muslim Indian men.

sīratu'l-nabī Literally, path of Prophet Muhammad; refers to following the example of Prophet Muhammad in conducting one's life.

sunnah Tradition; proper practice of Islam, following the example of the Prophet Muhammad.

swārāj Home rule; policy introduced by the Congress party in its struggle for independence.

tablīgh Missionary activity; propagation of Islamic teachings.

tajdīd Literally, renewal; refers to Muslim millenarian yearnings.

tarīqah Literally, the path; refers to the path of Sufism.

tawāzun Balance.

'ulamā' Those educated in Islamic law and capable of issuing opinions on religious matters.

ummah Community of Muslims.

zakāt A canonical tax, the payment of which is incumbent on all Muslims.

zımmı See *dhımmī* above.

Interviewees

'Abbası, Jan Muhammad. Deputy amır and amır of Sind. Karachı, May 8, 1990.

Afghanı, 'Abdu'ssattar. Former mayor of Karachı. Karachı, May 8, 1990.

Afzal, Muhammad. Former minister of education. Islamabad, February 20, 1990.

Ahmad, 'Abdu'l-Ghafur. Deputy amır. Karachı, May 3, 1990.

Ahmad, 'Azızu'ddin. Leftist intellectual, activist, and former member of the People's Party Lahore, March 17, 1990.

Ahmad, Israr. Former Jama'at member and leader of Tanzım-ı Islamı. Lahore, November 12, 1989

Ahmad, Khurshıd. Deputy amır. Islamabad, November 19, 1989

Ahmad, Qazı Husaın. Amır. Lahore, January 22, 1990.

Ahmad, Sultan. Former Jama'at leader. Karachı, May 11, 1990.

'Ali, Malik Ghulam. Former justice of the Shari'at Court. Lahore, January 31 and March 11, 1990.

'Ali, Sayyıd Amjad. Former minister of finance. Lahore, October, 5, 1989

'Ali Shah, Sayyıd Khawar. Member of the Punjab Assembly Lahore, March 9, 1990.

Ansarı, Zafar Ishaq. Director of the Islamıc Research Institute. Islamabad, October 21, 1989, and May 5, 1990.

Ashraf, Mawlana 'Abdu'l-Rahım. Former Jama'at leader. Faısalabad, November 18, 1989

Baluch, Lıaqat. Deputy secretary-general. Lahore, February 3, 1990.

Brohı, Allahbakhsh. Former minister of law Personal correspondence, 1985–1986.

Faruqı, Mahmud A'zam. Former amır of Karachı. Karachı, May 7, 1990.

Ghamıdi, Javıd Ahmadu'l- Former Jama'at member. Lahore, September 19, 1989

Gilani, Sayyid As'ad. Amir of Lahore. Lahore, December 4, 1989, and March 11, 1990.

Gurmani, Begum 'Abidah. Confidant of Mawlana Mawdudi. Lahore, April 8, 1990.

Hamidi, Khalil Ahmadu'l- Director of Daru'l-'Urubiyah. Lahore, February 4, 1990.

Haqqani, Husain. Former IJT leader. Lahore, January 9 and 28, 1990.

Hasan, Mawlana 'Abdu'l-Ghaffar. Former Jama'at leader. Faisalabad, November 17 and 18, 1989

Hasan, Sayyid Munawwar. Secretary-general, former amir of Karachi. Karachi, May 19, 1990.

Hashmi, Javid. Former IJT leader, former minister of culture, and member of the National Assembly Lahore, March 15, 1990.

Ilahi, Chaudhri Rahmat. Deputy amir. Lahore, March 12, 1990.

Iqbal, Javid. Former justice of the Supreme Court. Lahore, November 7, 1989

Islahi, Mawlana Amin Ahsan. Former Jama'at leader. Lahore, October 7, 1989

Khar, Ghulam Mustafa. Former governor and former chief minister of Punjab. Lahore, May 3, 1990.

Khwajah Amanu'llah. Confidant of Mawlana Mawdudi. Lahore, April 8, 1990.

Mahmud, Khalid. Editor of the Nation. Lahore, March 12, 1990.

Mawdudi, Begum Mahmudah. Mawlana Mawdudi's wife. Lahore, April 1, 1990.

Mazari, Sardar Shairbaz Khan. PNA leader. Karachi, May 20, 1990.

Muhammad, Mian Tufayl. Former amir. Lahore, September 21 and 23, 1989

Munir, Siraj. Former adviser to Nawaz Sharif. Lahore, October 20, 21, and 22, 1989

Murad, Khurram Jah. Deputy amir. Lahore, September 14, 1989, and January 22, 1990.

Nadwi, Mawlana Sayyid Abu'l-Hasan 'Ali. Nadwi leader and one of the Jama'at's founders. Lucknow, December 27, 1989

Nadwi, Mawlana Wasi Mazhar. Former member of shura' Personal correspondence, 1989–1990.

Niyazi, Kawthar. Former amir of Punjab and minister of religious affairs. Islamabad, October 3, 1989, and May 6, 1990.

Parachah, Farid Ahmad. Former IJT leader. Lahore, December 4, 1989

Pirzadah, 'Abdu'l-Hafiz. Former minister of law Karachi, May 23, 1990.

Qadri, Muhammad Tahiru'l- Leader of Minhaju'l-Qur'an. Lahore, March 7, 1990.

Qasmi, Ja'far. Former Jama'at follower. Faisalabad and Lahore, November 18, 1989, and January 23 and 25, 1990.

Quraishi, Altaf Hasan. Pro-Jama'at journalist and activist. Lahore, February 6, 1990.

Sadiq, Mustafa. Former Jama'at member. Lahore, March 6, 1990.

Safdar Mir, Muhammad. Leftist ideologist. Lahore, April 13, 1990.

Sa'id, Hakım Muhammad. Former minister of health. Karachı, September 27, 1989

Salahu'ddin, Muhammad. Pro-Jama'at journalist and political activist. Karachı, May 20, 1990.

Salimı, Chaudhrı Aslam. Former secretary-general. Lahore, October 8, 1989, and March 24, 1990.

Shamı, Mujibu'l-Rahman. Pro-Jama'at journalist and political activist. Lahore, February 10 and 14, 1990.

Siddiqı, Fazlu'l-Rahman Na'im. Jama'at leader. Lahore, September 30, 1989

Wali Khan, Begum Nasım. Pathan leader and politician. Lahore, March 28, 1990.

Zafar, S.M. Former minister of law Lahore, September 18, 1989

Bibliography

PRIMARY SOURCE COLLECTIONS

Archives of Institute of Islamic Culture (Idarah-ı Thıqafat-ı Islam), Lahore.
Archives of Islamic Studies Academy (Idarah-ı Ma'arif-ı Islami) of Jama'at-ı Islamı, Lahore.
Archives of the Khudabakhsh Library, Patna.
Archives of the Ministry of Culture, Government of Pakistan, Islamabad.
National Archives of United States of America, Washington, D.C., and Suitland, Maryland. Diplomatic correspondence and the collection of embassy and Department of State papers.
Public Record Office, London. Papers of the Foreign Office and Commonwealth Relations Office.

MAGAZINES, NEWSPAPERS, AND URDU JOURNALS

A'in, Lahore.
Akhlaqı Jang, Karachı.
Asıa, Lahore.
Awaz-ı Jahan, Lahore.
Chatan, Lahore.
Chıragh-ı Rah, Karachı.
Civil and Military Gazette, Lahore.
Crescent, Lahore.
Criterıon, Karachı.
Dawn, Karachı.
Frıday Times, Lahore.
Al-Furqan, Lucknow
Haftrozah Zindagı, Lahore.
Hamqadam, Karachı.

Herald, Karachı.

Iqdam, Lahore.

Jang, Lahore, Rawalpındi.

Jasarat, Karachı.

Kawthar, Lahore.

Al-Ma'arif, Lahore.

Mithaq, Lahore.

Al-Nadwah, A'zamgarh.

Nation, Lahore.

Nawa'-ı Waqt, Lahore

Newsline, Karachı.

Nida, Lahore.

Nigar, Delhı, Karachı.

Pakıstan Observer, Karachı.

Pakıstan Times, Lahore.

Qaumı Digest, Lahore.

Sayyarah, Lahore.

Sharq, Karachı.

Takbır, Karachı.

Tarjumanu'l-Qur'an, Hyderabad, Pathankot, Lahore.

Tasnım, Lahore.

Thınker, Karachı.

Times of Karachı, Karachı.

Urdu Digest, Lahore.

Wifaq, Lahore.

URDU AND PERSIAN SOURCES

'Abd, Chaudhrı 'Abdu'l-Rahman. Mufakkır-ı Islam: Sayyıd Abu'l-A'la Mawdudi (Thınker of Islam: Mawlana Sayyıd Abu'l-A'la Mawdudi). Lahore: Islamıc Publications, 1971.

'Abdu'l-Shakur. "Jahan-ı Tazah kı Takbırın" (The New World's Invocation of Greatness), ın Salim Mansur Khalid, ed., Talabah Tahrikaın (Student Movements) 2: 69–112. Lahore: Al-Badr Publications, 1989

Abu'l-Afaq. Sayyıd Abu'l-A'la Mawdudi: Sawanih, Afkar, Tahrik (Sayyıd Abu'l-A'la Mawdudi: Biography, Thought, and Movement). Lahore: Islamıc Publications, 1971.

Abu Tarıq, ed. Mawlana Mawdudi kı Taqarır (Mawlana Mawdudi's Speeches). 2 vols. Lahore: Islamıc Publications, 1976.

Ahmad, 'Abdu'l-Ghafur. Pher Martial Law A-Giya (Then Came Martial Law). Lahore: Jang Publications, 1988.

Ahmad, Anas. "Jami'at ka Ta'sısı Pasmanzar" (Background to the Jami'at's Establishment), ın Salim Mansur Khalid, ed., Talabah Tahrikaın (Student Movements) 1: 109–20. Lahore: Al-Badr Publications, 1989

Ahmad, Israr. *Islam Awr Nash'at-ı Jadid* (Islam and Renaissance). Lahore, 1968.

———— *Islam Awr Pakıstan: Tarikhı, Siyası, 'Ilmı Awr Thıqafati Pasmanzar* (Islam and Pakıstan: Historıcal, Political, and Cultural Background). Lahore: Maktabah-ı Markazı-ı Anjuman-ı Khuddamu'l-Qur'an, 1983.

———— *Tahrik-ı Jama'at-ı Islamı: Ik Tahqıqı Mutala'ah* (The Movement of the Jama'at-ı Islamı: A Critical Study). Lahore: Daru'l-Isha'ah-ı Islamı, 1966.

———— *Tarikh-ı Jama'at-ı Islamı: Ik Gumshudah Bab* (History of Jama'at-ı Islamı: A Lost Chapter). Lahore: Maktabah-ı Jadid Press, 1990.

———— "Naghz-ı Ghazal" (Felicity of the Ode). *Mithaq* 39, 1 (January 1990).

Ahmad, Khurshıd. *Tazkırah-ı Zindan* (Prıson Log). Karachı: Chıragh-ı Rah, 1965

———— ed. *Adabıyat-ı Mawdudi* (Mawdudi's Literature). Lahore: Islamıc Publications, 1972.

Ahmad, Qazı Husaın. *Shari'at Bill: Uskı Zarurat Awr Us Par I'tirazat Ja'izah* (Shari'at Bill: Its Necessity and an Examınation of the Objections to It). Lahore: Mutahhıdah Shari'at Mahaz, 1986.

'Ali, Malik Ghulam. "Professor Mawdudi ke Sath Sath Islamıyah College Se Zaildar Park Tak" (With Professor Mawdudi from Islamıyah College to Zaildar Park). *Haftrozah Zindagı*, Mawdudi Number (September 29–October 5, 1989): 118–27

'Ali, Naqı. *Sayyıd Mawdudi ka 'Ahd* (Sayyıd Mawdudi's Covenant). Lahore, 1980.

'Ali, Nawwab Sadiq. *Bi Tiq Sipahı* (Armless Army). Karachı: Allied Books, 1971.

Amınu'l-Haq, K.M. "Al-Badr Commander Bulta Hi" (Al-Badr Commander Speaks), ın Salim Mansur Khalid, ed., *Talabah Tahrikaın* (Student Movements) 2: 326–54. Lahore: Al-Badr Publications, 1989

Amıru'l-'Azım. "Talabah Huquq Bihali kı Jadd'u Jahd" (Struggle for the Rights of Students), ın Salim Mansur Khalid, ed., *Talabah Tahrikaın* (Student Movements) 2: 357–63 Lahore: Al-Badr Publications, 1989

Ansarı, Zafar Ahmad. "Tahrik-ı Pakıstan Awr Ulama" (Pakıstan Movement and the Ulama). *Chıragh-ı Rah* 14, 12 (December 1960): 232–34.

Badr, Khurram. *Qazı Husaın Ahmad.* Karachı: Saba Publications, 1988.

Baluch, Lıaqat. "Rushanıyun ka Safar" (Journey of Enlightenment), ın Salim Mansur Khalid, ed., *Talabah Tahrikaın* (Student Movements) 2: 219–30. Lahore: Al-Badr Publications, 1989

Baraku'llah Khan. "Maın ne Sayyıd ke Sath Jail Kati" (I Was Jailed with the Sayyıd). *Haftrozah Zindagı*, Mawdudi Number (September 29–October 5, 1989): 88–90.

Bhuttu, Muhammad Musa. *Chaudhrı Ghulam Muhammad: Ik Shakhsıyat, Ik Tahrik* (Chaudhrı Ghulam Muhammad: A Personality, a Movement). Hyderabad: Daru'l-Islam Publications, n.d.

Bidar Bakht. "Jama'at-ı Islamı ka Paygham Purı Dunıya Maın Pahila Raha Hey" (The Message of Jama'at-ı Islamı Is Spreading across the World). *Awaz-ı Jahan* (November 1989): 32–34.

Brohı, Allahbukhsh K. "Mawdudi: Pakıstan ka Sab Se Bara Wakil" (Mawdudi: Pakıstan's Greatest Advocate). *Haftrozah Zindagı:* Mawdudi Number (September 29–October 5, 1989): 33–36.

Bukharı, Zahıd Husaın. "Talabah Tahrik ka Ik Almıyah" (A Tragedy ın the Student

Movement), in Salim Mansur Khalid, ed., *Talabah Tahrikain* (Student Movements) 1. 137–44. Lahore: Al-Badr Publications, 1989

Chiragh-i Rah. Tahrik-i Islami Number (November 1963).

Dastur-i Jama'at-i Islami, Pakistan (Constitution of Jama'at-i Islami of Pakistan). Lahore: Jama'at-i Islami, 1989

Faruqi, 'Abdu'l-Ghani. "Hayat-i Javidan" (Eternal Life). *Haftrozah Zindagi*, Mawdudi Number (September 29–October 5, 1989): 23–31.

Gauhar, Altaf. "Pakistan, Ayub Khan, Awr Mawlana Mawdudi, *Tafhimu'l-Qur'an* Awr Main" (Pakistan, Ayub Khan, Mawlana Mawdudi, *Tafhimu'l-Qur'an*, and I). *Haftrozah Zindagi*, Mawdudi Number (September 29–October 5, 1989): 41–45

Ghafarlahu, Ahqar Mazhar Husain. *Mawdudi Jama'at ki 'Aqa'id par Ik Tanqidi Nazar* (A Critical Review of the Ideas of Mawdudi and the Jama'at). Jhelum, n.d.

Gilani, Chaudhri Ghulam. "Ik Chatan" (A Rock), in Salim Mansur Khalid, ed., *Talabah Tahrikain* (Student Movements) 2: 15–20. Lahore: Al-Badr Publications, 1989

Gilani, Sayyid As'ad. *Qafilah-i Sakht Jan* (The Tenacious Caravan). Sargodha: Idarah-i Adab-i Islam, 1965

———— "Jama'at-i Islami, 1941–1947 " Ph.D. dissertation, University of Punjab, 1989–1990.

Haftrozah Zindagi. Mawdudi Number (September 29–October 5, 1989).

Hamidi, Khalil Ahmadu'l- *Tahriki Safar ka Dastan* (Story of the Journey for the Movement). Lahore: Idarah-i Ma'arif-i Islami, 1989

———— "Iran Main Din Awr La-Dini Main Kashmakash" (The Struggle between Religion and Secularism in Iran). *Tarjumanu'l-Qur'an* (October 1963): 49–62.

———— "Jama'at-i Islami ki Dasturi Jadd'u Jahd" (The Constitutional Struggle of Jama'at-i Islami). *Chiragh-i Rah*, Tahrik-i Islami Number (November 1963): 337–55

Hashmi, Javid. "Ik Jur'at-i Rindanah" (A Maverick's Daring), in Salim Mansur Khalid, ed., *Talabah Tahrikain* (Student Movements) 2: 47–58. Lahore: Al-Badr Publications, 1989

Idris, Hafiz Muhammad. "Sarmayah-i Millat ki Nigahban" (Protectors of the National Resources), in Salim Mansur Khalid, ed., *Talabah Tahrikain* (Student Movements) 1: 249–92. Lahore: Al-Badr Publications, 1989

Ijtima' Se Ijtima' Tak (1963–1974): Rudad-i Jama'at-i Islami, Pakistan (From Convention to Convention (1963–1974): Proceedings of the Jama'at-i Islami of Pakistan). Lahore: Jama'at-i Islami, 1989

Ijtima' Se Ijtima' Tak (1974–1983): Rudad-i Jama'at-i Islami, Pakistan (From Convention to Convention (1974–1983): Proceedings of the Jama'at-i Islami of Pakistan). Lahore: Jama'at-i Islami, 1989

Ilahi, Chaudhri Rahmat. *Pakistan Main Jama'at-i Islami ka Kirdar* (Jama'at-i Islami's Activities in Pakistan). Lahore: Markazi Shu'bah-i Nashr'u Isha'at-i Jama'at-i Islami, Pakistan, 1990.

Iqbal, Shaikh Muhammad. *Jama'at-i Islami par Ik Nazariyah* (A Look at the Jama'at-i Islami). Karachi, 1952.

Isma'il, Tariq. *Election '88.* Lahore: Maktabah-ı Nawa'-ı Waqt, 1989

Kashmırı, 'Ashıq. *Tarikhı Tahrik-ı Islamı, Jamun'u Kashmır* (The Historıcal Islamıc Movement of Jamu and Kashmır). Lahore: Idarah-ı Ma'arif-ı Islamı, 1989

Khalid, Salim Mansur. *Al-Badr* Lahore: Idarah-ı Matbu'at-ı Talabah, 1985

————— "Shahıd Fazl-ı Rabi" (Martyr Fazl-ı Rabi), ın Salim Mansur Khalid, ed., *Talabah Tahrikaın* (Student Movements) 2: 298–310. Lahore: Al-Badr Publications, 1989

————— "Talabah Awr I'lan-ı Tashqand" (Students and the Tashkent Declaration), ın Salim Mansur Khalid, ed., *Talabah Tahrikaın* (Student Movements) 1: 216–23. Lahore: Al-Badr Publications, 1989

————— "Talabah Awr Tahrik-ı Khatm-ı Nubuwwat" (Students and the Anti-Ahmadi Movement), ın Salim Mansur Khalid, ed., *Talabah Tahrikaın* (Student Movements) 2: 159–75. Lahore: Al-Badr Publications, 1989

————— "Tin Salah Degree Course Awr Unıversity Ordinance" (Three-Year Degree Course and the Unıversity Ordinance), ın Salim Mansur Khalid, ed., *Talabah Tahrikaın* (Student Movements) 1: 160–75 Lahore: Al-Badr Publications, 1989

————— ed. *Talabah Tahrikaın* (Student Movements). 2 vols. Lahore: Al-Badr Publications, 1989

Khan, Hafiz. "Zawq-ı 'Amal" (Enthusıasm for Action), ın Salim Mansur Khalid, ed., *Talabah Tahrikaın* (Student Movements) 2: 21–28. Lahore: Al-Badr Publications, 1989

Khukar, Mas'ud. "'Uqabun kı Nishıman" (Eagles' Nest), ın Salim Mansur Khalid, ed., *Talabah Tahrikaın* (Student Movements) 2: 199–218. Lahore: Al-Badr Publications, 1989

Mansur, 'Umar. "Talabah Awr Qaumi'u Milli Masa'il" (Students and National Issues), ın Salim Mansur Khalid, ed., *Talabah Tahrikaın* (Student Movements), 1. 159–76. Lahore: Al-Badr Publications, 1989).

Mashrıqı Pakıstan Talib-ı 'Ilm Rahnıma [an East Pakıstanı student leader]. "Mashrıqı Pakıstan Akhrı Lamhih" (East Pakıstan's Final Tragedy), ın Salim Mansur Khalid, ed., *Talabah Tahrikaın* (Student Movements) 1. 311–38. Lahore: Al-Badr Publications, 1989

Mawdudi, Begum Mahmudah. "Mawlana Mawdudi Apne Ghar Maın" (Mawlana Mawdudi ın His Own House), ın Muhammad Yusuf Buhtah, *Mawlana Mawdudi: Apnı Awr Dusrun kı Nazar Maın* (Mawlana Mawdudi: In His Own and Others' Views), 261–64. Lahore: Idarah-ı Ma'arif-ı Islamı, 1984.

Mawdudi [or Maududi or Maudoodi], Sayyıd Abu'l-A'la. *Dakter ka Nishtar Ya Daku ka Khanjar* (Doctor's Lancet or the Dacoit's Dagger). Lahore: Daru'l-Fikr, n.d.

————— *Da'wah Awr 'Amal* (Calling and Action). Lahore, n.d.

————— *Islamı Hukumat Kis Tarah Qa'im Huta Hey* (How to Establish the Islamıc State). Lahore, n.d.

————— *Islamı Riyasat.* Lahore: Islamıc Publications, 1969

————— *Islam ka Nazrıyah Siyası* (Islam's Political Views). Delhı, 1967

————— *Jama'at-ı Islamı kı Untis Sal* (Twenty-nıne Years of the Jama'at-ı Islamı). Lahore: Shu'bah-ı Nashr'u Isha'at-ı Jama'at-ı Islamı, Pakıstan, 1970.

—— Jama'at-ı Islamı: Tarikh, Maqsad, Awr La'ihah-ı 'Amal (Jama'at-ı Islamı: History, Aims, and Plan of Action). Reprint. Lahore: Islamic Publications, 1963.
—— Al-Jihad Fi'l-Islam (Jihad ın Islam). Reprint. Lahore: Idarah-ı Tarjumanu'l-Qur'an, 1986.
—— Jihad fi Sabil Allah (Jihad ın the Path of God). Reprint. Lahore: Islamic Publications, 1989
—— Khilafat'u Mulukıyat (Caliphate and Monarchy). Lahore: Islamic Publications, 1966.
—— Mas'alah-ı Qaumıyat (The Question of Nationality). Reprint. Lahore: Islamic Publications, 1982.
—— Musalman Awr Mawjudah Siyası Kashmakash (Muslims and the Current Political Struggle). 3 vols. Lahore, 1938–1940.
—— Musalman ka Mazı, Hal Awr Mustaqbal (Muslims' Past, Present, and Future). Lahore: Islamic Publications, 1963.
—— Qadiyanı Mas'alah (Ahmadi Issue). Lahore, 1954.
—— Rasa'il'u Masa'il (Queries and Responses). 4 vols. Lahore, 1951–1965
—— Risalah-ı Dinıyat (Treatise on Religion). Hyderabad, 1932.
—— Shakhsıyat (Personalities). Sami'u'llah and Khalid Humayun, eds. Lahore: Al-Badr Publications, n.d.
—— Sunnat'u Bid'at kı Kashmakash (The Struggle between Tradition and Innovation). Lahore: Idarah-ı Tarjumanu'l-Qur'an, 1950.
—— Tafhımat (Explanations). 3 vols. Lahore: Islamic Publications, 1965.
—— Tahrik-ı Azadi Hind Awr Musalman (India's Independence Movement and the Muslims). 2 vols. Lahore: Islamic Publications, 1973.
—— Tahrik-ı Islamı ka A'indah La'ihah-ı 'Amal (The Islamic Movement's Future Course of Action). Lahore: Islamic Publications, 1986.
—— Tahrik-ı Islamı kı Akhlaqı Buniadin (The Basic Ethical Principles of the Islamic Movement). Lahore: Islamic Publications, 1968.
—— Tahrik-ı Pakistan Awr Jama'at-ı Islamı (The Pakistan Movement and the Jama'at-ı Islami). Multan: Ikhwan Publications, n.d.
—— Tajdid'u Ihya'-ı Din (Renewal and Revival of Religion). Lahore, 1952.
—— Tanqihat (Inquiries). 22d ed. Lahore: Islamic Publications, 1989
—— Watha'iq-ı Mawdudi (Mawdudi's Documents). Lahore: Idarah-ı Ma'arif-ı Islamı, 1986.
—— "Ham ne Tahrik-ı Pakistan ke Sath Nehın Diya Tha" (We Were Not with the Pakistan Movement). Nawa'-ı Waqt (August 15, 1975): 3.
—— "Ihya'-ı Nizam-ı Islami" (Revival of the Islamic Order). Al-Furqan, Shah Waliu'llah Number (1940): 16–20.
—— "Khud Nivısht" (Autobiography), ın Muhammad Yusuf Buhtah, ed., Mawlana Mawdudi: Apnı Awr Dusrun kı Nazar Maın (Mawlana Mawdudi ın His Own and Others' Views), 23–29 Lahore: Idarah-ı Ma'arif-ı Islamı, 1984.
Mawdudi Sahab Awr Unkı Tahrırat ke Muta'aliq Chand Ahamm Mazamın (A Few Important Points about Mawlana Mawdudi and His Writings). Karachı: Daru'l-Isha'at, n.d.

Mir, Sajjad. "Wahıd-ı Shahıd" (Martyr Wahıd), ın Salim Mansur Khalid, ed., *Tala-bah Tahrikaın* (Student Movements) 2: 59–64. Lahore: Al-Badr Publications, 1989

Muhammad, Chaudhrı Ghulam. "Pakıstan kı Kharji Palsı Awr Jamaʿat-ı Islami" (Pakıstan's Foreıgn Policy and the Jamaʿat-ı Islami). *Chıragh-ı Rah* (November 1963): 10–15

———— "Pakıstan Maın Jumhurı Iqdar kı Baqa Awr Furugh" (The Emergence and Establishment of Democracy ın Pakıstan). *Chıragh-ı Rah*, Tahrik-ı Islamı Number (November 1963): 200–204.

———— "Sind Maın Jamaʿat-ı Islami" (The Jamaʿat-ı Islamı ın Sind), ın Muhammad Musa Bhuttu, ed., *Mawlana Jan Muhammad Bhuttu: Shakhsıyat Awr Kirdar* (Maw-lana Jan Muhammad Bhuttu: Personality and Deeds). Hyderabad: Sind National Academy, n.d.

Munır, Ahmad. *Mawlana Abu'l-Aʿla Mawdudi.* Lahore: Atashfishan Publications, 1986.

———— "Punjab Unıversity Se Shahı Qila Tak" (From Punjab Unıversity to the Lahore Fort), ın Salim Mansur Khalid, ed., *Talabah Tahrikaın* (Student Movements) 1: 198–214. Lahore: Al-Badr Publications, 1989

Munır, Sıraj. "Azadi ka Ik Nia Mur" (Freedom's New Turn). *Urdu Digest* (August 1988): 211–17

Mutaqqıu'l-Rahman, Sayyıd, and Salim Mansur Khalid, eds. *Jab Vuh Nazım-ı Aʿla The* (When They Were Nazım-ı Aʿla). 2 vols. Lahore: Idarah-ı Matbuʿat-ı Talabah, 1981.

Nadwı, Sayyıd Abu'l-Hasan ʿAli. *ʿAsr-ı Hazır Maın Din Ki Tafhım'u Tashrih* (Explana-tion and Understanding of Religıon ın Contemporary Times). Karachı: Majlis-ı Nashrıyat-ı Islam, n.d..

Nasru'llah Khan, Nawwabzadah. "Ham Unke, Vuh Hemarah Sath Rahe" (He Is with Us and We with Him). *Haftrozah Zindagı*, Mawdudi Number (September 29–October 5, 1989): 37–41.

Niyazı, Kawthar. *Awr Lıne Kat Ga'i* (And the Lıne Was Cut). Lahore: Jang Publica-tions, 1987

———— *Jamaʿat-ı Islamı ʿAwamı ʿAdalat Maın* (The Jamaʿat-ı Islamı ın the Court of the People). Lahore: Qaumı Kutubkhanih, 1973.

Nizamı, Rana Sabır. *Jamaʿat-ı Islamı Pakıstan: Nakamıyun ke Asbab ka ʿIlmı Tajzıyah* (The Jamaʿat-ı Islamı of Pakıstan: A Rational Analysıs of Its Failures). Lahore: Idarah-ı Tafhımu'l-Islam, 1988.

Nuʿmanı, ʿAsım. *Mawlana Mawdudi Par Jhuti Ilzamat Awr Unkı Mudallil Jawabat* (False Accusations agaınst Mawlana Mawdudi and the Responses to Them). Lahore: Maktabah-ı Faısal, n.d.

———— *Tasawwuf Awr Taʿmır-ı Sirat* (Sufism and the Building of the Prophetic Way). Lahore: Islamıc Publications, 1972.

———— ed. *Makatib-ı Sayyıd Abu'l-Aʿla Mawdudi* (Correspondence of Sayyıd Abu'l-Aʿla Mawdudi). 2 vols. Lahore: Islamıc Publications, 1977

Nuʿmanı, Mawlana Muhammad Manzur. *Mawlana Mawdudi Mirı Sath Rifaqat kı*

Sarguzasht Awr Ab Mira Mauqaf (The Story of My Friendship with Mawlana Mawdudi, and My Position Now). Lahore: Quraishi Book Agency, 1980.

Qadri, Mahiru'l. "Nuqush-i Zindagi" (Sketches of Life), in Muhammad Yusuf Buhtah, *Mawlana Mawdudi: Apni Awr Dusrun Ki Nazar Main* (Mawlana Mawdudi: In His Own and Others' Views), 234–46. Lahore: Idarah-i Ma'arif Islami, 1984.

Qasmi, Ja'far. "Mujhe Yad Hey Sab Se Zara Zara   " (My Recollections, Little by Little). *Nida* (April 17, 1990): 28–34.

Qaumi Digest. Mawdudi Number (1980).

Rahi, Akhtar. *Mas'ud 'Alam Nadwi: Sawanih'u Makatib* (Mas'ud 'Alam Nadwi: Biography and Works). Gujrat, Pakistan: Maktabah-i Zafar, 1975.

Ra'if, Ahmad. *Pakistan Awr Jama'at-i Islami* (The Jama'at-i Islami and Pakistan). Faisalabad: Al-Mizan, 1986.

Rana, Jalil Ahmad, and Salim Mansur Khalid, eds. *Tazkirah-i Sayyid Mawdudi* (Biography of Sayyid Mawdudi). Lahore: Idarah-i Ma'arif-i Islami, 1986.

Rashidi, Abu Sufyan Muhammad Tufayl. *Tahaffuz-i Khatm-i Nubuwwat Awr Jama'at-i Islami* (Protecting the Finality of Prophethood and the Jama'at-i Islami). Lahore: Majlis-i Ta'zim-i Sahabah, n.d.

Rudad-i Jama'at-i Islami (Proceedings of the Jama'at-i Islami). 7 vols. Lahore, 1938–1991.

Rudad-i Jama'at-i Islami Pakistan, 1972 (Proceedings of the Jama'at-i Islami of Pakistan, 1972). Lahore: Jama'at-i Islami Pakistan, n.d.

Safdar Mir, Muhammad. *Mawdudiyat Awr Mawjudah Siyasi Kashmakash* (Mawdudism and the Current Political Crisis). 2d ed. Lahore: Al-Bayan, 1970.

Salahu'ddin, Muhammad. *Peoples Party: Maqasid Awr Hikmat-i 'Amali* (Peoples Party: Objectives and Plan of Action). Karachi: Matbu'at-i Takbir, 1982.

Salimi, Sa'id. "Furugh-i Subh" (Morning Light), in Salim Mansur Khalid, ed., *Talabah Tahrikain* (Student Movements) 2: 311–24. Lahore: Al-Badr Publications, 1989

Sarwar, Muhammad. *Jama'at-i Islami Awr Islami Dastur* (The Jama'at-i Islami and the Islamic Constitution). Lahore, 1956.

Sayyarah. Sayyid Mawdudi Number (April–May 1980).

Shahid, Zia. "Amiriyat, Talabah, Awr Garmi Guftar" (Dictatorship, Students, and the Intensity of Their Discourse), in Salim Mansur Khalid, ed., *Talabah Tahrikain* (Student Movements) 1: 177–90. Lahore: Al-Badr Publications, 1989

Shahpuri, Abad. *Tarikh-i Jama'at-i Islami* (History of the Jama'at-i Islami). Vol. 1. Lahore: Idarah-i Ma'arif-i Islami, 1989

Shair 'Ali Khan, Nawwabzadah. *Al-Qisas* (Tales). Lahore, 1974.

Shami, Mujibu'l-Rahman. "Jama'at-i Islami Awr Peoples Party: Fasilah Awr Rabitah, Ik Musalsal Kahani" (The Jama'at-i Islami and the People's Party: Distance and Relations, a Continuous Story). *Qaumi Digest* 11, 2 (July 1988): 11–26.

——— "Karan Se Aftab Tak" (From Rays to the Sun). *Haftrozah Zindagi*, Mawdudi Number (September 29–October 5, 1989): 31–33.

Shirazi, Sayyid Ma'ruf. *Islami Inqilab ka Minhaj* (Path of the Islamic Revolution). Chinarkut: Manshurat-i Islami, 1989

Siddiqi, Manzuru'l-Haq. "Tahrik-i Pakistan Talib-i 'Ilm ki Yadain" (Recollections of

Students from the Pakistan Movement), in Salim Mansur Khalid, ed., *Talabah Tahrikain* (Student Movements) 1. 91–104. Lahore: Al-Badr Publications, 1989

Siddiqi, Na'im. *Al-Mawdudi*. Lahore: Idarah-ı Ma'arif-ı Islami, 1963.

Siddiqi, Na'im, and Sa'id Ahmad Malik. *Tahqiqat-ı 'Adalat ki Report Par Tabsarah* (Analysis of the Report of the Court of Inquiry). Lahore: Shu'bah-ı Nashr'u Isha'at-ı Jama'at-ı Islami, 1955

Siddiqi, Rahman. "Mawlana Azad Awr Mawlana Mawdudi ki Mabain ik Gumshudah Kari" (A Lost Link in the Relations between Mawlana Azad and Mawlana Mawdudi). *Nida* (February 7–13, 1990): 20–22.

Sindihlawı, Mawlana Muhammad Ishaq. *Islam ka Siyasi Nizam* (Islam's Political Order). A'zamgarh: Daru'l-Mussanifin, n.d.

Wahidu'ddin Khan, Mawlana. *Din Ki Siyasi Ta'bir* (Political Interpretation of Religion). Lahore: Al-Maktabah Al-Ashrafiyah, n.d.

———— *Din Kiya Hey* (What is Religion?). Delhi: Maktabah-ı Risalah, 1978.

———— *Ta'bir ki Ghalti* (Mistaken Interpretation). Delhi: Maktabah-ı Risalah, 1975

Yahya, Muhammad. "Sikandarpur Se Lahore Tak." *Qaumi Digest*, Mawdudi Number (1980): 169–89

Yusuf, Muhammad. "Mawlana Mawdudi Bi Haithiyat-ı Ik Adib" (Mawlana Mawdudi as a Literary Figure). *Sayyarah*, Sayyıd Mawdudi Number (April–May 1980): 115–17

Zaidi, Sayyıd Nazar. *Qiyam-ı Pakistan Main Mawlana Mawdudi ka Fikri Hissah* (The Intellectual Role of Mawlana Mawdudi in the Pakistan Movement). Lahore: Idarah-ı Ma'arif-ı Islami, 1983.

PRIMARY ENGLISH SOURCES

'Abdu'l-Hakım, Khalifah. *Islamic Ideology*. Lahore: Institute of Islamic Culture, 1951.

Ahmad, Khurshıd. *The Movement of Jama'at-e-Islami, Pakistan*. Lahore: Jama'at-e-Islami, Pakistan, 1989

———— *Studies in the Family Law of Islam*. Karachı: Chıragh-ı Rah Publications, 1961.

Aijaz, S. Zakır. *Selected Speeches and Writings of Mawlana Mawdudi*. Karachı: International Islamic Publishers, 1981.

The Annual Report of Islami Jami'at-ı Tulabah. Lahore: Islami Jami'at Tulabah, 1988.

Constitution, Islami Jamiat-e-Talaba Pakistan. Lahore: Islami Jamiat-e-Talaba Pakistan, 1979

Correspondences between Maulana Maudoodi and Maryam Jameelah. 4th ed. Lahore: Muhammad Yusuf Khan and Sons, 1986.

Documents from the U.S. Espionage Den, Nos. 45 and 46: U.S. Intervention in Islamic Countries: Pakistan. 2 vols. Tehran: Muslim Students Following the Line of the Imam, n.d.

ESTA CODE: Civil Service Establishment Code. Islamabad: O and M Division. Public Administration Research Center, Government of Pakistan, 1983.

Foreign Broadcast Information Service, Daily Reports, Near East and South Asia. (Washington, D.C.)

Jameelah, Maryam. *Islam in Theory and Practice*. Lahore: Mohammad Yusuf Khan, 1973.

———— *A Manifesto of the Islamic Movement*. Lahore: Mohammad Yusuf Khan, 1969

Manifesto of Jama'at-i Islami of Pakistan. Lahore: Jama'at-i Islami, 1970.

Manifesto of Jamaat-e-Islami, Pakistan. Karachi: Jamaat-e-Islami, 1958.

Mawdudi [or Maududi or Maudoodi], Sayyid Abul A'la. *Islamic Law and Constitution*. Khurshid Ahmad, ed. Karachi: Jamaat-e-Islami Publications, 1955

———— *The Islamic Movement: Dynamics of Values, Power, and Change*. Khurram Murad, ed. and trans. Leicester: Islamic Foundation, 1984.

———— *The Islamic Way of Life*. Khurram Murad and Khurshid Ahmad, eds. and trans. Leicester: Islamic Foundation, 1986.

———— *Islam Today*. Beirut: International Islamic Federation of Student Organizations, 1985

———— *Kashmir: A Call to the Conscience of Humanity*. Lahore: Jama'at-e-Islami, 1966.

———— *The Political Situation in Pakistan*. Karachi: Jamaat-e-Islami, 1965

———— *The Process of Islamic Revolution*. 8th ed. Lahore: Islamic Publications, 1980.

————. *A Short History of the Revivalist Movement in Islam*. Al-Ash'ari, trans. Reprint. Lahore: Islamic Publications, 1963.

———— *System of Government under the Holy Prophet*. Lahore: Islamic Publications, 1978.

———— *Towards Understanding Islam*. Khurshid Ahmad, trans. and ed. Reprint. Indianapolis: Islamic Teaching Center, 1977

———— *Witness unto Mankind: The Purpose and Duty of the Muslim Ummah*. Khurram Murad, ed. and trans. Leicester: Islamic Foundation, 1986.

———— "Muslim Women Must Participate in Islamic Movement." *Criterion* 5, 5 (Rajab-Sha'ban 1390/1970): 40–75

Mirza, General Iskandar. "Memoirs." Unpublished manuscript.

Muhammad, Chaudhri Ghulam. *Jamaat-e-Islami and Foreign Policy*. Karachi: Rajab Ali, 1963–1964.

Muhammad, Mian Tufayl. "General Zia ul-Haq Shaheed," in *Shaheed ul-Islam: Muhammad Zia ul-Haq*, 45–53. London: Indus Thames Publishers, 1990.

———— ed. and trans. *Statement of 209 Ulema of Pakistan on the Muslim Family Law Ordinance*. Lahore, 1962.

Report of the Court of Inquiry Constituted under Punjab Act 11 of 1954 to Enquire into the Punjab Disturbances of 1953. Lahore: Government of Punjab, 1954.

Report on the General Elections, 1985. 3 vols. Islamabad: Election Commission of Pakistan, n.d.

Report on the General Elections, Pakistan 1970–1971. 2 vols. Islamabad: Election Commission of Pakistan, n.d.

Short Proceedings of the 2nd Annual Conference, Jamaat-e-Islami, East Pakistan. Dacca: Jamaat-e-Islami, Pakistan, 1958.

Statement of Syed Abul Ala Maudoodi before the Punjab Disturbances Court of Inquiry. Karachi, n.d.

White Paper on Electorate Issue. Karachi: Jama'at-i-Islami of Pakistan, 1957

SECONDARY ENGLISH SOURCES

Abbott, Freeland. *Islam and Pakistan*. Ithaca, N.Y.. Cornell University Press, 1968.
——— "The Jama'at-ı-Islamı of Pakistan." *Middle East Journal* 11, 1 (Winter 1957): 37–51.
——— "Pakistan and the Secular State," in Donald E. Smith, ed., *South Asian Religion and Politics*, 352–70. Princeton: Princeton University Press, 1966.
——— "Pakistan's New Marriage Law· A Reflection of Qur'anic Interpretation." *Asian Survey* 3 (January 1962): 26–32.
Abd, Abdur Rahman. *Sayyed Maududi Faces the Death Sentence*. Reprint. Lahore: Islamic Publications, 1978.
Adams, Charles J. "The Ideology of Mawlana Mawdudi," in Donald E. Smith, ed., *South Asian Politics and Religion*, 371–97 Princeton: Princeton University Press, 1966.
——— "Mawdudi and the Islamic State," in John L. Esposito, ed., *Voices of Resurgent Islam*, 99–133. New York: Oxford University Press, 1983.
Ahmad, Aziz. *Islamic Modernism in India and Pakistan, 1857–1964*. London: Oxford University Press, 1967
——— "Mawdudi and Orthodox Fundamentalism of Pakistan." *Middle East Journal* 21, 3 (Summer 1967): 369–80.
Ahmad, Eqbal. "Islam and Politics," in Yvonne Y. Haddad et al., eds., *The Islamic Impact*, 7–26. Syracuse: Syracuse University Press, 1984.
Ahmad, Khurshid. "The Nature of Islamic Resurgence," in John L. Esposito, ed., *Voices of Resurgent Islam*, 218–229 New York: Oxford University Press, 1983.
Ahmad, Khurshid, and Zafar Ishaq Ansari. "Mawlana Sayyid Abul A'la Mawdudi: An Introduction to His Vision of Islam and Islamic Revival," in Khurshid Ahmad and Zafar Ishaq Ansari, eds., *Islamic Perspectives: Studies In Honour of Mawlana Sayyid Abul A'la Mawdudi*, 359–84. Leicester: Islamic Foundation, 1979
Ahmad, Mumtaz. "Islam and the State: The Case of Pakistan," in Mathew Moen and Lowell Gustafson, eds., *The Religious Challenge to the State*, 239–67 Philadelphia: Temple University Press, 1992.
——— "Islamic Fundamentalism in South Asia: The Jamaat-ı-Islamı and the Tablighı Jamaat," in Martin E. Marty and R. Scott Appleby, eds., *Fundamentalisms Observed*, 457–530. Chicago: University of Chicago Press, 1991.
——— "The Politics of War: Islamic Fundamentalisms in Pakistan," in James Piscatori, ed., *Islamic Fundamentalisms and the Gulf Crisis*, 155–87 Chicago: American Academy of Arts and Sciences, 1991.
Ahmad, Syed Riaz. *Maulana Maududi and the Islamic State*. Lahore: People's Publishing House, 1976.
Ahmad Khan, 'Ali. *The Jama'at-e-Islamı of Pakistan*. Introduction Series, no. 2. Lahore, 1954.
Ahmed, Akbar S. *Discovering Islam: Making Sense of Muslim History and Society*. London: Routledge and Kegan Paul, 1988.
Ahmed, Ishtiaq. *The Concept of an Islamic State: An Analysis of the Ideological Controversy in Pakistan*. New York: St. Martin's Press, 1987

Ahmed, Zafaryab. "Maudoodi's Islamic State," in Asghar Khan, ed., *Islam, Politics and the State: The Pakistan Experience,* 95—113 London: Zed Press, 1985

Ajmal Khan, Mohammad. "A Note on *Adab* in the *Murshid-Murid* Relationship," in Barbara D. Metcalf, ed., *Moral Conduct and Authority: The Place of Adab in South Asian Islam,* 241—51. Berkeley and Los Angeles: University of California Press, 1984.

Akhavi, Shahrough. "Shi'ism, Corporatism, and Rentierism in the Iranian Revolution," in Juan R.I. Cole, ed., *Comparing Muslim Societies: Knowledge and the State in a World Civilization,* 261—93. Ann Arbor: University of Michigan Press, 1992.

Alavi, Hamza. "The State in Postcolonial Societies: Pakistan and Bangladesh," in Kathleen Gough and Hari P Sharma, eds., *Imperialism and Revolution in South Asia,* 145—73. New York: Monthly Review Press, 1973.

Amin, Tahir. *Ethno-National Movements of Pakistan.* Islamabad: Institute of Policy Studies, 1988.

Amjad, Rashid. *Pakistan's Growth Experience: Objectives, Achievement, and Impact on Poverty, 1947—1977* Lahore: Progressive Publishers, 1978.

Anderson, Benedict. *Imagined Communities: Reflections on the Origin and Spread of Nationalism.* 2d ed. New York: Verso, 1991.

Ansari, Sarah F.D. *Sufi Saints and State Power· The Pirs of Sind, 1843—1947* Cambridge: Cambridge University Press, 1992.

Anwar, Zainah. *Islamic Fundamentalism in Malaysia.* 2d ed. Kualalampur: Pelanduk Publications, 1989

Arjomand, Said Amir. *The Turban for the Crown: The Islamic Revolution in Iran.* New York: Oxford University Press, 1988.

———— "Social Change and Movements of Revitalization in Contemporary Islam," in James B. Beckford, ed., *New Religious Movements and Rapid Social Change,* 87—112. Beverly Hills: Sage Publications, 1986.

Ayub Khan, General Mohammad. *Friends, Not Masters: A Political Autobiography.* London: Oxford University Press, 1967

Ayubi, Nazih. *Political Islam: Religion and Politics in the Arab World.* New York: Routledge, Chapman and Hall, 1991.

Bahadur, Kalim. *The Jama'at-i Islami of Pakistan.* New Delhi: Chetana Publications, 1977

Binder, Leonard. *Islamic Liberalism: A Critique of Development Ideologies.* Chicago: University of Chicago Press, 1988.

———— *Religion and Politics in Pakistan.* Berkeley and Los Angeles: University of California Press, 1961.

Brohi, Allahbukhsh K. "Mawlana Abul A'la Mawdudi: The Man, the Scholar, the Reformer," in Khurshid Ahmad and Zafar Ishaq Ansari, eds., *Islamic Perspectives: Studies in Honour of Sayyid Abul A'la Mawdudi,* 289—312. Leicester: Islamic Foundation, 1979

Burki, Shahid Javed. *Pakistan: A Nation in the Making.* Boulder, Colo.. Westview Press, 1986.

———— *Pakistan under Bhutto, 1971—1977* London: Macmillan, 1980.

———— "Pakistan under Zia, 1977–1988." *Asian Survey* 28, 10 (October 1988): 1082–1100.

Callard, Keith B. *Political Forces in Pakistan, 1947–1959* New York: Institute of Pacific Affairs, 1959

Chishti, Lt. General Faiz Ali. *Betrayals of Another Kind: Islam, Democracy, and the Army in Pakistan.* Cincinnati, Ohio: Asia Publishing House, 1990.

Chaudhry, Kiren Aziz, and Peter McDonough. "State, Society, and Sin: The Political Beliefs of University Students in Pakistan." *Economic Development and Cultural Change* 32, 1 (October 1983): 11–44.

Choudhury, G. W *Constitutional Development in Pakistan.* Lahore: Longmans, Green, 1959

Cohen, Stephen P *The Pakistan Army.* Berkeley and Los Angeles: University of California Press, 1984.

Dabashi, Hamid. "Symbiosis of Religious and Political Authorities in Islam," in Thomas Robbins and Ronald Robertson, eds., *Church-State Relations: Tensions and Transitions,* 183–203. New Brunswick, N.J.. Transaction Books, 1987

Denny, Fredrick M. "Fazlur Rahman: Muslim Intellectual." *Muslim World* 79, 2 (April 1989): 91–101.

El-Affendi, Abdelwahab. "The Long March from Lahore to Khartoum: Beyond the 'Muslim Reformation.' " *British Society for Middle Eastern Studies Bulletin* 17, 2 (1990): 137–51.

Enayat, Hamid. *Modern Islamic Political Thought.* Austin: University of Texas Press, 1982.

Esposito, John L. *Islam and Politics.* 3rd ed. Syracuse: Syracuse University Press, 1991.

———— *The Islamic Threat: Myth or Reality?* New York: Oxford University Press, 1992.

———— "Islam: Ideology and Politics in Pakistan," in Ali Banuazizi and Myron Weiner, eds., *The State, Religion, and Ethnic Politics: Afghanistan, Iran, and Pakistan,* 333–70. Syracuse: Syracuse University Press, 1986.

Esposito, John L., and James P Piscatori. "Democratization and Islam." *Middle East Journal* 45, 3 (Summer 1991): 427–40.

Esposito, John L., and John O. Voll. "Khurshid Ahmad: Muslim Activist-Economist." *Muslim World* 80, 1 (January 1990): 24–36.

Ewing, Katherine. "The Politics of Sufism: Redefining the Saints of Pakistan." *Journal of Asian Studies* 42, 2 (February 1983): 251–68.

Faruqi, Misbahul Islam. *Introducing Maudoodi.* Karachi, 1968.

Friedmann, Yohanan. *Prophecy Continuous: Aspects of Ahmadi Religious Thought and Its Medieval Background.* Berkeley and Los Angeles: University of California Press, 1989

———— "The Attitude of the Jamiyyat-i 'Ulama'-i Hind to the Indian National Movement and the Establishment of Pakistan," in Gabriel Baer, ed., *The 'Ulama' in Modern History,* 157–83. Jerusalem: African and Asian Studies, Israeli Oriental Society, VII, 1971.

Geertz, Clifford. *Interpretation of Cultures.* New York: Basic Books, 1973.

Gilani, Sayyid Asad. *Maududi: Thought and Movement.* Lahore: Islamic Publications, 1984.

Gilmartin, David. *Empire and Islam: Punjab and the Making of Pakistan.* Berkeley and Los Angeles: University of California Press, 1988.

———. "Pakistan, the Pastoral and Panjabiyat." Paper presented at the Association for Asian Studies, 1993.

———. "Religious Leadership and the Pakistan Movement in Punjab." *Modern Asian Studies* 13, 3 (July 1979): 485–517

———. "The Shahidganj Mosque Incident: A Prelude to Pakistan," in Edmund Burke III and Ira M. Lapidus, eds., *Islam, Politics, and Social Movements,* 146–68. Berkeley and Los Angeles: University of California, 1988.

Graff, Violette. "La Jamaat-i-Islami en Inde," in Oliver Carré and Paul Dumont, eds., *Radicalismes Islamiques,* vol. 2, 59–72. Paris: L'Hartmann, 1986.

Haeri, Shahla. "Obedience versus Autonomy· Women and Fundamentalism in Iran and Pakistan," in Martin E. Marty and R. Scott Appleby, eds., *Fundamentalisms and Society: Reclaiming the Sciences, the Family, and Education,* 181–213. Chicago: University of Chicago, 1993

ul-Haq, Mahbub. *The Poverty Curtain: Choices for the Third World.* New York: Columbia University Press, 1976.

Hardy, Peter. *The Muslims of British India.* Cambridge: Cambridge University Press, 1972.

Hasan, Masudul. *Sayyid Abul A'ala Maududi and His Thought.* 2 vols. Lahore: Islamic Publications, 1984.

Hasan, Mushirul. "The Muslim Mass Contact Campaign: An Attempt at Political Mobilization." *Economic and Political Weekly* 21, 52 (December 27, 1986): 273–82.

Herring, Ronald J. "Zulfiqar Ali Bhutto and the 'Eradication of Feudalism' in Pakistan." *Comparative Studies in Society and History* 21 (1979): 519–57

Huntington, Samuel P *The Third Wave: Democratization in the Late Twentieth Century.* Norman: University of Oklahoma Press, 1991.

Hussain, Akmal. "The Karachi Riots of 1986: Crisis of State and Civil Society," in Veena Das, ed., *Mirrors of Violence: Communities, Riots, and Survivors in South Asia,* 185–93. Delhi: Oxford University Press, 1990.

Hussain, Syed Shabbir. "Inayat Ullah Khan El-Mashriqi," in *The Muslim Luminaries: Leaders of Religious, Intellectual, and Political Revival in South Asia,* 246–75 Islamabad: National Hijrah Council, 1988.

Hussain, Zahid. "The Campus Mafias." *Herald* (October 1988): 51–65

Ibrahim, Saad Eddin. "Anatomy of Egypt's Militant Islamic Groups: Methodological Note and Preliminary Findings." *International Journal of Middle East Studies* 12, 4 (December 1980): 423–53

Ikram, S.M. *Modern Muslim India and the Birth of Pakistan.* 2d ed.. Lahore: Institute of Islamic Culture, 1965

Iqbal, Afzal. *Islamization of Pakistan.* Lahore: Vanguard Books, 1986.

Jahan, Rounaq. *Pakistan: Failure in National Integration.* New York: Columbia University Press, 1972.

Jalal, Ayesha. *The Sole Spokesman: Jinnah, the Muslim League, and the Demand for Pakistan.* Cambridge: Cambridge University Press, 1985
———— *The State of Martial Rule: The Origins of Pakistan's Political Economy of Defence.* Cambridge: Cambridge University Press, 1990.

Jameelah, Maryam. *Who Is Maudoodi?* Lahore: Mohammad Yusuf Khan, 1973.
———— "An Appraisal of Some Aspects of Maulana Sayyıd Ala Maudoodi's Life and Thought." *Islamic Quarterly* 31, 2 (Second Quarter 1987): 116–30.

Kennedy, Charles H. "Islamization and Legal Reform in Pakistan, 1979–89 " *Pacific Affairs* 63, 1 (Spring 1990): 62–77
———— "Islamization in Pakistan: Implementation of the Hudood Ordinances." *Asian Survey* 28, 3 (March 1988): 307–16.
———— "Judicial Activism and Islamization after Zia: Toward the Prohibition of Riba" in Charles H. Kennedy, ed., *Pakistan 1992*, 57–73. Boulder, Colo.. Westview Press, 1993.
———— "The Politics of Ethnicity in Sind." *Asian Survey* 31, 10 (October 1991): 938–55

Lapidus, Ira M. "Islamic Political Movements: Patterns of Historical Change," in Edmund Burke III and Ira M. Lapidus, eds., *Islam, Politics, and Social Movements*, 3–16. Berkeley and Los Angeles: University of California Press, 1988.

Laroui, Abdallah. *L'idéologie arabe contemporaine.* Paris: Françoise Maspero, 1967

Lerman, Eran. "Mawdudi's Concept of Islam." *Middle Eastern Studies* 17, 4 (October 1981): 492–509

Lewis, Stephen R. *Economic Policy and Industrial Growth in Pakistan.* Cambridge: MIT Press, 1969

Malamud, Margaret. "The Development of Organized Sufism in Nishapur and Baghdad from the Eleventh to the Thirteenth Century " Ph.D. dissertation, University of California, Berkeley, 1990.

Malik, Hafeez. "Islamic Political Parties and Mass Mobilization." *Islam and the Modern Age* 3, 2 (May 1972): 26–60.

Mayer, Ann Elizabeth. "The Fundamentalist Impact on Law, Politics, and Constitutions in Iran, Pakistan, and the Sudan," in Martin E. Marty and R. Scott Appleby, eds., *Fundamentalisms and the State: Remaking Polities, Economies, and Militance*, 110–51. Chicago: University of Chicago Press, 1993.

Mehdi, Safdar. *Politics without Parties: A Report on the 1985 Partyless Elections in Pakistan.* Lahore: SAHE, 1988.

Metcalf, Barbara D. *Islamic Revival in British India: Deoband, 1860–1900.* Princeton: Princeton University Press, 1982.
———— "Islamic Arguments in Contemporary Pakistan," in William Roff, ed., *Islam and Political Economy of Meaning*, 132–59 Berkeley and Los Angeles: University of California Press, 1987

Minault, Gail. *The Khilafat Movement: Religious Symbolisms and Political Mobilization in India.* New York: Columbia University Press, 1982.

Mottahedeh, Roy *Mantle of the Prophet: Religion and Politics in Iran.* New York: Simon and Schuster, 1985

Mujahid, Sharif al- "The 1977 Pakistani Elections: An Analysis," in Manzooruddin Ahmad, ed., *Contemporary Pakistan: Politics, Economy, and Society*, 63–91. Karachi: Royal Books Company, 1980.

———— "Pakistan's First General Elections." *Asian Survey* 11, 2 (February 1971): 159–71.

Munir, Muhammad. *From Jinnah to Zia*. Lahore: Vanguard Books, 1979

Munson, Henry, Jr. *Islam and Revolution in the Middle East*. New Haven: Yale University Press, 1988.

Naseem, S.M. "Mass Poverty in Pakistan: Some Preliminary Findings." *Pakistan Development Review* 12, 4 (Winter 1973): 315–35

Nasr, Seyyed Hossein. *Sufi Essays*. London: George Allen and Unwin, 1972.

Nasr, Seyyed Vali Reza. "Democracy and the Crisis of Governability in Pakistan." *Asian Survey* 32, 6 (June 1992): 521–37

———— "Pakistan: Islamic State, Ethnic Polity " *Fletcher Forum of World Affairs* 16, 2 (Summer 1992): 81–90.

———— "The Politics of an Islamic Movement: The Jama'at-i Islami of Pakistan." Ph.D. dissertation, Massachusetts Institute of Technology, 1991.

Niazi, Kausar. *Zulfiqar Ali Bhutto of Pakistan: The Last Days*. New Delhi: Vikas Publishing House, 1992.

Nur, Syed Ahmad. *From Martial Law to Martial Law: Politics in the Punjab, 1919–1958*. Craig Baxter, ed., and Mahmud Ali, trans. Boulder, Colo.. Westview Press, 1985

Oldenburg, Philip. " 'A Place Insufficiently Imagined' Language, Belief, and the Pakistan Crisis of 1971." *Journal of Asian Studies* 44, 4 (August 1985): 711–33.

Papanek, Gustav F *Pakistan's Development: Social Goals and Private Incentives*. Cambridge: Harvard University Press, 1967

Piscatori, James P *Islam in a World of Nation-States*. New York: Cambridge University Press, 1986.

Poston, Larry *Islamic Da'wah in the West: Muslim Missionary Activity and the Dynamics of Conversion to Islam*. New York: Oxford University Press, 1992.

Qureshi, Ishtiaq Husain. *Education in Pakistan: An Inquiry into Objectives and Achievements*. Karachi: Ma'aref, 1975

———— *Ulema in Politics: A Study Relating to the Political Activities of the Ulema in South Asian Subcontinent from 1566–1947* Karachi: Ma'aref, 1972.

Rahman, Fazlur. *Islam*. Chicago: University of Chicago Press, 1966.

———— "The Controversy over the Muslim Family Laws," in Donald E. Smith, ed., *South Asian Religion and Politics*, 414–27 Princeton: Princeton University Press, 1966.

———— "Islam in Pakistan." *South Asian and Middle Eastern Studies* 8, 4 (Summer 1985): 34–61.

Ramadan, Abdel Azim. "Fundamentalist Influence in Egypt: The Strategies of the Muslim Brotherhood and the Takfir Groups," in Martin E. Marty and R. Scott Appleby, eds., *Fundamentalisms and the State: Remaking Politics, Economies, and Militance*, 152–83 Chicago: University of Chicago Press, 1993.

Richter, William L. "The 1990 General Elections in Pakistan," in Charles H. Kennedy, ed., *Pakistan 1992*, 19–42. Boulder, Colo.. Westview Press, 1993.

Rizvi, Hassan Askari. "The Civilianization of Military Rule in Pakistan." *Asian Survey* 26, 10 (Summer 1986): 1067–81.

Robinson, Francis. *Separatism among Indian Muslims: The Politics of United Provinces' Muslims, 1860–1923* Cambridge: Cambridge University Press, 1974.

Rosenthal, Erwin I. J. *Islam in the Modern Nation State*. Cambridge: Cambridge University Press, 1965

Roy, Olivier. *Islam and Resistance in Afghanistan*. 2d ed. New York: Cambridge University Press, 1990.

Saeed, Muhammad. *Lahore: A Memoir*. Lahore: Vanguard Books, 1989

Saulat, Sarwat. *Maulana Maududi*. Karachi: International Islamic Publishers, 1979

Sayeed, Khalid B. *Politics in Pakistan: The Nature and Direction of Change*. New York: Praeger, 1980.

———— "The Jama'at-i-Islami Movement in Pakistan." *Pacific Affairs* 30, 1 (March 1957): 59–69

Selznick, Philip. *The Organizational Weapon: A Study of Bolshevik Strategy and Tactics*. New York: McGraw-Hill Books, 1952.

Shaheed, Farida. "The Pathan-Muhajir Conflict, 1985–1986: A National Perspective," in Veena Das, ed., *Mirrors of Violence: Communities, Riots, and Survivors in South Asia*, 194–214. Delhi: Oxford University Press, 1990.

Shaikh, Farzana. *Community and Consensus in Islam: Muslim Representation in Colonial India, 1860–1947* Cambridge: Cambridge University Press, 1989

Sivan, Emmanuel. *Radical Islam: Medieval Theology and Modern Politics*. New Haven: Yale University Press, 1985

Smith, Donald E. *Religion and Political Development*. Boston: Little, Brown, 1970.

Smith, Tony *Thinking Like a Communist: State and Legitimacy in the Soviet Union, China, and Cuba*. New York: W W Norton, 1987

Smith, Wilfred Cantwell. *Islam in Modern History*. 2d ed. Princeton: Princeton University Press, 1977

———— *Modern Islam in India: A Social Analysis*. 3d ed. New Delhi: Usha Publications, 1979

Stephan, Alfred. *The State and Society: Peru in Comparative Perspective*. Princeton: Princeton University Press, 1978.

Syed, Anwar Hussain. *The Discourse and Politics of Zulfikar Ali Bhutto*. London: Macmillan, 1992.

———— *Pakistan: Islam, Politics, and National Solidarity*. New York: Praeger, 1982.

———— "Factional Conflict in the Punjab Muslim League, 1947–1955 " *Polity* 22, 1 (Fall 1989): 49–73.

von der Mehden, Fred. *Religion and Modernization in Southeast Asia*. Syracuse: Syracuse University Press, 1986.

Waseem, Mohammad. "Pakistan's Lingering Crisis of Dyarchy " *Asian Survey* 32, 7 (July 1992): 617–34.

Weinbaum, Marvin. "War and Peace in Afghanistan: The Pakistani Role." *Middle East Journal* 45, 1 (Winter 1991): 71–86.

Weiss, Anita M. "The Historical Debate on Islam and the State in South Asia," in Anita M. Weiss, ed., *Islamic Reassertion in Pakistan*, 1–20. Syracuse: Syracuse University Press, 1986.

Wolpert, Stanley *Jinnah of Pakistan*. Oxford: Oxford University Press, 1984.

——— *Zulfi Bhutto of Pakistan: His Life and Times*. New York: Oxford University Press, 1993.

Zafar, S.M. *Through the Crisis*. Lahore: Book Center, 1970.

Ziring, Lawrence. *The Ayub Khan Era: Politics of Pakistan 1958–69* Syracuse: Syracuse University Press, 1971.

——— "From Islamic Republic to Islamic State in Pakistan." *Asian Survey* 24, 9 (September 1984): 931–46.

Index

Printed in the United States
133522LV00001B/246/A